American Studies in a Moment of Danger

D0558777

CRITICAL AMERICAN STUDIES SERIES

GEORGE LIPSITZ
UNIVERSITY OF CALIFORNIA–SAN DIEGO
SERIES EDITOR

American Studies in a Moment of Danger

George Lipsitz

Critical American Studies

University of Minnesota Press
Minneapolis • London

Frontispiece (across from "Introduction"): *Self-Portrait a.k.a. Untitled*, by Diane Gamboa, 1984. Serigraph, 34 × 25 inches. Copyright 1984 Diane Gamboa. Reprinted with permission.

See pages 353–54 for permissions and previous publication information.

Published by the University of Minnesota Press
111 Third Avenue South, Suite 290
Minneapolis, MN 55401-2520
http://www.upress.umn.edu

Printed in the United States of America on acid-free paper

Library of Congress Cataloging-in-Publication Data

Lipsitz, George.
  American studies in a moment of danger / George Lipsitz.
    p. cm. — (Critical American studies series)
Includes bibliographical references and index.
  ISBN 0-8166-3948-5 (HC : alk. paper) — ISBN 0-8166-3949-3 (PB : alk. paper)
1. United States—Study and teaching. 2. Learning and scholarship—Social aspects—United States. 3. United States—Intellectual life—20th century. 4. Social movements—United States—History—20th century. 5. Minorities—Study and teaching—United States. 6. United States—Social conditions—1945- 7. National characteristics, American. I. Title. II. Series.
  E175.8 .L76 2001
  973'.07'2—dc21   2001003292

12 11 10 09 08 07 06 05 04 03 02 01   10 9 8 7 6 5 4 3 2 1

Contents

Acknowledgments

A life in the struggle can be a life of disappointment. Victories are rare, and defeats are regular occurrences. Sometimes allies turn out not to be allies, and friends turn out not to be friends. But a life in the struggle can also be a life of serene satisfaction. The solidarity and mutuality we find in the struggle enables us to share the most serious parts of our lives with some of the people we respect most. Struggles for social change enable us to learn from—and grow along with—people who reach out to others because they simply cannot endure the inequalities and injustices they see around them. I owe great debts to people who have helped me, taught me, tolerated me, and inspired me along the way. I thank all of them, but have space to acknowledge only a few.

Toni Cade Bambara predicted that guides and teachers would simply show up when I needed them, and she turned out to be right. Tom McCormick was there for me at the beginning, and he has been with me every step of the way. Marisela Norte has shown me how far you can go on a bus, if only you read the route maps and schedules in the right way. Robin D. G. Kelley's artistry always amazes me and inspires me. Tricia Rose reminds me to pop and lock, to scratch and mix. Stan Weir, Johnny Otis, Ivory Perry, and George Rawick never let me forget the lessons learned by their generation. Susan McClary and Rob Walser are superb ensemble players. David Roediger is always ready, willing, and able to do the right thing.

American Studies in a Moment of Danger came about in dialogue with many friends and colleagues, including Donald Pease, Robyn Wiegman, Rachel Buff, Joe Austin, Amy Kaplan, Jeff Chang, Adrian Gaskins, Kandice Chuh, Karen Shimakawa, William Deverell, Louis Chude-Sokei, Bennetta Jules-Rosette, Nick Browne, Marla Berns, Charles McGovern, Susan Strasser, Elizabeth Long, Jodi Dean, George Sanchez, Earl Lewis, Dana Takagi, and Peggy Pascoe. Conversations with the core and affiliated faculty from the Department of Ethnic Studies at the University of California, San Diego, have helped me understand what is at stake in the work we do as well as how to do it.

In the midnight hour, it helps to have companions capable of seeing the dawn. David W. Noble's uncompromising integrity and unique insights have paved the way for me and for many others. Paul Buhle and Mari Jo Buhle have always had the courage to ask the right questions. I appreciate the wise counsel and exemplary scholarship of Herman Gray, Rosa Linda Fregoso, Jose Saldivar, Devra Weber, Michael Omi, Emory Elliott, Avery Gordon, Melvin Oliver, Tom Shapiro, Farah Jasmine Griffin, Mary Helen Washington, Michael Awkward, Andrew Ross, Arlene Davila, Paul Lauter, Janice Radway, Dana Nelson, Lynn Spigel, Tania Modleski, and Roberta Hill. Barbara Tomlinson's guidance on matters of evidence and argument always improves my work, and I treasure her intelligence and integrity.

Talking about social change is easy; implementing it is difficult. The Fair Housing Council of San Diego is one of the organizations in our society that actually brings about change. By battling against housing discrimination, the council fights every day for a more open, inclusive, and egalitarian society. It does so largely because of the guiding vision and tireless work of its executive director Mary Scott Knoll. This book is dedicated to her, and to the organization she so skillfully leads.

Introduction

I stumbled into American studies the way most people do, by accident. There were no American studies programs on the campuses where I took my undergraduate and graduate courses. In retrospect, I now realize that I was assigned books crucial to the American studies tradition in my classes, but I never identified them as such. It was only while working as a labor historian researching the massive strike wave in the United States after World War II that I turned to the study of culture. The standard historical evidence I found in archives told me a great deal about the history of government agencies, trade unions, and businesses, but very little about the consciousness of the actual workers whose collective actions and mass mobilizations I was trying to study. I managed to find a few oral history interviews about the strikes and I conducted some of my own, but my most valuable evidence about how and why workers mounted the largest strike wave in American history came from analyzing and interpreting a wide range of working-class cultural practices and products—religion and roller derby, films and fiction, subcultural styles and speech, car customizing and country music.[1]

Researching culture led me to consult *American Quarterly*, the official journal of the American Studies Association. *American Quarterly* provided an inspiring array of methods and theories for connecting cultural texts to their social and historical contexts. It made me feel that the kind of scholarship I did might fit into American studies. When advertisements for jobs specified American studies as a desired area of expertise, I put in my application, even though I was not really sure what the term meant to others. My first full-time academic teaching job in the Humanities Program at the University of Houston at Clear Lake City required me to teach history, film studies, and American studies. I sometimes assigned my students articles from *American Quarterly*, but I did not think of myself as having an institutional connection to something called American studies until I was hired as an assistant professor of American studies at the University of Minnesota in 1986.

At Minnesota, American studies occupied a prominent position and boasted a proud history. Joining that department meant working in an institutional space once occupied by the founders of American Studies—Leo Marx, Henry Nash Smith, and Robert Penn Warren, among others. It meant having brilliant, productive, and congenial colleagues with deep commitments to the American studies project. It meant taking a footbridge across the Mississippi River as I walked from my office to classrooms where I taught students about Mark Twain or Miles Davis, whose art had been shaped by that very river.

This was a big change for me after Houston. When I moved there, Houston was in the middle of an incredible period of rapid growth. The local population had quadrupled in ten years; everything looked new, or more precisely everything looked not yet fully constructed. Population growth led to the expansion of local institutions and made my job at the university possible. But the huge influx of new residents also meant that few of the people I knew had any substantial memory of Houston's past. The presence of so many newcomers made the city a hard place to set down roots. I distinctly remember having lived in Houston for three months and thinking that the most personal thing anyone in the city had said to me in that time was "Attention, K-Mart shoppers!" Tradition at Minnesota meant walking in the footsteps of Leo Marx, living in F. Scott Fitzgerald's hometown, and visiting the cafés in Dinkytown where the great Bob Dylan got his start as a folksinger. In Houston, tradition was one of my senior colleagues trying to sell me his used car.[2]

It took me a while to understand Minnesota, but I liked it from the start. It was refreshing to move from Texas, where the game of football was serious business, to the upper Midwest, where football was only something to keep people busy between fishing seasons. In Texas, the teams had macho mascots like Cougars and Longhorns, but in the Midwest the mascots were merely Gophers and Badgers. Houston gave the world Kenny Rogers. Minneapolis produced Prince.

Yet it was only after I left Minnesota and moved to California that I came to understand fully its uniqueness. After working in Minnesota, I was startled to learn in California that 80 percent of college students are *not* named Anderson, that in other states Twins outfielder Mickey Hatcher is not considered a candidate for the Baseball Hall of Fame, and that in some states entire decades pass without anyone named Rudy being elected to high public office.[3]

Yet what endeared me most to Minnesota was its serious side. Inside the Program in American Studies, we had the privilege of teaching at a public university that combined egalitarianism and excellence. Our institution had been created and sustained by the people of Minnesota because of their respect for education, their faith in the future, and their principled commitment to opportunity and inclusiveness. We felt a sense of stewardship toward our department and our university because we knew how hard the people who came before us had to fight to create such a space. We owed our existence to the battles fought and won inside and outside the university by the social movements of the past, especially during the great upheavals of the 1930s and the 1960s.

In 1934, a labor dispute between Minneapolis truck drivers and their employers escalated into a general strike. Workers from nearly every industry and shop in the city walked off the job in a stunning demonstration of solidarity and power. They showed the world that everything stops without the labor that working people contribute. Like the general strikes the same year in Toledo and San Francisco, the Minneapolis General Strike was a dramatic manifestation of an even larger struggle for egalitarian and democratic change. The wave of work stoppages, street demonstrations, and direct action protests that confronted the nation during the Great Depression changed the balance of power in the United States for many years to come. Farmers took up arms to prevent sheriffs from auctioning off the land of neighboring farmers unable to keep up with mortgage payments. Tenement dwellers blocked the halls of their apartment houses to prevent landlords from evicting their neighbors. African American organizations mobilized against job discrimination by organizing boycotts based on the premise that you should not shop where you cannot work. Immigrants and their children fashioned a new and inclusive vision of America by participating in electoral coalitions and trade-union-organizing drives that celebrated the diverse and international origins of the nation's people.[4]

More than a watershed in the history of labor-management relations, the rambunctious self-activity embodied in actions like the 1934 Minneapolis General Strike played an important role in legitimating a more egalitarian and democratic direction for the nation. Workers and their allies won important institutional resources for themselves by persuading the government to take on new responsibilities to promote home ownership, provide retirement and disability insurance, and regulate collective bargaining between labor and management. But beyond any particular material gain, the social movements of the Age of the CIO won a new "social warrant"—a change in self-perception and social expectations. The "social warrant" of the 1930s took the form of a socially agreed upon understanding certifying that working people deserved respect, dignity, and self-determination, and that European American immigrants and their children (especially Catholics and Jews) had legitimate standing as "redemptive insiders" in America rather than probationary status as unwanted aliens.[5]

The social warrant of the Age of the CIO still influenced our lives in Minneapolis during the 1980s. The founding of academic American Studies was one of many responses to the "America" fashioned through collective struggle by the social movements of the 1930s. When a new era of mass mobilization during the 1960s attempted to redefine that "America" by addressing its racism, sexism, and nationalism, academic

American Studies responded with scholarship that spoke to those emerging challenges and concerns.

Within the Program in American Studies at the University of Minnesota during the 1980s, we inherited the legacies of these social movements. The struggles of the 1930s and 1960s played important roles in expanding access to education and in the development of high-quality egalitarian and inclusive universities like the one where we worked. The curriculum we taught had meaning because these social movements had made it necessary for all people in the United States to ask and answer questions about the nature of the national culture. We were authorized to study American culture because students and teachers in the 1930s and 1940s had waged successful battles to insert the study of American culture into humanities departments that had previously devoted their efforts exclusively to the study of Europe. The courses we taught and the research we conducted and supervised was shaped by 1960s efforts to diversify the curriculum, the faculty, and the student body, to include women, people of color, and other unrepresented or underrepresented groups in both the curriculum and the classroom.

Yet from the day I arrived at Minnesota, the future of universities and other democratic public institutions was in jeopardy. Unlike the mass mobilizations of the 1930s and the 1960s when the most important social movements came from the left, the most important mass mobilizations of the 1980s came from the right in the form of what Sidney Plotkin and William Scheuerman call "Balanced Budget Conservatism."[6] Believing that excessive public expenditures drained capital away from more productive investments, Balanced Budget Conservatives called for the complete privatization of public services when possible, but even when not possible they argued that public institutions should pay their own way by engaging in for-profit ventures in collaboration with private interests. This clash between the achievements of 1930s and 1960s social movements and the aims of the social movements of the 1980s shaped every aspect of our attempts to teach American studies at Minnesota in those years. If we had not realized it before, we came to understand that academic struggles over meaning are always connected in crucial ways to social movement struggles over resources and power. Social movements shake up social life; they reconfigure the horizons of individuals and groups by challenging old forms of knowledge and advancing new ones.

Understanding the conflicts of the 1980s as a clash between different social movements with different conceptions of society enabled us to see that the history of American studies was also a history of successive social movements. The myth-image-symbol school of the 1930s and 1940s with its recurrent questions about the true essence of the U.S. nation stemmed directly from the celebratory nationalism of the New Deal coalition. The turn toward social science methods of studying small groups and away from humanistic study of the nation at large emanated directly from the emphases on participatory democracy within civil rights, student, and feminist mobilizations during the 1960s, as well as on the ways in which the Vietnam War undermined the legacy of patriotic nationalism that had gone largely unchallenged during World War II and the cold war. The emphasis on ideological critique and cultural studies that characterized American studies scholarship in the 1980s emerged as a direct response to the rise of Balanced Budget Conservatism and to the success of Ronald Reagan and other politicians in wielding cultural symbols for political ends.

This book explores the links between American Studies and social movements. In Part I, "American Studies and Social Movements," I examine the ways in which the contemporary realities of globalization have disrupted the isomorphism of culture and place, giving new meaning to national and transnational identities. I try to trace the relationship between social movements in the 1930s, 1960s, and 1980s and the schools of American studies that emerged in their wake. I also try to show that each new social movement and each new paradigm for American studies have been shaped by the victories and the defeats of the previous era. If we are to fashion an American studies appropriate to our own era, we need to know what we want to retain from the past and what we want to discard. We need to know how scholarship and social movements influence each other, and we need to ask and answer hard questions about the project of national culture and our relationship to it.

In Part II, "Race, Culture, and Collective Struggle," I turn to the relationship between ethnic studies and American studies. The knowledges generated from within aggrieved ethnic groups can serve as a rich repository for understanding national, international, and transnational cultures, if we learn how to read them in the most fully theorized and knowing way. Aggrieved groups pay a terrible price for the hurts of history that they endure, but collective struggle generates organizational learning and produces new ways of knowing and new ways of being. For scholars in American studies, the situated knowledges of aggrieved racialized groups hold great promise for teaching us how to combine the particular histories of specific groups with the larger social processes that shape social identity and for understanding the connections that link separate oppressions to larger structures of power.

I explore the ways in which the concept of "panethnicity" within Asian American studies has generated a unique epistemological standpoint that can be of great utility in all inquiries about culture, power, and social identities. My discussion of sexuality, race, and national identity in popular music from Miami attempts to explore the ways in which globalization is being lived at the grass roots, how it creates unexpected antagonisms, but also unexpected affiliations and alliances. The graphic art of the Chicano movement offers me an opportunity to talk about the connections that link aesthetic choices to social structures, as well as to examine the role played by artistic imagination and expression within social movements. I conclude this section with a study of "genre anxiety" in 1970s cinema, of the ways in which disturbances about the meaning of race in U.S. society outside the motion picture theaters can be discerned through critical interpretation and analysis of changes in generic Hollywood productions.

In Part III, "Facing Up to What's Killing You," I explore the emergence of new social movements and their impact on cultural contestation today. New forms of capital accumulation and consumption have compelled artists and intellectuals to create new cognitive mappings about themselves and their relationships with other people. Dramatic changes in urban spatial relations have generated new kinds of spoken word and performance art. The rise of "flexible accumulation" and "on-time" production undermine the power of workers at the point of production, but create new dynamics around distribution and consumption that offer opportunities for struggles for social justice. Emerging dynamics within professional and technical training make educational institutions more closely connected to commerce than ever before, but they also engender alienations that might serve as a stimulus for social change. In the final chapter, I explore the ways in which contemporary nostalgia for the national past might inhibit the development of new and greatly needed forms of knowledge.

My emphasis on social movements might strike some readers as eccentric or misplaced. We do not generally think about social movements when we think about culture. Powerful corporations try to convince us that our only important identities are as individual consumers, not as members of cultural communities. Dominant political institutions encourage us to think of ourselves as atomized citizen-subjects, not as the beneficiaries of collective social movements from the past or as generators of new ones in the future. The pervasive nature of therapeutic advice we receive from newspaper columnists, talk-show hosts, authors of self-help books, and from trained therapeutic professionals themselves generally encourages us to seek self-improvement rather than social connection as our most important life project. Yet the legacies of past social movements still loom large in our lives, not only in our consciousness but also in our degree of access to institutional resources. I hope to show in this book that our identities as consumers, citizens, and therapeutic subjects have themselves been shaped by the actions of social movements past and present, by what they gain when they win and by the terrible price they pay when they lose.

Among those directly engaged in American studies teaching, learning, and research, my emphasis on social movements as part of the history of the field will probably be more familiar. Yet my arguments about the shortcomings of past social movements and the limits of previous paradigms for doing American studies may be less welcome. I think we can learn from all previous experiences and approaches;

we cannot afford to dispense with any of the paradigms from the past completely. Yet I am equally convinced that new problems require new solutions. I am not so much interested in rendering a judgment on others in the field, to create a distinguished lineage within which we might locate ourselves, as I am in discovering how we can use the experiences and understandings of the past to prepare ourselves adequately for the challenges that the future seems certain to present to us.

PART I
AMERICAN STUDIES AND
SOCIAL MOVEMENTS

In this sense, social science was very much a creature, if not a creation, of the
states, taking their boundaries as crucial social containers.

—Immanuel Wallerstein et al., *Open the Social Sciences:*
Report of the Gulbenkian Commission on the
Restructuring of the Social Sciences

CHAPTER 1

In the Midnight Hour

American Studies in a Moment of Danger

More than simply a superpower face-off having broad political
repercussions, the Cold War was also a form of knowledge and a
cognitive organization of the world.

—Katherine Verdery, *What Was Socialism, and What Comes Next?*

Senegalese singer Baaba Maal has a theory about midnight. Acknowledging that others view the middle of the night with trepidation and
dread, that they think of it as the time when despair reigns and a new
dawn is very hard to see, Maal nonetheless encourages us to embrace the
midnight hour. For him, "Midnight is the time when the spirit takes
stock and looks ahead to the new day. It's important for every person to
have a midnight in their life—to know what you have done and what you
have yet to do."[1]

For millions of people around the world, the present moment may
seem like midnight. The rapid movement across the globe of people,
products, ideas, and images seems to undermine foundational certainties
about the meaning of local and national identities, the value of personal
and collective histories, and the solidity of social relationships and social
networks. New forms of economic activity produce both astounding
wealth and appalling poverty—sometimes in the same locations. New
technologies liberate us from tiresome tasks yet create unprecedented
environmental dangers. In some respects global marketing brings the
people of the world closer together than ever before, yet consuming the
same products, enjoying the same entertainments, or working for the
same employers does not seem to make us any less divided, as old antagonisms and new enmities create violent conflicts on every continent.

Educational institutions have trained most of us to think largely in terms of national politics, national histories, and national cultures. Yet the present moment of global social and cultural transformation requires us to develop *trans*national and *post*national as well as national ways of knowing. We see now, if only in retrospect, that industrialization, nationalism, and the cold war were not just historical processes and events—they were also ways of knowing and ways of being. They had their own logics and optics; they encouraged us to see some things and prevented us from seeing others. They trained us to ask how each specific geographic location produced its own specific culture, to define politics largely in terms of citizenship and the nation-state, and to pursue social justice by seeking universal truths that could apply to all people and make us equal and interchangeable. Yet our actual experiences in today's postindustrial, postnationalist, and post–cold war era confront us constantly with cultural practices and political projects that cannot be pinned down to any one place, that supersede the purview of individual states, and that generate a seeming endless stream of new differences that frustrate strategies for social justice based on equivalence and interchangeability.

Older narratives about national identity, citizenship, and subjectivity do not disappear under these conditions, but they do become recontextualized in light of emerging understandings, ideas, and identities. For several hundred years, questions about social emancipation have been directly related to a relatively fixed understanding of spaces and places. Within fields like American studies, the nation-state has served as the logical—and seemingly inevitable—object of inquiry. Even within the state, physical places have taken center stage as sites of struggle— the frontier, the farm, the factory, and the city. In American studies, this approach emerged in part because of the centrality of the national landscape to the national imagination.[2] But it also originated in social struggles centered on place: in efforts by farmers to retain control over their land, from battles by factory workers to gain control at the point of production, from mobilizations by urban coalitions seeking solutions to shared problems through control over the regulatory and taxing activities of cities and states.

Yet many of the cultural and community crises we face today emanate from the ways in which the sense of place that guided social movements and scholarship in the past has now become obsolete. Containerization in shipping, computer-generated automation, outsourcing of production, Internet commerce, fiber-optic telecommunications, and satellite technologies seem to have terminated the "isomorphism" (the congruence or one-to-one relationship) between culture and place. In the process of losing this dominion over place, ordinary workers, consumers, and citizens have found it more difficult to influence the social allocation of resources and opportunities in their lives.

In the United States today, emerging patterns of migration, trade, investment, and military intervention affect everything from the national origins of babies available for adoption to the ethnic identities of clerks in convenience stores, from the ownership of downtown skyscrapers to the price of drugs on the streets. The most sophisticated and advanced technologies of our time generate new anxieties, but they also enable us to make novel and intimate connections that seem to transcend space and time.

Some affluent children in North American suburbs go to sleep wearing pajamas emblazoned with images from the Walt Disney film *Pocahontas*. The pajamas they wear are sewn under sweatshop conditions by women workers in Haiti who receive thirty cents an hour for their labor. At the same time, the chief executive officer of the Disney Corporation that markets the pajamas (and the film that they publicize) receives $97,000 per hour in direct compensation. The mechanisms of global cultural production and marketing provide low-wage women workers in Haiti, affluent suburban children, and the CEO of the Disney Corporation with a common frame of reference—the film *Pocahontas*—but these members of different social groups have very different relationships to the common object that seems to unite them.

Pocahontas pajamas, and the film they celebrate (or to be more precise sell-abrate), keep alive in the twenty-first century a story first fashioned in North America during the seventeenth century. Tales about marriage between an indigenous woman of color and a white male have long been a staple in Euro-American culture as a foundational myth of national origins. The native woman's love for the white man serves to establish the moral superiority of the conqueror's culture. Marriage allows the native woman to "assimilate" into the nation by disappearing, by becoming part of the genealogy of white society. The Pocahontas story, and others like it, turn the brutality and sadism of conquest into a voluntary romance.

The reemergence of the Pocahontas story in the present age of globalization unwittingly directs our attention to the similarities between our own time and the seventeenth century. The expansion of capitalism in both eras created new cognitive mappings of the world and brought diverse peoples into direct contact with one another. But in both eras, unequal power relations structured the terms of contact, communication, and commerce. The exploitation of Haitian women workers by the Disney Corporation enables that company to market worldwide a product that rationalizes conquest as a romance.[3]

Pocahontas pajamas turn bedtime into a marketing opportunity for a multinational corporation. They connect a shared moment of recognition between North American parents and children to legacies of imperial conquest and genocide from the past, as well as to the raced and gendered exploitation of contemporary workers in Caribbean garment assembly shops. Suburban children and their parents, the director of Disney's business operations, low-wage women workers in Haiti, and contemporary feminist and Native American activists are all united by their links to the film *Pocahontas*, but the gender, race, class, and national identity of each of them have everything to do with the nature of that connection and its consequences for their lives.[4]

The Pocahontas connection does not exist in isolation. Air Jordan athletic shoes made by low-wage women workers in Indonesia secure high prices from consumers in Boston, Berlin, and Buenos Aires largely because they symbolize "prestige from below" as icons evoking the sensibilities and style leadership of impoverished African American inner-city youths. The direct labor costs to Nike for a $90 pair of shoes are $1.20—only 1.3 percent of the retail price. A Nike worker would have to work 60,000 years making Air Jordans at $1.20 per hour to receive compensation equal to Michael Jordan's earnings from the company in 1998 alone.[5] But Jordan's endorsement is lucrative only because someone even richer can easily afford his fee. The profits made by paying Asian women workers less than subsistence wages enable Nike's top executive, Phil Knight, to hire the highly publicized Michael Jordan, but also to control entry into a vast network of jobs in marketing, design, management, and sales for employees in North America and Europe. Air Jordan shoes influence the lives of impoverished inner-city athletes and the style choices of wealthy suburban consumers, they have an impact on the earning power of well-paid corporate executives in Europe and North America and on low-wage women workers in Asia. They create a community of interest that stretches across continents and classes, yet they leave the individuals in that community with permanently hierarchical and segmented opportunities and life chances.

The generation of new points of commonality and new points of conflict among the world's people embodied in the production, distribution, and marketing of Pocahontas pajamas and Air Jordan athletic shoes occurs within a context of increasingly centralized power and control in the hands of a small group of corporate executives and investors. Economic policy decisions that used to be made by local legislative bodies are now implemented automatically in response to the activities of stocks and bonds markets. International treaties, agreements, and institutions including the North American Free Trade Agreement (NAFTA), the General Agreement on Tariffs and Trade (GATT), the International Monetary Fund (IMF), the World Bank, and the World Trade Organization (WTO) impose fatal constraints on national efforts at antitrust regulation, environmental protection, and fair labor practices.[6] International boards controlled by financiers and corporate executives have been given authority to void local, state, and national laws that impede the flow of capital, even when those laws protect public health, safety, and welfare.

The new spatial and social relations of our time have important consequences for knowledge. New social relations create new social subjects who inevitably create new epistemologies and new ontologies—new ways of knowing and new ways of being. New social subjects produce new archives and new imaginings. Demographic changes within nation-states, as well as the complex networks and circuits that connect identities, economies, and ideologies across national boundaries, all compel us to rethink some long-established beliefs and concepts. What happens to the individual citizen, worker, or community member at a time of such dramatic transformation and change in spatial and social identities? How do nationally inflected understandings of citizenship, race, class, gender, and sexuality change when they become international, transnational, and national all at the same time?

More than 125 million people around the globe currently reside outside their country of birth or citizenship. An additional 2 to 4 million others join their ranks every year.[7] Remittances sent home by overseas workers make up crucial components of the national economies of many countries in Asia, Africa, and Latin America. The exploitation and indignities suffered by immigrant low-wage workers in Europe and North America subsidize the standard of living enjoyed by educated urban professionals on those continents by providing them with low-cost goods and personal services. The remittances immigrant workers send home then subsidize the interests of transnational corporations by softening the impact of the devastation engendered by the low wages and low taxes that those firms enjoy in Asia, Africa, and Latin America.

Workers leave Kerala in southwest India to labor in Kuwait and become at one and the same time the poorest people in their new neighborhoods and the wealthiest in their home villages. Undercapitalized immigrant businesses in New York City produce revenue that finances new housing complexes and luxury automobiles in the cities of Baní and San Francisco de Macorís in the Dominican Republic, while small huts in Filipino villages feature video recorders and television sets paid for with money sent home by expatriate household laborers in Hong Kong, Saudi Arabia, and Rome. Urban professionals in metropolitan "world" cities in Europe, North America, and Asia enjoy lavish consumption-oriented lifestyles largely because of the inexpensive cooking, cleaning, child care, and other personal services provided by exploited immigrant workers.

A handful of multinational corporations now control more than one-third of the world's productive private-sector assets. Around the globe every day, more than thirty thousand children under the age of five die of starvation or completely curable diseases, some ten million every year—one every three seconds.[8] More than a billion people subsist on incomes less than a dollar per day. The richest fifth of the world's population controls 85 percent of the globe's wealth, leaving little more than 1 percent for the poorest fifth.[9] In Mexico, the twenty-four wealthiest families have more money than the twenty-four million poorest Mexicans.[10]

The global economic system is a class system, but it is also a racial system. Built upon the remnants of previous racial regimes, it now produces a proliferation of new forms of differentiation that exacerbate and expand old ethnic and racial conflicts. The shake-up in spatial and social relations in our time does nothing to dislodge long-standing forms of white supremacy. Instead, structural-adjustment policies, mass migration, and attacks on the social institutions traditionally responsible for creating greater equality all function together in our time to make "whiteness" a global as well as a national project, to insure the permanent supremacy of the largely "white" global north over the largely "non-white" global south, and even to restore power in the global south to the light-skinned elites who in the era of decolonization found themselves forced to make concessions to the dark-skinned masses of their own countries. At the same time, in North America and Europe, what Ghassan Hage calls the "psychopathology of white decline" draws on old and new forms of racism to portray hardworking and exploited immigrants as parasites rather than as producers.[11]

As the population of the United States becomes less white, the psychopathology of white decline influences the outcome of all public policy debates. U.S. citizens invested in the notion of their nation as essentially white and European confront a daunting demographic challenge. The population of the United States now includes thirty million Latinos and ten million Asian Americans.[12] African Americans, Native Americans, Asian Americans, and Latinos account for more than half of the populations of Los Angeles, Miami, San Antonio, Honolulu, and several other major cities. California, Hawaii, New Mexico, and Texas will be "majority minority" states by 2025. Nearly half of the children born in California and almost a third of the children born in New York in 1996 had immigrant mothers.[13] In 1997, the number of babies in California designated as "interracial" by their parents exceeded the number designated Black, Asian, or Native American.[14] The aggregate minority population in the United States exceeds the national population of many nations, including Great Britain, France, Italy, and Spain. If U.S. racial minorities had their own country, it would be the fifteenth largest nation on earth.[15]

The United States now houses the fifth largest Spanish-speaking population in the world. If present population trends in Colombia and Argentina continue, in five years the United States will become the third largest concentration of Spanish speakers on the planet.[16] Latino children make up more than 40 percent of the school-age population of California, and the Latino percentage of births in California has increased from 20 percent in 1975 to 46 percent in 1995.[17] Almost 10 percent of the population of the Dominican Republic lives in the United States.[18] Three million Puerto Ricans, close to 40 percent of the island's population, reside on the North American mainland.[19] Nearly one-third of the population of Belize lives in the United States.[20]

Secondary migration complicates the picture even more. Some Korean Americans and Chinese Americans in Los Angeles came to the United States after first migrating to Brazil and Panama. Significant numbers of Dominican, Haitian, and Leeward Islander immigrants to New York first migrated to Puerto Rico, the Bahamas, and the U.S. Virgin Islands. As early as 1970, nearly 40 percent of the population of the Virgin Islands had already moved to Canada or the United States, while the percentage of foreign-born residents of the islands climbed above 34 percent.[21] More than 1 million Haitians live in the United States, 150,000 in the Dominican Republic, and close to 40,000 in the Bahamas. Migration to the United States and the Bahamas has helped make English rather than French the second language of many *kreyol*-speaking Haitians.[22]

Immigrants make up 34 percent of the population of Miami and 27 percent of the population of Los Angeles.[23] Nearly half the people living in Miami and about one quarter of the people living in Houston are Latinos.[24] New York, Miami, and Boston each have more Haitian residents than Cap Haitien, Haiti's second-largest city.[25] Forty-five percent of the people in Los Angeles County speak a language other than English at home, and students who attend classes in the Los Angeles Unified School District include native speakers of more than 120 languages and dialects.[26]

Twenty years ago, the United States imported almost no mangos from anywhere in the world. But the food preferences of immigrants from Asia and Latin America have propelled a 200 percent increase in mango imports to the United States between 1986 and 1995, making the nation currently the world's largest importer of mangos. According to Robert Alvarez, nearly half of U.S. mango consumption takes place in Los Angeles.[27]

New York City is now the Caribbean's largest city, even though it is not in the Caribbean: New York has a larger Caribbean population than the combined populations of Kingston (Jamaica), San Juan (Puerto Rico), and Port of Spain (Trinidad).[28] Immigration from Guyana, Haiti, and Jamaica has made New York the second largest Guyanese, Haitian, and Jamaican city on the globe. More people from the Caribbean island of Nevis live in New York than live on Nevis itself.[29]

Approximately 3.7 million people of Mexican ancestry and 1.3 million people of Asian ancestry reside in Los Angeles. The city is also home to 300,000 Salvadorans and 159,000 Guatemalans.[30] Los Angeles is now the second-largest Mexican, Guatemalan, and Salvadoran city in the world, as well as the third-largest Canadian city.[31] The Los Angeles metropolitan area houses the largest Iranian population in the Western world and is home to what are generally considered the largest populations of Armenians outside of Armenia, Vietnamese outside of Vietnam, and Koreans outside of Korea.[32] More Samoans live in Los Angeles than in American Samoa itself.[33]

Immigration from Asia, Africa, the Caribbean, and Latin America since 1965 has transformed the demography of the United States, increasing the nation's nonwhite population significantly. But immigration has also changed the composition of aggrieved racial groups. Nearly one and a half million African Americans are now immigrants from the Caribbean. Their ranks include native speakers of English, French, Spanish, Dutch, and indigenous languages such as Garifuna. At least one-half million of the immigrants to the United States from Spanish-speaking countries alone between 1990 and 1998 were Black by North American standards, bringing the total number of Black Latinos to about 1.7 million. At the same time, 600,000 Asian Americans are also Latinos—mostly secondary migrants who stopped in Latin America before settling in the United States, but also products of interracial marriages.[34] California's American Indian population of 307,000 includes 118,000 Latinos, while nationwide an estimated 7 or 8 million people now classified by the census as Latino are probably also Native American.[35]

Under these conditions, immigrants inevitably experience new forms of racialization in the United States. Nationals from Asia and Latin America appear to be people of color by North American standards, and consequently face both nativist and racist hostility in their new surroundings. But immigrants also bring with them traditional forms of racism learned in their home countries from local practices as well as from global media. At the same time, competition for scarce resources in the North American context generates new racial enmities and antagonisms, which in turn promotes new variants of racism.

These dynamic transformations produce new kinds of social subjects, as people increasingly perceive themselves in need of new cognitive mappings and understandings. Yet these radically new reckonings do not erase the very old inequalities and injustices on which they are based.

Corporations at the present time are often wealthier than countries. According to Karen Brodkin, the Philip Morris Corporation is wealthier than Chile, and Wal-Mart is wealthier than Greece. The holdings of Chrysler and Nestle are about the same size as the economies of Pakistan and Hungary.[36] Yet the power of transnational corporations does not mean that the nation-state disappears under the present regime of globalization. Although political leaders everywhere plead powerlessness in the face of the imperatives of corporate profits in the transnational economy, the nation-state remains a crucial part of the architecture of transnationalism. The very existence of national borders allows employers to play one location against another, to ensure international investors that they can secure labor, markets, and raw materials worldwide, but in doing so confront only national political resistance.

U.S. consumers enjoy lower prices because of the exploitation of workers in the rest of the world. The tiny nation of El Salvador sends nearly three hundred million garments to the United States every year. In special export production zones, Salvadoran armed guards make sure that labor ministry officials cannot enter factory grounds to check on working conditions. Some sixty-five thousand *maquiladora* workers in that country labor fifteen hours a day, seven days a week in factories surrounded by ten-foot-high cinderblock walls with barbed wire on top. Workers are allowed one bathroom visit in the morning and one in the afternoon. Women employees are routinely given pregnancy tests and are fired if they test positive, so that the companies can avoid paying mandatory prenatal care and maternity-leave benefits. Salvadoran garment workers are paid sixty cents an hour, about one-third of the subsistence wage. A woman's jacket made in El Salvador and retailing for $198 in North American clothing stores includes a labor cost of eighty-four cents.

More than fifty thousand workers from China, the Philippines, and Bangladesh work twelve-hour days, seven days a week, for less than the legal minimum wage in Saipan (in the Mariannas, a U.S. possession), making garments for various U.S. apparel firms including Wal-Mart,

Sears Roebuck, and Tommy Hilfiger. These workers live seven to a room in barracks surrounded by barbed-wire fences. Their passports are confiscated on arrival to prevent escape or resistance to the compulsory overtime, low wages, and sporadic beatings that are a routine part of labor discipline in the production of garments that reach the public adorned with labels that read "Made in the USA."[37]

The export of production to low-wage countries overseas has a decided impact on wages and working conditions in the United States as well. Structural adjustment policies imposed on people in Asia, Africa, and Latin America by the International Monetary Fund and the World Bank exacerbate inequalities on those continents and provoke people to migrate to higher-wage countries like the United States. Asian American women, many of them recent immigrants, make up more than 50 percent of the entire labor force in the U.S. textile and apparel industries. They work for low wages in largely unregulated small shops, contracting respiratory illnesses at high rates because of repeated exposure to fiber particles, dyes, formaldehydes, and arsenic. On the assembly lines in California's "Silicon Valley," the production of "high-tech" computers depends upon the low-wage labor of Latino/as and Asian Americans. Forty-three percent of these workers are Asian Americans. At work on high-tech assembly lines, Asian and Latina women experience illness approximately three times as often as workers in general manufacturing—illnesses that often entail damage to reproductive and central nervous systems.[38]

Although they often complain about an immigrant "invasion," middle- and upper-class consumers are triply subsidized by the exploitation of low-wage workers. Immigrant labor assures them of lower-priced products and easily acquired personal services. Immigrant low-wage workers dominate household and personal service jobs in advanced high-consumption countries. They clean houses, cook food, and care for children and seniors for little monetary compensation. Their labor enables high-income professionals to sustain high-consumption lifestyles, to have more time for earning and spending. The low cost of immigrant labor makes child care, convalescent care, and old-age care less expensive for families and for the state; it discourages savings and encourages spending. Low-wage immigrant labor in North America and Europe even subsidizes capital flight. As Neferti Tadiar's important work demonstrates, remittances sent home by overseas workers often provide the crucial margin of difference that enables workers in Asia, Africa, and Latin America to survive on the below-subsistence wages paid them by transnational corporations.[39]

All U.S. consumers enjoy lower prices because of the exploitation of workers in poor countries, but the resulting benefits are not distributed equally. Despite a decade of extraordinary prosperity and economic growth, the net worth of the median U.S. family actually declined in the 1990s. The share of net worth of the richest fifth of families, however, rose from 83.5 percent to 84.5 percent. In 1972, the top 1 percent of the nation's families owned 27 percent of the country's wealth; by 1987 the richest 1 percent of families controlled 36 percent of the national wealth.[40] Economic inequality in the United States in 1998 was greater than at any time since the Great Depression of the 1930s. Nearly one half of the nation's income now goes to the wealthiest fifth of households.[41] The wealthiest 10 percent of families in the United States own 94 percent of the business assets, 90 percent of the bonds, 89 percent of the corporate stock and 78 percent of the nation's real estate.[42]

The globalization of economic production, distribution, and consumption transforms the nature of national politics and national cultures. Simple binary oppositions between the local and the global or the particular and the universal no longer seem useful; the isomorphism of place, culture, nation, and state can no longer be taken for granted.[43] Jean-Bertrand Aristede and other Haitian politicians compete for followers in each of their country's nine states (called *départments*), but they also seek support from what they refer to as *le dixième départment*, the tenth department—the more than one million Haitians living overseas in Miami, Brooklyn, Montreal, Paris, and other diasporic centers.[44] Major-league games in the United States use baseballs fabricated in small workshops by low-wage women workers in Haiti and other Caribbean and Central American countries.

Although contemporary and emerging economic, political, and cultural relations may give the impression that the power and practical utility of the nation-state has been superseded by transnational corporations and the global market, the state continues to be an indispensable component of the global system. The state serves as a crucial resource to multinational corporations by supplying mechanisms for capital accumulation and technological innovation through direct investment by governments, indirect support for research and development, tax abatements, and research and development spending on the infrastructure of global capital, especially containerization in shipping and the Internet, which were originally developed by the United States Navy and Department of Defense. The state also supplies transnational capital with political regulation through direct repression of insurrections and strikes as well as through agreeing to international treaties like the GATT agreements that deprive citizens of the power to use politics in order to challenge multinational corporate environmental pollution, labor exploitation, or market monopolization. The state helps discipline the labor force and imprisons surplus labor. As Etienne Balibar reminds us, "The state is the form through which nations enter the modern world system."[45]

Under contemporary conditions, it is important to understand the things that all nation-states have in common as well as the things that distinguish them. This might seem a sharp departure from the core categories and concerns of American studies under the pressure of present events, but in actuality such an inquiry will enable us to revisit traditional American studies scholarship with new insight and understanding. By looking at the state functionally as a transnational entity rather than as a discrete and atomized national body, we can learn that elites in every nation have a stake in perpetuating differences among nations.[46] The very existence of nation-states encourages cessation of internal hostilities in order to face outside foes. It justifies national inequalities and injustices while projecting anger and resentment against outside enemies rather than internal elites. The mere existence of national borders enables differential rates of pay for the same work and creates artificial *what about culture? (poverty)*

divisions among workers. In addition, ruling groups in every country have a stake in national exceptionalism—in attributing a unique character and destiny to the national project as a way of making actions taken in their own self-interest seem predestined, necessary, and even inevitable.[47]

The hegemony of the nation-state as the ultimate horizon in American studies (and other nationally based inquiries in the humanities and social sciences) has deadly consequences. It encourages us to confine politics to the realm of the citizen-subject, to view emancipatory movements for social change as primarily efforts to reform the state and its privileged institutions. This emphasis on the state as the primary (and often exclusive) site for political action occludes the unity of politics, culture, and economics in social life, leading us to an idealist and inaccurate view of culture as the site where economic and political exclusions become neutralized by the purported inclusiveness of cultural practices and stories. These acts of cognitive mapping leave us poorly prepared to understand the ways in which culture functions as a social force or the ways in which aesthetic forms draw their affective and ideological power from their social location.

Purely national studies may encourage comparisons between states, but they do too little to reveal the degree to which nation-states are formed by their relations with one another. By encouraging us to see the different ways in which nation-states make war or legitimate their rule through different racial and ethnic categories, purely national approaches have obscured the interests that states have in common, especially the ways in which the nation-state is so often a racial state and the racial state is so often a warfare state. Perhaps most important at the present time, excessive focus on unilateral national histories and national cultures directs our attentions away from polylateral relations between sites, from the very circuits and networks most likely to generate new imaginaries, identities, and intersubjectivities.

Anthropologist Katherine Verdery argues that the end of the cold war generates a particular crisis for well-established knowledge regimes. The cold war was not simply a face-off between two superpowers with contrasting economic and political systems, she argues, but also an impetus for cognitively mapping the world through strategically useful divisions between "east" and "west," "right" and "left," "north" and "south," and "first," "second," and "third worlds." From Verdery's perspective, these spatial metaphors do little to help us find the battleground where the decisive final conflict actually took place. She suggests that the decisive conflict was not one of geographic entities or even of social systems, but rather a clash between two different concepts of time.

Starting at least in the 1960s, new management techniques and new technologies generated a "speedup" in capitalism, a compression of time and space emblematized by computer-generated automation, instantaneous electronic transfers of money, and new forms of production based on "flexible accumulation" and on-time production. This speedup exacerbated faction fights inside socialist countries between government leaders committed to "socialist time" based on centralized planning methods and bureaucrats in charge of foreign trade who saw that increased turnover time cost them hard currency. The initial compromise between these factions revolved around borrowing from the West in order to meet the challenge of the capitalist speedup. But the massive debts incurred from this borrowing did not lead to commensurate increases in productivity. As a result, officials interested in production for export secured additional loans, which resulted in even larger debts. The collapse of socialism came about when party leaders and economic policy planners in socialist countries felt compelled to adopt capitalism as the only way to service their debt.

Verdery notes the irony of this turn of events: "If socialist economies had not opened up themselves to capital import and to debt servicing, perhaps their collision with capitalist speedup would have been less jarring—or at least would have occurred on more equal terms. But the capitalist definition of time prevailed as socialist debtors bowed to its dictates (even while postponing them) thereby aggravating factional conflicts within the elite. Because its leaders accepted Western temporal hegemony, socialism's messianic time proved apocalyptic." Thus, in its final stages, both sides in the cold war believed in the inevitability of capitalist time. Verdery points out that the socialist countries could have very probably brought down the world capitalist system simply by acting in concert and defaulting on their debts while encouraging other debtor nations to do the same. "That this did not happen," Verdery continues, "shows how vital a thing was capitalist monopoly on the definition of social reality."[48]

Verdery's account will do little to satisfy those who believe that the cold war was a righteous crusade against an "evil empire," who want to credit the defense buildup of the Reagan era for the "fall of Communism." Yet even the adherents to that view might want to explore what they have to gain from a transnational analysis like Verdery's that does not automatically grant the United States a messianic role at the center of history. Her explanation of the end of the cold war helps us understand why the demise of officially existing communism has left the world with so little democracy and so much plutocracy and profiteering. Following political scientist Ken Jowitt, Verdery argues that the extinction of Leninism in the Soviet Union is not merely a local problem of interest to Russia and its neighbors, but rather part of a process that requires us to redefine national identities as well as "the entire conceptual arsenal through which Western institutions and social science disciplines have been defined in this century."[49]

The end of the cold war, the rise of postindustrial forms of "flexible accumulation," production, and consumption, as well as the emergence of transnational cultural, economic, and political entities all require new ways of being and new ways of knowing. Scholars may still have the luxury of thinking in exclusively national terms, but workers, citizens, migrants, artists, and activists do not. They have become transnational as a matter of necessity. They can no longer assume the isomorphism of culture and place or of citizenship and the state. American studies scholars need to join them, to reckon with the vexations and challenges that we face with the emergence of new social relations and new social subjects.

We need to appreciate the ways in which new social, cultural, economic, and political practices are rupturing traditional connections between culture and place, making local identities both less and more important at the same time. We need to learn from people and cultures that have been forced to make themselves as mobile, flexible, and fluid as transnational capital, yet still capable of drawing upon separate histories, principles, and values. Fashioning scholarship in American studies appropriate to our time requires us to move beyond either simple celebration or categorical condemnation. Deciding on a new course for American studies obligates us to understand where our field has been in the past and where it might go in the future.

As Michael Denning demonstrates in his wonderful volume *The Cultural Front*, academic American Studies emerged out of the redemptive "America" fashioned in social struggle by the democratic mobilizations of the 1930s, out of the imagined America that social movements both asked for and authorized. As the product of a particular place and time, American studies shared its conditions of possibility with the emergence of the class-conscious interethnic coalitions during the 1930s, especially the organizing drives of the Congress of Industrial Organizations (CIO) and the political campaigns of the Farmer-Labor Party in Minnesota, the Anton Cermak coalition in Chicago, and the Fiorello La Guardia alliance in New York. Joined with the efforts of radical immigrant journalists like Louis Adamic who celebrated the multiethnic history of this country and aided by mass mobilizations like the general strikes of 1934 (which were central to the egalitarian accomplishments of that era), what Denning describes as the Age of the CIO helped restructure the contours of politics and culture in this country.

Mass mobilizations and electoral initiatives during the 1930s drew upon disparate sources of resistance and opposition. They forged uneasy alliances, linking antimonopoly capitalists with Popular Front Marxists, connecting desires for ethnic inclusion into mainstream society with proletarian self-activity. They met with mixed success in their efforts to redistribute wealth and power, but they won enduring victories on the terrain of culture. The New Deal coalition laid claim to the national legacy by celebrating the multiethnic and immigrant roots of the republic. In the process, it helped turn unwanted alien immigrant outsiders and their children into triumphant redemptive insiders, "rewriting" the past as well as the present. The "cult of the common person" that circulated inside the era's film, photography, fiction, and theater projects established a cultural consensus so powerful that its ideology permeated not only the work of Popular Front writers and artists, but the cultural expressions of monopoly capitalist filmmakers in Hollywood as well.

Academic American Studies was not an intentional creation of this social upheaval and cultural transformation, but the field emerged as one of many unintended aftershocks of the social and cultural struggles of the 1930s. That is the way history happens. Social movements shake up social life. They throw a pebble into a pond and produce ripples everywhere. Even when social movements fail to achieve their own stated goals, they send a message to people in other places about the potential for struggle and resistance. They provide tools for people to ask new questions, to settle old scores, to speak about parts of their lives that have been repressed and suppressed. The creation of American studies had everything to do with the cultural and intellectual spaces opened up by the mass movements of the 1930s.

Mass mobilizations during the Age of the CIO included southern segregationists and northern European American ethnics, old-line aristocrats and minority workers. During the 1930s these antagonistic elements worked together to help pass legislation initiating old-age pensions, aid for dependent children, and disability compensation. They established the National Labor Relations Board to regulate labor-management relations, and created agencies like the Federal Housing Administration, which put the full faith and credit of the federal government behind the home loan industry and made it possible for working people to borrow money to purchase their own homes. For the first time they could accumulate assets that might appreciate in value and subsequently serve as a source for intergenerational transfers of wealth.

An interracial "culture of unity" worked together to win these victories, but the spoils won in the struggle were apportioned according to white supremacist principles. The Social Security Act and the Wagner Act excluded farm workers and domestics from coverage, channeling benefits to white workers who secured jobs in manufacturing because of discriminatory hiring while denying segments of the labor force dominated by minorities the benefits of legislation that their activism had helped to produce. The Federal Housing Administration adopted explicitly racialized categories in determining eligibility for home loans, funneling 98 percent of federally supported home loans to whites between 1934 and 1965. The New Deal State became a racial state, and it evolved into a warfare state with the entry of the United States into World War II.[50]

President Franklin Delano Roosevelt himself declared that "Dr. New Deal" had to get out of the way and make room for "Dr. Win the War" after the Japanese military attacked Pearl Harbor on December 7, 1941. Mobilization for World War II co-opted the political radicalism of the social movements of the 1930s, quickly enabling the establishment of an undemocratic alliance among big business, big government, and big labor in the form of the postwar corporate liberal welfare/warfare state. But the cultural radicalism of the 1930s could not be suppressed completely. After the war, bureaucrats acting on behalf of the national security state used the excuse of anticommunism to direct the full force of legal and extralegal repression against activists, artists, and intellectuals in an effort to purge labor unions, universities, the media, and community groups of their "subversive" tendencies. Yet even in the darkest days of McCarthyism, social movements, cultural practitioners, and traditional intellectuals continued to draw on the legacy of the past to preserve oppositional thought.

At a time when history departments encouraged "consensus" school interpretations that celebrated the status quo and attempted to erase all memories of the oppositional interpretations advanced by New Deal–era scholars, in an era when English departments turned to New Criticism largely as a means of isolating cultural texts from their social and historical contexts, American studies prospered as an institutional site where literature could be studied in relation to history, and where historical inquiry concerned itself with the culture of ordinary people as well as the actions of elites. Whatever the limits of these endeavors by the 1930s generation—and there were many—they none-theless kept alive a critical tradition that proved itself extremely useful to a later generation looking to interpret and understand the many challenges to political and cultural hierarchies that emerged inside and outside the academy in the 1960s and 1970s. The myth-image-symbol school of American studies did not adequately address the nation's racial hierarchies or its imperial relations with the rest of the world—in large part because the social movements of the Age of the CIO failed to address those elements of the national life, but academic American Studies nonetheless functioned as a democratic, egalitarian, and progressive force because it preserved an institutional site for exploring the chasm between the ideal and the real in the United States.

The social movements of the Age of the Civil Rights Movement focused on what the 1930s generation did not—race, empire, and gender especially. For the participants in these movements, yesterday's solutions (the America fashioned by the New Deal and World War II) served as the source of today's problems (racism, imperialism, male privilege and power). The new paradigms that emerged within American studies after the 1960s drew their determinate shapes from these social movements outside the academy. Scholars have become accustomed to discussing "the new social history" and "the anthropological turn" of the 1970s in American studies as purely academic refinements of the myth-symbol-image school, as alterations in the field emerging entirely from within. But I would argue that the emancipatory and egalitarian social movements of the 1960s among women, youth, aggrieved racial minorities, workers, gays, lesbians, and opponents of the war in Vietnam instigated this paradigm shift by demonstrating through their actions the difference between the stories that society tells about itself from the top down and the realities of social relations as they might be understood from the bottom up. The emphasis on the everyday life experiences of ordinary people within the new social history as well as the concern for the uses and effects of culture in enabling people to make meaning for themselves evident in the anthropological turn in American studies did not emerge from the academy alone. Rather, they responded to the new view of culture in America made possible by social movements in the streets during the Age of the Civil Rights Movement, just as the Age of the CIO stimulated the emergence of the myth-symbol-image school in the 1930s.

The American studies that was forged in the 1930s and 1940s allowed scholars and citizens in the 1950s to understand and interpret the defeats of 1930s social movements. Similarly, the new social history and the anthropological turn of the 1970s emphasized links between micro-social experience and macrosocial institutions that proved extremely important in explaining how conservative mobilizations of the 1970s and 1980s succeeded in reversing many of the egalitarian victories won by the oppositional movements of the 1960s. Seen in this light, the cultural studies approach of the 1980s and 1990s was neither a rebuke of the anthropological and social history approaches of the 1970s, nor a rejection of the myth-symbol-image school of the 1940s and 1950s. Rather, it emerged out of a recognition of new conditions and new connections between culture and social structure.

Many of the victories of the New Deal social democratic era ignored or even exacerbated injustices based on race, gender, or sexuality. Even more important, the defeats suffered by the social movements of the 1960s and the victories secured by the successful countermobilization orchestrated by big business neoconservatives in the 1970s and 1980s placed new emphasis on the role of culture as a political force. The most important social movements of the 1980s coalesced around Balanced Budget Conservatism and the religious right with their shared antipathy to the egalitarian cultural and political changes identified with the 1960s. Because of the power and success of the right-wing counter-revolution of the 1980s, cultural studies scholars in American studies turned to the work of European theorists, including Antonio Gramsci, Michel Foucault, and Stuart Hall. Their work offered insights into the political popularity of Ronald Reagan and Margaret Thatcher because they helped show how cultural appeals could induce people to support policies that were diametrically opposed to their own material interests. They provided productive ways of understanding the ideological implications of seemingly apolitical practices and activities. The power of patriotism and patriarchy, of war and whiteness as cultural forces in the 1980s encouraged American studies scholars to see the price that previous movements for social change had paid by marginalizing issues of race, gender, and sexual identification, how cultural conservatism rooted in racialized, gendered, and sexualized hierarchies worked against egalitarian social change. At the same time, they also came to see the importance of oppositional, resistant, and negotiated cultural practices among subcultures, countercultures, and even groups within dominant culture itself.

The democratic self-activity of ordinary people is an extraordinarily powerful force. It influences every emancipatory hope and practice around it. When aggrieved populations fight to participate in the decisions that affect their lives, they not only act to free themselves, but also set in motion dynamics that help free others. But the current crisis we face compels us to rethink the role of democratic self-activity in relation to place. The connections between place and culture that have undergirded the cultural and political practices of the industrial era are becoming obsolete, and the current crisis demands a different imagination about culture, place, and power.

In order to combat the ways in which the new realities of social space have given management and investors the upper hand, we now need to think about places not only as specific geographic and physical sites, but also as circuits and networks of communication, physical movement, and commodity circulation. American studies scholarship can be a great help in rethinking the perils and prospects of the present because its history helps us understand the ways in which place has always been a strategic construct, a narrative creation as well as a physical reality. All places are produced by cognitive mappings that give physical realities their social functions and meanings. Arjun Appadurai argues that we should stop thinking solely in terms of physical spaces and landscapes, and instead realize that our world is now cognitively mapped into ethnoscapes, mediascapes, technoscapes, financescapes, and ideoscapes.[51] Thinking in terms of these "scapes" enables us to see how ethnic identities extend beyond national borders, how mass media creates common images with radically different local inflections, how technology gives workers in the heavy machinery plants of East Peoria the same labor conditions facing assembly-line laborers in Japan and Brazil, how the policies of the IMF and the World Bank impose a similar urban austerity on cities around the world, and how ideologies, religions, and market practices are both global and local at the same time.

In my view, Appadurai underestimates the enduring importance of local spaces, memories, and practices, and his framework does not account adequately for the degree of oppressive centralized power basic to the creation of these new spaces; but he does us a great service in fashioning new forms of thinking about circuits and networks, about their consequences for the meanings attached to physical places. In this respect, the study of global popular culture becomes an essential task of an American studies attuned to the realities of the present moment, because global popular culture is one of those "sites" that might be interrupted, inverted, or subverted for egalitarian purposes.

Intercultural and transnational cultural creations emblematize the dramatic transformations of our time. Something more than postmodern mixing and the juxtaposition of seemingly inappropriate entities is at work here. We are witnessing an inversion of prestige, a moment when diasporic, nomadic, and fugitive cultures from the "margins" seem to speak more powerfully to present conditions than do metropolitan cultures committed to the congruence of culture and place. Populations that suffer the anguish of exile and displacement—Filipinos and Jamaicans, Puerto Ricans and Punjabis—offer powerful expressions of code-switching and cultural fusion that attract followers from outside their own groups. cultural consumption?

The first serious challenge to NAFTA came in the form of an insurrection by Mayan Indians and their supporters in Chiapas, Mexico. The Zapatista movement did not seek state power in Mexico, but rather sought to delegitimate the Mexican state at home and abroad by pointing to the consequences that its submission to global neoliberalism had for indigenous people in Chiapas. Yet while taking direct military action in Chiapas, the Zapatistas also used the Internet and other modern means of communication to foment solidarity around the globe. On the very day they launched their military attack, posters supporting their demands appeared in Mexico City, Los Angeles, London, Paris, and in other cities. Supporters around the globe bypassed the corporate media and followed the struggle by finding their way to Subcommandante Marcos's communiqués on the Internet.

The feminist Gabriela network centered in the Philippines drew upon the worldwide Filipina diaspora for political support and publicity in the 1990s for their campaigns against sex tourism and against the ruinous effects of collaboration between the U.S. and Filipino governments in perpetuating the large-scale prostitution industry that flourished in that country to "supply" U.S. military personnel with access to Filipina women.

Leaders of the Hawai'ian Sovereignty movement in the 1990s assembled a worldwide coalition of indigenous representatives, feminists, environmentalists, and antinuclear activists in collective struggle on behalf of self-determination for indigenous peoples, limits on tourism and development on indigenous lands, and an end to the use of the Pacific as a nuclear testing zone.

What does this activism have to do with American studies today? It seems to me that there are two American studies traditions in existence. One is the institutional American studies canonized within easily recognized paradigms like myth-symbol-image, uses-and-effects anthropology, the new social history, and cultural studies. All of these offer vital, important, and even essential ways of understanding culture in the United States, but they are tied to connections between culture and place that no longer may be operative. The present moment and the present crisis threatening the connections between culture and place require us to draw upon what we might call the "other American studies," the organic grassroots theorizing about culture and power that has informed cultural practice, social movements, and academic work for many years. Much of this work has been created by exiles, migrants, and members of other groups that have been displaced and consequently are less likely to take for granted the automatic congruence between culture and place. This is the American studies of C. L. R. James, whose brilliant book *American Civilization*, written in the 1950s, has recently been reissued.[52] It is the American Studies of Duke Ellington, who used to respond to questions about "Negro" identity by playing a dissonant chord on the piano and saying, "That's us. That's our life in America. We're a thing apart, yet an integral part." This is the tradition of Americo Paredes, whose extraordinary 1958 book about the ballad of Gregorio Cortez, *With His Pistol in His Hand*, explains what culture means to people for whom displacement, bilingualism, code-switching, and struggle have been constant realities.[53]

The "other American Studies" takes on new meaning in this age of deindustrialization, economic restructuring, capital flight, and economic austerity. We face a crisis within all the institutions whose existence was established by the social movements of the 1930s and the 1960s—public schools and libraries, subsidized housing and health care, youth centers and arts organizations, among others. We face the planned shrinkage of the university as fee increases and attacks on affirmative action change the racial and class composition of our students, sending increasing numbers of poor people to prison rather than to school. Expensive patent sharing agreements and research and development subsidies for large corporations undermine the critical, creative, and contemplative agenda of liberal education, giving a mercenary and vocational cast to the future of higher education in this country. At the same time, millions of workers around the world face a future of low-wage labor, diminished public services, and the continuing disintegration of social networks and communities. This kind of crossroads can be confronted, understood, and mastered, but only by blending both versions of American studies into a new synthesis.

Reframing American studies may be a painful process. Change can always be unsettling, and changes in some of our most cherished ideas and theories may be especially threatening. But social activism and movements for social change can augment our understanding and aid our collective education. Change comes from the bottom up as well as the top down. Demographic alterations, migration patterns, new technologies, and attacks on the social wage are not the only sources of new social relations and social identities in our time. Many people who do not look or sound like the authority figures that run our society are determined to have a hand in shaping the future they will inherit. Their work, and ours, is important. As Grace Lee Boggs reminds us, "When people come together voluntarily to create their own vision, they begin wishing it to come into being with such passion that they begin creating an active path leading to it from the present."[54]

We have come to a place where displacement matters, where it produces profound insights as well as pain, survival strategies as well as suffering. We can remain rooted in nostalgia and mired in melancholy if we choose. We can fight the old battles forever. But the best work in American studies has always been willing to face the future without fear. We know from personal experience and scholarly study that people do not always accept passively the roles assigned to them by those holding economic, political, and cultural power. The present instability of "place" might help us make a different future take place; the moment of danger that we now face might also become a time of what David W. Noble refers to as "unpredictable creativity."[55] People who are displaced might not "know their place," but they might be precisely the people we need to help us discover exactly what time it is.

At one of the most frightening moments of the 1955–1957 Montgomery Bus Boycott, a time when it appeared that the civil rights activists would surely lose their fight, a group of parishioners came to Reverend Martin Luther King Jr. and asked him to call off the struggle. Pointing to the defeats they had suffered, and worried that the people on their side would continue to lose their jobs, their savings, and the ability to protect their families in the wake of massive reactionary retaliation from the city's segregationist establishment, these members of Dr. King's church expressed anguish about the predicament they faced.

Dr. King was surprised by their surprise. "What did you expect?" he asked, reminding them that entrenched power never surrenders without a fight. Dr. King explained that their shock revealed that they had failed to learn the most important lesson he had tried to teach them—that we stand in this life at midnight. Principled people in an unprincipled world always confront problems that seem too complex to solve; they always find themselves pitted against powers that seem too strong to defeat. But the very seriousness of the situation contains the seed of a solution. "Even the most starless midnight may herald the dawn of a great fulfillment," Dr. King explained.[56] We stand in this life at midnight, always on the verge of a new dawn.

CHAPTER 2

Sent for You Yesterday, Here You Come Today

Who Needs the Thirties?

> The history of America as a country is quite different
> from that of America as a State.
>
> —Randolph Bourne, *War and the Intellectuals: Collected Essays, 1915–1919*

At the first International Conference on Popular Music Research in 1981, one of the world's most distinguished musicologists, Charles Hamm, began his presentation with a startling admission. Gesturing toward the elusiveness of the term "popular music" and acknowledging the difficulty of identifying exactly what makes any particular piece of music "popular," Hamm told the gathering that they began their deliberations under a severe handicap. The handicap, he explained, was that "we're not sure what we're talking about."[1]

Probably all academic conferences and all scholarly books (including this one) should begin with a similar confession, especially in an amorphous field like American Studies, but not because American studies scholars are incompetent or uninformed. On the contrary, critical work emerging from American studies research has been richly generative of new archives, epistemologies, and analyses in recent decades. It is just that academic fields of study are always artificial constructs that inhibit as well as enable the development of new knowledge. Every optic opens up some possibilities while occluding others.

Disciplinary, subdisciplinary, and interdisciplinary designations attached to different areas of study generate distinct vocabularies and frames of reference. They divide the interdependent and mutually constitutive processes of social life into discrete, atomized, and isolated objects of study. In our everyday life experiences, everything happens at once. We cannot separate the historical from the rhetorical, the structural from the cultural, or the psychological from the sociological. But on campuses, our inquiries take place in separate sites. Disciplines are assigned to different buildings and the fruits of their research can be found on separate floors in the library and in separate sections of the bookstore. There is much to be gained by disciplinary (as well as subdisciplinary and interdisciplinary) specialization. Divisions by disciplines and fields will probably not disappear in our lifetimes. That makes it all the more urgent, however, for us to define our terms and understand the consequences of the choices we make about research methods and objects of inquiry. Within American studies, this means that we need to be self-aware and self-reflexive about the questions our field has encouraged us to ask and answer.

American studies is an unusual field because it enjoys both an institutional and an extrainstitutional life. It has its own academic departments, professional associations, and scholarly journals, but also a constituency among artists, activists, and educated general readers.[2] In addition, even more than other interdisciplinary fields, American studies draws its collective identity from its specific local incarnations, from the form it takes in hundreds of dispersed sites, each with its own history influenced by a chaotic chain of circumstances, events, incidents, and accidents. At one time, the uneven activities and plural practices conducted under the name of American studies could be thought of as cohering around a common set of questions about national culture and national identity, about the congruence between place and culture in the United States. At this moment in history, however, we face new conditions and circumstances that demand new ways of knowing.

The end of the cold war, the transformation of industrial production-based economies into postindustrial information-based systems, and the seeming eclipse of the nation-state by powerful new multinational and transnational institutions call into question the reigning assumptions within American studies. The relationships linking culture to place seem particularly disrupted by the emergence of new social relations and new social subjects. Efforts to explain the unique (or at least the singular) qualities of national culture seem less important now when the global nature of the forces shaping national life can no longer be ignored.

In a curious inversion, however, asking and answering questions about locality and place can take on even greater importance in a globalized world, because the effects of globalization are most fully felt and most comprehensively understood through the distinctly local and national inflections given to processes that seem to take place everywhere. Rather than becoming obsolete, the field of American Studies has become home to some of the most original, insightful, and generative contemporary research. Its annual conventions and quarterly journals are venues of choice for a brilliant body of young scholars from traditional disciplines as well as from hybrid fields like cultural studies, women's studies, and ethnic studies. The institutional identity of American studies provides protective cover for many paradigm-breaking innovators, and the field's activities offer valuable dialogue, support, and social connection to many who would otherwise find themselves isolated and disconnected from collegial advice and encouragement.

The traditions of academic inquiry honed and refined within American studies still have much to teach us about the enduring importance of national cultures and national identities, about the reasons why the "local" and the "national" still matter. Scholars are always susceptible, however, to becoming trapped in our own traditions, constrained and confined by our own categories. To be certain that we know (in Hamm's words) "what we're talking about," we need to define the terms that bring us together, to acknowledge and understand the legacies that we inherit, and to speak directly and intelligently to the rapidly changing nature of national and transnational identities and interests.

Scholarship in American studies under contemporary conditions evokes the tension in the words that Little Jimmy Rushing used to sing in the 1930s as the vocalist for Count Basie's band: "Sent for you yesterday, here you come today." [3] Just as we have become more and more expert about defining national culture, the question of national culture itself must now undergo revision and critique.

Yet discontinuity between the past and present can also serve as a generative source of insight and understanding. In times of crisis we often see that we need a new understanding of the past as well as the present, that developments which might strike us as fundamentally new and unexpected also have a long history of their own. Rather than being obsolete, American studies scholarship might help us understand the ways in which better knowledge about suppressed elements of the past might make us better prepared for the present and the future that we face from the effects of globalization.

In his provocative and profoundly important book *The Cultural Front*, Michael Denning reminds us that "American Studies" originated in responses by intellectuals to the social upheavals of the 1930s and 1940s. Denning establishes a lineage of enormous importance for contemporary academic practitioners of American studies by uncovering a hidden history of the field replete with surprising links between professional academics and social movement institutions. He demonstrates the ways in which cultural production, consumption, and criticism enabled academics, artists, and activists to work together in a variety of institutional sites ranging from college classrooms to evening adult-education courses, from literary magazines to trade-union meetings, from Hollywood film studios to amateur camera clubs, from mass-circulation magazines to discussion groups at neighborhood bookstores. His research recovers important international, interethnic, and antiracist elements of the original American studies project in a way that offers important lessons for the present and the future.

Most important, Denning compels us to think of American studies not just in terms of academic inquiry and arguments, but also in terms of social movements, spaces, and institutions. In a time when nascent social movements are articulating some of the most important cultural, economic, and political critiques of globalization, scholarship connecting academic research to the work of social movements holds great promise for the generation of new knowledge as well as for the development of resistance against the increasingly indecent global social order.

Denning reminds us that at the very time that Charles Beard served as professor of history at Columbia University—and secured a professional and popular following through arguments that identified the antagonism between democracy and capitalism as the core contradiction within the U.S. national narrative—he also taught evening adult-education classes at the Workers University in New York sponsored by the International Ladies Garment Workers Union (ILGWU). F. O. Matthiessen not only defined the American Renaissance of the nineteenth century through his work as a professor of literature at Harvard University, but also served as a founder, trustee, and teacher at the trade-union-sponsored Samuel Adams School for evening adult education in Boston. Kenneth MacGowan established his scholarly reputation during the 1930s at UCLA as one of the first academic analysts of cinema, but in the evenings he taught at the ILGWU's Los Angeles and Hollywood adult-education schools along with screenwriter John Howard Lawson, composer Earl Robinson, and People's Songs activist Harry Hay.[4]

Associating themselves with trade-union night schools enabled these scholars and artists to secure a broader audience for their work, but it also offered them opportunities to learn from workers whose cultural tastes, political allegiances, and social activities played a crucial role in the "discovery" and "invention" of something called American culture during the New Deal and World War II eras.[5]

In some cases, intellectual work and artistic production emerged directly out of activism. Novelist H. T. Tsiang and other Chinatown writers in New York participated enthusiastically in mobilizing support for the Chinese Hand Laundry Alliance. In 1941, filmmaker Orson Welles joined with F. O. Matthiessen and music producer John Hammond as cochairs of a citizens committee protesting the deportation of Harry Bridges, the Australian-born leader of the International Longshore Workers Union. Filipino Labor Union organizers Chris Mensalvas and Carlos Bulosan worked together as labor activists and as copublishers of a literary magazine, *The New Tide*, in the 1930s. Twenty years later, as president of a local cannery workers union in Seattle, Mensalvas hired Bulosan to edit the union yearbook.[6]

After receiving a doctorate in economics from Columbia University,

Ernesto Galarza worked with Luisa Moreno throughout the southwest in the mid-1930s as an organizer for the Pan-American Union. In 1937, he became editor of *Photo-History*, a picture magazine dedicated to telling the story of CIO-organizing to a mass audience. The Socialist Party's Rebel Arts Group in New York City included dancers, musicians, writers, and artists. It sponsored a drama club, chess club, camera club, and a puppet group while also broadcasting dramas on radio station WEVD (a station that selected the initials of Eugene Victor Debs as its call letters). In Carmel, California, the John Reed Club, supported by the Communist Party, brought together photographer Edward Weston, sculptor Jo Davidson, playwright Orrick Johns, and writers Ella Winter, Lincoln Steffens, and (for a time) Langston Hughes to sponsor lectures by radical intellectuals and labor leaders as a means of mobilizing support for trade-union struggles by farm workers, cannery employees, and longshoremen.[7]

The story of depression-era activism, Popular Front art, and the political culture of the 1930s and 1940s has been told many times, but in his carefully researched and wide-ranging account Denning develops original interpretations of four key relationships that contain extraordinary import for our understanding of the problems and possibilities within contemporary American studies scholarship.[8] Although he does not always develop fully the theoretical implications of the issues he raises, Denning's evidence and analysis leads logically to reconsideration and retheorization of the relationships between politics and culture, between ethnic identity and class consciousness, between the myth of American exceptionalism and the always international identities of the U.S. nation-state and its inhabitants, and between cultural practice and cultural theory.

Denning's first major contribution is to move the discussion of links between politics and culture in the 1930s and 1940s beyond sectarian disputes about the Communist Party and its enemies into a broader and more productive exploration of the ways in which social crises create new cultures and foment new forms of cultural expression. Denning locates sectarian rivalries and strategic contestation among Stalinists, Trotskyists,

Socialists, and Liberals within a broader context that he describes as "the Age of the CIO," a designation designed to demonstrate the power of social movements to create the conditions that make new forms of cultural production and cultural criticism both necessary and inevitable.

Working from concepts developed by Raymond Williams and Antonio Gramsci, Denning depicts the "America" and the "American Studies" created in the 1930s and 1940s as a product of new ways of "feeling and seeing reality" brought into being by the egalitarian and inclusionary social movements that emerged in the Age of the CIO. He calls attention to the argument advanced by Gramsci that "a new social group that enters history with a hegemonic attitude, with a self-confidence

"Battle of Bull Run," Minneapolis General Strike, May 21, 1934. The social warrant of the 1930s was won in the streets by militant direct-action protests and demonstrations such as this one, during the Minneapolis General Strike. Courtesy of Minnesota Historical Society.

which it initially did not have, cannot but stir up from deep within it personalities who would not previously have found sufficient strength to express themselves fully in a particular direction."[9] Thus, for Denning the Popular Front during the New Deal and World War II is not so much the creation of the Communist Party and its front organizations but rather the visible manifestation of a new popular imagination provoked by the experiences of everyday life, labor, politics, and culture in a time of turmoil and transformation.

Denning's second major contribution to our understanding of the origins of depression-era "Americanism" and the rise of American studies comes from his recuperation of ethnicity as a powerful independent generator of radical politics during the 1930s and 1940s rather than as simply one site where class consciousness emerged. American studies scholars in recent years have emphasized the extraordinary energy unleashed by the affirmation of ethnicity in that era through events as diverse as the interethnic electoral coalitions that secured Fiorello La Guardia's election as mayor of New York and Anton Cermak's election as mayor of Chicago, the culture of unity celebrating ethnic difference within CIO-organizing drives, the radical journalism of Louis Adamic and his campaign to make the Statue of Liberty a sacred symbol of national inclusion, and ethnic festivals that portrayed immigrants and their children as "redemptive outsiders" rather than as unwanted aliens.[10] Denning delineates the broad base developed for an inclusionary and pluralistic vision of the American nation through the extraordinary self-activity of ethnic American organizations and individuals including the Japanese Proletarian Artists' League and the Japanese Workers Camera Club in Los Angeles; magazines including Adamic's *Common Ground*, Ralph Ellison's *Negro Quarterly*, Dorothy West's *Challenge*, and the League of American Writers' *The Clipper*; as well as the efforts of a broad range of artists and writers including Mine Okubo, Jacob Lawrence, Ollie Harrington, Mario Suarez, Mari Tomasi, Toshiro Mori, Hisaye Yamamoto, Gwendolyn Brooks, Paule Marshall, Milton Murayama, Zora Neale Hurston, Roshio Mori, Carlos Bulosan, Arna Bontemps, and Younghill Kang among others.[11]

Denning's innovative approach to ethnicity enables him to ground the efflorescence of ethnic cultural creativity in the 1930s in a common class experience rather than as solely ethnic phenomenon. He shows that what united these diverse expressions of ethnic identity and affiliation was a shared historical experience with "ethnic formation" produced by "the restructuring of the American peoples" by labor migrations ranging from the movement of Asian immigrants across the Pacific to the journeys across the Atlantic by people from southern and eastern Europe, from the exodus enacted by the Mexican Revolution and the development of railroads in the U.S. southwest to the great migration from the sharecropping South to the industrialized North and West by African Americans. While the identities created through these processes of ethnic formation contained powerful working-class inflections, they are not reducible to class. As Denning explains, by the 1930s "ethnicity and race had become the modality through which working-class peoples experienced their lives and mapped their communities.... The invention of ethnicity was a central form of class consciousness in the United States."[12] Consequently, no atomized class consciousness completely independent of ethnic identity could exist in the United States, but at the same time, many seemingly discrete ethnic identities contained a sedimented class content.

Yet affirmation of ethnic identity during the 1930s and 1940s as part of strategies for addressing and redressing the humiliating subordinations of working-class life and inverting the ideological formulations that rendered immigrants and their children as unworthy and unwelcome participants in American politics eventually evolved into an uncritical cultural pluralism after World War II. European Americans secured a significant measure of ethnic inclusion for themselves at the price of becoming complicit in the racialized exclusion of communities of color through the policies of trade unions, New Deal social welfare agencies, immigration officials, and private Realtors, lenders, and employers.[13] The militaristic and expansionist commitments of the U.S. government during the cold war transformed the egalitarian nationalism of the Popular Front into jingoistic expansionism, setting the stage for anticommunist purges of progressives from public and private institutions as well as for an imperialist foreign policy that exported the class antagonisms of U.S. society to countries all around the globe.[14]

It has been tempting for scholars to view the politics and the culture of the Popular Front as innately assimilationist, xenophobic, and nationalistic.[15] American Studies itself has been implicated in this project because of its inattention to the role of imperialism in U.S. history and because its core questions about "what is an American" have assumed the existence of an unproblematized, undifferentiated, and distinctly national "American" identity that differs from the identities open to individuals from other national contexts.

Denning offers some cautionary obstacles to these readings through his third major contribution in *The Cultural Front*, his recuperation of the expressly internationalist content of the cultural politics of the Popular Front. He shows how the literary journal *Front* printed articles in three languages and featured contributions by Peruvian Marxist theoretician José Carlos Mariategui as well as Japanese proletarian poet Kei Mariyama. A trip to Haiti in 1931 energized Langston Hughes and initiated his commitment to blending art and activism in works that included his play *Emperor in Haiti* and his collaboration with composer William Grant Still on the opera *Troubled Island*. African American units of the Federal Theatre Project performed works set in Haiti, including *Black Empire* performed in Los Angeles and *Haiti* in New York. Jacob Lawrence painted a series of historical paintings about Toussaint L'Ouverture, while Arna Bontemps set his novel *Drums at Dusk* in Haiti. Young Filipinos in Hollywood managed to publish one issue of *The New Tide*, a literary magazine that featured a prose poem about leaving the Philippines by Chris Mensalvas, a story by Filipino American writer José Garcia Villa, a story protesting against lynching, and a poem by William Carlos Williams. Émigré Japanese writer and feminist Ayako Ishigaki published the autobiography *Restless Wave* under the pen name Haru Matsui with the left-wing Modern Age Books.[16] Joseph Freeman argued that the interest in national identity among popular front writers did not originate in an uncritical and unproblematic nationalism and cultural pluralism, but from the converse. "If you lose an arm, you are likely to think a great deal about arms," Freeman opined, "and if you are born into an oppressed nationality you are likely to think a great deal about oppression and nationalism. Freeman went on to contend "The native-born American takes his Americanism for granted; the 'alien' absorbing America into his heart, being absorbed into its culture, thinks about the meaning of America day and night."[17]

Denning demonstrates that this internationalist presence not only added on a global dimension to the better-known regionalist and nationalist cultural expressions of the popular front, but also served as an independent site for theorizing about the antagonisms and affinities emerging from questions of citizenship, nationality, culture, and class. For example, he shows how Carey McWilliams's location in Los Angeles encouraged him to view race relations from a West Coast perspective that contained profound consequences for his understanding of the United States as an always international entity. Confronted with the internment of Japanese Americans and the "zoot suit riots" with their violence against Mexican Americans, McWilliams in 1943 saw the United States as increasingly oriented toward Central America, South America, and the Pacific. This understanding provoked him to rethink U.S. history and to propose a new periodization, one that traced the origins of the modern era to 1876 and its aftermath—the time when the U.S. government abandoned African Americans by ending Reconstruction, excluded Asians through the Chinese Exclusion Act of 1882, began to place Native Americans on reservations, and set the stage for global expansion through successive moves to secure control over Hawaii, Cuba, the Philippines, and Puerto Rico. Similarly, African American sociologist Oliver C. Cox traced the unequal life chances confronting African Americans to the participation by the United States in a world capitalist system "in which racialization is a fundamental economic and political process." Even the discovery of U.S. ethnicities often had an international dimension. Denning notes that Joseph Freeman and Richard Wright first became interested in Marxism because they felt that the writing of Lenin and Stalin on oppressed nationalities helped them understand their ethnic experiences as a Jewish American and as an African American.[18]

Denning's fourth major contribution comes from his extraordinary success in using evidence about cultural expressions to advance our understanding of culture as a social force. Rather than representing either transparent truths about social relations or functioning as transmission belts to send the unmediated ideology of the owners of the commercial culture industry, Popular Front culture constituted a complex site where a variety of social identities could be arbitrated and negotiated. Denning explains, for example, how critics Kenneth Burke and C. L. R. James interpreted the prevalence of brutality, violence, and sadism in 1930s fiction and film as a register of a historically specific kind of crisis brought on by the depression—in Burke's words, a time when "the perception of discordance is perceived without smile or laughter."[19] Drawing on Burke's formulation, Denning calls our attention to the importance of a genre of films and fictional tales that he characterizes as "ghetto pastorals," as examples of "the proletarian grotesque." He identifies these allegorical stories of urban terror—often dismissed by previous critics as middle-class misrepresentations of working-class life—as important expressions of a social reality aimed less at direct descriptions of social class than at attempts to represent a "cityscape composed in a pidgin of American slang and ghetto dialect, with traces of old country tongues."[20] Aiming neither for socialist realism nor for bourgeois romanticism, the ghetto pastorals in Denning's view attempted to rebuild and transcend modernism through a contradictory blend of the magic and the real, of the allegorical and the empirical. They relied on "the proletarian grotesque" to interrupt the ideological closures enacted by traditional narrative form and ideologies about the autonomy of art as well as to reflect and shape the resentments of their audiences.

Denning also shows how difficult it can be for intellectuals to understand their own social location in an era of intense class conflict. The Age of the CIO not only involved mass mobilizations by workers on issues important to their class, but also provoked a broader identity crisis about the relationships between people from different classes and strata. Denning makes productive use of John Dos Passos's ruminations in a 1930 article about the nature of intellectual work in which the author describes his social role as a writer as similar to the work performed by engineers, scientists, independent manual craftsmen, artists, actors, and "technicians of one sort or another." Dos Passos observed that this group of people tended to belong to their jobs regardless of their individual ideas, that their lives were defined by a core contradiction emanating from "the fact that along with the technical education that makes them valuable to the community they have taken in a subconscious political education that makes them servants of the owners." Denning builds on Dos Passos's argument to analyze his emphasis in the *U.S.A.* trilogy on "the contradictory lives of those who traded in the speech of the people."[21] More than a site for choosing sides in an already declared class war, responsible intellectual work emerges in this analysis as an effort to understand the problems and the potential of the contradictory allegiances that characterize the lives of intellectuals.

In our time, when the social role of intellectuals remains undertheorized and when images of the grotesque play a central role in cultural expressions of all kinds, Denning's discussions of the Cultural Front contain compelling insights about the present as well as about the past. It makes a difference for our work in the present for us to acknowledge that the origins of American studies lie both inside and outside the academy, that the social movements of the 1930s were both an inspirational stimulus and an empirical site for the construction of the field. It makes a difference for our work in the present when we understand that class and ethnicity have always been linked in the United States, that each identity is experienced through the other—as well as through gender, sexuality, religion, and many other social identities—and that there can be no valid mutually exclusive opposition between ethnic studies and American studies. It makes a difference for our work in the present when we enable ourselves to see that globalization is not new, that a long history of labor migration, imperial expansion, and international solidarity have shaped the American nation in ways that cannot be reversed by political, cultural, or intellectual projects that remain purely national in scope. It makes a difference for our work in the present when we encounter the evidence Denning offers about the power of the ghetto pastoral and the proletarian grotesque in the 1930s, and how difficult, yet how necessary, it was for intellectuals to theorize their relationship to social movements and oppressed populations in that era. For these reasons and many more, it is impossible to overestimate the importance of Michael Denning's achievements in *The Cultural Front;* it is a book certain to transform American studies in significant and lasting ways.

Yet the same qualities that make Denning's fine work so compelling require us to ask how the rich and full past that he describes has become the impoverished present. What has happened to separate specialized academic inquiry from social movement activism? Why do desires for ethnic inclusion and empowerment now seem so divorced from concerns about social class? How did the inclusionary nationalism and international solidarity of the depression and World War II eras become transformed into the imperial expansionism of the cold war? Which elements of Popular Front culture continue to inform and inspire egalitarian social movements and which ones now serve other purposes? What price did the Popular Front culture pay for its association with the Communist Party, not just through the impact of anticommunism in the postwar period but also through the internal deficiencies of the undemocratic "vanguard party" model as a stimulus for effective social change? Most important, why were the emancipatory visions of the Popular Front so concentrated on redemptive views of "America" as an island of virtue in a degraded and corrupt world?

Not all of these questions can be answered here, but we can make a good start by asking about the causes and consequences of the emphasis on "American" identity by the Popular Front. Certainly the long history of anti-immigrant nativism in America, the stigmatization of outsiders, and the countersubversive hysterias deployed against communities of color had something to do with the desire among aggrieved groups to escape the terms by which they had been stigmatized and to claim insider status for themselves. Anton Cermak's opponent in the Chicago mayoral race in 1932 bragged that he could trace his own ancestry back to the landing of the *Mayflower* in Massachusetts in 1620, deriding Cermak as "Pushcart Tony, the son of immigrants." Cermak scored a great public relations victory by replying that he regretted that his ancestors had not come over on the Mayflower, but assured his listeners that "they got here as fast as they could." With this quip, Cermak inverted the terms of the debate by presenting immigrants as more deserving than the native-born because they came to America by choice rather than by the accident of birth. New York's Mayor La Guardia successfully assembled a coalition of outsiders partly because his own identity so clearly reflected the idea of a culture of unity. As urban historians Dennis Judd and Todd Swanstrom note about La Guardia, "Half Jewish and half Italian, married first to a Catholic and then to a Lutheran of German descent, himself a Mason and an Episcopalian, he was practically a balanced ticket all by himself."[22]

In addition, as Denning points out, by associating themselves with the "Lincoln Republic"—the republican-era America before the dawn of corporate capitalism—Popular Front patriots could deploy the contrast between a producer democracy and a parasitical capitalism for their own purposes, and they could present their mostly white, Anglo-Saxon, and Protestant enemies as interlopers and radicals betraying the "true American" mission. Yet for all its utility, it was precisely the invocation of an ideal America that set the stage for the defeat of the Popular Front and for the inversion of its icons and symbols in the cold war era. Coupled with the crippling vanguardism of the Communist Party, which as often as not repressed rather than released the egalitarian energies erupting from the grass roots in the Age of the CIO, the effort to "let America be America again" (in the words of Langston Hughes) contained contradictions that allowed for the transformation of the Popular Front into the cold war.[23]

Denning's identification of the origins of "America" and "American Studies" within the Popular Front of the 1930s needs to be placed in the broader context of American Exceptionalism, which Amy Kaplan does in her original and generative introduction to the book she co-edited with Donald Pease, *Cultures of United States Imperialism.* Kaplan constructs another genealogy of American studies, one that identifies the construction of an exceptionalist America as part of a project intended to evade responsibility for the nation's imperial practices and ambitions. Kaplan points to Perry Miller's 1956 preface to his pathbreaking study of Puritan intellectual history, *Errand into the Wilderness*, where Miller traces the origins of his thinking about the Puritans to his experiences in the 1920s as a college dropout unloading drums of oil on the banks of the Congo River in Africa. He testifies to an "epiphany" about the coherence and uniqueness of American identity because of his encounter with what he perceived as the "blankness" of Africa and the difference between its "jungle" landscape and the early American frontier. Kaplan notes that the binary opposition between a blank jungle and a noble frontier provides the conditions of possibility for the core narrative of American Exceptionalism—the belief in America as an island of virtue in a corrupt world, and the contrast between the inevitable decline of European empires and the "illimitable capacity for self-renewal and expansion" of the United States.[24]

Kaplan's categories help us discern the hidden contradictions within some of the Popular Front politics celebrated by Denning. She observes that the American Exceptionalism articulated by Perry Miller (and I would argue embraced by the Popular Front) depends upon the occlusion of America's role in the world. It proceeds on the belief that American nationality is what Kaplan describes as "a monolithic and self-contained whole."[25] Consequently, the progressive celebration of the nation's diverse national origins also worked conservatively to endorse the building of an American nationality as an atomized identity detached from its own history of conquest, slavery, and genocide, as well as from its role in denying the national aspirations of people in the Caribbean, Latin America, Africa, and Asia. Thus even the progressive multiculturalism and polyvocality of the Popular Front contains the seeds for an imperial consensus capable of reconciling diverse groups into a common national project through shared participation in warfare. This reconciliation of diverse national groups into a unified totality forms the subtext of an astounding range of war novels and motion pictures from World War II through to the Gulf War, and it helps explain how the Popular Front of the New Deal eventually became incorporated into World War II and then the cold war.

Kaplan's emphasis on American Exceptionalism helps us understand the limits of the Popular Front version of American studies, especially with respect to its uninterrogated emphasis on the nation-state as the logical object of intellectual and political activity, its ultimately conservative racial and gender politics, and its inadequacy as a basis for retheorizing American studies in an age of globalization. It was the reliance on the "Lincoln Republic" as the lost ideal erased by contemporary capitalism that prevented the Popular Front from addressing adequately the legacies of slavery, conquest, and overseas imperialism in the American past and present. It was the reliance on a masculinized vision of class struggle that occluded the feminist possibilities implicit in the actions of radical women activists and artists in the 1930s. Perhaps most important, it was the emphasis on "ethnic" unity and the incorporation of racialized minorities into an "ethnic" paradigm that made the Popular Front at one and the same time a focal point for class unity *and* an instrument for increasing the privileges and power of whiteness and masculinity, an indisputably important moment in the history of American egalitarianism *and* an impediment to genuinely global and postnational politics.

Several years before President Roosevelt admitted that "Dr. New Deal" had to give way to "Dr. Win the War," the great scholar W. E. B. Du Bois saw clearly the connections between the unresolved racial agenda of the New Deal at home and the likelihood of war overseas. In his 1935 book, *Black Reconstruction in America*, Du Bois presented a history of the 1860s and 1870s with prophetic implications for the 1930s. Looking back at the nation's previous great era of reform, Du Bois noted that white racism destroyed the "abolition democracy" of the post–Civil War era. It was not only black people who were hurt by the betrayal of Radical Reconstruction through the establishment of "Jim Crow" segregation, Du Bois argued, but egalitarian democracy itself. White workers in the 1870s may have believed they were securing a measure of inclusion for themselves by excluding African Americans; they may have believed that by investing in their whiteness they created a floor below which they could not fall. But by accepting the naturalized hierarchies of white supremacy, they could no longer join with blacks and other aggrieved groups to challenge class and social inequalities. The death of Radical Reconstruction was the death of public education, public roads, and public health care in the South and the end of worker solidarity in the North. By making sure that blacks would be poor, white workers guaranteed their own poverty.

Yet Du Bois went a step beyond the national story. He argued that the defeat of Radical Reconstruction was a global rather than just a national defeat. The racialized hierarchies of the United States shaped by what Du Bois called the victory "of the South" made the United States a defender of new forms of slavery in new disguises both at home and abroad. "The South is not interested in freedom for dark India," Du Bois argued. "It has no sympathy with the oppressed of Africa or Asia." Consequently, the racial state at home was supported by a worldwide racialized economy, and that world economy found a friend in the resurgent racism of the United States. Du Bois explained, "Imperialism, the exploitation of colored labor throughout the world, thrives upon the approval of the United States, and the United States has given that approval because of the South."[26]

The analysis offered by Du Bois was prophetic in both senses of the word: prophetic in that it spoke truth to power as the prophets of the Old Testament had done, but prophetic as well in the way that it anticipated the direction of national and global politics in the 1930s and 1940s. The penultimate paragraph of *Black Reconstruction in America* offers a description that linked the failures of the 1870s to the emerging problems of the 1930s. In that paragraph, Du Bois asks his readers to see what is happening in their world by telling them, "Immediately in Africa, a black back runs red with the blood of the lash; in India, a brown girl is raped; in China, a coolie starves; in Alabama, seven darkies are more than lynched; while in London, the white limbs of a prostitute are hung with jewels and silk. Flames of jealous murder sweep the earth while brains of little children smear the hills."[27]

By linking the demise of "Abolition Democracy" at home to global imperialism, Du Bois recognized the limits of a purely national approach. What happened in the United States mattered, because the U.S. racial system had global ramifications. The betrayal of Radical Reconstruction led to the opening of more western lands and to intensified warfare against Native Americans as a way of defusing competition for scarce resources and reuniting former Union supporters and former Confederate citizens in a common enterprise. The military officials who supervised campaigns against indigenous people in the western part of the United States soon found themselves conducting operations against "native" forces in the Philippines. The plantation system of the South spread to Hawaii and Puerto Rico.

The lessons of the nineteenth century held tremendous import for the twentieth in Du Bois's view. The battles of the 1930s led to genuine victories for the "culture of unity," but those victories were apportioned along race, gender, and national lines. The social welfare system implemented by the New Deal treated the class injuries of the 1930s as injuries to manhood and whiteness, which is why it channeled unemployment benefits, social security, federal home-loan assistance, and the protections of the Wagner Act mostly to white men, rather than distributing universal benefits. This consolidation around gender subordination and racial privilege came to full fruition during and after World War II when the wartime gains in employment and income by women and members of aggrieved racialized minorities were treated as temporary, while the GI Bill and FHA housing offered extensive new subsidies to masculinity and whiteness.

The war also transformed the culture of unity from an oppositional grassroots movement into a national patriotic mobilization by the state. Wartime military spending ended the depression by supplying capital to industry and guaranteeing full employment and full production, while the unity necessitated by war provided an appealing model of a state and economy largely untroubled by internal division. U.S. policy makers attempted to institutionalize these structures in the postwar world through the cold war with great success. But that very success guaranteed that the next wave of social movements would address both the resolved and unresolved problems of the 1930s by questioning the links between patriotism and patriarchy, between war and whiteness that were solidified in the 1940s.

Attempts to separate progressive articulations of "America" and "American Studies" from their history as building blocks for hierarchical, exploitative, and imperial projects need to reckon with the history of the 1930s and 1940s as well as with the ideological origins of American Exceptionalism and their conflation of culture and place. David W. Noble provides the best analysis to date of both in his 1986 book, *The End of American History*.[28] Noble locates the origins of American Exceptionalism in the metaphor of two worlds, in the identification of an innocent and virtuous America (the new world) alone and embattled against the forces of European corruption.

Ironically enough, this metaphor of two worlds was a European rather than an American invention. Drawing on the scholarship of Sacvan Bercovitch and J. G. A. Pocock, Noble explains that classical republican theorists in England viewed their own country as corrupt because they felt that the rise of capitalism had elevated the private, particularistic, and selfish interests of a few over the public universal interest needed to preserve the social contract. They discerned their loss of freedom in many ways, but especially through the introduction of a particular kind of time. They perceived that previous to the capitalist era, time had belonged to God—that the days and nights, seasons, and years marked a temporal flow ordained by the deity. But the emergence of capitalism gave time a different meaning. Capitalists could divide the day into hours, minutes, and seconds of labor that could be bought and sold. Even worse in the republican view, interest-bearing loans and investments made time itself a commodity; capitalist time forced them to mortgage the future, to trade time they did not yet have in return for resources they needed. To classical republicans, feudalism had been ruled by space, by the land one tilled or the community in which one lived, but capitalism was ruled by time.

Dreams of escape to America not only aimed at a change of spaces, but also at an escape from time. Classical republicans (and generations of republican theorists who followed them) believed that European space had been corrupted by time, but that a producer-oriented yeoman democracy was still possible in America. They saw the American space as sacred because it might be a place where one could escape the corruptions of time by living within the timeless physical space of American nature. Even though the trading companies that financed British settlement in the colonies clearly sought profitable returns on their investments, the ideologies of commercial property and capitalist time coexisted uneasily in North America with a republican ideology that became more powerful in the colonies that it had ever been in England.

When skilled artisans and land-owning farmers resisted the eclipse of the "Lincoln Republic" by the rise of industrial capitalism after the Civil War, they often justified their anticapitalism through republican ideology.[29] Owning land (and the tools with which to work it) seemed to insure economic and political independence through control over space, while working for wages or incurring debts brought dependency and obligation in the arenas of time. Frederick Jackson Turner's articulation of the frontier thesis in the 1890s predicted a threat to American freedom from the closing of western lands (limiting access to space); as Noble explains, Turner believed that the escape from European time to American space had been temporary, and that the closing of the frontier proved in the long run that time had been more powerful than space.

Noble's work provides an important context for the anticapitalism of Denning's Popular Front. Activists of the 1930s could draw upon several centuries of anticapitalist and antimonopoly republicanism which argued that American space had to remain free of European time. Charles Beard's conception of American history as a struggle between democracy and capitalism rested on a belief that democracy emerged out of agrarian life in America and that capitalism's corruption came from Europe. Beard objected to the dynamism of capitalism, arguing that it was the enemy of tradition, that it brought immigrants from Europe to work in America as a way of replacing free Americans with subservient Europeans accustomed to domination. Beard changed his mind many times—about industrialization, about the New Deal, about overseas expansion and imperialism—but his many changes all stemmed from a consistent search for a way to escape the tyranny of capitalist time. Despite his participation in ILGWU evening-education courses, Beard cannot be confused with the entire Popular Front, but his premises help explain the nationalism within the Popular Front that made "America" such a powerful symbol. By associating themselves with the American landscape, literally and figuratively, Popular Front artists and intellectuals activated powerful symbols of freedom. Yet by maintaining a Manichean split between an innocent American space and a corrupt European time, they simply inverted rather than superseded the nationalist sense of American Exceptionalism held by their capitalist opponents as well as their anticapitalist allies.

Noble's study revolves around the search by historians for a national narrative that might fulfill republican hopes for a free space outside of the corruptions of time. But historians by definition deal with change over time, with competition over scarce resources, with political conflicts that endlessly indicate the futility of a universal or national narrative capable of expressing the interests of all. The five historians Noble examines—Frederick Jackson Turner, Charles Beard, Reinhold Neibuhr, Richard Hofstadter, and William Appleman Williams—all fail to one degree or another, but the nature of their failures has much to teach us about the core questions posited in Denning's book.

Turner and Beard distrusted capitalism deeply, but they could not envision any actual social group capable of acting unselfishly and universally. Turner accepted that Native Americans should be conquered in the name of freedom, but admitted that European settlement from the East Coast and Europe soon overwhelmed free spaces with the considerations of capitalist time. It should not be surprising that Turner's frontier thesis struck many capitalists as decidedly in their interests because it could justify overseas expansion as necessary to American freedom, as the moral equivalent of the settling of the West, which Turner considered the crucible of American freedom.

The historical writings by Turner and Beard attempted to call an oppositional constituency into being through prophecy, through warnings about the impending loss of freedom that Americans faced, and through appeals to the creation of a powerful national identity capable of overcoming selfish divisions. Turner died during the Progressive Era, but Beard became an important figure in the Age of the CIO, although not always in alignment with its dominant political forces. Hofstadter and Neibuhr participated in Popular Front politics and pursued anticapitalist stances in the 1930s. But World War II convinced them that most of the ideals of republicanism were impractical, that an imperfect capitalism was more desirable than fascism or communism, and they became virulent anticommunists and enthusiastic advocates of cold war militarism and expansion in the postwar era. Yet even here, they drew upon residual elements of republicanism. The very same features of republicanism that lauded America's isolation from the rest of the world also contained impulses toward imperialism. Because they viewed America's differences from the rest of the world as both the source of the nation's virtue and its peril, from the early nineteenth century through the twentieth some republican thinkers concluded that the only way to preserve freedom would be to make the American system universal, to spread its political and economic systems to the rest of the world. Although they resigned themselves to the inevitability of inequality and injustice in the world, Hofstadter and Neibuhr drew upon the Manichean oppositions between innocence and evil at the heart of republicanism in their support for U.S. foreign policy during the cold war era.

William Appleman Williams was the only one of the historians studied by Noble who experienced at least partial success in reconciling anticapitalist goals with historical methods, but he did so only through radical critique of the core categories of space and time so central to both historians and republican theorists. Williams argued that the capitalists and the anticapitalists (or at least the Marxist left) shared the same false premises—that affiliations to particular places had to proceed at the level of the nation-state, that time had to be defined as the present as it would look to the future, that the spaces in which humans acted embraced the whole world.

Williams believed that many different kinds of places could be created as social units that would be superior to the nation-state. He felt that formulations about time should evade either stasis or simplistic narratives of progress, but allow for the possibility of conceptions of time that unite the past, present, and future into an ongoing dialogue. Williams emphasized that the lure of global trade and global profits led inevitably to totalitarianism and war. He objected to the cold war because he thought that both the United States and the Soviet Union believed that their particular systems must become universal—an error that he viewed as common to capitalism, Marxism, *and* republicanism. Williams came to these conclusions at a time when many veterans of the Age of the CIO had become corporate liberals, anticommunist conservatives, and Cold Warriors. But his insights did not belong to him alone, they emerged from antiwar, feminist, and Native American social movement groups of the 1970s and 1980s whose perspectives drew his attention.

Denning argues that the Popular Front inserted politics into popular culture so effectively that the culture remained radical, egalitarian, and democratic, even when the movement that originally generated it no longer existed. But Williams allows us to see another dimension of that achievement. In their emphasis on entertainment and spectacle, the Popular Front not only brought politics to culture, but also demonstrated the power of bringing culture to politics. Through their hero worship of the living Franklin Delano Roosevelt and the deceased Abraham Lincoln (suspending for a moment discussion of those who revered Joseph Stalin) the Popular Front's politics invited citizens to share in the reflected glory of their leaders, to perceive sharing the leader's charisma as equivalent to the sharing of power. Williams observes that this process makes citizens consumers of politics in much the same way that they become consumers of goods. The radio broadcasts of FDR and the connection between the CIO and commercial culture worked effectively in the 1930s for egalitarian ends, but they also set the stage for the mixture of Hollywood glamour and global adventurism practiced by later "heroes," most notably John F. Kennedy in the 1960s and Ronald Reagan in the 1980s, both of whom drew their models of leadership from Roosevelt's history with the Age of the CIO and World War II.

By affirming their desire to help build a redemptive America, the immigrants and children of immigrants in the Popular Front remained securely within the ideological confines of the metaphor of two worlds and as a result remained susceptible to substituting a program of national glory for one of social justice. Noble argues that the search for a unified national narrative lies at the heart of American Exceptionalism, but that human freedom depends upon an unpredictable creativity that cannot be found within historical narratives of any one nation. This does not mean that the nation-state is irrelevant to political or intellectual action, only that it cannot provide the ultimate terrain for imagination and contestation.

In social movement struggles in the United States and around the world today, new historical formations can teach us lessons about culture and politics that are both old and new at the same time. The important victories of the Popular Front came through the power of social movements and their institutions, through unexpected alliances and affiliations across and within social categories, through the ability of culture to reflect and shape past, present, and future social relations, and through understanding of the always international aspects of U.S. identity. But the social movements of the Age of the CIO also suffered from uninterrogated assumptions sedimented within their inherited vocabulary about time, space, and the nation-state, from the limits of the political vanguard and the artistic avant-garde, from an underestimation of the importance of direct democracy and continuous cultural renewal, and from their embeddedness in a kind of time with too little room for unpredictable creativity.

No critique from the past ever becomes completely obsolete, but no critique from the past can ever be adequate for the purposes of the present and future. Our time could become a time of unpredictable creativity, but only if we acknowledge the ways in which yesterday's solutions can become today's problems, and only if we accept the necessity for each generation to fashion a social warrant appropriate to its own historically specific needs and circumstances.

CHAPTER 3

Dancing in the Dark

Who Needs the Sixties?

> Of course, Chester longed for justice and was incensed
> by its absence, but he was too pragmatic to spend his time
> waiting for the justice-Santa to come down the chimney
> with a stocking full of equality.
>
> —Melvin Van Peebles, *"His Wonders to Perform"*

In an eloquent and moving reminiscence about the 1960s, Marshall Berman recalls that decade as a *time* that produced new kinds of *spaces*. For Berman, civil rights and antiwar demonstrations created a new kind of public life that brought to "many of us an ease and confidence in public spaces that we had never had before, and never expected to have at all."[1] He remembers that public gatherings at that time had a special charge to them because they served as important sites for the transformation of individual and collective consciousness.

I understand what Berman means. I have a few of those memories myself—memories of a March afternoon in 1965 in front of the state capitol building in Montgomery, Alabama, linked arm and arm with others in a crowd of twenty-five thousand people singing "We Shall Overcome." We had marched through the city in the morning and spent the afternoon listening to Dr. King, who told us that although the moral arc of the universe was long, in the end it would inevitably curve toward justice.

I remember a cold October night in 1967 in Washington, D.C., sitting on the Pentagon steps with several hundred demonstrators as a combined force of federal marshals, military police officers, and soldiers holding bayonets tried to drive us away. We vowed to hold our ground in hopes of dramatizing our opposition to the Vietnam War. After midnight we realized that Pentagon officials had called the press inside for a "briefing" so that no one would see or hear anything that happened to us. We withdrew in disappointment and shame.

I remember a tumultuous February morning in 1968, taking over the mayor's office in the St. Louis city hall as part of a coalition of students, civil rights activists, and welfare recipients. We demanded that the mayor support our demands for welfare payments adequate enough to meet the food and shelter needs of poor families. One of the women in the group got down on her knees and led us in prayer as nervous members of the mayor's staff phoned the police.

Most of the time our activism grew out of desperation, out of a feeling that words alone were not enough. I remember my feelings of fear and powerlessness as I watched Fannie Lou Hamer testify on national television about being beaten brutally in a Mississippi jail for the "crime" of attempting to register to vote. I remember my sorrow and anger over the murder of Bill Moore, a white postal worker who attempted to strike a blow for civil rights by marching through the Deep South "to deliver a letter" to Governor Ross Barnett of Mississippi, urging him to end his allegiance to racism. I remember my confusion and guilt when I read about Norman Morrison burning himself to death in front of the Pentagon to protest the war in Vietnam. He asked the rest of us how we could continue to live while our government brought systematic death and destruction to the people of Vietnam. It seemed as if each day brought another tragedy, another challenge that made us ask ourselves what were we going to do and what kind of people we were going to be. Activism provided one answer to that question.

Most sixties activists will recognize the aura that Marshall Berman invokes, a warmth, trust, and intimacy with strangers, a newfound ease and confidence in public spaces, an exhilarating sense of social connection and citizenship. But the power of these memories stems not so much from a sense of personal recognition as from their reminder of the transformative power of public political action. It is not as if we remember storming from victory to victory. Almost none of my own recollections involve moments of victory. Less than twelve hours after Dr. King's speech in Montgomery, white racists (and an FBI informant) murdered Mrs. Viola Liuzzo on an Alabama highway. The war in Vietnam continued for eight years after the confrontation at the Pentagon. Our demonstration in the St. Louis city hall won no benefits for the working poor, the disabled, or children on welfare. Even worse, more than thirty years later, it is hard to look at the nation in which we live and feel that we have progressed in any meaningful sense. We did not think then that we were winning very much, but I do think that we would have been shocked if we knew that in the ensuing decades we would see an unprecedented rise in military spending and devastating cuts in expenditures on housing, health care, education, and public works. We would not have guessed that the gaps in income and power between races and classes would expand rather than contract, or that young women and children would become the fastest growing and largest segments of the poor.

But even if they brought little in the way of concrete victories, those moments from the 1960s remain important because they involved action, because in those moments people without position or prestige tried to change themselves and others through politics. In demonstrations and direct action protests, they tried to respond to the terrifying challenges raised by the social turmoil around them. They turned public spaces into political stages and discovered close connections to others who shared their commitments at the same time.

Yet it would be foolish to become nostalgic about the 1960s. Along with gratifying memories of struggle and resistance, the decade also leaves many of us with memories of another sort—memories of our own egotism and arrogance, of our vulnerability to police agents and provocateurs, of the faction fights and frustrations of a movement composed largely of children with too little knowledge, too limited an imagination, and too narrow a base of support to effect meaningful and lasting change. It was one thing to believe that we lost because the other side had more power, force, and resources. It was quite another to believe that we lost because we deserved to lose, that at the times we were tested the most we had insufficient resolve, insufficient courage, and insufficient love for others to see the struggle through to the end.

Our enemies often accused us of being out of touch with the mainstream of U.S. society, but in reality we actually shared too many of the values of the society we wanted to change. Within our own ranks, we reproduced our country's social hierarchies, its fascination with violence, its ignorance and disregard for the rest of the world, and its fear of egalitarian and democratic decision-making. We saw ourselves as the creators of a new society, but all too often our actions were merely symptoms of the bankruptcy of the old. To borrow a metaphor from Debussy's description of Wagner's music, in many ways we were a sunset that thought we were a sunrise.

Nonetheless, we learned something important in those years. From sharecroppers and students, from inmates at Attica and Indian insurgents of AIM, from feminists and farm workers—we learned about the possibilities of politics, the importance of taking a stand, and the necessity of standing together. It is precisely this *political* dimension of the 1960s that disappears when the decade is invoked by contemporary commentators. In an emblematic statement, Kentucky Senator Mitch McConnell exclaimed, "You remember the 60s. That's when they built up the Berlin Wall and tore down America."[2] In similar accounts by Allan Bloom, Robert Bork, and Newt Gingrich, the 1960s emerge as a kind of organized lunacy grounded only in the Oedipal rage and hedonistic desires of spoiled rich kids.

Separating culture from politics, these commentators recall (and invent) with loving detail a decade of flag burning, drug taking, and sexual promiscuity. But they remain conspicuously silent about the lasting changes in consciousness and behavior secured by that era—by a woman's movement that educated us about our self-defeating attachments to unfair and unjust ways of dealing with one another, by antiracist organizers who exposed the enormity of white supremacy in our society, by soldiers and civilians resisting an unjust and immoral war who made us face up to the ruinous consequences of individual and collective violence, and by rank-and-file factory workers who exposed the alien-ations and indignities of wage labor and who brought the principles of participatory democracy so important to that decade to shop-floor dis-cussions and community gatherings all across the country.

In the mass media, in political advertising, and to a significant degree in the popular imagination of ordinary Americans, a *rhetorical* 1960s fabricated by countersubversive conservatives has erased the *his-torical* 1960s that actually took place. Too much is at stake to leave unchallenged these accounts that demonize the 1960s and distort its his-tory. They forget, for example, that during the 1960s Martin Luther King Jr. *lost* most of the important battles he fought. From the drive to desegregate department stores and register voters in Atlanta and Albany (Georgia) to the Meredith March in Mississippi, from the fair-housing campaigns in Chicago suburbs to the sanitation workers strike in Mem-phis, from the struggle to stop the bombing and urge a negotiated set-tlement to the war in Vietnam to the economic demands of the Poor People's March on Washington, the United States of America that remembers Dr. King so lovingly in death defeated him time and time again when he was alive.[3]

Most retrospective accounts of the 1960s forget that a majority of Americans opposed almost all of the specific objectives of the civil rights movement throughout the 1960s, that a majority supported the war in Vietnam throughout the decade, that U.S. voters cast more ballots for Richard Nixon during the 1960s than for any other individual. By the time a majority of Americans turned against the Vietnam War, it was largely because a significant plurality believed that the war was unwin-nable, not that it was illegal or immoral.

Even the often-celebrated "counterculture" of the 1960s looms larger in retrospect than it deserves. Contemporary accounts recall the successes of Janis Joplin and Jimi Hendrix, but rarely remember that Connie Francis, Elvis Presley, Brenda Lee, and Ray Charles joined the Beatles to form the five best-selling artists of the 1960s. Psychedelic acid rock and folk rock stand out as signature musical styles of the era, but the single best-selling song of the 1960s was the Percy Faith Orchestra's (overorchestrated) ballad "Theme from a Summer Place." Jimi Hendrix's searing "Star Spangled Banner" and Country Joe and the Fish's sardonic "Feel Like I'm Fixin' to Die Rag" in the motion picture *Woodstock* leave us with an impression of popular music as a central institution in the oppositional consciousness of the decade, but while some songs certainly played a role in progressive political mobilizations, the best-seller charts also reveal a long list of countersubversive classics including Sergeant Barry Sadler's "The Ballad of the Green Berets," Pat Boone's "Wish You Were Here Buddy," Victor Lundberg's "Open Letter to My Teenage Son," and Merle Haggard's "Okie from Muskogee" and "Fightin' Side."

Alice Echols's riveting biography of Janis Joplin, *Scars of Sweet Paradise*, offers an antidote to the amnesia that hinders our understanding of the 1960s. Echols deftly captures the contradictory realities of the decade through her moving account of Joplin's efforts to find an identity for herself in a society that offered precious few models of success to women. Instead of a simple story about Dionysian excesses and uninhibited indulgence in "sex, drugs, and rock 'n' roll," Echols emphasizes the ordinary nature of Joplin's upbringing, the contradictions of middle-class life, and the relentless and excruciating pressure on young women to conform to the qualities most prized by the "beauty system" in our society. Joplin commanded the attention of her generation because of her extraordinary artistry as a singer, to be sure, but also because her efforts to fashion her own forms of self-expression and sexuality resonated with other young people who came out of similar battles with high school cliques, community college instructors, and mass-mediated images of normativity. Echols explains how war overseas and racial upheaval at home created a time of turmoil, terror, and torment for many middle-class and working-class white youths, but she also delineates in precise detail how difficult it was for them to avoid replicating within the counterculture the very sexism, individualism, and materialism against which they thought they were rebelling.[4]

Demographic growth and targeted marketing had a great deal to do with the emergence of the counterculture in the 1960s. Seventeen-year-olds became the largest single age group in the United States in

1964. Increases in wages and in the gross national product every year since 1946 had produced a group of teenagers with considerable market power. In addition to parental spending on their children, the average teen paid out $555 in 1964 for products or services. Sales of rock music propelled the rise of the music business. By 1968, the sales of music by the Beatles alone had netted $154 million in revenues. In 1970, sales of recorded music exceeded $2 billion, making the music industry more lucrative than motion pictures or professional sports.[5]

The emerging youth market contributed to the commercial viability of FM radio stations and underground newspapers. While affecting an alternative if not oppositional stance toward politics, the new communications media also worked to create, solidify, and expand a distinct youth market by advertising the wares of merchants selling bell-bottom pants and paisley shirts, cigarette papers and black lights, and, of course, recorded popular music. The dominant players in the music business quickly discovered that they could secure significant sales as a result of favorable commentary in alternative newspapers or on FM broadcasts. They funneled advertising dollars to these venues, sometimes providing the overwhelming share of their revenues.[6] To the extent that young people in the 1960s shared a common culture, it was largely as a result of their constitution as a distinct market segment, not because of their own activity and imagination.

The counterculture of the 1960s expressed both a rejection of U.S. culture and a profound embrace of it at the same time. Exploration of hallucinogenic drugs promised the possibility of blocking out the everyday ugliness of news about peasants' bodies scorched by napalm and ghettos set on fire. Yet it also imitated the "quick fix" mentality of a society accustomed to tobacco, alcohol, and prescription drug solutions to personal worries and problems. The lure of setting up rural communes spoke to deep-seated desires for new ways of organizing work, family, and community relations. But the rural commune also replicated the retreat to suburbia as a personal escape from shared social problems about city life. The adoption of practices and beliefs originating in Buddhist and Hindu traditions raised the possibility of non-Western and non-Christian ways of knowing and being, but largely by emphasizing retreat from the world and avoidance of authority at a time when political engagement was becoming increasingly risky and costly.

From this perspective, it may be difficult to see why the 1960s serves as such a powerful locus for contemporary countersubversive mobilizations. Seemingly, never have so many been frightened by so little. Yet is important to remember as well that many young people in the 1960s entered adulthood in contexts far removed from the college campuses and countercultural encampments that appear most prominently in contemporary rhetorical reconstructions of the decade. The new social warrant that emerged during the Age of the Civil Rights Movement was not really the creation of countercultural hippies and campus rebels, but rather came from the sense of self-worth and raised expectations resulting from participation in social movements by workers, women, military personnel, and members of aggrieved racial groups.

During the 1960s, a sustained series of wildcat and sanctioned strikes, acts of sabotage, and insurgent challenges to union leadership largely by young workers raised serious opposition to management control over the purpose, pace, and nature of production in workplaces all across the country. Women's consciousness-raising groups promoted processes of social critique and self-examination that demonstrated the links between macrosocial institutions and microsocial practices. Young people on active duty in a shooting war thousands of miles away from home and those stationed at military bases in the United States mounted serious campaigns against the authority of their commanding officers by leaving their units, forming affinity groups with like-minded friends inside and outside the service, and in some cases disobeying direct orders. Antiwar GI coffeehouses and newspapers created spaces for criticism of the war from inside the military. Black soldiers stationed at Fort Hood in Texas resisted serving as a counterinsurgency force to suppress ghetto rioters. Even in Vietnam, the large number of desertions, orders not implemented, and mysterious frequent casualties suffered by front-line officers unpopular with their own troops all contributed materially to the end of the war.

At the same time, youthful residents of inner-city neighborhoods burned buildings and fought with law enforcement officers to challenge police brutality, job discrimination, and housing segregation. Movements for racial justice generated a new sense of self among their participants, and in the process produced an entire generation of activists, artists, and intellectuals committed to collective decision-making, and radical egalitarianism. They went far beyond simply seeking removal of legal impediments to their full participation in U.S. society. The social struggles of the Age of the Civil Rights Movement taught their participants about the need to make radical transformations in U.S. society in general. As black activist, scholar, and theologian Vincent Harding explains, "This people has not come through this pain in order to attain equal opportunity with the pain inflictors of this nation and this world. It has not been healed in order to join the inflictors of wounds. There must be some other reason for pain than equal opportunity employment with the pain deliverers."[7] Harding's formulation leads us to what was truly radical about the 1960s: the belief in participatory democracy, the recognition of the connectedness of different kinds of oppressions, and the search for a "beloved" community.

The social ferment of the 1960s drew directly on the legacies and resources of political institutions created in the 1930s. The Students for a Democratic Society emerged out of the League for Industrial Democracy and the Socialist Party.[8] Veterans of CIO and Communist Party organizing in Alabama during the 1930s created the infrastructure of civil rights activism in Alabama in the early 1960s.[9] Key activists in the early days of the women's movement had learned about the dynamics of organizing as staff members for CIO unions.[10] Ernesto Galarza's experiences in the CIO during the 1930s informed Cesar Chavez's organizing efforts for the United Farm Workers union.[11] The leaders of the rank-and-file resistance to automation on the San Francisco waterfront in the 1960s claimed legitimacy by stressing their fidelity to the social warrant secured during the 1934 west coast longshore strikes.[12]

The culture of the 1960s also displayed debts to the Age of the CIO. Bob Dylan followed in the footsteps (and copied the speech) of

Woody Guthrie. Allan Ginsberg admired and emulated William Carlos Williams. Janis Joplin contributed to the cost of a headstone for the previously unmarked grave of Bessie Smith. Warren Beatty and Arthur Penn drew upon the iconic value of New Deal FSA photography for the visual imagery in *Bonnie and Clyde*, a film set in the 1930s but filled with the rebelliousness and libidinal concerns of the 1960s counterculture.

Yet while owing a great deal to the enduring presence of the Cultural Front in U.S. society, the politics and culture of the Age of the Civil Rights Movement also made decisive breaks with the past. The effectiveness of anticommunism as a countersubversive strategy in the post–World War II years created a rupture between generations on the left and relieved the right of the responsibility of developing credible arguments on behalf of the status quo. The very solidity of the cold war consensus made it difficult for liberals and conservatives, for the old left and the old right, to engage the concerns and arguments of people trying to critique that consensus's assumptions and suppositions. But the "New Left" was not prepared either. Countersubversion and anticommunism made it difficult for them to locate themselves in history, to offer systemic analyses of social problems, or to critique and counter the dominant ideology. Consequently, the New Left lived in what seemed like an infinitely renewable present shaped by shared desires rather than sustained historical analysis and understanding.

The New Left relied on spontaneity and direct democracy as their great equalizers, and for a time, that was enough. In some ways it is amazing that they went as far as they did, cobbling together coalitions that crossed seemingly insurmountable barriers, building unity across national, racial, and class lines with surprising success. Educated to believe that ideology was a thing of the past and deprived of direct contact with an older generation of experienced activists, the New Left make marvelously creative use of the few theoretical writings that became popular among them, especially the sexual radicalism of Norman O. Brown, the critique of bureaucratic society advanced by C. Wright Mills, and the revisionist diplomatic history of William Appleman Williams. But when

St. Louis civil rights activists Percy Green and Richard Daly climb the base of the Gateway Arch in order to chain themselves to the structure to dramatize their protests against the all-white construction crews hired for the project. Their protest changed the image of the arch for many people; after the protest, it became hard to view the monument and *not* think of it as a symbol of black exclusion from jobs and other opportunities, even projects financed by the federal government. Photograph by James A. Rackwitz from the Missouri Historical Society, St. Louis, Mercantile Library collection; reprinted with permission.

their idealistic efforts led to crushing defeats, the New Left had no backup plan and precious little analysis of why they had failed.

Activism during the Age of the Civil Rights Movement produced a new social warrant that challenged the supremacy of war, whiteness, patriarchy, and patriotism within U.S. society. Within American studies, this social warrant undermined the legitimacy of the myth-image-symbol school. Grassroots community activists fought for social change from the bottom up, and their success in showing how much is already known by people without power or position motivated scholars to try to view culture and history from the bottom up as well. Direct-action protesters attacked symbols of national or local unity in order to dramatize the extent of their own exclusion. John Carlos and Tommie Smith raised their fists in the "black power" salute and bowed their heads when the national anthem was played after their medal-winning performances at the 1968 Olympics. Their protest hijacked a moment of national glory and revealed the deep divisions within the nation. Two members of a St. Louis civil rights group stopped construction on the Jefferson National Memorial Gateway Arch in that city by chaining themselves to the monument hundreds of feet above the ground. From that moment on, the 630 foot stainless steel arch that was supposed to symbolize the common heritage all St. Louisans shared because westward expansion started in their city, instead became a site that no local resident could look at without thinking of the civil rights activists and their demonstration.

Within American studies, the social warrant of the 1960s appeared most powerfully in the form of an anthropological turn. Moving away from essentially literary analyses of unifying national symbols, scholars in American studies rejected questions about the singular character of American nationality to pursue instead studies of how small groups of people make meaning for themselves. Bruce Kuklick's 1972 *American Quarterly* article, "Myth and Symbol in American Studies," forced a move beyond the myth-image-symbol school because it revealed the empirical weaknesses and untheorized assumptions that had guided the field from the start. Myth-image-symbol approaches did not disappear—to this day they are the source of true and useful works within American studies, but they lost their centrality to the field, in part because they no longer spoke to the generational experience of younger scholars and students.[13]

In an address commemorating the fiftieth anniversary of American studies at the University of Minnesota in 1994, Leo Marx advanced an argument about the links between social movements and American Studies that resonates powerfully with my own observations and experiences. Although I disagree emphatically with some of Marx's conclusions, I believe that he asks all the right questions and provides many useful and generative answers to them as well. His framework enables us to see why the American Studies scholarship emanating out of the civil rights movement differed so sharply from the scholarship generated during the Age of the CIO.

Marx argued that scholars have not paid sufficient attention to the relationship between scholarly debates in American studies and the history of social movements. Looking back on the sectarian battles between the "context"-oriented American studies scholars of the 1940s and their "text"-oriented Southern Agrarian or New Critical opponents, Marx minimizes the differences between the two approaches. Both sides knew that social contexts framed aesthetic choices and that textual content played a large role in determining the effectiveness of any given work. Yet a larger and more fundamental disagreement motivated this debate, Marx contends. The New Critics and Southern Agrarians held elitist, conservative, and sometimes reactionary and racist views about politics and society, while the American studies scholars shared a generational affinity for the secular, left-liberal, progressive, and sometimes explicitly socialist or Marxist ideas of the New Deal era.

Marx explains that both the New Critic/Southern Agrarian scholars and the myth-image-symbol/American studies scholars had a stake in avoiding, concealing, and denying their real differences, in disguising deep political disagreements as simply matters of opinion about literary criticism. To acknowledge their ideological differences openly would have threatened to rupture the collegial and harmonious relations that made professional work pleasant for members of both groups and that facilitated promotion and reward within the structure of the academic system. Perhaps more important, neither side wished to risk revealing their doubts about the corporate liberal cold war state that emerged out of World War II, and consequently exposing themselves to charges of disloyalty to the national project. Collegiality between the two groups was also based upon some very real things that they did share; they were all well-educated white professionals (and almost all were male) with a common faith in the "exceptional" nature of the American nation. They shared a critical stance toward the gap between the American promise and the American reality. Although they recommended different remedies, neither side doubted that their core mission was "to recover, reaffirm, and redefine the foundational ideals of a democratic republic."[14]

Marx's honest and self-reflexive insights about the centrality of the New Deal era to the consciousness of his generation and to the myth-symbol-image school they created, led him to periodize subsequent methodological changes in American studies in relation to social movements as well. The turning point, in his view, came during the Vietnam War with its disclosures of systematic dishonesty and misconduct on the part of highly placed government officials, and the rise of insurgent movements against established institutions. Marx endorsed the ways in which this climate of insurgency "lifted the heavy lid of cultural repression that had effectively silenced many groups in American society" and gave many previously excluded groups a significant political presence for the first time.[15] Yet while acknowledging these changes as "necessary and fruitful," Marx nonetheless depicted them as the beginning of the end for American Studies, as the first step in an evasion of duty and an abdication of responsibility.

Marx contended that the oppositional thinkers of the Age of the Civil Rights movement became so disillusioned with the nation-state that "the original and holistic agenda of American Studies was largely discredited and replaced." From his perspective, this disillusionment led American studies scholars to shy away from the big and important questions about the nation as a whole, its institutions, and its shared beliefs and values, to focus instead on "small-scale particularities." While such studies have a legitimate place in Marx's world, he claimed that their emergence at the expense of focus on the nation-state led to political quiescence and moral cowardice. Instead of "activist political radicalism," Marx lamented that American studies scholars today seem immersed in what he called the "merely conceptual radicalism characteristic of poststructural critical theory, social construction, and their variants." He went on to present multiculturalism as the main enemy of holistic study. Multiculturalism is self-serving, Marx alleged, because it enables scholars to celebrate their own groups without having to confront "the unpleasant macroscopic developments in American life today—for example, the increasingly plutocratic concentration of wealth and power."[16]

I have the greatest respect for everything we have learned from Leo Marx in the past and for everything we will be continue to learn from him in the future. His writings enlightened me long ago, long before I ever encountered him personally. When I did meet him, he was exceedingly kind and generous, reading my work and talking to me about it at length even though he had absolutely nothing to gain by doing so. At that time, I had no other access to any kind of critical scrutiny and collegial conversation, so being able to dialogue about my research with Leo Marx meant a great deal to me. Yet it would hardly honor the serious challenge that Marx has posed to American studies scholars if we avoided open debate out of personal loyalty or affection. Instead, I want to show here how we can use Marx's core insight about the links between American studies and social movements to identify a scholarly trajectory in the field that leads in a very different direction than the one he describes.

Marx believes that the patriotic nationalism of the Age of the CIO served important epistemological purposes. Because the original American studies generation turned to Jeffersonian and Lincolnian ideals as the antidote to the ills of the depression, they connected local and particular grievances to the social totality. Imagining "American culture and society as a putative whole" remains essential for Marx because it enables us to critique the "powerful macrocosmic institutions" and its "partly shared beliefs and values."[17] Critical stances toward nationalism and patriotism in his view require a prior commitment to the national project to be legitimate.

Leo Marx presents the experience of his academic generational cohort as if it were a universal truth, while dismissing the experiences of later generations as indicative largely of their failures of nerve and morality. Marx's powerful attachment to the redemptive America fashioned by the Cultural Front during the Age of the CIO reveals how profoundly his generation embraced the political-cultural-intellectual project of their day. It reminds us of the degree to which the mass activism of the CIO's "culture of unity" produced a "social warrant" for an entire generation that revolved around an ideal and redemptive "America."[18] But Marx now presents the object of study that emerged from that ideal—the distinctive character and promise of the U.S. nation-state—as "an ineluctable premise of American Studies."[19]

By sticking dogmatically to his own generation's understanding, Marx neglects the legacy left by the New Deal generation to subsequent social movements and to subsequent cohorts of American studies scholars. He fails to see how the Age of the CIO left the nation with a renewed and expanded commitment to whiteness and war, to patriotism and patriarchal privilege as the nation-state's dominant project. By attributing the epistemologies of subsequent generations of American studies scholars to fear or loss of faith, he forecloses the possibility that the creative new approaches that emerged during the 1960s emerged from that decade's social movements and their activism *against* the legacy of the 1930s generation.

Marx's analysis fails to see that a scholarship based on an unquestioning allegiance to the premise of American exceptionalism presumes what it should be proving (or disproving). In this formulation, American Exceptionalism becomes an article of faith rather than a falsifiable hypothesis. Moreover, while "activist" in a certain way, Marx's American studies is innately reformist, aimed at fulfilling already existing ideals or restoring lost qualities of the republic, but never capable of testing whether the republic itself and its ideas may be at the heart of the problems we face. Marx fails to see the degree to which the bargain that ended the ferment of the 1930s relied upon the creation of a corporate liberal state capable of ensuring U.S. corporations global access to markets, raw materials, and labor. It left us with a state that granted a measure of ethnic and class inclusion to white men of Marx's generation, but only on the condition that they demonstrate fidelity to the state's systems of racial exclusion, gender subordination, and imperial domination.

The new social warrant that emerged from the Age of the Civil Rights Movement made a break with the metaphor of two worlds, arguing that the myths of American Exceptionalism and American Innocence, which may have served progressive purposes in the 1930s, now obscured the actual role of the U.S. nation-state at home and abroad. Through political mobilizations as well as through scholarly inquiry, the 1960s generation fashioned a new social warrant that made a distinction between the nation-state and the nation's people, and that understood racial exclusion, gender subordination, and imperial domination as constitutive of the New Deal state, not as aberrations from it or as evidence of incomplete reforms yet to be implemented. The social movements of the Age of the Civil Rights movement had none of the nostalgia for the preindustrial, preurban, slave-holding republic that captured the imagination and allegiance of the New Deal generation, and as a result they located their project as the future fulfillment of present goals rather than as a return to the lost (but still valid) ideals of the early republic.

Most important, Marx makes an inexcusable error in seeing the self-interested project of white male critics as macrosocial and universal, while dismissing the critiques of aggrieved racial groups as microsocial and particular. The specific and situated knowledge that emerged from civil rights struggles propelled the Student Nonviolent Coordinating Committee, Martin Luther King Jr., Malcolm X, and the Black Panther Party to emerge as early opponents of the Vietnam War, not out of parochialism or particularism but from a systemic analysis that argued for structural links between U.S. counterinsurgency against social change overseas and defense of the status quo at home—just as Du Bois had argued about the emerging corporate liberal state during the 1930s.

The radical Asian American movement of the 1960s developed in the context of the cold war corporate liberal state's efforts to control the rimlands of Asia through wars in Japan, Korea, China, and Vietnam that increasingly defined domestic "American" identity in opposition to Asian "outsiders." The powerful anti-Asian bias that emerged from these conflicts compounded already existing slurs against Asian Americans as "forever foreign," a designation written into U.S. law between 1790 and 1953 through exclusionary immigration policies and embedded in the national culture through the xenophobia consistently directed at people viewed as phenotypically Asian. The Movimiento Chicano challenged the Vietnam War, in part because of the disproportionate number of Mexican Americans in combat as well as because of the ways in which military expenditures diverted resources away from fighting poverty at home. But the movement also connected the current status of Chicanos in the 1960s to the national legacy of conquest and colonization that made it logical to seek solidarity with other people of color throughout the hemisphere and around the world.

The social warrant generated by the social movements of the 1960s could not look to the redemptive America of the 1930s for guidance. In fact, the celebratory America that provided the solution for the social movements of the Age of the CIO had become the major problem for the social movements of the 1960s. By refusing induction into the military to declare his opposition to the Vietnam War, Muhammad Ali had to break with the example of Joe Louis who fought exhibitions for the United States Army during World War II. Kate Smith's recording of "God Bless America," a song written by Russian Jewish immigrant Irving Berlin, could emblematize the transformation of the Cultural Front of the 1930s into support for the military struggle against fascism during World War II, but Bob Dylan's "With God on Our Side" marked the 1960s generation's perception that the civil rights struggle led logically to antiwar rather than prowar politics.

When the social movements of the 1960s confronted residential segregation, job discrimination, and state-sponsored violence, they found themselves in direct opposition to the key components of the New Deal coalition—the federal government's housing policies, trade-union support for discrimination, the Democratic Party's reliance on Southern segregationists, and whites who believed that their success at securing ethnic inclusion during the 1930s allowed them to act as agents of racial exclusion during the 1960s. George Mariscal notes that the antiwar movement among Chicanos enacted a particularly wrenching generational rift, because it pitted young activists against their community's key institutions—the Catholic Church, the trade unions, and the Democratic Party.[20]

Furthermore, by focusing exclusively on "multiculturalism" as the source of the 1960s generation's break with American Exceptionalism, Leo Marx neglects the importance of the ideas of the Wisconsin School of diplomatic history in challenging the American studies framework. The scholarship of William Appleman Williams and his students at the University of Wisconsin during the 1950s and 1960s advanced a revisionist critique of the metaphor of two worlds, and especially of its institutionalization after World War II through the cold war warfare state. Williams and his students explained that domestic economic tensions and the imperatives for profit within the capitalist system motivated U.S. elites to search for overseas markets, raw materials, and labor as early as the nineteenth century. For them, the "triumph" of the New Deal led to an increasingly centralized, militarized, and undemocratic state dominated by big business leaders and their labor allies. Williams and his students were hardly multiculturalists; they were all white males from conservative midwestern backgrounds. Williams himself came from Iowa and received his undergraduate education at the United States Naval Academy. Readers of the Wisconsin School's scholarship sometimes had trouble determining if Williams and his students were so far right wing that they were on the left, or so far left wing that they were on the right. Part of this confusion stemmed from the hegemony of corporate liberal thought after the New Deal, a hegemony so strong that it created unexpected alliances among those who opposed it. Members of aggrieved racial groups and the descendents of midwestern nationalists opposed to the New Deal may have had little else in common, but for different reasons they both resisted the idea of imposing American Exceptionalism on the entire world.

Leo Marx and other representative thinkers of his generation bemoan the demise of the original American studies project. But much of the most creative, courageous, and committed scholarship of our time owes its origins to the new social warrant that emerged during the 1960s out of struggles against the social warrant of the 1930s. Yet, as we shall see, the 1960s generation also failed to understand the contradictory outcomes of its own project, and often stood in the way of the unpredictable creativity of the 1980s that came from the new social warrant of that period.

The "anthropological turn" of the 1970s enabled American studies scholars to come into closer contact with the diversity and plurality of U.S. society. But it left scholars ill prepared to grapple with the importance of ideology within the production and reception of culture. The field received an education on this topic, however, from an unexpected source—from the emphasis placed on culture by the mobilization of conservative social movements during the ensuing Age of Balanced Budget Conservatism in the 1970s and 1980s. Images of the 1960s played a central role in this struggle. In fact, much of the politics of the 1980s and 1990s would be framed as a kind of retroactive referendum on the culture of the 1960s.

For more than thirty years, countersubversive ideologues have been blaming the "excesses" of the 1960s for an astonishing range of social problems, from declines in student test scores and worker productivity to increases in sexually transmitted diseases, homelessness, and drug addiction. By presenting the 1960s as a deranged aberration, they are able to place the unjust distribution of wealth, power, and opportunities in the present beyond critique. What disappears from these accounts is politics, not only the politics of the 1960s as they emerged in response to racism, militarism, and sexism, but also any acknowledgment of who has held political power in America in the 1970s, 1980s, 1990s, and beyond—as well as any discussion of what they have done with that power.

The most revolutionary political mobilization of our lifetimes did not take place in the 1960s, but rather in the 1970s. In that decade, restructuring of the American economy, a new politicization of capital, deindustrialization, and profound alterations in the role of the state initiated convulsive changes in American life and culture. Most of what countersubversives today attribute to the 1960s—changes in gender roles, the fiscal crisis of the state, the paralysis of public institutions, the pervasive demoralization and resignation among growing segments of the population, and increasing gaps between blacks and whites and between rich and poor—in actuality have taken place since the 1970s under neoconservative and neoliberal stewardship. Conveniently enough, the more chaos that contemporary policies promote, the greater the affective power of condemnations of the 1960s.

Thus for conservative author Allan Bloom in his best-selling 1987 book *The Closing of the American Mind*, the memory of black student demonstrators brandishing (but not firing) guns at Cornell University in the 1960s serves as a symbol of the breakdown of reason and the rise of violence in our society. Yet actual attacks on women trying to enter abortion clinics or on minorities singled out for hate crimes at the time he was writing completely escaped his censure. The memory of a few black men with guns twenty years ago evidently continued to trouble Bloom more than the plight of hundreds of thousands of black men in his own time without jobs, education, or shelter. Similarly, former Secretary of Education and Director of the National Endowment for the Humanities William Bennett was so concerned about children who had not read *The Federalist Papers* before they got out of school, that he had nothing to say about children who had not been able to have breakfast before coming to school because of their families' poverty in the wake of the "triumphs" of Reagan-era economics and politics.

The curricular agenda for higher education advanced by Bloom and Bennett reflected an attempt to effect a similar erasure of politics in the present. They recommended that students read Plato and Shakespeare much in the way that fundamentalist Christian parents encourage their children to listen to Christian rockers like Amy Grant or Stryper, not because they understand them or even like them, but in the hope that they will distract their children from things that are more relevant to their lives and more threatening to their parents' interests and beliefs.

Countersubversives still need to attack the 1960s. It provides them with a legitimating narrative for avoiding the social chaos produced by their own policies. It enables them to displace onto the terrain of culture anxieties that emerge from political and economic realities. Along with neoliberal allies like Arthur Schlesinger Jr., they decry "the dis-uniting of America" purportedly enacted by feminism and by what they call multi-culturalism, but they remain silent about the disuniting of America effected by racial discrimination, sexism, and class hierarchies. Their policies leave us with fragmented lives, but they demand a school curriculum and a culture that gives us a unified story.

This dominant discourse aims to transform popular memory about the democratic movements for change that shook society during the Age of the Civil Rights Movement into a temporary moment of madness described as "the 1960s" and comprised of two parts—a legitimate "civil rights movement" aimed only at de jure segregation whose gains were satisfied by civil rights legislation in 1964 and 1965, and an illegitimate aftermath during which feminists, gays, and racial minorities went too far by creating mechanisms aimed at actually implementing the "victories" of the civil rights movement, mechanisms like school busing, affirmative action, and fair housing enforcement.[21]

The popular mobilizations that emerged under the broad umbrella of "civil rights" did not view racism as an aberrant phenomenon in an otherwise just society. Rather, these mobilizations identified racism as one of the key social mechanisms for teaching, institutionalizing, legiti-mating, and naturalizing hierarchy, inequality, and exploitation. They saw that many of their society's mechanisms for social, political, and eco-nomic exclusion relied on racism for their deep structure and practical legitimacy. The movement produced integrationists to be sure, but it also nurtured and sustained broad social critiques—not just of racist hier-archies, but of all hierarchies, not just of racist dehumanization but of the broader dehumanization integral to a society where the lives of humans count for less than the concerns of capital.

Curiously enough, the origins of the contemporary attacks on the 1960s lie in the 1960s themselves. In 1968, Richard Nixon turned himself into a successful presidential candidate by creating a countersubversive consensus organized around opposition to the countercultures and oppositional movements of that time. Nixon found that voters disliked the antiwar movement even more than they disliked the war, and that his traditional campaign strategy of denigrating his opponents could provoke an outpouring of anger that had important political implications.

Consequently, Nixon selected Spiro T. Agnew as his running mate, not so much because of the Maryland governor's fitness for high office (Agnew, after all was the politician who, according to Gore Vidal, once called America "the greatest nation in the country" as well as a man who took kickbacks on construction projects while serving as governor of Maryland and who continued to receive payments from them while serving as vice president of the United States) but because of Agnew's much publicized scolding of black leaders in Baltimore after a riot in their community on the night Dr. King was assassinated. In that speech Agnew presented himself as a self-made man who had overcome humble beginnings through hard work, even though his father owned several restaurants and had enough money to send his son to Johns Hopkins University during the Great Depression for three years before Agnew flunked out. Agnew went on to assert that he had never asked anyone for a handout, even though he returned to college and attended law school on a GI loan, bought his first house with VA and FHA financing, and made a fortune investing in real estate on land he helped zone as an appointed member of his county's board of supervisors. While Agnew's lecture failed to represent accurately the details of his own biography, it did conform to a larger American master narrative, and consequently won him widespread approval among whites longing for a show of paternal authority and discipline in response to riots and demands for black power.

Agnew's humiliating scolding of black leaders in Baltimore secured him a place as Nixon's running mate, and it situated him in a role within the administration as "Nixon's Nixon,"—a one man strike force capable of enunciating the visceral rage necessary for mobilizing a countersubversive consensus. Although clearly tied to a longer history of nativist and anticommunist attacks on the "other" in American politics, Agnew's paternal scolding (which included preventing his own daughter from wearing an antiwar armband on Moratorium Day) and his masculinist hyperbole (he baited the antiwar movement as "effete snobs") fit perfectly into an administration headed by Richard Nixon, the man who after his reelection described the American people "like children" as he vowed to move this country so far right you won't recognize it.[22]

What we can recognize about this country today is that over the past three decades, neoconservative and neoliberal economic policies have dismantled the industrial and social capital of America, undermined the nation's medical and educational infrastructures, and subsidized extravagant spending by the rich while imposing onerous burdens on the poor. Yet at the upper levels of our society, nothing succeeds like failure. Each sign of social disintegration becomes evidence in favor of even more oppressive versions of the policies that have created crises in the first place. When restructuring of the state and the economy undermined employment and housing in inner cities during the 1970s, neoconservatives responded with treatises about the negative effects of welfare on the self-esteem of poor people. When a decade of cuts in welfare benefits only left the poor with fewer resources, the New Right responded with arguments about the moral deficiencies of the black family. Yet when speculators and swindlers looted the savings and loan industry we heard no corresponding lectures about the moral deficiencies of the families of white capitalists; on the contrary, our government funneled federal funds to pay for the party that rich people had at our expense. Evidently here was one problem that *could* be solved by "throwing dollars at it." The more these policies fail, the more they centralize power in the hands of multinational corporations, the more they fuel feelings of alienation and powerlessness among the populace. They incite a longing for paternal power and authoritarian order to soothe the frustrations and fears of a life that leaves people with few firm connections to others. In this context, ideological legitimation plays a crucial role in making this system work, because the sadistic rage vented against transgressors provides the pleasures of power without the responsibility and intersubjectivity of politics. But the very need for legitimation shows the instability of the system. These policies perpetually subvert the stability their narrative extols; they make us long for unified narratives but leave us with fragmented lives.

By couching their political and economic agendas in the language of restoring patriarchal authority, Nixon and Agnew succeeded in launching the most radical transformation of our lifetimes. Even their own personal disgraces did not discredit the master narrative or the policies for which it provided ideological cover. In our own day, the legacy of this strategy has turned American political discourse into what one critic calls "sadism in search of a story"—an ever more aggressive venting of rage against demonized others coupled with promises of patriarchal protection against further pollution. Of course, this rhetoric does nothing to solve actual social problems, but it provides a ready scapegoat for present and future failures.

Under these circumstances, our memories of the 1960s will not be enough. The 1960s have been distorted, not forgotten. Politically they serve a vital function for neoconservatives. Without losing sight of the many things we can learn from the activism of that decade, we would also be well advised to connect it to the politics of the decades that preceded and followed it. The exceptionalism of the 1960s serves the right as the linchpin of a very powerful social text, a case in which, as Bertolt Brecht once counseled, both the text and the audience need to be rewritten.

Those of us who are in the American Studies Association are in a fortunate position to contest these stories. In our scholarship about American culture and in our classrooms we encounter an America that is very different from the stable, static, and unitary society conjured up by neoconservative ideology. We know that the monolithic definitions of citizenship, patriotism, knowledge, and sexuality prescribed for us collapse immediately in the face of the plurality of practices that actually exist in American society past and present.

In the 1960s, when a series of fortuitous experiences shaped my political perspective, I thought I had the opportunity to be part of a time that produced the new kinds of spaces that Marshall Berman remembers as the key characteristic of the 1960s. Since that time, however, counter-subversive mobilizations have revolved around efforts to prevent a social movement like that from ever emerging again. They may be successful. Perhaps the darkness that has enveloped this country over the past thirty years is here to stay. Certainly the experiences of the 1960s have been so distorted beyond recognition that it is difficult to imagine how they might still serve as a source of inspiration and education for anyone. But the fact of activism itself remains interesting and important. No one in the early stages of a social movement knows whether his or her efforts will ultimately succeed. But something makes them prefer activity to passivity, something makes them choose action over inaction. We have no way of knowing if the social movements of our time will attain any of their ultimate goals or produce lasting social changes. But at least some people will feel compelled to try to turn the discord of our world into a new kind of harmony, to attempt to ignite a spark—as Bruce Springsteen used to sing—"even if we're just dancing in the dark."[23]

CHAPTER 4

Listening to Learn and Learning to Listen

Who Needs the Eighties?

> The constriction of political alternatives actually promotes the
> mindless obsession with self in contemporary America—
> whether in its hard, Reaganite or soft, therapeutic versions.
> Both the new right and the new subjectivity gratify the self at
> the expense of the community, and treat claims for social justice
> as threats to personal well-being. Both inhabit, as starved selves,
> a world of scarce resources, in which there is not enough love
> or money to go around. Both are therefore punitive toward
> others and indulgent toward themselves. Law and order and the
> narcissistic self flourish in symbiosis, not opposition.
>
> —Michael Rogin, *"Pa Bell"*

American studies scholars today face a culture characterized both by continuity with the cultures that emerged during the Age of the CIO and the Age of the Civil Rights Movement and by dramatic ruptures from them. During the 1970s and 1980s, conservatives in the United States fashioned a powerful coalition that united executives from multinational corporations, suburban small property holders, independent entrepreneurs, and religious fundamentalists to mobilize around a broad range of economic, political, and cultural concerns. Support from some of the wealthiest families (Coors, Mellon) and some of the most richly endowed foundations (John M. Olin, Bradley, Scaife) enabled this movement to build an extensive network of interrelated institutions including research centers, direct-mail solicitation companies, public relations outlets, magazines, newspapers, prayer circles, and public interest law firms. This coalition secured impressive political gains—moving the Democratic Party away from the liberalism of the 1972 McGovern campaign and toward the moderation of the Carter administration, defeating liberal Democrats in the 1978 and 1980 elections to give Republicans control of the Senate (and by 1994 the House of Representatives), and laying the groundwork for the election of Ronald Reagan as president. Yet even more important than the political reversals enacted by the conservative coalition of the 1970s and 1980s were the cultural changes it brought about at both the macropolitical and microsocial levels.

Although this coalition was initiated from the top down, from some of the most affluent and powerful sectors of U.S. society, it also attempted to nurture and sustain conservatism from the bottom up. The welfare/warfare state that emerged in the wake of the New Deal protected the aggressive pursuit of markets, labor, raw materials, and investment opportunities overseas by multinational corporations through a combination of defense spending and military intervention. It secured the popularity of that program by encouraging large corporations to pay high wages and grant substantial benefits to organized workers, and by using the power of the federal treasury to stimulate consumer spending, promote home ownership, and ease suffering while discouraging excessive savings by subsidizing old-age pensions and medical care for the elderly. But by the early 1970s, the combination of increased social demands from aggrieved groups (workers, racial minorities, women, youth) and decreasing profits and growth made it appear to some business leaders that the costs of government aid on behalf of social legitimation now exceeded the benefits of government aid to capital accumulation. They sought to free up capital for private investment by campaigning for lower taxes, less government regulation, privatization of public services, and sparser social welfare benefits. Sidney Plotkin and William Scheuerman sum up these goals as the politics of Balanced Budget Conservatism, and the 1980s come into clearer focus if we think of the decade as the Age of Balanced Budget Conservatism.

The enduring popularity of the culture of the Age of the CIO and the legitimacy and respect accorded to the culture of the Age of the Civil

Rights Movement stood in the way of the conservative coalition's agenda. They recognized that it would not be easy to mobilize the clients of a welfare state around the idea of lower benefits and reduced services. It would not be easy to convince a culture transformed by the struggle for direct democracy that the nation was suffering from what political scientist Samuel P. Huntington described as an excess of democracy.[1] But they found that it was possible to divide and conquer, to mobilize the winners of the social wars of the 1930s against the forces challenging them in the 1960s. Conservatives built a countersubversive coalition in the 1970s by purporting to rescue the patriotic nationalism of the New Deal from the "anti-Americanism" of the 1960s, by deploying the egalitarian anti-elitism of the 1930s (which had at that time been directed against the "economic royalists" of big business) against "special interests," which in the conservative lexicon of the 1970s and 1980s came to mean trade unions, civil rights groups, public employees, and the poor.

The contradictions of the 1930s Popular Front made the task of 1970s and 1980s conservatives easier. The enthusiastic nationalism of the 1930s could easily be channeled into cold war anticommunism and support for military interventions overseas. The built-in biases inside New Deal social welfare programs that sought protection for white male employment and wages at the expense of women and nonwhite workers made it easier to portray the social programs of the 1960s as radical departures from the world of the New Deal. The people who profited most from the commitments to social welfare won by the New Deal coalition had no intention of surrendering their own protections, the benefits they derived from Social Security or the assets they acquired as a result of federally subsidized home loans and the federal mortgage interest tax deduction. But they were willing to turn against extending the welfare state to others, to oppose public expenditures and public institutions once "public" became a synonym for nonwhite, while "private" became a code word for white.

The most important grassroots movement experiences for the "new right" of the 1970s and 1980s came in the context of "antibusing" organizations—efforts to prevent court-ordered school desegregation and to preserve the advantages enjoyed by residents of the mostly white suburbs that had been created by public and private housing policies during and since the New Deal.[2] The opponents of court-ordered desegregation realized that whiteness has a cash value in U.S. society as well as a psychic value. Whiteness is the key that enables some people to enter those exclusive areas of society that enjoy a better quality environment, receive better government services, and secure access to better educational, employment, and consumption opportunities. Antibusing campaigns enabled these people to claim these privileges as if they were not privileges at all. Instead, these beneficiaries of thirty years of government aid (especially subsidies to suburban home ownership) presented themselves as oppressed victims of government "meddling" in their lives.[3]

Sociologist Clarence Lo demonstrates that most of the activists in the antibusing movement believed that blacks had already made too many gains as a result of the 1960s, that blacks no longer suffered from discrimination, and that government support for black rights constituted discrimination against whites. Moreover, Lo reveals that people who supported the antibusing movement almost always connected that opposition to antitax sentiment. He shows how Boston antibusing activists attributed increased property tax assessments solely to the costs of school busing and other programs designed to help blacks, not to the regressive nature of the U.S. tax code.[4] Antibusing and antitax campaigns provided the training ground for subsequent "anti" campaigns central to the conservative crusade to change U.S. culture and politics in the 1980s: efforts to defeat the Equal Rights Amendment, to resist gun control, to destroy affirmative action, to deny women freedom to make choices about contraception and abortion, and to prevent the passage of legislation banning discrimination against gays and lesbians.

Antitax activists, such as the supporters of California's Proposition 13 in 1978, provided an ideal source of defections from the New Deal coalition for conservatives. The activists' focus on blacks and on the federal courts kept them from ever raising broader questions about tax equity (like the share of the tax burden paid by the wealthy or by corporations). Antitax sentiment revolved around preserving access to "consumption" in the broadest sense of the term, and did nothing to challenge corporate plans for generating growth, expansion, and change through outsourcing production, redirecting capital overseas, and deregulation. Most important, antitax and antibusing movements combined a possessive investment in whiteness with the preservation of private privilege, elevating private desires over public needs. Where the Age of the CIO had encouraged Americans to think of themselves as workers and producers, and the Age of the Civil Rights Movement had encouraged Americans to think of themselves as citizens and community members, the Age of Balanced Budget Conservatism placed its greatest emphasis on American identities as consumers and accumulators.

Balanced Budget Conservatism encouraged well-off communities to hoard their advantages, to use their tax base only for themselves, while displacing onto less wealthy areas the costs of remedying complex social problems. This put every subunit of government in competition with every other unit, strengthening the hand of wealthy individuals and corporations seeking to evade their civic responsibilities and obligations. In addition, by emphasizing the insulation of local taxing units from the broader needs of city, county, state, and federal bodies, the antitax activists found they could be fiscal liberals at home, enjoying high spending on services they consumed directly, but fiscal conservatives elsewhere, demanding cuts in services that went to "others." Their self-interest was served twice over, increasing public spending in well-off districts to increase their property values, while reducing spending in poorer communities and making residence in them worth even less to their inhabitants. Once in place, this logic could be implemented even at the federal level. Conservative Congressman Newt Gingrich saw to it that his home district received more federal funds than any other district while he was Speaker of the House of Representatives, even though he presented himself as a resolute opponent of federal taxation and government spending. Similarly, the wealthy and mostly white west side of Los Angeles routinely voted for liberal candidates who spoke out in favor of aid for the poor, yet the west side received more federal "antipoverty" funds at the time of the 1992 Los Angeles insurrection than did the poverty-stricken areas of South Central Los Angeles with their largely Latino and black populations.[5]

A certain amount of cynicism and self-interest permeated conservative antitax and antibusing mobilizations, but they succeeded in large measure because they correctly understood the contradictions of the culture of this country, especially the unresolved contradictions between the Age of the CIO and the Age of the Civil Rights Movement. It was no accident, therefore, that the conservative coalition found its fullest expression in Ronald Reagan, who (as Michael Rogin points out) voted four times for FDR, practiced imitations of Roosevelt during his private moments to enhance his public performances, and translated Roosevelt's intimate and warm radio mannerisms to the medium of television.[6]

Reagan proved himself adept at using cultural symbols for political ends. He began his "law and order" campaign for the presidency in 1980 with a speech in Philadelphia, Mississippi, the town where civil rights workers James Chaney, Andrew Goodman, and Michael Schwerner were brutally murdered by a coalition of Klansmen and law enforcement officers during "Freedom Summer" in 1964.[7] Clearly, the man viewed by his supporters as a white knight was prepared to become a white nightmare to his enemies. At the Republican National Convention in 1984, convention managers presented a celebratory film about Reagan's life that started with clips from western movies starring John Wayne. The transformation of Wayne's on-screen characters from the democratic Ringo Kid in 1939's *Stagecoach* to the vengefully racist Ethan Edwards in *The Searchers* in 1956 and the authoritarian countersubversive who moved the frontier to Vietnam in 1968's *The Green Berets* replicated Reagan's off-screen transformation from New Deal disciple to New Right representative.[8]

Reagan's visibility during the 1930s and 1940s as a Hollywood union activist and as an actor who portrayed labor activists (especially in *Juke Girl* with Ann Sheridan in 1942) made him an iconic representative of the Age of the CIO. His resentment of the high taxes he had to pay as he moved into the upper-income brackets fueled his movement to the right, however, and by the 1960s he had become a corporate spokesperson for General Electric and a visible supporter of conservative Senator Barry Goldwater's 1964 campaign for the presidency. That same year, Reagan used his prominence as an opponent of California's first Fair Housing Act as the springboard for his successful campaign to be elected governor of the state in 1966. In that post, he presented himself as a resolute opponent of the student, civil rights, and antiwar movements, prefiguring at the state level President Nixon's national politics of countersubversion.

Throughout the 1980s, Reagan used the mechanisms of public relations, especially photo opportunities and carefully scripted cinematic "performances," as effectively as John F. Kennedy had used the televised press conference during the 1960s and Franklin Delano Roosevelt had used radio "fireside chats" during the 1930s. His performances were larger than life. For the majority of Americans, Reagan came to symbolize Christian piety even though he rarely went to church and his wife regularly consulted an astrologer to help advise the president on decisions of state. He came to symbolize family values, even though he had been once divorced, was estranged from three of his children, and did not recognize one of his grandchildren at a family gathering. Reagan epitomized the grandeur of military heroism to many of his admirers, even though he had spent World War II in Hollywood (like John Wayne), never actually served in any military unit, and drew his examples of military valor largely from the plots of old movies.

When Reagan met with Soviet leader Mikhail Gorbachev to negotiate about the nuclear arms race, the first matter the president wanted to raise with his Russian counterpart was a comment Gorbachev had made dismissing Reagan as a former B-movie actor. "They weren't *all* B movies," Reagan noted to the startled Gorbachev. Reagan praised the secret (and illegal) activities of Oliver North delivering weapons to Middle East terrorists in order to raise money for the (equally illegal) operations of the Nicaraguan contras. He told North that his experiences would make a great film. After seeing the Sylvester Stallone movie *Rambo* in 1985, Reagan asserted that now he knew what he should do the next time U.S. citizens were taken hostage.[9]

Reagan's ability to seem like a character from a Frank Capra film from the 1930s or 1940s softened the harsh impact of his policies as president. Reagan looked and sounded so much like George Bailey, the hero of Capra's 1946 *It's a Wonderful Life* who saves his small town from greedy bankers and developers, that it was difficult for many Americans to realize that it was precisely Reagan's deregulation of the Savings and Loan industry in the 1980s that allowed speculators to loot the savings of ordinary citizens and leave taxpayers with a five-hundred-billion-dollar obligation, or to see that his policies effected a complete takeover of U.S. politics by the nation's wealthiest individuals and corporations.[10]

These moments of synergy between Reagan's film career and his presidency symbolized part of a broader pattern during the 1980s. The focus on consumption within Balanced Budget Conservatism, the growth of the entertainment industry, and Reagan's adroit appropriation of egalitarian cultural symbols for conservative ends gave entertainment and popular culture a central role in the political life of the nation. Perhaps nothing encapsulates the new character of the nation's political culture during the 1980s so emblematically as the succession of *Rocky* films made by Sylvester Stallone. In *Rocky* (1976) and *Rocky II* (1979), the humble, modest, and downwardly mobile white working-class hero, Rocky Balboa, symbolically reverses the 1960s by triumphing over the fast-talking, flashy, and obscenely wealthy Apollo Creed—obviously an evocation of Muhammad Ali. In *Rocky III* (1980), Apollo Creed joins with Rocky Balboa to defeat Clubber Lang, an obnoxious, arrogant, and savage thug whose Mohawk haircut and vulgar gold necklaces mark him as a "typical" ghetto dweller, presumably an unintended and unwanted creation of the Apollo Creeds of the world who are now horrified by what they have produced. *Rocky IV* followed the logical trajectory of the Reagan years by fusing vengeance against the symbolic decline of white masculinity with a battle against foreign adversaries. In this film, Rocky gets vengeance for a fallen comrade by battling against a superhuman Russian boxer. No longer a humble working-class boxer from South

Philadelphia, the Rocky Balboa in this film is introduced into the ring by means of a Las Vegas production number featuring red, white, and blue bunting, American flags, and James Brown singing about the glories of "Living in America."

During the 1930s, the actual ring triumphs of heavyweight boxing champion Joe Louis seemed to embody the experiences of a generation. Louis was an African American autoworker from Detroit whose quiet humility and patriotic decision to fight exhibitions for soldiers during World War II symbolized the Age of the CIO and its link between egalitarianism and celebratory nationalism. Muhammad Ali's victories during the 1960s inside and outside the ring seemed to embody a markedly different generational experience. Ali's flamboyant self-confidence, his rejection of Christianity and embrace of Islam (which included changing his name from Cassius Clay), and his principled refusal to join the army or support the Vietnam War resonated with the social warrant of the Age of the Civil Rights Movement. But in the Reagan years of the 1980s, the nation's most popular boxer was not a boxer at all, but a simulacrum, an actor playing a boxer in order to spin out fantasies designed to salve the wounds caused by a perceived decline in the status and prestige of white men as a result of the changes of the 1960s. MYTH

As the *Rocky* series indicates, part of the conservatism of the 1980s depended upon images and ideas from the 1930s. Reagan's followers remembered a New Deal that had fused consumption with celebratory nationalism. For them, the New Deal had created valuable opportunities for ethnic inclusion and equally lucrative mechanisms for racial exclusion. They recalled a New Deal that gave them faith in the future in the form of patriotism and national unity forged through symbolic identification with a charismatic leader.

Many of the leading spokespersons for neoconservatism in the 1980s had been socialist radicals in the 1930s and 1960s, including Irving Kristol, Gertrude Himmelfarb, Midge Decter, Norman Podhoretz, David Horowitz, and David Stockman.[11] Reaganism enabled them to pursue power in a new setting, to remain true to the elitist and vanguardist practices they had learned from Leninism, and to get rewarded by the nation's wealthiest individuals and corporations at the same time. They disavowed the revolutionary ends they had espoused in earlier decades, but never came to grips with the ways in which their fear of genuine democracy lent continuity between their later politics and their youthful selves.

Reagan also learned from the New Deal about the importance of using nationalism to entice labor leaders to become defenders of the status quo and the capitalist system. During the Reagan presidency, the AFL-CIO received nearly forty million dollars per year from outside sources to spend on "foreign activities." Ninety percent of this money came directly from the government, channeled to the unions through cold war government agencies including the National Endowment for Democracy. This infusion of cash nearly equaled the entire domestic budget of the federation and almost matched the AFL-CIO's income from dues payments by individual workers and their unions.[12]

Why did one of the most antiunion presidents in history funnel millions of dollars every year to the labor bureaucracy? Ostensibly the funds were to be used to fight communism by exporting democratic unionism overseas, but the AFL-CIO did not use this money to organize the unorganized around the world or to establish channels of communication to help workers employed by the same multinational companies coordinate strategies of resistance. Instead, the money went to ensure the institutional survival of the AFL-CIO. The unions suffered a devastating decline in membership during the 1980s as a result of capital flight, automation, outsourcing, and union-busting measures by private industry and government. Money from the Reagan administration and sources it supervised cushioned the blow for the labor bureaucracy by adding money to its treasury.

Organized labor opposed the Reagan administration politically, donated money to Democrats, and organized a few demonstrations against Reaganomics. Yet labor leaders did not mobilize their own memberships at the point of production or in communities, did not conduct mass organizing drives, and undermined local militancy by workers everywhere across the country. During the Reagan years, AFL-CIO

President Lane Kirkland kept such a low public profile that some groups of local militants thought of offering a prize to anyone who had seen him.

During the 1930s, the sharp decline in dues-paying members throughout the previous decade led reluctant and conservative union leaders to change their policies to support aggressive mass organizing campaigns. These drives unleashed the energy and enthusiasm of rank-and-file activists and created the CIO's "culture of unity." Without new members, the unions would not have survived. During the 1980s, however, the unions did not have to recruit new members, nor become more militant, because Ronald Reagan and the Cold Warriors around him used government and private funds to ensure the institutional survival of the unions, but also to neutralize them as a political force on the homefront.

The political successes of conservatives during the 1980s did not translate into complete control over U.S. culture, despite their effective manipulations of cultural symbols. On the contrary, the conservative focus on culture led to an intensification of oppositional cultural practices that directly challenged the conservative agenda. From Bruce Springsteen's egalitarian populism (which constantly referenced egalitarian memories of the 1930s and 1960s) to the popularity of feminist "women of color" writers, including Toni Morrison, Leslie Marmon Silko, Maxine Hong Kingston, and Sandra Cisneros, from the postmodern parodies of celebrity culture in art by Hans Haacke and Cindy Sherman to the enthusiasm for ambiguity and hybridity embodied in the commercial viability of musicians Madonna, Boy George, Michael Jackson, and Prince, cultural production during the 1980s offered opportunities for airing ideas and identities that were being precluded in politics by the political power of the right.

American studies scholarship changed during the Age of Balanced Budget Conservatism in order to address the new relationships linking culture, the nation, and social power. An emphasis on ideology and on the counterhegemonic uses of commercial culture informed many of the most influential works in the field, most notably Janice Radway's *Reading the Romance* and Michael Denning's *Mechanic Accents*. The rise of global commerce and culture, the end of the cold war, and the emergence of new centers of economic and cultural power in Asia and Europe seemed to turn Henry Luce's predicted "American Century" into something like the "American Half-Century," rendering analyses of American Exceptionalism less credible than ever.[13] The ever increasing reach and scope of commercialized leisure eclipsed both "high culture" art and "folk culture" artifacts, replacing them with cultural products resistant to traditional methods of criticism. In addition, the cultural politics of neo-conservatism and the political economy of higher education in an age of deindustrialization undermined the very constituencies historically most closely associated with critical examination of the myths and realities of American culture—women, ethnic minorities, and the working class.

The 1980s also encouraged American studies scholars to think about the ways in which the field had too easily conflated the national culture with the needs and interests of the state. The 1940s and 1950s emphasis on the American Renaissance seemed at the time to many in the field a progressive extension of the politics of the 1930s, a search for the "Lincoln Republic" and the democracy it might have enabled in the years before the rise of industry and monopoly capital.

But in retrospect, it now seemed possible that the rebirth of scholarship on the American Renaissance has been more of an effort to turn away from realism and regionalism, from the documentary art that focused attention on the nation's flaws and frustrations. Some of the founders of American studies on particular campuses had close ties to the Central Intelligence Agency, and several international centers promoting American studies bore the unmistakeable stamp of the U.S. Information Agency and the CIA.[14]

Moreover, the critical understanding within American studies during the 1950s of Herman Melville's *Moby Dick* as a story about a battle between a free individual and a totalitarian state now appeared to conform too closely to the cold war agenda of the nation-state. Celebrations within American studies of Melville's masterpiece and of abstract expressionist art affirmed a necessary autonomy from the state for art, but it became clear by the 1980s that this "art for art's sake" mentality played an important role in the project of the very state from which art was sup-posed to be independent.[15]

American studies originally emerged as a field because of the his-torical crises of the 1930s, and it responded sensitively to subsequent crises during the 1960s and 1980s. Confronted by a country where cul-ture seemed to play a more significant role in politics than ever before, American studies scholars sought approaches, methods, and theories adequate to explain the ideological importance of nationalism, material-ism, and patriarchy during the Reagan years.

European cultural theory emerged as an especially important com-ponent of American studies scholarship during the 1980s. Since the 1960s, European critics from a variety of perspectives had been theoriz-ing about a "crisis of representation" that called into question basic assumptions within the disciplines central to the American studies pro-ject—literary studies, art history, anthropology, geography, history, and legal studies. From the structuralist-Marxism of Louis Althusser to the psychoanalytic interventions of Jacques Lacan, from Foucauldian post-structuralism to the French feminism of Luce Irigaray and Hélène Cixous, from Derridean deconstruction to the dialogic criticism of Mikhail Bakhtin, European theory revolutionized the study of culture in the second half of the twentieth century.

The frequently confusing and often acrimonious debates engen-dered by the rise of European cultural theory within academic disciplines had important ramifications for all scholars of culture, but they were especially important for those in American studies because they chal-lenged so many of the theoretical assumptions and methodological prac-tices of the field. These challenges to the project of the Enlightenment involved a radical skepticism about the utility and wisdom of rationality, language, and history as neutral mechanisms for understanding the world. At its best, European cultural theory offered radical interrogation of concepts too often undertheorized within American studies, especially the utility of national boundaries as fitting limits for the study of culture, the reliability of categories identifying a canon of "great works," the wis-dom of dividing "high" and "low" culture, the ability of art and literature to mirror a unified and homogeneous national culture, and the value of collapsing the intentions and subjectivities of artists with those of their audiences.

As Michael Ryan explained with elegant precision, much of European cultural criticism revolved around one central dialectical premise, that cultural texts are inescapably part of social processes and that social processes are themselves always textualized in some form. The 1980s "crisis of representation" stemmed from the recognition of the inevitability of representation, and from an attendant acceptance of the necessity for understanding how the mechanisms of representation contained covert as well as overt ideological messages.[16]

When confronted with radically new information, the women in Toni Morrison's wonderful novel *Beloved* "fell into three groups: those that believed the worst; those that believed none of it; and those, like Ella, who thought it through."[17] American studies scholars confronted European cultural theory in much the same way. Some believed all of it, some believed none. Others thought it through, like Morrison's Ella. Far from representing the end of American studies, European cultural theory offered an important opportunity for scholars to reconnect with some of the founding aims and intentions of their field in new and exciting ways.

European cultural theory reproblematized and reframed essential categories about communication and culture. For example, Lacanian psychoanalysis and Althusserian structuralist-Marxism enabled British film critics in the 1970s to begin challenging the "naturalness" of film narrative conventions and of cinematic subject positions, identifying them as social and historical constructs rather than essential and inevitable properties of storytelling or filmmaking. The sophisticated works of Laura Mulvey and Stephen Heath drew upon Althusser for theories of the subject as socially constructed by "ideological state apparatuses," and upon Lacan for explanations about how individual subjects are "hailed" by visual, verbal, and social forms of address.[18] British cultural studies theorist Stuart Hall tempered the structuralist and essentialist implications of Lacanian and Althusserian criticism by blending them with the concept of hegemony advanced by the Italian Marxist Antonio Gramsci.[19] This combination enabled Dick Hebdige, Angela McRobbie, and Iain Chambers (among others) to produce studies of British subcultural practices that treated popular culture as a crucial site for the construction of social identity, but also as a key terrain for ideological conflict.

These inquiries into the nature of subjectivity and the relationship between culture and power helped prepare many American readers for French deconstruction, poststructuralism, and postmodernism. Deconstruction, as articulated by Jacques Derrida, challenged the very fiber of criticism and interpretation by revealing the metaphysical priority given to language within Western thought. This "logocentrism" presumes that careful naming can uncover fixed meanings about the world, but deconstruction's interrogation of language reveals the provisional, contingent, and unstable nature of naming. Derrida found Western thinkers to be uncritical about their "standpoint," about their insistence on unifocal and univocal investigations outward from a privileged center that deny opportunities for reciprocal perspectives and multivocal dialogues. Uncritical acceptance of language as an unmediated vehicle for understanding experience underlies much of the arrogance of Western thought for Derrida—its privileging of written texts over other forms of discourse, its dangerous instrumentality, its crude dismissal of competing systems of thought as "primitive" and "barbaric." In short, the logocentrism of Western culture undergirds the "humanism," which presents the experiences of modern Europeans and North Americans as "human," while dismissing much of the rest of the world as some kind of undifferentiated "other." Logocentrism establishes a symbolic order that naturalizes oppression and injustice.[20] Deconstruction helped cultural critics to break with logocentrism, to be self-reflexive about the tools they wielded, and to investigate the ways in which language positioned the subjects and objects of knowledge.

Similarly, the poststructuralism advanced in the work of Michel Foucault challenged radically the traditional premises of cultural investigation and interpretation. Foucault demonstrated how discursive

categories constitute sites of oppression, for example, how the medicalization of sexuality or the criminalization of "antisocial" behavior
constructed the body as a locus of domination and power. Thus, for Foucault, centralized economic and political power rested not so much on
direct authority, force, or manipulation, but more on the capacity to
disperse power to localized sites where the symbolic order constrains,
contains, silences, and suppresses potential opposition. This approach
called attention to marginal social positions, to diffuse sites of oppression
and resistance, and to practices capable of resisting or at least interrupting
domination.[21]

The concept of postmodernism as developed in the work of Jean-
François Lyotard helped American studies scholars locate the work of
Derrida and Foucault within the contemporary cultural crisis of representation. Although Lyotard implied that postmodernism is more of a
sensibility than a time period, he does acknowledge that the delight in
difference, self-reflexivity, detached irony, and "incredulity toward meta-
narratives" that define the postmodern "condition" stemmed from the
modern sense of living in a "post" period characterized by the exhaustion
of modernism and Marxism as ways of understanding and interpreting
experience.[22] Thus, the rejection among deconstructionists and poststructuralists of the "grand master narratives" emanating from the Enlightenment represented more than methodological or theoretical novelty
in culture studies. Rather, the fragmented, decentered, and divided world
uncovered by cultural theory reflected a recognition of contemporary
social and economic crises including deindustrialization in the West,
de-Stalinization in the East, and imperatives imposed on the third
world by first and second world imperialisms, austerity, hunger, debt,
and dependency.

Lacanian psychoanalysis, Althusserian structuralist-Marxism, British
cultural studies, deconstruction, poststructuralism, and postmodernism
represented the most important strains of European cultural theory
influencing American studies during the 1980s, but this list is hardly an
exhaustive one. Explorations into taste cultures by the French sociologist
Pierre Bourdieu, the rediscovery of the body and the insistence on

gender as an independent frame of inquiry by Luce Irigaray and other French feminists, the theories of communicative rationality advanced by the German sociologist Jürgen Habermas, and the scholarly exhumation of Russian literary critic Mikhail Bakhtin's "dialogic criticism" each played an important role in redefining cultural studies in America.[23]

Yet American studies scholars could not regard European cultural theory uncritically, as if it were a panacea. Gayatri Chakravorty Spivak demonstrated how poststructuralists, in their ignorance of the Third World and their unwillingness to search out other voices, often shared the Eurocentric biases they presume to challenge.[24] Those who privileged "marginality" as an abstraction often forgot that what may seem marginal from one perspective might be central to another. Michèle Lamont demonstrated to scholars how the emergence of an oppositional intellectual like Jacques Derrida as a "dominant" philosopher owed a great deal to his ability to benefit from the "cultural capital" institutionalized in the power structures of academic discourse.[25]

Similarly, Judith Lowder Newton noted the disturbing unwillingness among many European cultural theorists to acknowledge their debt to feminism and to the women's movement, which initially raised the issues of subjectivity and representation that served as the basis for the more generalized critique of power raised within cultural theory.[26] Beyond the problem of internal contradictions within European cultural theory lay larger questions about its reification as a method and its application to the American context.

Few scholars engaged in any form of cultural studies during the 1980s were able to avoid the acrimonious debates provoked by the rise of European cultural theory.[27] At one extreme, some scholars rejected all theory through an antiintellectual dismissal of new methods and approaches (especially of deconstruction and poststructuralism). At the other extreme, some scholars seemed to embrace theory as a "magic bullet" that could by itself position scholars outside the oppressions and exploitations of history. One can understand the appeal of a critique that worried about theorists becoming (in the words of one of my colleagues) "spiritless automatons designing ever more elaborate theoretical machines."[28] On the other hand, what might have seemed like self-serving jargon and "intellectual-speak" to nontheorists was often in reality an important effort to create a language capable of interrupting and opposing dominant ideologies. The best work in American studies built on the best of both sides, grounding itself in the study of concrete cultural practices, extending the definition of culture to the broadest possible contexts of cultural production and reception, recognizing the role played by national histories and traditions in cultural contestation, and understanding that struggles over meaning are inevitably struggles over resources.

One of cultural theory's great contributions was to challenge the division between texts and experience. Literary critic Terry Eagleton especially took pains to affirm that the construction of texts is a social process, while at the same time insisting that no social experience existed outside of ideology and textualization. However, Eagleton's healthy warning sometimes led to an unhealthy result, to fetishizing texts by interpreting reality as if it were simply one more text. It is one thing to say that discourse, ideology, and textualization are inevitable and necessary parts of social experience, but it is quite another thing to say that they are the totality of social experience. As phrased in a quip reported by Jon Wiener, those who think everything is a text should "tell that to the veterans of foreign texts."[29]

Stuart Hall described the goal of cultural criticism as the reproduction of the concrete in thought, "not to generate another good theory, but to give a better theorized account of concrete historical reality."[30] Hall's formulation combined "high" theory and "low" common sense and was an essential corrective to uses of theory that lost touch with particular historical and social experiences. It prevented the self-reflexivity of 1980s cultural theory from degenerating into solipsism, seeing theoretical work itself as a part of larger social processes. Finally, it enabled cultural critiques to evolve into cultural interventions by engaging dominant ideology at the specific sites where it was articulated and disarticulated.[31]

Although European cultural theory seemed to threaten traditional practices within American studies, it flourished because it brought a specialized language to bear on key questions about the creation and reception of culture in modern societies. The methodological sophistication of European cultural theory enabled American studies scholars to move beyond questions about what is American. Yet it also resonated with the core categories and questions of the American studies tradition. Indeed, it is fair to say that the development of American studies itself anticipated many of the crossdisciplinary epistemological and hermeneutic concerns at the heart of European cultural theory.

Anticommunism and uncritical nationalism during the early years of the cold war transformed the study of American culture in significant ways, imposing a mythical cultural "consensus" on what previously had been recognized as a history of struggle between insiders and outsiders.[32] Yet while the hegemony of the consensus myth in the 1950s and 1960s served conservative political ends, it did not prevent American studies scholars from asking critical questions about the relationship between the social construction of cultural categories and power relations in American society. As Giles Gunn so convincingly demonstrates, scholars of the myth-image-symbol school consciously sought to "overcome the split between fact and value" by explaining how value-laden images influence social life. He points out that the principal project of these scholars revolved around increasing "comprehension of the historical potentialities and liabilities of different ways of construing the relationship between consciousness and society." Most important, Gunn reminds us that their project was both diagnostic and corrective because they recognized the interpenetration of symbolism and semiotics with power and privilege.[33]

In their sensitivity to language as a metaphorical construct with ideological implications, the myth-image-symbol scholars anticipated many of the concerns of contemporary cultural theory. In his introduction to the 1970 edition of *Virgin Land*, Henry Nash Smith claimed that "our perceptions of objects and events are no less a part of consciousness than are our fantasies," and he described myths and symbols as "collective representations rather than the work of a single mind."[34] Similarly, in his 1965 study of the Brooklyn Bridge, Alan Trachtenberg insisted that "surely the conventions of language themselves suggest predispositions among Americans to react in certain ways at certain times."[35] Yet for all their attention to the role of language in shaping and reflecting social practice, the myth-image-symbol scholars still tended to make sweeping generalizations about society based upon images in relatively few elite literary texts, and they never adequately theorized the relationship between cultural texts and social action.

Bruce Kuklick's devastating 1972 critique of the myth-image-symbol school provided the focal point for an emerging anthropological approach within American Studies, advancing the field's reach and sophistication in significant ways. Yet without an adequate interrogation of the ways in which all communication is metaphorical and by which all language inscribes a sedimented subjectivity in researchers, these efforts did not do enough to show how Americans made meaning for themselves out of cultural practices. Moreover, they tended to stress the uses and effects of cultural artifacts at the expense of their ideological and historical meanings.[36] Reviewing the field in 1979, Gene Wise argued for a new American Studies, one that would be self-reflexive, pluralistic, and focused on the particular and concrete practices of American everyday life, while at the same time remaining comparative and crosscultural.[37]

European cultural theory aided in the implementation of Wise's goals. While most directly relevant to the "new historicism" within literary criticism, cultural theory's location of language within larger social and discursive contexts inevitably led it toward cultural practices beyond literature, especially to popular culture. Many of the most effective applications of European cultural theory within American studies during the 1980s appeared within analyses of popular culture. This affinity between "high" theory and "low" culture may seem surprising at first, but each category contained elements of great importance to the other. Cultural theorists trained to see literary texts as "multivocal" and "dialogic" found rich objects of study within the vernacular forms and generic recombinations collectively authored within commercial culture. The fragmented consciousness, decentered perspective, and resistance to narrative closure that postmodernists labored so diligently to produce within "high" cultural forms were routine and everyday practices within popular music and television. On the other hand, investigators of popular culture found their objects of study so implicated in commercial and practical activities, that it was sometimes difficult to distinguish the texts from their conditions of creation, distribution, and reception. For those engaged in research about commercialized leisure and electronic mass media, the approaches advanced within European cultural theory provided critical frameworks for exploring and theorizing the full implications of their objects of study.

For scholars working in the American studies tradition, the affinity between European cultural theory and American popular culture offered an opportunity to reconnect American studies to its original purpose and potential. Writing in *The Negro Quarterly* in 1943, Ralph Ellison suggested that "perhaps the zoot suit conceals profound political meaning; perhaps the symmetrical frenzy of the Lindy-hop conceals clues to great political power."[38] Two years later, Chester Himes incorporated Ellison's sense of the specific in his novel *If He Hollers Let Him Go*. In that book, Himes's characters negotiate identities of race, gender, and class in dialogue with the icons and images of popular music, film, folklore, and fashion.[39] Less than a decade after Ellison wrote his article, the great jazz musician Charlie Parker argued for a necessary connection between his art and his experience, explaining "if you don't live it, it won't come out of your horn."[40]

In the decade 1943–1953, which proved so crucial to the development of scholarly research in American studies, Ellison, Himes, and Parker all understood something important about their historical moment, about the ways that popular culture, political economy, and cultural theory defined new possibilities for studying and understanding American culture. Provoked by the social and cultural changes of the 1940s, Ellison, Himes, and Parker fashioned works of art and criticism that pointed to the obsolescence of old boundaries dividing popular culture from "high" culture. By focusing on the contexts and processes of cultural creation rather than just on validated texts, they recognized that the generation and circulation of ideas and images pervades all forms of social life. They conceived of art and culture as a part of everyone's everyday life, not just as the domain of artists and critics. The zoot suit, the Lindy-hop, and bop music constituted commodities within commercial culture, but they also served as cultural practices, as critiques of dominant values. They disclosed what Albert Murray, rebuking white supremacist assumptions, later would call "the inescapably mulatto nature of American culture."[41] These African Americans revealed the importance of popular cultural texts and practices in the construction of individual and group identity, challenging a reductionism that concentrated solely on social and economic categories as crucibles of interests and ideas. They exposed an interaction between art and life that refuted formalist assumptions about the autonomy of art.

Perhaps most important, in their understanding of the ways in which the zoot suit, bop music, and the Lindy-hop manifested a new kind of "prestige from below" made possible by the migrations and shop-floor interactions of the war years, these artists illustrated the ways in which changes in political economy necessitated new forms of cultural practice and new theories of cultural studies. The immediate, emotional, and participatory aspects of this new popular culture privileged coded, indirect, and allegorical propensities deeply embedded within the art, music, dance, and speech of aggrieved populations. The expanded reach and scope of electronic mass media called into being a fundamentally new audience, one that was unified and diverse at the same time. Describing the postwar world and its culture, Ellison wrote prophetically, "There is not stability anywhere and there will not be for many years to come, and progress now insistently asserts its tragic side; the evil now stares out of the bright sunlight. New groups will ceaselessly emerge, class lines will continue to waver and break and re-form."[42]

Some of the best early work in American studies addressed topics of cultural production in broad-minded and sophisticated fashion. The first issues of the *American Quarterly* featured important discussions by David Riesman and Charles Seeger on popular music, by Parker Tyler on film, and by Gene Balsley on subcultural practice.[43] Yet despite this early impetus within American studies to investigate popular culture, the field like the rest of the scholarly community became isolated from the social bases and oppositional ideologies necessary for a break with the past. Consequently, despite significant accomplishments over the years, American studies scholars too often have been accomplices in an unjust representation of American culture, depicting it as more monolithic and less plural than the realities of American life and history warrant.

The positions advanced by Ellison, Himes, and Parker during the decade that gave birth to the discipline of American studies call attention to a lost opportunity for scholarship and criticism. Had they been fully understood by American studies scholars, these provocations by African American artists and critics might have helped to shape the field along radically different lines. They might have led to an American cultural criticism that did more to resist the idea of a unified and static American identity, one that more thoroughly explored the complicated relationship between social processes and cultural texts, one that inquired more effectively into the sedimented subjectivities of language and thought that lay beneath the surface appearances of texts or social processes. What might have been a watershed for scholarship and criticism turned out to be merely a detour, one of those many "turning points" in history that failed to turn.

For many years, American Studies needed more explorations into popular culture grounded in political economy and guided by theoretical critique. Despite the field's recurrent preoccupations with myths and symbols (even with the eclipse of the myth-image-symbol school) as well as with the sociology of cultural production and reception, most scholarly work by the 1980s still focused on validated literary and historical texts, and one can understand why. How, for example, can we begin to fathom Rupert Murdoch's directive as the new publisher of *TV Guide* that the editors make the publication "less cerebral and more popular"? Was this a problem with the old *TV Guide*, too much Baudrillard and not enough *Baywatch?*[44] Exactly what can scholars add toward understanding a popular song such as the Angry Samoans' "My Father Is a Fatso"? Yet our inquiries into literary and historical texts take place within a society where people like Rupert Murdoch and the Angry Samoans have extraordinary influence, and we neglect them only at our peril.

Even if popular culture contained only debased and banal images it would be necessary for us to understand and explain them; but we know that popular culture also reflects the extraordinary creativity and ingenuity of grassroots artists and intellectuals. American studies scholars read Ralph Ellison's *Invisible Man* but still know too little about the Lindy-hop. We identify Chester Himes as the author of popular detective novels, but not as the important theorist of race and culture that he was. The 1988 motion picture *Bird* (directed by Clint Eastwood) revived the importance of Charlie Parker, but it did so in a manner so oblivious to the specific historical and social contexts essential to the development of bop music that the film just as well might have been titled *Amadeus and Andy* or *Every Which Way But Black*.

The popular culture of the 1980s evoked memories of the 1940s within American studies: once again the work of artists from seemingly marginal communities called attention to unprecedented opportunities for serious study of popular culture, for explorations into politics and economics, and for renewed theoretical inquiry. Fourteen-year-olds with digital samplers may not have known Jacques Lacan from Chaka Khan, but they could access the entire inventory of recorded world music with the flick of a switch. The music of Laurie Anderson and David Byrne presumed that artifacts of popular culture circulate within the same universe as artifacts of "high" culture, and they built their dramatic force from the juxtaposition of these seemingly incompatible discourses. Motion pictures such as David Lynch's *Blue Velvet* anticipated viewer competence in the codes of popular culture as well as in the concerns of contemporary cultural criticism.

As Horace Newcomb observed, the industrial mode of television production in the United States during the 1980s favored serial narratives, resisting ideological closures in a manner that had profound influence on the nature of narrative itself in our culture.[45] At the same time, postmodernism in literature and the visual arts followed some of the sensibilities of electronic mass media, especially through forms of intertextuality and interreferentiality that call attention to the entire field of cultural practices surrounding any given cultural utterance. Indeed, one might argue that the most sophisticated cultural theorists in America during the 1980s were neither critics nor scholars, but rather artists—writers Toni Morrison, Leslie Marmon Silko, Rudolfo Anaya, and Maxine Hong Kingston, or musicians Laurie Anderson, Prince, David Byrne, and Tracy Chapman. Their works revolved around the multiple perspectives, surprising juxtapositions, subversions of language, and self-reflexivities explored within cultural theory. Their creations came from and spoke to contemporary cultural crises about subjectivity and nationality. Issues that critics discussed abstractly and idealistically seemed to flow effortlessly and relentlessly from the texts of popular literature and popular culture.

For example, Toni Morrison's radical interrogation of commodities and collective memory along with her relentless critique of the role of language and textuality in maintaining social hierarchies in *Beloved* provided readers with a work of art that fundamentally resisted traditional methods of criticism.[46] Morrison's book presented a particularly vivid illustration of the necessary connection between the basic categories of European cultural theory and the basic concerns of American cultural discourse. The entire novel revolved around the core issues evident in European cultural theory—desire, fragmentation, subjectivity, power, and language. One of Morrison's villains was a schoolteacher who beats a slave "to show him that definition belonged to the definers not the defined" (190). The schoolteacher also silences those whom he oppresses: "The information they offered he called backtalk and developed a variety of corrections (which he recorded in his notebook) to reeducate them" (220).

This "power to define" that Morrison reflected on, constructs subjectivity from the white perspective, leaving African Americans as the objects of the white gaze. Whites possess "the righteous Look every Negro learned to recognize along with his ma'am's tit," while blacks know that when their pictures appear in the newspaper it means trouble because those pictures are always constructed from within white subjectivity (157). Consequently, black subjectivity is problematized and fragmented. In a Derridean moment, one character ruminates on his identity "when he looks at himself through Garner's eyes, he sees one thing. Through Sixo's another. One makes him feel righteous. One makes him feel ashamed" (267). At times in the novel, desire and selfishness define individual subjectivity, but in the end it is recognition of a collective subjectivity and a collective project that resolves the dilemmas posed by power and language. Perhaps most significantly, the resolution of *Beloved* came through song and sound, "the sound that broke the back of words" (261).

The issues that informed Morrison's *Beloved* pervaded 1980s European cultural theory as well: a focus on diversity, difference, and fragmentation and an understanding that both centralized and localized sources of oppressive power require dynamic, fluid, and polylateral forms of struggle and resistance. Her work, like so much else in contemporary culture, underscores the necessity of theoretically informed criticism capable of examining the processes and contexts of cultural creation as well as its products.

The dynamism of popular culture sparked an attendant sensitivity among scholars to the importance of cultural studies. Six significant anthologies about American popular culture appeared between 1987 and 1990. These anthologies rode the crest of a wave of fine monographs and articles about popular literature by Janice Radway, Michael Denning, and Elizabeth Long; on television by Lynn Spigel, John Fiske, and David Marc; about film by Dana Polan, Michael Ryan, and Rosa Linda Fregoso; on music by Lisa Lewis, Herman Gray, and Leslie Roman; and about sports by Jeff Sammons, Steve Hardy, and Elliott Gorn. In addition, graduate student research in programs all across the country in the late 1980s addressed new and exciting areas of research, such as Brenda Bright's study of Chicano low-riders, Barry Shank's exploration of local music communities, Joe Austin's work on graffiti artists, Tricia Rose's explorations into rap music, and Henry Jenkins's examination of commercial network television.[47] This work was not confined solely to cultural criticism either; it also took the form of cultural intervention. Reebee Garofalo's involvement with "Rock against Racism" in Boston, Doug Kellner's activism with "Alternative Views" on public access television, and Ed Hugetz's efforts on behalf of independent filmmakers with the Southwest Alternate Media Project in Houston all combined important cultural criticism with creative cultural practice.

Much of what seemed new in American studies cultural criticism during the 1980s came from self-conscious recognition of the "crisis of representation."[48] The inevitable gap between cultural accounts and cultural experiences honed an extraordinary sensitivity among researchers about the ways in which scholarly conventions of representation are not complete, objective, or impartial, but rather partial, perspectival, and interested. Problematizing representation was especially important to scholars in feminist and ethnic studies as they challenged the unconscious sexism and racism sedimented within presumably neutral scholarly methods and perspectives. Indeed, one might argue that the friendly reception accorded European cultural theory in the United States during the 1980s stemmed mostly from the political and cultural struggles waged by women and ethnic minorities inside and outside of universities.

These struggles called attention to a crisis of representation in a different sense of the word, not as artistic representation through characters and symbols, but rather as political representation through action and speech on behalf of particular groups. Scholarly commitments to the agenda raised by European cultural theory were often belittled as "trendy," "careerist," and "arcane," but their emergence in America was tied directly to real crises confronting key constituencies, including women, people of color, blue-collar workers, state employees, and scholars themselves. The emergence of European cultural criticism on this continent was less the product of internal debates within American studies and related disciplines than of a recognition of changing conditions in American society brought on by the crises of deindustrialization and the rise of neoconservatism.

Just as the African American art and criticism of the 1940s both reflected and shaped a concrete historical moment, cultural creation and criticism during the 1980s took place within a cultural and social matrix made possible by social change. In the 1980s, the transition to a "high tech" service and sales economy deindustrialized America, fundamentally disrupting the social arrangements fashioned since the 1930s. Structural unemployment, migration to the Sunbelt, and the radical reconstitution of the family all worked to detach individuals from the traditional authority of work, community, and family, while the individualistic ethic of upward mobility encouraged a concomitant sense of fragmentation and isolation. As the economy focused less on production and more on consumption, services like cable television, and appliances like video recorders, digital samplers, and compact discs expanded both the reach and scope of media images.

Popular culture intervened in the construction of individual and group identity more than ever before as presidents won popularity by quoting from Hollywood films ("Make my day," "Read my lips"), while serious political issues such as homelessness and hunger seemed to enter public consciousness most fully when acknowledged by popular musicians or in made-for-television movies. It should not be surprising then that radical changes in society and culture in the 1980s provoked an emphasis on popular culture within American studies. Part of the revived interest in popular culture stemmed from victories by women and racial minorities in winning access to university positions and their consequent interest in those voices silenced in "high" culture but predominant within some realms of popular culture.

Defeats for the democratization of society also played a major role in shaping American studies approaches during the 1980s. In the decades after World War II, the university could be seen as part of an ascendant social formation. As educators of a new class of technicians and administrators, scholars in the 1950s could see themselves as a plausible part of an expanding elite and as beneficiaries of dominant ideology. Six times as many students attended college in 1970 than in 1930, and the faculty numbers rose from 48,000 in 1920 to 600,000 by 1972. Between 1965 and 1970 alone, the college faculty numbers grew by 138,000.[49] These years also witnessed a dramatic growth in student enrollments, especially among women and ethnic minorities. Yet the economic recessions of the 1970s, the attendant fiscal crisis of the state, and efforts by Balanced Budget Conservatives to "defund the left" drastically curtailed this growth. Neoconservative ideologues launched attacks on public sector employment, arguing that such jobs drained capital from the private sector and functioned to subsidize what neoconservatives described as the "adversary culture" (a phrase borrowed from Lionel Trilling and F. O. Matthiessen in the early days of American studies). Budget cuts served to undermine the economic base of public education, while reversals of hard-won commitments to equal opportunity for women and ethnic minorities undermined some of the constituencies bringing new voices and concerns to academic life. In addition, while raising payroll and sales taxes, neoconservative policies for the cutting of income and capital gains taxes left the United States with the most regressive tax structure of any Western nation. This economic situation pitted educators against low- and middle-income taxpayers and allowed wealthy individuals and large corporations to reap most of the benefits of higher education, while paying ever smaller proportions of its costs.[50]

In the 1980s, it became clear that most academics were tied to a declining social formation, to the residues of commitments to increased access to education that characterized some aspects of the politics of the 1930s and 1960s. Despite lavish salaries paid to a few scholars with international reputations, and despite increasing total budgets for higher education, the social power of most scholars involved in cultural studies had declined drastically by the 1980s. Since the economic crises of the 1970s, a radical reallocation of capital voided unilaterally the social bargain made in the postwar years, marginalizing almost all but the most technical and vocational forms of education. Between 1975 and 1986 the percentage of current-fund revenue for higher education coming from federal, state, and local governments dropped from 51.3 percent to 44.9 percent. This decline led to serious increases in student tuition, which further skewed the class base of student populations. As shown in a late 1980s survey by the American Council on Education, there were severe declines in the numbers of minority and poor students enrolled in college between 1976 and 1988.[51]

Of course, private sector donations to education increased during the 1980s, but in such a way as to put the resources of the university at the disposal of the highest bidders. Distinguished universities eliminated entire geography, linguistics, and sociology departments, not because of declining enrollments, but to finance the ever-increasing costs of scientific research that might lead to lucrative licensing and selling of patent rights.[52] Military and business research thrived, while other areas faced severe budget shortages, which was a problem not just for the humanities. Funding for social science research from the National Science Foundation fell 75 percent in the early 1980s, and between 1975 and 1982 the number of social science graduate students receiving federal support at leading research universities fell 53 percent, while federal support for students in other scientific fields rose by 15 percent.[53] Like industrial workers and inner-city dwellers, scholars in cultural fields not only confronted a power structure hostile to their ideological interests during the 1980s, they faced as well a political and economic apparatus determined to undermine public education, cultural diversity, and mechanisms for equal opportunity—in short, the entire social base necessary for their survival.

Neoconservatives knew full well that academics suffering from the transformations in culture and economics during the 1970s and 1980s posed a potential threat to the emerging hegemony of neoconservatism. From attacks on critical scholarship by William Bennett and Lynne Cheney from their posts as heads of the National Endowment for the Humanities to corporate funding for neoconservative scholarship (the Olin Foundation's backing of Allan Bloom and the Exxon Foundation's support for E. D. Hirsch) to Senator Jesse Helms's disgraceful efforts to cut off federal funding for controversial works of art, neoconservatives demonstrated their understanding of how struggles over meaning are also struggles over resources.[54] As Michael Denning observes, "The post–World War Two university is a part of 'mass culture,' of the 'culture industry,' a central economic and ideological apparatus of American capitalism."[55] As such, its battles resonate with the struggles over resources operative in society at large.

Under these conditions, struggles over meaning were also struggles over resources. They arbitrated what would be permitted and what would be forbidden; they helped determine who would be included and who would be excluded; they influenced who got to speak and who got silenced. Investigations into popular culture during the 1980s were not merely good-hearted efforts to expand the knowledge base of the field, they were also inevitably a part of the political process by which groups—including scholars—sought to reposition themselves in the present by reconstituting knowledge about culture and society in the past.

According to a story often told among jazz musicians, when trumpet player Clark Terry first joined the Duke Ellington Orchestra in 1951, he rehearsed in his mind every complicated technical maneuver that might be expected of him. The young musician waited anxiously for instructions from the legendary bandleader, but all his new boss asked him to do was "to listen." When Terry complained that anyone could just sit and listen, the ever-enigmatic Ellington informed him that "there's listening, and then there's listening, but what I want from you is to listen." [56]

Eventually, Terry came to understand what Ellington wanted. Terry had been so preoccupied with what he might contribute to the orchestra as an individual, that he had not taken time to hear what the other musicians needed. He had not yet learned to hear the voices around him or to understand the spaces and silences surrounding them. Ellington knew that his young trumpeter had talent as a virtuoso, but he felt that Terry had to learn how to bring his virtuosity in harmony (literally and figuratively) with the rest of the orchestra.

Ellington's admonition might serve as a useful way of conceptualizing the challenges posed to scholarly research in American studies since the 1980s. In this period of creative ferment and critical fragmentation, virtuosity entails listening as well as speaking; it requires patient exploration into spaces and silences as much as it demands bold and forthright articulation. As a field, American studies always has been at its best when engaged in dialogue with the complex and conflicted realities of American life and culture. Yet too often its dominant paradigms have suffered from an overemphasis on what has been articulated from within the profession, and a consequent underemphasis on the voices, power struggles, and ideological conflicts outside it. The complicated relationship between scholarly methods and the social movements, popular cultures, political economies, and ideologies of "America" demand a scholarship capable of adopting Duke Ellington's advice and learning how to do careful and comprehensive listening.

Traditional American studies inquiries about "what is an American" have insufficiently problematized the ways in which scholars perceive culture being produced and received in any given circumstance. These questions have imposed premature closures on open questions and have presumed a more unified American experience than the evidence can support. Yet questions of national identity are crucial to culture, and American Studies has an important role to play by applying the categories raised within European cultural theory to the American context, as well as by raising new questions that emerge from the particular complexities and contradictions within American culture.[57]

Most important, a theoretically informed American studies would begin by listening for the sounds that Toni Morrison describes, the sounds capable of "breaking the back of words." These sounds cannot be summoned up by theoretical expertise alone. They cannot be constructed out of idealized subject positions emanating from reforms in discursive practices. They are to be found within the concrete contests of everyday life. Accessible by listening to what is already being said (and sung and shouted) by ordinary Americans, these sounds hold the key to understanding the zoot suit and the Lindy-hop, and so much more. To paraphrase Ellison's narrator in *Invisible Man*, Who knows? Maybe they speak for you.

PART II
RACE, CULTURE, AND
COLLECTIVE STRUGGLE

While the study of culture attracted people in almost all the disciplines, it was particularly popular among three groups; among scholars in literary studies of all kinds, for whom it legitimated a concern with the current social and political scene; among anthropologists, for whom the new emphases offered a domain to replace (or at least compete with) that of ethnography, which had lost its commanding role within the discipline; and among persons involved in the new quasi-disciplines relating to the "forgotten" peoples of modernity (those neglected by virtue of gender, race, class, etc.) for whom it provided a theoretical ("postmodern") framework for their elaborations of difference.

—Immanuel Wallerstein et al., *Open the Social Sciences: Report of the Gulbenkian Commission on the Restructuring of the Social Sciences*

CHAPTER 5

Like Crabs in a Barrel

Why Interethnic Anti-Racism Matters Now

You know, the hardest thing about pan-Asian solidarity
is the "pan" part. It forces us outside of our comfort zones,
whether they are constructed by ethnicity, class,
home city, identity, whatever.

—Naomi Iwasaki, *"Pan-Asian What?"*

In places near the ocean where merchants sell live crabs, they display their wares in open barrels without tops. When the crabs try to escape by climbing up the sides of the barrel they always fail. As soon as one starts to climb up, the others who are also trying to escape pull it back down.

When we try to overcome racism, sexism, homophobia, or class oppression, we often find ourselves in the position of crabs in a barrel. We work as hard as we can, but all our efforts fail to free us. We cannot get at the people who really have power, but we can reach someone from our own group or someone from another group no more powerful than our own. Instead of pulling ourselves up, we only pull someone else down.

It is not hard to figure out why this happens. People with power want those they rule to be divided and to fight each other so they will not unite and fight side by side against their true enemy. If forced to make concessions to aggrieved groups, the powerful want the gains of one group to come at the expense of another, instead of acceding to a fundamental redistribution of resources and power.

This "divide and conquer" strategy has been used more and more in recent years. Unlike the relatively simple segregation and one-dimensional white supremacy of the past that produced a relatively uniform and unified system of exclusion, the racism of today proceeds through practices that produce differentiation rather than uniformity, that give excluded groups decisively different relations to the same oppression.

Yet these new divisions can also produce unexpected affiliations and alliances. Attacks on bilingual education and immigrant rights harm *both* Latinos and Asian Americans. Irrational and alarmist policies about AIDS stigmatize *both* homosexuals and Haitians. Puerto Ricans on the mainland are Spanish speakers from a colonized homeland like Mexicans *and* suppressed second-class U.S. citizens like Blacks. Filipino Americans may be noncitizen immigrants from Asia like Korean Americans, but they are also like Mexicans in that they are immigrants from a Catholic nation colonized by Spain whose patron saint is the Virgin of Guadalupe.

For scholars in ethnic studies, the prospect of alliances among groups with similar but nonidentical experiences holds special import. In a world that produces a seemingly infinite amount of differentiation and division, interethnic antiracist alliances emerge as a crucial site for the generation of new forms of affiliation, identification, and social mobilization. Researchers specializing in the study of race and ethnicity have been producing significant new works every year. Ethnic studies programs and departments are proliferating at an accelerated pace. At every level of instruction, lesson plans and curricula reflect an unprecedented attention to issues of identity and power. Yet while ethnic studies is doing very well, ethnic people are faring very badly.

It has proven easier to desegregate libraries and reading lists than to desegregate college classrooms or corporate boardrooms. Images of ethnic people (and ideas about them) circulate widely, but many of the people themselves remained confined in ghettos, barrios, and prisons. The literature, art, and music created in communities of color frequently command more respect than the communities that created them. Businesses seem more interested in managing diversity than in diversifying management. The dominant institutions of our society may be willing to make room for some version of "multiculturalism," but they remain unwilling to give members of aggrieved racial groups fair and equal access to jobs and justice, to housing and health care, to education and opportunities for asset accumulation.

The contrast between the successes of ethnic studies and the crises facing ethnic communities is especially galling because academic Ethnic Studies emerged as a field precisely because of movements for social justice during the 1960s and 1970s. The institutional spaces we occupy exist because community activists and organizations won them through sustained collective struggle. Poor people burned down their neighborhoods thirty years ago to protest intolerable inequalities and injustices. They won little for themselves through their efforts, but among the concessions granted in response to their anger were departments of ethnic studies.

Some of the disparity between the status of ethnic studies and the status of ethnic communities stems, in part, from the personal failings of individual scholars, from the elitism and ideological conservatism at the core of academic career hierarchies, and from the isolation of many ethnic studies scholars from the activities of actual social movements. The routine practices of training, employment, and evaluation that prevail in jobs that rely on "mind work" encourage a competitive individualism rooted in the imperative to surpass others in accomplishment and status. No one working in academia remains unaffected by those imperatives. We are allowed, and sometimes even encouraged, to take positions opposed to dominant power, but we are also pressured to separate ourselves from aggrieved communities and to confine our work within institutions controlled by the powerful and wealthy.

The ethnic studies paradigm itself, as it has emerged historically, is also partly responsible for the problems we face. Competition for scarce resources among aggrieved groups, and the success of our enemies in keeping us divided, has often led ethnic studies scholars to pursue a one-group-at-a-time story of exclusion and discrimination rather than an analytic, comparative, and relational approach revealing injustice to be the rule rather than the exception in our society. The sense of sameness that holds ethnic groups together, builds organic solidarity, and makes ethnic mobilization logical and desirable can also lead us to suppress differences and demand uniformity within our own groups. We have inherited much from the past, but some of it ill serves us under present circumstances.

Malcolm X used to say that racism was like a Cadillac: they make a new model every year. There is always racism, but it is not always the same racism. Just as an owner's manual for a 1970 model would be of little help in repairing a new Cadillac, today's racism cannot be combated with theories, methods, and strategies from the 1960s or 1970s. Global migration, the evisceration of the welfare state, and the increasing importance of new categories of "unfree" laborers (unable to bargain about their wages and working conditions as a result of the growth prison labor, undocumented immigrant labor, and punitive welfare-to-work "reforms") have led to a new era in racialized exploitation. The racism of postindustrial society proceeds through practices that produce differentiation rather than uniformity. It pits outsider groups against each other. It gives racialization distinctly different meanings for different groups. This new era demands new methods, theories, and strategies. It calls into question received wisdom and traditional ways of knowing and being.

Ethnic studies scholarship can play a progressive role in this context by exploring the interconnectedness of oppressions, by complicating the neoconservative and neoliberal paradigms that recognize only a "legitimate" civil rights paradigm (one that advanced the interests of individuals) and an "illegitimate" group politics paradigm based on "identity." At the present moment, many different groups suffer from racism, but it is not always the same racism. Gains made through the antiracist efforts of any one group might come at the expense of another aggrieved community. Conservatives ask blacks to mobilize against bilingual education and social services for immigrants, while inciting Latinos and Asian Americans against affirmative action. Rather than being united by racial oppression into a coherent and unified polity, members of aggrieved racialized groups experience seemingly endless new forms of conflict, competition, division, and differentiation.

African Americans, for example, suffer especially harsh levels of housing segregation, unemployment, and political disenfranchisement. Consequently, a seemingly race-neutral reform like "term limits" for elected officials has especially disastrous consequences for their group. African American elected officials represent large population blocks even when voter turnout is low, and consequently are able to channel resources through the state to communities otherwise deprived of access to private capital and intergenerational transfers of wealth. Pervasive racial discrimination in housing, employment, and education makes public-sector influence especially valuable to black people. By limiting the seniority that accrued to these officials, by making government weaker and therefore less able to compensate for racial discrimination in the private sector, and by denying African Americans the advantages that came from the block voting imposed on them by housing segregation, term limits seriously dilute the power of black communities, further augmenting the privileges garnered by the already advantaged.

Latinos, in contrast, have been less successful than blacks in turning demographic strength into political power. Barriers of language and citizenship, the forced mobility imposed on low-wage labor, and the astoundingly youthful median age of most Latino communities have all worked to dilute Latino political power. Consequently, they have been less damaged by term limits than blacks have been. But educational inequality, segregation of students in low-income schools, lack of access to prenatal care, and environmental hazards with particular impacts on children impose inordinate burdens on Latinos.

Attacks on bilingualism and immigrant rights harm both Latinos and Asian Americans, but not in the same ways. The narrative of national decline most frequently used by neoconservatives to justify their policies has a special anti-Asian edge to it, in part because decline is traced to the U.S. defeat in Vietnam, but also because of the rise of economic competition from Japan and new industrializing countries in Asia, as well as the perceived threat to white privilege posed by immigrant Asian successes. The hate crimes that emanate from what Yen Le Espiritu calls "the new yellow peril-ism" are racist and anti-immigrant in general, but have a specific meaning when carried out against Asian Americans because of the past and present roles played by Asia and Asians in the civic and cultural imagination of the United States. At the same time, the ways in which this narrative of national decline is often presented as a threat to white masculinity gives anti-Asian hate crimes an affinity to attacks on women, and on gays and lesbians in a way that is not exactly parallel to hate crimes against other racialized or immigrant groups.[1]

The proliferation of new low-wage-labor jobs affects all communities of color, but especially women immigrants from Asia, Mexico, Central America, and South America. Unemployment has hit African Americans harder than it has hit Latinos or Asian Americans. Welfare reform has been couched in directly racist and sexist terms through the use of images about excessive procreation among black women and Latinas, even though these groups provide two of the largest sectors of hard working laborers while the majority of people receiving welfare are white. Discourses about crime focus attention on black and Latino males who are incarcerated in numbers far greater than their percentage of the general and the criminal population, but this discourse consequently hides the rapidly increasing numbers of minority women incarcerated in penal institutions.

Environmental racism harms all aggrieved racialized populations, but Native Americans live in places that make them more susceptible to cancer than other racial groups. Latinos are the group most likely to breathe polluted air. In Los Angeles County, Asian Americans and Pacific Islanders are more than seven times as likely as whites to have tuberculosis.[2] Lead poisoning affects black children more than children from any other group.[3]

Yet precisely because no single identity encompasses anyone's social world, interethnic antiracist activism offers an opportunity for new struggles for social justice that might one day become as mobile, fluid, and flexible as the new forms of oppression, hierarchy, and exploitation generated by the current global balance of power. The panethnic concept of "Asian American" identity offers the quintessential model for interethnic antiracism in both activism and scholarship. Originating in a self-conscious strategy for maximizing resources at a specific historical moment, members of different Asian national groups worked together during the 1960s to build a movement emphasizing common concerns even though they understood fully that many things also divided them. Created by people from different national backgrounds who spoke different languages, practiced different religions, and occupied very different places in the U.S. social order, the Asian American movement flaunted its constructedness in order to emphasize a common political project. The "identity" of being Asian American never presumed experiences that were identical. But for groups whose past rivalries had produced pernicious forms of disidentification with one another, coalescence on the basis of a common experience of racialization by the U.S. nation-state and economy served progressive political ends.

Because of this history, Asian American studies remains grounded in a politicized notion of identity. This grounding has enabled the field to raise unique questions about the nature of general concepts like citizenship and racial formation, rendering race less a matter of personal injury or personal affirmation than a shared social reality and structured social dynamic. Embodied individual experience counts for less in this constellation than collective epistemological position. In a characteristically complex and insightful discussion, Lisa Lowe explains that Asian American studies emerges from specific historical realities and draws its determinate force from continuing engagement with the recuperation of otherwise occluded histories of U.S. nationalism, gendered social stratification, labor exploitation, and racialized exclusion. The narratives and cultural practices of Asian immigrants and their descendants, according to Lowe, include displaced memories that become "refigured as alternative modes in which immigrants are the survivors of empire, its witnesses, the inhabitants of its borders."[4]

Asian American studies scholars do not simply "add on" previously ignored evidence about Asian Americans, but rather generate new ways of knowing by concentrating on objects of study that confound conventional modes of inquiry. Consequently, Asian American studies is not limited to the study of Asian Americans, but rather uses the specific historical experiences of Asian Americans to produce comparative studies of the role national cultures play in forming citizens and gendered subjects, in linking patriotism to patriarchy, and in disciplining and precluding alternative sexual and social identities. Rather than presuming a primordial homogenous, atomized, and discrete Asian American identity, Asian American studies encourages exploration of all the differences that define any group—ethnic differences within specific national-origin groups, differences caused by social identities and sexuality, gender and generation, class and religious conviction, and point of origin and political orientation.[5]

Asian American studies also challenges scholarly and civic practices that define social identities within the confines of single nation-states. The historically specific experiences of people of Asian origin in the United States cannot be understood in isolation from the global history of empire building, war, transnational commerce, and migration that brought Asian America into existence in the first place.[6] Contemporary Asian American identities are part of a broader Asian diaspora that includes Asians in Africa, South America, Europe, Australia, the Caribbean, and Asia as well as North America. Asian American culture reveals these links in clear and irrefutable forms, from the ruminations by composer Jon Jang on political repression in China to the blend of Filipino "folk" instruments with Western avant-garde forms in the compositions of Eleanor Academia; from the country-western singer Neal McCoy who calls himself a Texapino to the hip-hop group the Boo Yaa Tribe made up of Samoans from Carson, California (some of whom lived briefly with cousins in Japan), enjoying commercial success playing a music based in African American aesthetic forms for largely Chicano audiences.

The model of interethnic antiracism pioneered with the Asian American movement is emerging as a tactical necessity for many people at the present time. Interethnic alliances do not erase purely national or racial identities, nor do they permanently transcend them. There is always room for more than one tactical stance in struggles for social justice, and ethnic nationalism especially will always be legitimate and meaningful for some people at some times. But the current historical moment is generating new forms of struggle, forms identified by Lowe as "alternative forms of practice that integrate yet move beyond those of cultural nationalism."[7]

There are many obvious reasons for interethnic antiracist activism, but the obvious reasons may not be the most important ones. Certainly alliances of this type produce strength in numbers. We are more powerful with allies than we are alone. These alliances demonstrate solidarity in the present in order to reap its benefits in the future; if we are there for other people's struggles today, there is a greater likelihood that they will be there for us tomorrow. This solidarity also enables us to avoid the dangers of disidentification and disunity. By standing up for someone else we establish ourselves as people with empathy for the suffering of others. Common experiences in struggle also make it harder to play aggrieved groups against one another. These experiences are a hedge against what John Okada described as "persecution in the drawl of the persecuted"—the tendency to defend oneself from unfair treatment by directing that unfairness onto someone else.[8]

Yet some of the less obvious advantages of interethnic antiracism may be even more important to its logic at the present historical moment. Coordinated attacks against racist privilege enable individual racialized groups to move beyond defensiveness about their own specific identities and to focus attention on the actions of those doing the discriminating rather than solely on the victims of discrimination. They make visible the new forms of racial formation being created every day in the present, not just those directly attributable to the histories of slavery, conquest, genocide, immigrant exploitation, and class oppression. Interethnic antiracism shifts the focus away from a diagnosis of minority disadvantages to an analysis of "majority" advantages. Unlike many other kinds of antiracist work, it aims at peace and justice rather than at peace and quiet, attacking racism in order to face its consequences responsibly rather than merely trying to be free of the burdens that its long history imposes on us.

By proposing reallocation of resources and structural changes in institutions, interethnic antiracism reveals racism to be about interests as well as about attitudes, and about finances rather than just feelings. By acknowledging the differentiated experiences of aggrieved racialized populations, it avoids the simplistic binary opposition that neoconservatives offer in response to racism—stupefied and uncomprehending "color blindness" versus primordial attachment to kin and kind.

Ultimately, the most important reason for interethnic antiracism is its epistemological value in enabling us to understand how power actually works. We will always misread our situatedness in the world unless we are able to view power from more than one perspective, unless we are able to look through multiple, overlapping, and even conflicting standpoints on social relations. In order to challenge the differentiated deployment of power in the contemporary world, we need to create places where our differences and our common interests remain in plain sight. We need places like those described by Patrick Chamoiseau in his epic novel about antiracist struggle in Martinique—"Those places in which no one could foresee our ability to unravel their History into our thousand stories."[9]

The Asian American project helps us remember that *all* ethnic groups are coalitions and that purely national categories do little to explain anyone's identity. Asian Americans sometimes worry that American studies will not become sufficiently international, that the field's foregrounding of the U.S. citizen-subject establishes a norm that automatically marginalizes the international and transnational dimensions of the Asian American experience, and that it disavows the ways in which that citizen-subject has been constructed in opposition to Asia and to Asian Americans. African Americans, on the other hand, may worry that American studies will become *too* international, that studies of globalization might enable scholars to once again evade the unique history of antiblack racism in the United States by making all categories of difference interchangeable. African Americans also worry sometimes that directing attention away from the citizen-subject and the nation marginalizes the struggle for citizenship rights, which has been such an important focus of political activism among African Americans. Such a move away from citizenship might also be a move away from politics, away from challenging the U.S. nation-state to keep its promises and to implement fully the concessions that black people have wrested from it over the years through ferocious struggle and at a terrible cost.

Yet no group in the United States is any more international than African Americans. Direct and indirect cultural connections link blacks in the United States to Africa in myriad ways, but the African diaspora itself was a global phenomenon that entailed an African presence in South and Central America, in the Caribbean, in Europe, and in Asia as well. People of African origin in the United States have been shaped by polylateral politics within this diasporic space as well as by their bilateral relationship to white supremacy in North America.

The *Plessy v. Ferguson* decision by the United States Supreme Court endorsing Jim Crow segregation played a pivotal role in U.S. history, but as the research by Michel S. Laguerre demonstrates it was an important moment in Haitian history as well.[10] When Homère A. Plessy purchased a round-trip ticket from New Orleans to Covington, Louisiana, with the express intention of testing the legality of the Louisiana Separate Car Act of 1890 mandating the segregation of black and white passengers on railroad cars, he acted as part of a coordinated attack on segregation by the New Orleans Comité des Citoyens, an organization composed of New Orleans residents of Haitian origin or ancestry.

For the Comité des Citoyens, the Plessy case was only the latest in a long line of legal battles for equality initiated by their black and mulatto grandparents in Haiti and carried on by their parents in the United States. The Comité had previously mounted a successful legal challenge in 1892 to the constitutionality of the Louisiana Separate Car Act as it applied to interstate commerce. The judge in that case ruled that the state of Louisiana could not segregate passenger-car seating on trains headed for another state. The plaintiff in that case was Daniel Desdunes, whose father Rudolphe Lucien Desdunes founded the Comité. Plessy purchased his ticket for travel from New Orleans to Covington as part of the Comité's strategy to challenge the law's validity within the state of Louisiana. When the case reached the United States Supreme

Court, the justices knew full well about the Haitian origins of the plaintiffs. They issued their decision upholding the constitutionality of the Louisiana Separate Car Act on May 18, 1896, Haitian Flag Day. Laguerre notes that this date was selected by the Court in order to teach the Haitians a lesson in humility.[11]

Haitian immigrants played a prominent role within nineteenth-century African American communities in Baltimore, New York, Philadelphia, and Charleston, in addition to New Orleans. Laguerre documents the extraordinary transnational dynamics that shaped Haitian participation in politics, commerce, and social life in both the United States and Haiti. The founder of Chicago, Jean Baptiste Point du Sable, came from Haiti. The chief armorer of the Haitian army's Port-au-Prince arsenal in 1861 had been born in St. Martin's Parish, Louisiana. Haitian Americans were not simply binational either. Many came to the U.S. only after first migrating from Haiti to Cuba, Jamaica, Martinique, Guadeloupe, and France.[12]

Winston James demonstrates how much we can learn by appreciating the transnational nature of African American history. It makes a difference to our cognitive mapping of "America" to remember that South Carolina originated as a colony largely to provide supplies to sustain sugar cultivation in Barbados, and that it grew to maturity as a supplier to slave plantations in Jamaica. Nearly all of the productive labor performed in the southern American colonies during the seventeenth century was carried out by slaves from Barbados and other Caribbean islands. Prince Hall from Barbados established black freemasonry in Boston in the eighteenth century at a time when Caribbean-born immigrants made up 20 percent of that city's population. Slave rebel Denmark Vesey and black nationalist Edward Wilmot Blyden came to the United States from the Virgin Islands. Journalist and advocate of colonization in Liberia, John Russworm, originally lived in Jamaica. Nineteenth-century inventor and entrepreneur Jan Earnst Matzlinger migrated to the United States from Surinam. In the twentieth century, entertainer Bert Williams was from Antigua, while journalist and historian J. A. Rogers and poet and author Claude McKay came from Jamaica.[13]

Not all African Americans possess African ancestry. Paul Quinn, the fourth Bishop of the African Methodist Episcopal Church enjoyed prominence within the African American community in the nineteenth century. But Quinn became black in America by an unusual route. Born an upper-caste Hindu in India, this son of a Calcutta mahogany merchant became a Christian and consequently was disowned by his parents. Traveling to England, he secured help from sympathetic Quakers who helped him reach Bucks County, Pennsylvania, where he became a sawmill worker. Quinn became "Negro" through white ascription and his own conviction, joining the AME church and serving as its most celebrated "missionary to the west" before ascending in the denomination's hierarchy.[14]

Just as Paul Quinn started out South Asian and ended up black, historically some black Americans became members of other groups out of necessity or choice. Edward Rose was the son of a black/Cherokee mother and a white father who grew up near Louisville, but later lived in New Orleans and St. Louis. Enlisting in a fur-trading expedition in 1805, he lived and traded with the Absaroka (Crow) Indians during his first winter away from St. Louis, and eventually became a trusted leader of the tribe, even distinguishing himself in combat against rival nations. Similarly, a seventeen-year-old African American known only as Bob jumped from a New England ship in 1816, surfacing three years later in Santa Barbara, California, as a Spanish citizen where he was baptized under the name Juan Cristobal. Some four thousand fugitive slaves lived south of the Rio Grande River in the 1850s under the protection of the Mexican government, which viewed their presence in the area as a way to discourage further U.S. expansion. They joined with Native Americans and Mexicans in border settlements such as the one established and governed by Seminole Indian chief Wild Cat.[15]

The international and interracial histories of Homère Plessy, Paul Quinn, Edward Rose, Juan Cristobal, and the fugitive slaves in Wild Cat's border settlement offer evidence that Asian Americans have not been the only U.S. "racial" group with an international, panethnic past. No matter how fixed by law and custom, the constructed nature of racial identities always allows for racial passings and masquerades serving a variety of purposes. Most important for our discussion here, however, is the question of what circumstances make it desirable to rally around a common *identity* and what circumstances make it desirable to rally around a common *ideology* or political *project*.

In a recent interview, Angela Davis identified the epistemological importance of political activism that incorporates perspectives from diverse identities and experiences.[16] From her point of view, too much solidarity can actually weaken a group's political power, while openness about differences can augment it. Davis shows how the deep structural problems currently confronting African Americans become distorted by simplistic analyses based on single identities. To view the current crisis in the black community as a crisis about black manhood, for example, in some ways acknowledges the harm done to black male employment and black male wages by deindustrialization. But describing the crisis in terms of the declining value of black manhood mistakes consequence for cause and leads to "remedies" that privilege the private sphere like rites-of-passage ceremonies, special schools for black males, and condemnation of black women for "succeeding" in ways that diminish the relative power of black males. These responses all hide the broader structural causes of the crisis facing black men and the black community. They encourage black men to seek more power *within* their community but not outside it, to seek redress from other aggrieved people rather than from those whose power has enabled them to profit from the decline in black male wages. This approach hides the ways in which black women and children have also been devastated by the effects of deindustrialization, and it renders invisible black gays and lesbians.

Davis shows how a positive politics might still emerge from the specific experiences of black men. They could, she argues, support the reproductive rights of women in their communities, could help black lesbians adopt children, and could lead a struggle against violence against women. But these actions would require an intersectional and multiply positioned perspective on identity and social power. Similarly, Davis urges us to think of race and class as intersectional realities rather than competing categories. She praises the activist centers in Chinatown run by Asian Immigrant Women Advocates and other groups that combine lessons in literacy with legal advice about domestic violence, and that address issues about hours, wages, and working conditions, but refuse to detach the workers' lives as workers from their other identities as women, as racialized subjects, and as family members. In addition, these cross-class coalitions linking the concerns of immigrants with the struggles of ethnic women born in the United States also lead to interethnic antiracism since issues like low-wage women's labor and domestic violence cut across racial lines.

Davis's own role in mobilizing support among diverse populations for a worker–instigated boycott against a prominent garment maker exemplifies the positive possibilities of this kind of coalition work. Women of color often play prominent roles in these movements because their situatedness in relation to power has always required this kind of supple and creative thinking. As Lisa Lowe argues, "The Asian American woman and the racialized woman are materially in excess of the subject 'woman' posited by feminist discourse, or the 'proletariat' described by Marxism or the 'racial' or ethnic subject projected by civil rights and ethno-racial movements."[17]

Precisely because so much of the revolution enacted by the right depends upon historical revision and the occlusion of contemporary social vision, interethnic antiracist politics inside and outside institutions of higher learning take on special significance in the present. At a time when ethnic studies seems to be doing very well but when ethnic people are experiencing extraordinary hardships, we confront an era that requires new ways of knowing, that demands us to go beyond the neoconservative framework of de jure desegregation and property-based individualism to retheorize social relations and social possibilities. From within the neoconservative optic, all the key developments of our time remain untheorized. The political regime of Balanced Budget Conservatism and its attendant augmentation of the possessive investment in whiteness has emerged in part to hide the radical new social, cultural, economic, and political realities produced by globalization and the increased mobility of capital that it entails. As Randall Robinson argues, this epistemology of ignorance has material implications. If you want the horse to work, you first put blinders on him.[18] One thing scholars can do is take the blinders off.

The "civil rights paradigm" deployed by neoliberals and neoconservatism inaccurately describes the past in order to paralyze people in the present and prevent them from raising serious questions about who holds power in our society and what they do with that power. A perspective that pretends that "discrimination" is an individual act rather than a structured social reality has little to offer in the current moment characterized by new communications technologies, economic austerity, global migration, the evisceration of the welfare state, the growth of unfree labor evidenced by the expansion of production within prisons, the widespread hiring of undocumented workers, the welfare "reforms" that create new categories of workers unable to bargain about their wages and working conditions, and the return of actual slavery as experienced by the Thai garment workers held in a sweatshop against their will in El Monte, California, and the exploitation of deaf Mexican immigrant workers by their "sponsors" in New York City. Unlike the simple segregation and one-dimensional white supremacy of the industrial era, postindustrial racism proceeds through practices that give racialization a distinctly different meaning for different groups, that produces differentiation rather than uniformity.

Solidarity based upon identity is limited; solidarities based upon identities are unlimited. People who have to see themselves as exactly the same in order to wage a common struggle will be ill positioned for the ferocity of impending struggles, but those capable of connecting their own cause to the causes of others by seeing families of resemblance capable of generating unity will be better positioned to make the kinds of unlikely alliances and unexpected coalitions that the differentiated struggles of the future will require.

Battles to better the conditions of low-wage workers in the current context automatically entail connections with movements for immigrant rights, challenges to sexism, and references to historical traditions of anti-imperialism. Fights for better education for aggrieved populations quickly lead to questions about housing segregation and intergenerational transfers of wealth and opportunity through closed racial networks. Increasing incarceration of large numbers of minority youth raises questions about how property rights and legal rights have been increasingly racialized, just as concerns about the health and safety of children reveal the racialized and gendered encoding of such seemingly neutral social concepts as "the family." Mobilization by women against common grievances about sexuality and gender quickly bring into view the ways in which race inflects gender, but antiracist struggles waged by women also increasingly expose the sexualized and gendered qualities at the root of white supremacy.

Fights for fair housing opportunities can play an especially important role in interethnic antiracism. This cause is innately interethnic because housing discrimination takes place against all groups. A political struggle built around fair housing could mobilize urban populations to pressure their elected officials to sue mortgage lenders, insurance companies, and realtors for the harm done to cities by illegal patterns of discrimination, much in the way that municipalities, cities, and states have sued manufacturers of tobacco products and firearms. Fair housing cases and campaigns could go beyond the language of individual injury and demand that punitive damages paid by those guilty of illegal discrimination be allocated for construction of new units of affordable housing to be made available to the public on a nondiscriminatory basis.

Interethnic antiracist struggles for social justice bring together diverse populations in a way that makes visible previously hidden aspects of social relations. Within the structure of business unionism that prevails in the United States, for example, it is hard for workers to win gains that do not hurt other workers. The concessions made to workers within individual labor-management negotiations are often passed on to consumers in the form of higher prices or at the very least still force unorganized workers to experience a new disadvantage in relation to workers who are organized. Angela Davis presents the historical struggles for the eight-hour work day and for shorter work weeks as models from the past that could be emulated in the present. She notes that the demand for a shorter work day and a shorter work week helps *all* workers by relieving the toil of some and opening up new jobs to unemployed and undocumented workers. By increasing the absolute number of wage earners and at the same time increasing the amount of leisure time for each, a shorter work day and week would also be good for the economy because it would stimulate spending from the bottom up.

In coming to this conclusion about the kind of demands suited to forging a unified struggle out of diverse identities, Davis reconnects us with the experiences of the past and shows that the "new social movements" are very much like the old. The original struggle for the eight-hour day in the late nineteenth century came about because of conditions very much like our own—a differentiated and divided workforce looking for common ground.[19]

Identifications within racial groups remain powerful for very understandable reasons. Shared experiences with discrimination and negative ascription by outsiders can build especially close bonds. A common language, religion, culture, or cuisine can make solidarity seem natural and inevitable. Yet this organic solidarity can come at a high price. It can make us expect to find more uniformity in our own groups than actually exists. It can encourage us to substitute ethnosympathy and ethnosubjectivity for social analysis, and often leads to the politics described by Los Angeles activist Charlotta Bass as settling for "dark faces in high places" instead of struggling for substantive reallocations of social resources and social power.

All politics is about identity, but not all politics is identity politics. Political mobilization takes place when people share a common image of themselves as members of an identifiable group. Mutual identification (as citizens, workers, or subjects of any sort) takes place strategically, out of a perception that it makes sense for the moment to emphasize the things that build unity and to ignore temporarily the things that undermine it. Racial identity can be a unifying factor, but only if nonidentical people with diverse experiences agree politically that their common exclusion from power and opportunity on the basis of race matters more than their differences. Black nationalism of the 1960s, like the American Indian movement, the Chicano movement, and the Asian American movement, depended on winning adherents to a newly politicized definition of identity, not by presuming that common histories or physical features automatically guaranteed unity and solidarity.

The antiracist mobilizations of the 1960s did not view racism as an aberrant phenomenon in an otherwise just society, but rather they identified racism as one of the key mechanisms for teaching, naturalizing, institutionalizing, and legitimating hierarchy, inequality, and exploitation. These "ethnic" movements realized that racism did not simply injure people of color, but that it provided the deep structure and legitimating logic for all forms of social, political, and economic exclusion. The movement had its share of integrationists, to be sure, but it also nurtured and sustained broad social critiques—not only of racist hierarchies but also of all hierarchies, not only of racist dehumanization but also of the broader dehumanization integral to a society where the lives of humans consistently count for less than the concerns of capital.

No simple formula will suffice to conquer the contradictions we face. In political strategy as in scholarship no single solution will fit all situations. But we can draw creatively on the very contradictions we face to find solutions for ourselves and for others. Part of the racial problem today is a knowledge problem. The educational institutions in which we work are not irrelevant to the racialization of opportunities and life chances in our society. In fact, they are important sites for the generation and legitimation of forms of knowledge that support and strengthen the racial status quo. Ethnic studies scholars are in an advantageous position to subject dominant regimes of knowledge to critical scrutiny, to identify and nurture activist sites where new knowledges are being created, and to play an active role in transforming social relations by helping build the forms of knowledge and action capable of creating quite different kinds of social relations. The origins of ethnic studies scholarship in social movements serves to remind us that the academy and the community can help each other, that social movements can win institutional spaces in colleges and universities, but also that educational institutions can provide valuable resources to movements for democratic social change.

Many activist academics and artists participate in struggles that use our differences in creative and productive ways by building unexpected alliances and affiliations. Glenn Omatsu shows how scholarly research and community-based activism mutually reinforce one another within the Asian American activist movement. Community groups organizing among low-wage immigrant workers remain community-based in their mobilizations against racism, sexism, and class oppression, but they draw on the intellectual and material resources of Asian American studies programs, on theories of popular literacy and democratic pedagogy advanced by Paulo Freire and his followers, and on unexpected alliances and affiliations across class, race, and gender lines.[20] Important research by Laura Pulido, Robert Bullard, Clarice Gaylord, and Elizabeth Bell reveals how campaigns against environmental racism have entailed alliances among representatives of aggrieved communities of color, academic experts, and organized social movement groups.[21] Manning Marable heads a scholarly research center at a prestigious Ivy League university and writes well-received books about racism and power, but he also writes a regular column syndicated in African American newspapers across the country.[22]

Connections between academics and artists also play a vital role in the possible politics of the present moment. In his prophetic work, *The Wretched of the Earth*, Frantz Fanon described how artistic expressions sometimes anticipate political upheavals:

> Well before the political fighting phase of the national movement, an attentive spectator can thus feel and see the manifestations of a new vigor and feel the approaching conflict. He will note unusual forms of expression and themes which are fresh and imbued with a power which is no longer that of invocation but rather of the assembling of the people, a summoning together for a precise purpose. Everything works together to awaken the native's sensibility of defeat and to make unreal and unacceptable the contemplative attitude or the acceptance of defeat.[23]

In our time, evidence of this cultural creativity exists in abundance. Community-based cultural production in Los Angeles exemplifies this phenomenon; on one weekend in 1995, for example, college students from the California State University at Northridge chapter of Moviemiento Estudiantil Chicano/a se Aztlan (MEChA) staged a "happening" to raise money to fund a suit against the University of California by a prominent Chicano professor. The evening's entertainment featured Chicano rap artists, comedians, musicians, and the Teatro por la Gente (Theatre for the People/Community) performing what they described as "social/political/cultural Edu-drama-dies." On the same weekend, Chicano poets, visual artists, and singers joined with Japanese taiko drummers and the Watts Prophets, an African American spoken word/ hip-hop ensemble, to stage a benefit at a warehouse loft owned by Chicano heavy metal musician Zach de la Rocha of the musical group Rage Against the Machine to raise money for the Los Angeles chapter of the National Commission for Democracy in Mexico, the support arm of the EZLN rebels fighting the Mexican government in Chiapas. Writing for the hip-hop magazine *Urb*, journalist Gerry Meraz described the weekend's events as "a new culture with roots in the old and appreciation for the art of people who need to be heard whether anyone likes it or not."[24] The broader culture of performance art, graffiti writing, and hip-hop from which these events emerged has been carefully catalogued and assessed in exemplary work by innovative scholars including C. Ondine Chavoya, Michelle Habell-Pallan, and Tricia Rose, among others.[25]

In Richmond, California, young immigrant Laotian women still in their teens lead panethnic and interethnic struggles against environmental racism. They feel the sting of antiforeign and antiracist resentment through comments they hear on the streets, through the ever present danger of anti-Asian hate crimes, and through the "neighborhood race effects" that leave them to deal with underfunded schools, polluted air and water, and low-wage jobs that they and their families share with their black, Latino, Arab American, and even poor white neighbors. The cumulative and intersectional injuries of class and race allow them no simple oppositional identity. To the Asian Pacific Environmental

Network (APEN) and its Japanese American and Chinese American feminist organizers that sponsor their activism, the young Laotian women are "Asian American women" or "Laotians." Within the alliances organized by the African American–led West County Toxics Coalition against environmental racism, they speak as "people of color." Their neighbors know them through their kinship ties and ethnic identities as Lao, Mien, Hmong, and Khmu youths. But to their immediate families they may seem quintessentially "American." The activism offered within APEN does not just speak to already existing identities, but rather offers a forum for staking out new positions as people with complex interests and identities. As group member Fam Linh Saechao (aka Fam Mulan) explains, "APEN gives us a place where we can come together and identify as Asian women. It gives us a place to be both Laotian and American, some kind of middle ground to talk about the struggles we have with our families, no matter if we are Lao, Mien, Hmong, or Khmu."[26]

The young Laotian women activists in APEN are not alone in creating new identities and new institutions to address the conditions they confront in their everyday lives; they share with millions of people around the world an urgent need to fashion dynamic new forms of struggle. The alienations and injustices they face are not only of importance to them; rather they are part of a system of generalized subordination that is most effectively named, defined, and challenged by those exposed to its most indecent acts. The most important thing about aggrieved groups is not who they are, but what they know, and what they have to teach about the struggle for a better world.

Scholars in ethnic studies and American studies can sometimes become weighted down by what they know, can be overcome by hopelessness and despair. But aggrieved communities do not have the luxury of despair; they have battles to fight every day. We can help them remember what has been done to them and what they have done for themselves. But most important, they can help us and we can help them answer the most important question of all: What must we now do?

CHAPTER 6

The Lion and the Spider

Mapping Sexuality, Space, and Politics in Miami Music

> The world economy is not a self-regulating globally invariant
> system whose social formations can be regarded as mere local effects;
> it is a system of constraints, subject to the unforeseeable
> dialectic of its local contradictions.
>
> —Etienne Balibar, *Race, Nation, Class: Ambiguous Identities*

Diverse ethnic, racial, regional, and national traditions come together in Miami, and they inflect the city's musical culture with a dazzling array of distinctive styles, figures, and forms. As a key crossroads for trade between the United States and Latin America, and as a magnet for migration from all over the hemisphere, Miami has become a privileged place for the generation of music marked by transnational networks, affiliations, and identifications. From rap to reggae, from disco to dancehall, from salsa to soft rock, and from jazz to junkanoo, Miami's popular music provides a rich catalogue of the different histories and experiences that have long divided its constituent population groups. But the music also presents a tantalizing picture of how the very things that divide people might paradoxically serve as a stimulus for creating new interethnic and transnational forms of cultural coalescence and consciousness.

Popular music made in Miami offers an important example of the promise and peril of globalization and its implications for the future of social movements. When read diagnostically as a symptom of broader transformations in social identities, popular music in Miami allows us to understand the complicated nature of contemporary racial and national identities, as well as the importance of gender and sexuality as the modalities through many of the most significant changes of our time are experienced.

Of course, it can be dangerous to take music too literally, to assume that it can be understood by its surfaces. The song "St. Louis Blues" contains a blues section, but it is really a tango. "Begin the Beguine" is not actually a beguine, but a bolero. Listeners hoping to experience the "warm" San Francisco nights evoked in the lyrics of the Animals' 1967 hit song "San Franciscan Nights" may have a long wait if they actually visit that chilly city. Louis Jordan's "Tympany Five" usually had seven members; gospel quartets routinely contain five singers. The Statler Brothers are not brothers, and none of them are named Statler.[1]

Yet while unreliable when taken at face value, music can contain significant evidence about important changes in social relations when interpreted properly. Contemporary popular music shapes and reflects the emerging realities of global cities like Miami. Social identities and social relations not yet possible in political life often appear first within popular culture. Important evidence about the world that is emerging all around us can be discerned in the ways in which popular music in Miami registers changes in black and Latino identities as well as disturbances in gender roles and sexuality provoked by new social relations in global cities.[2] Perhaps most important, the complexities of popular music production, distribution, and reception in Miami reveal the ways in which complicated social processes and powerful social institutions combine to shape our plural identities as cultural creators and consumers, as the inheritors of past social movements and as the potential organizers of new ones.

Miami grew into a "global" city in the second half of the twentieth century on the strength of its status as a center for regional, hemispheric, and international trade. Cuban American investors and entrepreneurs positioned Miami to fill a leadership role in the economies of the Caribbean and South America by starting banks, import-export companies, transportation, and service companies. Of course overt and covert subsidies to anticommunist Cubans from cold-war national security agencies played a huge role in the initial capitalization and subsequent expansion of Cuban capital in Miami. At the same time, low wage labor by Cuban American men and especially Cuban American women generate high profits for investors and low prices for consumers in the city's construction and apparel industries.[3]

Nearly 50 percent of the residents of Miami and Dade County are Latino, and nearly 20 percent are black. Cuban Americans comprise the largest single national group, yet the Cuban population is internally diverse, including more than twelve thousand Jewish Cubans, five thousand Chinese Cubans, and an undetermined but significant number of Afro-Cubans who face very different opportunity structures in the United States than do their lighter-skinned fellow nationals. Miami's population also includes more than two hundred thousand Latinos *not* from Cuba—Puerto Ricans, Nicaraguans, Venezuelans, Colombians, Ecuadorans, Panamanians, Mexicans, Argentinians, and Dominicans. In addition, large numbers of West Indians, including Haitians, Jamaicans, and Bahamians, contribute to the cultural and demographic diversity of the city, giving its African American population a simultaneously national *and* international inflection.[4] As early as 1980, foreign-born individuals accounted for 20 percent of Miami's black population, which at that time included seventy thousand Haitians, eight thousand Jamaicans, four thousand Bahamians, and seventeen thousand immigrants from other Caribbean, South American, and African countries.[5]

Half of all of the Miami area's two million residents are foreign-born. Every month some two hundred cargo ships and five thousand cargo planes transport commercial goods through Miami. The city's airport and seaport account for 70 percent of the trade conducted between the United States and Latin America. Trade-related businesses employ 98,000 workers and net more than thirteen billion dollars annually in Miami. The city boasts more foreign-owned banks than any U.S. city except New York. Under these circumstances, "local" life and culture in Miami has decidedly international dimensions.[6]

The demographic diversity of Miami shapes the city's popular music in decisive ways. Local radio stations, jukeboxes, and nightclubs offer samples of distinct musical forms from around the nation and the world, especially Caribbean salsa, son, soca, reggae, rara, and chutney; African American rhythm and blues, hip-hop, jazz, and gospel;

Anglo-American rock, pop, and folk; and a wide assortment of Asian, Middle Eastern, African, South American, and European styles. Inevitably, these distinct and separate forms blend together in Miami, inflecting each with elements of the others.

Yet this cultural diversity does not persist in isolation from other realms of human endeavor. Miami's complex musical culture also reveals the enduring power of social struggles and social movements in people's memories, even when those movements themselves are no longer around. Memories of the U.S. black power and civil rights movements loom large in the cosmologies of hip-hop, jazz, and rhythm and blues. Anticolonialism and Pan-Africanism provide a key subtext for contemporary reggae, rara, and soca. Controversies about sexism and misogyny in hip-hop or dancehall reggae resonate with class, caste, and generational tensions within communities of color in the United States and in the Caribbean, but they also emerge out of the very different kinds of cultural critiques advanced by feminists and the religious right. Salsa and son music today remain marked by the histories of progressive struggles for national liberation throughout the Americas—their failures as well as their successes—as well as by the aftermath of the Cuban Revolution, which brought Fidel Castro to power in 1959, and the ways in which that event has shaped the contours of culture for Cubans as well as other Caribbean people. In Miami, these different social movement histories interact with one another, and they confront as well the history of other social movements and causes ranging from free love to abstinence, from gay and lesbian activism to homophobic mobilizations and crusades.

The popular music of Miami provides us at one and the same time with visible markers of social division and powerful examples of cultural coalescence and coalition. For example, Latinos and African Americans in Miami have often seen each other as competitors for political power and wealth, but their worlds merge neatly in the music of Puerto Rican rapper Lisa M. She enjoys particularly strong popularity in the Miami market largely because of her song "Jarican Jive," with its blend of English and Spanish lyrics celebrating the benefits of mixing Jamaican and Puerto Rican music.[7] Similarly, one of the most popular recordings produced by Miami African American rapper Luther Campbell featured an interlingual hip-hop song by his group 2 Live Crew featuring Debbie Bennett, the group's Honduran-born publicity director rapping (obscenely) in Spanish.[8] The ways in which the presence of West Indians in Miami inflects the meaning of African American identity in the city may not be legible in the actions of community groups and institutions, but they appear boldly in the instrumentation and rhythms of songs by local rhythm and blues and disco artist Harry Casey (of KC and the Sunshine Band), in Luther Campbell's "Miami Bass" sound, and in the similarity of Campbell's song lyrics to the same kinds of sexual imagery prevalent in Jamaican dancehall reggae songs.[9]

Probably the most widely visible contemporary icon of "Latin" identity in the United States comes from the self-tropicalization at the heart of the music and performances of Gloria Estefan and the Miami Sound Machine. This group, with its strong allegiance to traditional Cuban music, occupies a powerful position within Miami's Cuban American community. Yet the group projects a strangely market-centered notion of *Latinidad*—a fusion more responsive to the marketing ambitions of entrepreneurs than to the cultural history that it purports to represent. The Miami Sound Machine first found popularity during the late 1970s using Spanish-language lyrics fused with largely Anglo-American pop sounds. When increased immigration from Latin America expanded the audience for "Latin" music, it enabled them to carve out a unique niche in the pop market by "mainstreaming" the sounds of salsa for Anglophone pop audiences. In the words of Gustavo Perez Firmat they transformed themselves from "a hispanophone soft-rock group" to "an anglophone soft-salsa group."[10]

Gloria Estefan and the Miami Sound Machine secured enormous success in the local and national pop music markets during the 1980s, aided by the emergence of Miami's Super Q (WQBA-FM) as an extremely successful radio station programming Cuban American music. The group's popularity and media prominence also stemmed from lead singer Gloria Estefan's much publicized anti-Castro and anticommunist views, which in the years of the Reagan presidency won the band coveted spots as the official U.S. cultural representative to events like the Pan-American games. (The role of Estefan's family members as high-level officials in the brutal and corrupt Batista dictatorship that preceded the Castro regime was of course almost never mentioned by government officials or journalists as they portrayed Estefan as a fighter for "democracy" and "freedom.") The Miami Sound Machine and Estefan went on to fashion an even more Latin sound in the 1990s, in part through Estefan's recording of a collection of beloved traditional Cuban songs, but also through their mid-nineties revival of Vicki Sue Robinson's 1976 disco hit "Turn the Beat Around." The new version foregrounded the song's rhythm and percussion in such a way as to recover the important (but often ignored) Latin elements within the original disco version. Gloria Estefan and her band became strangely *more* "Latin" through the act of "covering" a disco song with English-language lyrics originally recorded by a mixed-race rhythm and blues singer than they had been when the Miami Sound Machine made either Hispanophone soft rock or Anglophone soft salsa.

Gloria Estefan's blend of salsa and disco had roots in Miami as well as Havana. Many of disco's distinctive stylistic elements found their first expressions in Miami among Latino, African American, and Anglo musicians working at Henry Stone's TK Studios in Hialeah. George McCrae, Gwen McCrae, Betty Wright, and KC and the Sunshine Band turned out hit after hit based on these musical forms during the 1970s. Stone started out in the record business with Tone Records in Miami in 1946, and over the years recorded a dazzling array of artists, including Hank Ballard, Ray Charles, and James Brown. But by the mid-1970s, he was reduced to operating a four-track machine in a primitive studio on the second floor of a warehouse, not exactly the kind of set-up poised for significant commercial success. Stone drew upon the diverse local cultures of Miami, however, to fashion a distinctive sound. He fabricated a blend of Latin cowbells and timbales, North American "soul" vocals, and Afro-Caribbean whistles to create disco and rhythm and blues records punctuated by the distinctive pulsating riffs of the musicians who made up the Sunshine Band, and by the unique guitar stylings of the multi-talented Willie Hale, who recorded under the name Little Beaver.[11]

The leader of KC and the Sunshine Band (Harry Casey) was a white Pentecostal raised mostly by his mother, a woman who loved African American rhythm and blues music. Casey developed the band's distinctive sound after he attended fellow Miami musician Clarence Reid's wedding, where he became transfixed by a Bahamian band's "junkanoo" music—featuring cowbells, steel drums, and whistle flutes. Casey relied heavily on those instruments in his band's first two recordings ("Sound Your Funky Horn" and "Blow Your Whistle"), which he recorded under the name KC and the Sunshine Junkanoo Band.[12] Casey's band also featured the percussion of Havana-born Fermin Goytisolo, a black Cuban. It has become general knowledge by now that the fusion of Latin rhythms, Anglo-Caribbean instrumentation, North American black "soul" vocals, and Euro-American melodies gave rise to the disco music, which enjoyed enormous popularity in the 1970s, first within black, Latino, lesbian, and gay subcultures, but later with a mass "pop" audience. This popularity made Estefan's version of "Turn the Beat Around" legible to a mass audience even while it recuperated the subordinated Afro-Latin basis of the song. But the enduring power of the Bahamian and Anglo-Caribbean content in Miami music is less well known.

Clarence Reid not only introduced Harry Casey to Bahamian junkanoo music but also cowrote "Sound Your Funky Horn." Reid had been a successful rhythm and blues artist in the late 1960s and early 1970s, placing four songs recorded on Henry Stone's Alston label on the best-seller charts between 1969 and 1974.[13] In the late 1970s and early 1980s, Reid recorded a series of X-rated "party" records under the name Blowfly. The sexually explicit lyrics of Blowfly's songs influenced many young rappers in the 1980s. As Miami's Luther Campbell rose to fame as the guiding inspiration of 2 Live Crew, he blended together parts of Blowfly, dancehall reggae, and the powerful bass sounds and beat popularized by Jazzy Jay and other associates of Afrika Bambaataa in New

York. The Bahamian connection came full circle in 2000, when the Baha men, a soca-calypso band from that country, added Campbell's "Miami Bass" sound to Trinidad-Tobago singer Anselm Douglas's composition "Who Let the Dogs Out?" and secured an international hit. The music made at TK subsequently influenced artists throughout the Caribbean, and played a generative role in the emergence of disco, a musical form and social site originally nurtured and sustained largely inside communities of color and among white gays and lesbians.

Miami's proximity to the Caribbean is not the sole source of the city's musical fusions. Perez Firmat remembers hearing a performance by Willie Chirino that featured a Cuban *guaguanco* rhythm behind the Hebrew song "Hava Nagila," a sure-fire commercial combination in a city populated by so many Cuban Americans *and* so many Jewish Americans.[14] Notorious hip-hop group 2 Live Crew benefited from a similar cultural intersection when they hired retired Jewish American businessman Joseph Kolsky as their manager in the late 1980s. A former senior executive of Roulette Records in New York (the label that featured one of the first African American/Puerto Rican groups—Frankie Lymon and the Teenagers), Kolsky retired and moved to Florida with the sole intention of playing golf and listening to big band tunes. But Luther Campbell of 2 Live Crew coaxed him out of retirement, aware of Kolsky's successful track record with rhythm and blues and disco artists in New York. Under the guidance of Kolsky—an elderly Jewish American man described by his son as a conservative and prudish person—Campbell's outrageously vulgar 2 Live Crew made best-selling recordings with memorable titles like "Me So Horny" and "Pop My Pussy."[15]

Campbell and 2 Live Crew described themselves as a "comedy act" rather than a hip-hop group, and given their leader's limited skills as a rapper this was probably the right decision. Yet the stylistic features they chose to incorporate into their music revealed a good understanding of hip-hop, especially its affinities for contemporary immigrant music from the Caribbean, particularly the music that Jamaicans refer to as dancehall, a style that emerged in the 1970s and 1980s where vocalists and rappers perform to the accompaniment of prerecorded rhythms. In Jamaica and Miami, the lyrics of dancehall songs foreground what the Jamaicans call slackness, by which they mean explicit sexuality. As residents of Miami, Luther Campbell and 2 Live Crew would have had extensive exposure to the slackness of Jamaican dancehall music and to the possibilities of fusing it with hip-hop.

The fame of 2 Live Crew rested on their sexually explicit lyrics, but the vehicle for delivering those words was the distinctive bass-oriented sound created by blending Latino and African American musical forms. Campbell grew up in Miami's Liberty City ghetto and saw his first turntable artists and rappers in African Square Park and at local radio station WEDR. Desperate for money, he quickly sized up the profit-making potential in commercialized leisure. As a teenager, Campbell leased a pacman video game from a distributor and made money by inviting his friends over to play (with their quarters). At a time when Miami's dancehalls favored disco over hip-hop and offered few opportunities for new talent, Campbell created his own sound system and rented out his services as a DJ. He refused to perform for free in the park like the other rappers in his neighborhood, but secured paying jobs instead at skating rinks and school dances.

Discussions of hip-hop as an artistic form often neglect its economic significance as one of the very few sites in our society where the knowledge and talents of inner-city youth have a cash value and where they have the opportunity to translate their skills into opportunities for economic upward mobility. For ghetto youths like Campbell, hip-hop is about reality *and* about a salary.

Many hip-hop artists have surpassed Campbell artistically, but few have displayed his ability to attract lawsuits or to profit from the ensuing controversies. The Sheriff of Broward County sued him for performing obscene lyrics. George Lucas sued him for taking the stage name Luke Skywalker from the film *Star Wars* without permission. Nashville publishing house Acuff-Rose sued him for an unauthorized parody of Roy Orbison's "Pretty Woman." Despite setbacks at lower levels, Campbell was eventually vindicated in all but one of these actions—the case involving Lucas, which forced him to change his label name to Luke Records and his stage name to Luke instead of Luke Skywalker.[16]

In 1990, a federal district court judge in Fort Lauderdale agreed with the complaint of conservative activist Jack Thompson by declaring 2 Live Crew's rap album *As Nasty as They Wanna Be* obscene. Two years earlier, Thompson had been a candidate for the position of prosecuting attorney in Dade County, Florida, on the Republican Party ticket against the incumbent (and later United States Attorney General) Janet Reno. At one campaign appearance, Thompson handed Reno a prepared statement and asked her to check the appropriate box. The statement read "I, Janet Reno, am a ___ homosexual, ___ bisexual, ___ heterosexual." It continued, "If you do not respond ... then you will be deemed to have checked one of the first two boxes." Luther Campbell supported Reno and conducted voter registration drives on her behalf during that race.[17] Six weeks after the election, Thompson wrote letters to Reno and to Florida Governor Bob Martinez demanding an investigation of 2 Live Crew for possible violation of state obscenity statutes and racketeering codes, allegedly because of *As Nasty as They Wanna Be*.[18]

Two days after the federal court ruling that declared *As Nasty as They Wanna Be* in violation of federal obscenity laws, the Broward County Sheriff arrested Charles Freeman, a twenty-eight-year-old black businessman who owned a music store, for selling a record and tape version of *As Nasty as They Wanna Be* to an adult undercover deputy. Officers put Freeman in handcuffs and took him to the county jail; he was later convicted of a first-degree misdemeanor. Sheriff's deputies also arrested two members of 2 Live Crew later that week for singing lyrics from the album at an adults-only concert.[19] An appeals court later overturned the district court's ruling and held that *As Nasty as They Wanna Be* was not obscene after all, but Thompson's efforts did persuade the Musicland stores with 752 outlets and the Trans World Stores with 450 branches to drop 2 Live Crew's album from their inventories.[20] At the same time, United States Marine Corps officials (in a rare moment of alarm about pornography in the ranks) ordered the removal of the group's albums from shelves in on-base stores in Arizona, South Carolina, North Carolina, and California.[21]

While most critics have seen Campbell's repeated contests in the courts as self-induced, publicity stunts tailored to his astute business strategies, it is also clear that he has been targeted for attack because of his political activism. Campbell points to local political conditions—especially to fears by whites and Cubans that his business success and political organizing represent potential competition for political power and economic resources—as the reason for his troubles with the law. Yet recognizing the Caribbean content of Miami's culture leads to another explanation. Part of Campbell's emphasis on sexuality comes from the engagement that he and his audiences have with the complicated sexual politics emanating from the effects of globalization on the Caribbean as a whole, including—but not limited to—the city of Miami.

West Indian dancehall music by artists like Bounty Killer, Beenie Man, and Buju Banton provides a focal point for a vibrant immigrant dancehall subculture in Hallandale and other Miami neighborhoods. Miami has become, in fact, the second largest dancehall market outside the West Indies, trailing only New York City. Jamaican-born Miami DJ Waggy Tee draws huge audiences to his weekly dances at the Cameo Theater where he specializes in hip-hop-style mixing and scratching. Shabba Ranks, Patra, and Mad Cobra all record for Miami-based Shang Records. Company president Luther McKenzie claims, "Miami is very important. There's a lot happening behind the scenes, and there's more to come, believe me."[22]

Dancehall in Miami is not just another immigrant subcultural music, but rather an import that blends perfectly with hip-hop in a fusion that leaves both musical styles transformed. As one of Miami's leading DJs, Rory of Stone Love, explains, "Hip-hop and dancehall have the same beats. You can mix the records, and they will groove."[23] Jamaican musician Super Cat sees important affinities between dancehall and rap. "They're both ghetto music," he explains, noting that dancehall is "all about the hard core: survival, facts of life."[24]

Like West Indian dancehall artists—or for that matter like

Jamaican-born Richard Shaw (aka Bushwick Bill) of the Houston rap group the Geto Boys, also known for their frank lyrics—Campbell's misogynist "toasting" evidences new ideas and attitudes about sexuality within aggrieved communities at a time of extraordinary economic austerity. The frank celebrations of sexuality and the homophobia and misogyny that permeate hip-hop music and dancehall reggae lead many observers to see this music as irredeemably sexist or even pornographic. In the United States, some of the most vehement attacks on hip-hop have come from successful professionals in the Black Congressional Caucus and the National Political Congress of Black Women.[25] Similarly, opposition to dancehall reggae in Jamaica has been particularly prominent among members of the nation's light-skinned elite.[26] Yet even sworn enemies of these elites such as Mutabaruka, a veteran Jamaican reggae artist and revolutionary speaks for many progressives when he describes dancehall as "the worst thing that ever happen to Jamaican culture" because of the "lewdness, the downgrading of women, the slackness, materialism, gun violence."[27] At the same time, dancehall reggae in Jamaica and hip-hop in the United States have also become focal points of collective pride that connect black identity to the creativity and social struggles of some of the most oppressed members of the group. In these instances, "ghettocentricity" is less an embrace of licentiousness than a gesture of solidarity forged out of a refusal to disidentify with the greatest victims of globalization, deindustrialization, and economic restructuring.[28] The deep and real divisions over the morality of popular music in both countries testifies to the weaknesses of once unified national and racial identities and to the emerging importance of the proliferation of new and seemingly contradictory identities that seem to be a formative feature of contemporary capitalism and contemporary culture.[29]

While understandable, and perhaps even accurate as evaluation and critique, negative judgments about the role of sexuality in hip-hop and dancehall reggae evade why these expressions have emerged at this time and what they mean for the people producing and consuming them. Luther Campbell and other male performers do not monopolize discussions of sexuality in hip-hop; in fact they have been surpassed by more talented (if equally troubling) female artists including TLC, Foxy Brown, and L'il Kim. Similarly, references to sexuality by male dancehall artists Beenie Man or Buju Banton need to be seen in the light of the "bare as you dare" outfits and sex-affirmative lyrics of female singers Carlene Smith, Tanya Stephens, Patra, and Lady Saw. What do we make of music that some people read as a means of luring oppressed and aggrieved populations into celebrating the worst features of the system that oppresses them, while others see the exact same music as a brilliant form of contestation built upon the appropriation and recontextualization of dominant discourses and values?

In a discussion of dancehall reggae that contains great import for understanding Miami hip-hop, Louis Chude-Sokei claims that dismissals of "slackness" lyrics as sexist and/or pornographic miss the point. He notes the ways in which the sexuality of black women stands at the center of dancehall reggae's world. Along with Carolyn Cooper, he detects a strong strain of female self-affirmation in women's responses to the lyrics of male dancehall artists on the dance floor as well as in the lyrics of women artists who take to the microphone themselves. Chude-Sokei explains that women buy more of these recordings than men do, and that in Jamaican dancehalls women control the dance floor. Conceding that dancehall lyrics are offensive to metropolitan feminist sensibilities, Chude-Sokei nonetheless argues that women dancehall fans "find both affirmation and power in the fear that their sexuality creates in the men. It allows them the freedom and security to navigate in and around a world of brutality, violence, and economic privation."[30]

Like Chude-Sokei, Cooper argues that sexual topics in dancehall lyrics provide a positive alternative to the erasure of female desire and sexuality in most popular music. New York music critic Frank Owen endorses Cooper's claims, comparing favorably the overt and unconscious demands for sexual pleasure by women in dancehall music with gangsta rap's negative demonization of women as "ball breakers" and "gold diggers."[31] Cooper also argues that sex-affirmative songs by women in dancehall music need to be understood as a reaction against the masculinist and patriarchal politics of reggae with its biblically inspired Rastafarianism. The visionary black nationalism of 1970s Jamaican reggae with its antiracist and anti-imperialist content appealed enormously to political radicals in North America and Europe, many of whom failed to notice that reggae and Rastafarianism privileged male perspectives, advocated the subordination of women, and preached an asceticism that associated the female body with impurity.[32] Reggae fans around the world have often seen the rise of dancehall music as a degeneration from the moral and political superiority of "conscious" reggae of the Bob Marley years. But critics living outside the Caribbean have not had to confront directly the failures of 1970s Afro-Caribbean radicalism, the costs of the Structural Adjustment Policies of the IMF and the World Bank, or the social disintegration and restructuring of gender roles imposed on Caribbean society and much of the low-wage world over the past two decades.

Yet very little of Miami's hip-hop is performed by women, and Luther Campbell's lyrics and samples of dialogue from motion pictures like *Full Metal Jacket* contain the crudest kinds of objectification of sex and contempt for women. "Slackness" songs that may have positive implications for women performers, dancers, and listeners might have very different meanings for men because of the threat posed to traditional masculine privileges by changes in contemporary gender roles. Like Dominican merengue and bachata, Mexican banda, and West Coast gangsta rap, "slackness" dancehall reggae reveals that one of the ways in which men experience a global economy increasingly organized around the low-wage labor of women is through affirmations of masculine privilege and denigrations of female independence. Yen Le Espiritu notes that in the current global economy men generally lose social status and prestige through migration while women often secure advances in their status. Immigrant men of color suffer additional assaults on their dignity because of the racism in U.S. society.[33] Pierrette Hondagneu-Sotelo's brilliant research on Mexican immigrants finds that while immigrant men maintain more status and remain more mobile than women, they still feel that they lose power and status in the public sphere through migration. This loss undermines their standing within the family as well.[34] Misogyny is an understandable if ultimately foolish and counterproductive response to this status anxiety and perceived loss of respect and dignity.

Globalization does not just change relations between countries, it also upsets relations between genders. In Jamaica, over 60 percent of women worked full-time even before the Structural Adjustment Policies advocated by the IMF and the World Bank in the late 1970s. Efforts by global finance to restructure the Jamaican economy to give foreign investors a better rate of return on their Jamaican holdings caused the elimination of previously secure high-wage jobs held by men and instigated the proliferation of low-wage female jobs in garment, textile, light assembly, data processing, and electronics work.[35] The growth of "white collar" work in the new economy also opened up new categories of professional, technical, and administrative employment for Jamaicans. These jobs became "feminized" so that management could save money on educated labor. As a result, women constituted more than 45 percent of the labor force in Jamaica by the 1990s. They had desirable work histories and some economic mobility, enabling them to pursue employment as domestics, nurses, and child-care workers in global cities like New York and Miami in the 1980s and 1990s. Women also quickly recognized the ways in which migration from Jamaica to the United States could provide favorable opportunities for social independence through separation or divorce as well as for economic upward mobility through the pursuit of professional credentials.[36]

One manifestation of the misogyny exacerbated by new social relations comes through the symbolic value given to male perspectives in immigrant music, especially bachata, merengue, and dancehall reggae and rap. In addition, the same loss of male self-respect that leads to incisive critiques of racialized capitalism can also lead to a vicious homophobia. Slackness dancehall performer Buju Banton brilliantly connected declining educational opportunities and the rise of drug use in inner-city ghettos to a plot by the rich who "no want see ghetto youth elevate out a the slum" and consequently "give we all type a things [drugs], try turn we down."[37] Yet in 1992, Banton also recorded "Boom Bye Bye," a song inciting antigay violence. Similarly, dancehall *reggaespanol* artist Rude

Girl (La Atrevida) attacks lesbians in "Lesbiana" because she thinks they "harass woman" and refuse "procreation." When Shabba Ranks attempted to distance himself from the homophobic lyrics that characterized some of his songs, he lost street credibility and commercial power inside Jamaica, losing sales to the unrepentant Buju Banton. Part of Ranks's decline in popularity came from his eclipse by more talented artists, but part also stemmed from the perception among his fans that he had been made to bow to the wishes of foreigners—and gay and lesbian ones at that.

The important scholarship of Jacqui Alexander explains how postcolonial economic and political elites have used heterosexuality, nuclear families, and traditional roles for women as key symbols of national independence and integrity. Originally intended to displace slurs by colonialists that stereotyped third world men as hypersexualized rapists while portraying third world women as sexually aggressive Jezebels, this discourse of sexual respectability has become the last refuge of neocolonial scoundrels as they sell out the political and economic autonomy of their nations to global capital. They attempt to render their own nations as modern, safe, and appealing to outsiders (especially tourists) by persecuting homosexuals, suppressing women, extolling the nuclear family, and policing sexuality.[38]

Alexander's approach enables us to see some of the strategic purposes that homophobia might serve in the lives of dancehall artists and audiences. Above and beyond its sanction through traditional religious and moral codes, homophobia functions as a node in a network of power that shapes social relations and life chances. Functional uses of homophobia do not make it justified; any dehumanization of others should be condemned. Making others lower in order to make your group higher always makes things worse, because no matter how satisfying it might be for oppressed people to temporarily adopt the attitudes of their tormentors, in the long run they will only reinforce the domination and victimization that the oppressed need to overcome. Yet we remain powerless to fight homophobia unless we understand how and why it comes so easily to so many people.

For the working-class Jamaicans who comprise the core of dance-hall reggae's following, homophobia offers opportunities to deflect scorn away from oneself and onto others. Condemned by elites as immoral and indecent because they pursue pleasure, expressive displays of homophobia might give working-class Jamaicans an opportunity to redraw the lines of inclusion and exclusion; by participating in the expulsion of gays and lesbians from respectable society they might imagine that they become respectable defenders of the "nation." By connecting sex to procreation rather than pleasure, they might be staking a claim for their own sexual displays as virtuous and necessary rather than uncontrolled, undisciplined, vain, narcissistic, and sinful. In addition, radical transformations in contemporary gender and power relations raise enormous anxieties in people because behaviors once believed to be natural or necessary are clearly neither. Homophobia might help to ease anxieties about the seeming fluidity of gender roles by resurrecting a fixed and firm binary based on sexual behavior. People no longer able to demarcate the male-female boundary clearly might become more attached emotionally and ideologically to their imagined opposition between gay and straight.

Yet the disavowal of same sex desire that seems so central to dancehall reggae should not be accepted at face value. It may conceal more than it reveals. The open assertion of female desire within dancehall reggae might well raise the possibility of women desiring other women. Homophobic statements might well serve to police that possibility, to warn women against behavior perceived to threaten the interests and privileges of heterosexual men. Dancehall lyrics also foreground expressions of shared sexual desires among men who are focused on their mutual lust for women. Yet the peculiarly social and collective nature of these expressions represents a degree of same sex attachment that might be read as "homosexual," a reading so unsettling that it might require open homophobia as the only effective form of disavowal. It is a familiar paradox of sexual politics that overt homophobia often serves as an important form of homosocial bonding among heterosexual men.

Similarly, some of the hatred of women and gays expressed by male entertainers may stem from efforts to project an image of exaggerated masculine heterosexuality, to compensate for the possible stigma of engaging in behaviors generally coded as female—wearing costumes and makeup, preening for the gaze of others, revealing interior thoughts and emotions. Male dancehall entertainers and fans might be especially attracted to these strategies because the dance floor has so frequently been culturally coded as a space for women and as a site where many of the style leaders have been gay males.

Andrew Ross argues effectively that the homophobia of dancehall reggae plays into the hands of neocolonial cultural elites, while at the same time noting that the sex-affirmative propleasure politics of Lady Saw, Patra, Lady Apache, and Shelly Thunder might still create cultural and social spaces with distinctly feminist and counterhegemonic possibilities.[39] Yet neither side of this coin can remain static or isolated. Dancehall artists and audiences occupy a distinctive space in Jamaican cities, but they also participate in a global industry. Their competitors are international as well as national.

Marketing imperatives lead to perpetual transgressions of existing moral norms to give new "products" (in this case artists) a novel appeal. Yet at the same time, the economies of scale basic to global marketing encourage the production of goods that do not drive off potential consumers, that do not provoke censorship, and that can be safely and interchangeably marketed in many settings. In this system, places like Miami are where the seams show, where Jamaican dancehall meets North American gangster rap, where Caribbean black nationalism meets feminism and queer theory, where the post–civil rights generation and the post-Rastafarian generation interact with members of many other groups to forge new signs, symbols, and sensibilities.

The "obscene" lyrics of 2 Live Crew need to be seen, at least in part, in the context of Miami's location in the hemisphere. At one of Luther Campbell's obscenity trials, Harvard Professor Henry Louis Gates correctly noted the long history of misogynist and sexually explicit rhymes within African American oral traditions like playing the dozens. But part of Campbell's interest in salacious topics comes as well from his blending of African American traditions with the influences from Jamaica, influences that often have both cultural and political significance. The influence of Jamaican culture on Campbell's lyrics may have been indirect, but it was determined in part by the important role that Jamaica and its culture play in the broader African diaspora. More than two decades ago Afro-Guyanese intellectual Walter Rodney observed with admiration that all African and Caribbean people owed a debt to the vitality of Jamaican culture. Commenting on what he had seen as a student in England and as a professor at the University of the West Indies, Rodney noted, "Jamaicans can curse more proficiently than any other Caribbean people. They have such a range of words describing phenomena so neatly and I think this is a testimony to their combativeness. So that I always felt that there must be tremendous revolutionary potential in that island."[40]

In the process of connecting with the sexual politics of racialized low-wage work that Caribbean immigrants might share with American-born blacks, Campbell's engagement with Afro-Caribbean music inevitably also intersects with the specific and local histories of social movements in Jamaica and other Caribbean countries and territories. Understanding Miami hip-hop's fusions with dancehall reggae necessarily entails an engagement with the recent history of social movements in Jamaica.

Andrew Ross explains that the emergence of dancehall reggae in Jamaica reflected both the demise of the progressive political project advanced by Michael Manley (first signaled by his embrace of reggae) during his first term in office as Jamaica's president, and by recognition of the victory of the IMF and the World Bank over progressive grass-roots efforts in Jamaica to correct the nation's maldistribution of wealth. Subsequent regimes have implemented the austerity demanded by the U.S. government and the international financial community with devastating results. These measures increased pressures to migrate to the United States, transforming not only Jamaican society, but African American life and culture as well.[41]

Chude-Sokei notes that dancehall has refigured the African

diaspora, moving beyond the Rastafarian vision in reggae that portrayed the present as only a temporary sojourn—as exile in Babylon, preparatory to returning to Africa sometime in the future. In this worldview, the African past and future stood at the center of the diasporic imagination while the "here and now" of the present disappeared. Dancehall reggae, in contrast, focuses on the here and now, on the documentary realities of poverty and racism confronting Africans around the world, and on desires for immediate pleasure and gratification.[42] Ross points out that this sense of time is one that dancehall reggae shares with hip-hop. Both musics also share a sexual hedonism that certainly involves large doses of sexism, but at the same time exhibits a profoundly sex-affirmative commitment to sexual pleasure as an emotional and physical antidote to the aching muscles, frayed nerves, and psychic insults of lives oriented around low-wage labor.[43]

Affinities between hip-hop and dancehall can be seen directly in the music itself, for example, in collaborative recordings featuring hip-hop artists and dancehall stars: Salt-n-Pepa with Patra, KRS-1 with Shabba Ranks, Special Ed's hip-hop remix of Beenie Man's "slam," and Bounty Killer's 1996 album *Xperience* with guest appearances by Busta Rhymes, Raekwon, Jeru the Damaja, and the Fugees (themselves a fusion of Haitian-American and Afro-American music.)[44] Of course, these fusions also resonate with the long history of Caribbean influence on hip-hop dating back to its origins in the South Bronx in the 1970s when the culture's leading artists included Kool DJ Herc (who was born in Jamaica), Grandmaster Flash and Afrika Bambaata (whose families came from Barbados) and "Crazylegs" Ritchie Colon of the Rock Steady Crew (whose family came from Puerto Rico).[45]

The backgrounds of the members of 2 Live Crew displayed directly the links between North American hip-hop and the Caribbean. DJ David Hobbs (Fresh Kid Ice) hailed from California, Mark Ross (Brother Marquis) from New York, Chris Wong Won from Trinidad, and Campbell from Miami.[46] In his autobiography—copublished in Jamaica by Kingston Publishers—Campbell identifies Jamaican immigrants to New York as the originators of turn-table mixing and scratching.[47] Chris

Wong Won's name also reminds us that the Caribbean is itself multicultural, that upwardly mobile middle-class Asian Caribbeans like Jamaica's Leslie Kong and Byron Lee have played important roles in the origins and evolution of music that has become emblematic of working class Pan-Africanism.

Campbell's music also drew upon Miami's important long-standing relationship with the anglophone Caribbean. In the 1960s, Miami-based clear channel AM radio stations played a key role in exposing Jamaican musicians to North American black music via broadcasts of "soul" music. Reggae emerged as a blend between North American rhythm and blues and Jamaican Burru, Kumina, Pocomania, and Nyabinghi rhythms. At the same time, reggae rhythmic patterns and chord progressions have formed an important subtext of many different forms of soul music in Miami, a connection that has been particularly evident in the recorded work of Betty Wright.[48] Bob Marley bought a house in Miami in 1976; Ciddy Booker, his mother, has lived there since 1982. Marley's son Rohan played football for the University of Miami Hurricanes, participates in the local musical productions and performances of his brothers Ky-mani, Ziggy, Julian, Stephen, and Damian, and attracted national attention in the late 1990s when he started dating hip-hop artist Lauryn Hill.[49]

To North American ears, the rise of Latin rap and dancehall reggae may signal a declension from the golden age of "conscious" reggae. By contrast with the great reggae songs of the 1970s, the popular music of today contains lyrics that seem to do little more than celebrate misogyny and materialism. Reggae music and Rastafarian ideology informed and inspired many of the most radical currents of the worldwide "black power" movement of the 1960s, 1970s, and 1980s. Bob Marley's music in particular has served as a model of self-affirmation and solidarity with broader struggles for diverse people around the globe including Algerian rai singer Cheb Khlaed, the Australian aboriginal band No Fixed Address, African reggae singer Alpha Blondy from Cote d'Ivoire, and the thousands of American Indians who to this day congregate every year at the Hopi Veterans Center in Kykotsmovi, Arizona, to listen to reggae artists from Jamaica play music at the Spirit of Unity festival.[50] Yet while carefully crafted by believers in interethnic antiracism like Marley to appeal to a global audience, "conscious" reggae music also emerged from the historically specific problems confronting Afro-Jamaicans in the 1960s and 1970s.

By embracing reggae music from Jamaica, black militants around the world effected a radical break with the "trickster" tradition of covert resistance to power exemplified by Anancy the Spider, the character in Afro-Caribbean folklore whose triumphs over more powerful opponents depend upon trickery and guile. The Rastafarians rejected the trickster tradition, explaining "Rasta no jesta!" Instead, they identified with the Lion of Judah—literally Emperor Haile Sellassie of Ethiopia, but figuratively a character who confronts enemies directly, does not back away from a fight, and attempts to pursue self-realization and self-discovery independently of the oppressor's categories and institutions.[51]

The "lion" that emerged from reggae and Rastafarianism in the 1970s and 1980s produced an extraordinary moment in the history of resistance and struggle. Rastas subverted the language of the "Babylon" system at every turn. They refused to use pronouns like "me" that might make them appear to be passive objects or isolated monads, insisting on "I and I" instead, because the phrase connoted solidarity, activity, and creativity. In the Rastafarian vocabulary, the pejorative label given "the Third World" nations of Asia, Africa, and Latin America thought to be underdeveloped and "behind" the first and second worlds in Europe and North America became a positive demographic description connoting its percentage of the world's population—"the Two Thirds World." Politics became "poli-tricks," not "the Black man's lot" but rather "the white man's plot." They viewed the universe as the "I-an-I-ni-verse" and the university as the "I-an-I-ni-versity." A building filled with the oppressor's books might be called the library appropriately enough, but a building filled with one's own books had to be considered the "true"-brary not the "lie"-brary. Others might "understand" things, but Rastafarian wisdom is something that one must "overstand." The burial cemetery in Kingston known as May Pen, became "Must Pen" to the Rastas, because they knew that everyone dies and so one "must" go there.[52]

Attention to the ideological consequences of language choices among Rastafarians corresponded with their attentiveness to other aspects of personal demeanor and dress. The "dread stare" of Rastafarians that might be interpreted as simply a hostile gaze is in fact an expression of an obligation to "see" the truth, to "distinguish sincerity from superficiality."[53] The sacrament of smoking marijuana or *ganja* (the Hindu word for the herb) functions to affirm the value of all things made by God that are *ital* (natural) and to provide an alternative to the alcoholism that takes such a deadly toll on the health, income, and quality of life of impoverished Jamaicans.[54] Beards, matted hair, and dreadlocks presented the Rastafarians to Jamaican society as voluntary outcasts disinterested in assimilation, but wearing dreadlocks also served to express solidarity with the Mau Mau freedom fighters in Kenya after photos of dreadlocked Mau Maus appeared in the local press.[55] Dreadlocks also subverted the self-hatred signified by hair texture hierarchies among blacks in Jamaica and elsewhere that values fine silky hair over thick curly hair. The Rastas rejected chemical shampoos and hair straighteners in favor of washing their hair in clean water and locally grown herbs to encourage the hair to "do what it wills."[56]

Rasta customs enacted the world they envisioned, inscribing counterhegemonic thinking within the micropractices of everyday life. They also spoke powerfully to the alienations and indignities of racialized low-wage labor. The time-consuming rituals required for food preparation, personal grooming, and prayer among Rastafarians have their own internal logics, but they also encourage a daily existence that resists regimentation and on-the-job time-work discipline. Even the inclusive Pan-Africanism of Rastafarianism has clear implications in respect to wage labor.[57] Dark-skinned poor people in Jamaica are forced to compete with one another for low wage jobs. They are hired by the state as police officers and soldiers to police their own brethren. Every day, they see the signifiers of their own oppression in the faces and bodies of other blacks.

Under these circumstances it becomes easy to disidentify with one's own group, to channel anger and rage toward someone who is every bit as powerless and every bit as despised as you. Rastafarianism, however, provides a counternarrative to disidentification. It channels self-hatred not into hatred of another, but rather into self-love and group solidarity.

Bob Marley proved himself to be a particularly effective representative of Rastafarianism and a particularly influential symbol of "black power" radicalism before and after his untimely death in 1981 at the age of thirty-six. As the light-skinned offspring of a white father and a black mother, he drew his credibility as a black militant from his intellectual, spiritual, and cultural contributions, not from his skin color. Although raised in poverty in Jamaica and disciplined by a stint on the Chrysler Assembly Line in Newark, Delaware, he cared little for the material goods he acquired as a successful recording artist. Marley supported an enormous number of people with his earnings and gave away most of his wealth. The only possession he embraced as his own was a BMW automobile, which he claimed he needed because BMW stood for "Bob Marley and the Wailers." As a public figure, he brought together the leaders of Jamaica's warring political parties at a concert to promote an end to factional violence within the country, and he attained international recognition as the featured artist at the ceremonies marking the independence of Zimbabwe in 1980.[58] Marley's influence helped establish reggae music as a powerful political and social force among aggrieved populations around the world, not only in "Babylon" (the West Indies, Europe, North America), but in Central America, Africa, Australia, and Oceania as well.[59]

The distance between Bob Marley's highly spiritual and political oeuvre and the highly sexualized and occasionally homophobic dancehall reggae that has come to influence Miami musicians in the 1990s seems enormous. Yet it may well be the change is less from conscious politics to commercialism than it is from the Lion back to the Spider. The murder of Walter Rodney in Guyana in 1980, the coup against the New Jewel government in Grenada in 1983 (and the subsequent U.S. invasion), and the capitulation to Structural Adjustment Policies by the once militant and populist Michael Manley in Jamaica, all reflect the perils facing those who choose the Lion strategy. They make powerful enemies, provoke repression, and leave their supporters with little more than an ever-increasing list of martyrs to the cause—surely an ineffective recruiting device. Oppositional movements pay a terrible price for failure.

The Spider strategy, on the other hand, thrives especially well in times of repression and retreat. It relies on trickery and guile, on disguise and dissembling. Rather than attempting to return to a storied past or build a utopian future, it embraces the present in hopes of living to fight another day. Instead of seeking escape to a realm of purity uncontaminated by the oppressor's beliefs, institutions, and tools, it attempts to work from within to transform the very structures of oppression into mechanisms for liberation.

Louis Chude-Sokei attributes the evolution of conscious reggae into dancehall reggae partly to the political transformations of the 1980s and 1990s, to the ways in which they undermined the logic of the Lion and opened the door to the strategies of the Spider. As economic austerity devastated black communities and political repression and counterrevolution reversed the gains made by previous liberation movements the promises of black nationalism seemed more and more utopian to people struggling simply to survive. The "here and now" of hip-hop and dancehall reggae testifies to the importance of the daily battles over local resources and spaces engendered by globalization. By exploring what Chude-Sokei calls the "micro-realities, the obsessive minutiae of Jamaican urban life which holds little meaning for outsiders," dancehall reggae singers confront a standardized global culture with a music that expresses how that culture is received in a particular place and at a particular time.[60] North American hip-hop artists like Miami's Luther Campbell fulfill the same function for their listeners.

Dub poet Linton Kwesi Johnson, as eloquent as anyone in speaking like the Lion, seems to understand the strategic shift toward the Spider that has taken place in his assessment of dancehall reggae. He notes that as reggae has become increasingly influenced by Latin rap and African American hip-hop, it also paradoxically enough has become *more*

Jamaican in its rhythms. The drums and bass guitars beneath the singing of Buju Banton and Shabba Ranks clearly evoke Afro-Jamaican religious musical forms that predate reggae, especially etu, pocomania, and kumina. As the technology becomes more advanced, the rhythms become more roots-based, containing "a resonance even for quite old listeners, because it evokes back to what they first heard in rural Jamaica."[61] Perhaps the most important politics in dancehall reggae today lies in the drums and their ability to link different generations by evoking a distinct feeling of place in a world permeated by global marketing and seemingly interchangeable cultural creations. But dancehall also speaks to and from new gendered relations enacted and enabled on the dance floor, articulations of propleasure sex-affirmative sentiments in songs savored by hardworking and underpaid people, and the fusion cultures fashioned out of global migration by today's low-wage laborers everywhere around the world.

Lyrics on recent recordings by dancehall artists indicate a trend away from progun and antigay and antiwoman sentiments in favor of a more "conscious" sound that blends some of the political and moral concerns of 1970s reggae with the consumption, display, sensuality, and self-assertion of 1990s dancehall. Shootings that took the lives of key players in the dancehall scene, especially DJs Panhead and Dirtsman led Shabba Ranks, Buju Banton, and other artists to a different consciousness about violence.[62] Capleton transformed himself from a "slackness" DJ to an openly Rastafarian "cultural" artist.[63]

The popularity of Capleton and other gospel-influenced artists proved the market viability of "softer" lyrics. Yet the "hardness" of dancehall reggae remains important because it emerges from the hard and harsh realities of urban life facing people all around the world.

Miami music in recent years reveals the complex political realities that emerge from the new cognitive mapping made necessary by the rapid movements of people and products across and within national borders. Latin rap songs like Lisa M's "Jarican Jive" testify to the presence of Puerto Ricans and Jamaicans in south Florida and to the bilingual and interlingual realities and possibilities in the region. In Florida, a Puerto

Rican artist like Lisa M can be pro-Jamaican and pro-black more easily than she can in Puerto Rico where part of the nationalist project relies on suppression of Africa's contributions to the history and culture of the island.[64] Yet Miami's Latin rap can sometimes be more intercultural and progressive than the local culture would seem to produce, because they borrow from more progressive cultures in other world cities, especially New York where, as Peter Manuel points out, "Latinos, Jamaicans, and Afro-Americans have spliced their music together like a set of patchwork designer jeans."[65]

Gloria Estefan and the Miami Sound Machine's remake of "Turn the Beat Around" brings to the surface some of the repressed Cuban elements in the song, but does so by drawing on the African American soul of TK Records and Bahamian junkanoo that are the particular products of black Miami's diversity. Yet Estefan's popularity often serves to remind Miami's African Americans of the political, economic, and cultural favoritism shown to the anticommunist and anti-Castro Cuban immigrants who receive a broad range of direct and indirect government subsidies unavailable to blacks whether they are citizens or immigrants.

Luther Campbell's "Miami Bass" sound drew directly on West Indian elements in Miami's music culture, especially the "slackness" of dancehall reggae. Lyrics that would be considered mild by Jamaican standards provoked sustained legal harassment in the United States. Yet the voter registration drives that Campbell organized clearly provoked his opponents as much as his music did. At the same time, homophobic "slackness" lyrics by Shabba Ranks and Buju Banton that might not cause comment in Jamaica, raised sustained opposition in the United States where social justice advocates and gays and lesbians themselves make up significant parts of the potential constituency for dancehall music.

Contemporary Miami music cannot help but draw upon local histories of cultural connections that are both old and new at the same time. Reggae music drew some of its initial influences from rhythm and blues songs brought back to Jamaica by immigrant cane cutters in Florida as well as from broadcasts by clear-channel Miami radio stations. African American musicians like Little Beaver and Betty Wright in turn enjoyed more commercial success in the United States because of the popularity of "imported" reggae from Jamaica. KC and the Sunshine Band drew upon the Latin and rhythm and blues musics that came before them, but function today as a foundational source for nearly all Miami musicians: from Gloria Estefan and the Miami Sound Machine to Luther Campbell and 2 Live Crew, from Lisa M to Buju Banton.

Music in Miami today comes from a particular time and place. But it also reveals traces of past travel across spatial and temporal dimensions. Dancehall reggae, the Miami Bass sound in hip-hop, and a myriad of other musical styles emerging from the cultural crossroads of Miami emerge from a complicated political and social matrix. It may well be that they represent the ultimate triumph of consumer consciousness over oppositional identities. At the same time, the opposite may be true, they may represent the appropriation of the most advanced commercial and cultural technologies for oppositional ends. They reflect and shape the lived realities confronting low-wage laborers, migrants, and their families in an age of global austerity and inequality. Miami music does not sound much like the song of the Lion—at least not now, but its many forms of camouflage and covert resistance may well be singing the song of the Spider.

Yet without social movements, even the most militant oppositional impulses ultimately serve dominant purposes. The Rastafarian mobilization in Jamaica sought to create a better way of living in this world and it played an important role in a key moment of radical black nationalism. But the Rastafarians also acted to provide an alternative to self-hatred and disidentification, to lessen the deadly competition among poor and working-class blacks, to give people alternatives to the poisonous practices of consumer culture and social hierarchy. The propensities for misogyny, homophobia, and materialism within hip-hop and dancehall lyrics, and the class, caste, and national tensions that surround controversies about them, will not disappear on their own. They need to be addressed and resolved through the collective struggle and critique made possible by movements for social change.

It may be that such a movement is on the horizon, that the complex contradictions within Miami music are making it possible for people to envision and enact a shared struggle against the injustices and inequalities of the global system. It may be that like the Spider, the creators and consumers of transnational cultural forms in Miami are working behind the scenes to link the interests of low-wage workers with those of sexual minorities, to fuse the legacies of radical nationalisms with the transnational concerns of feminists, environmentalists, and anti-racists. The spider, however, always has a problem. In the course of fooling the enemy, it is possible to fool yourself at the same time. At some point, on some day, at some place, even the craftiest spider eventually has to learn to act like a lion.

CHAPTER 7

Not Just Another Social Movement

Poster Art and the Movimiento Chicano

> Changing the rules of art is not only an aesthetic problem; it
> questions the structures with which the members of the artistic
> world are used to relating to one another, and also the customs
> and beliefs of the receivers.
>
> —Néstor García Canclini, *Hybrid Cultures*

Early in January 2001, the University Art Museum at the University of
California–Santa Barbara opened the exhibition "Just Another Poster,"
celebrating thirty years of Chicano poster art. The posters on display
revealed a hidden history of the Chicano movement. They documented
the struggles of *braceros* and Brown Berets, of boycotts and ballot initiatives, of antiwar activism and immigrant self-defense. They presented a
permanent record of mass mobilizations and community coalitions
against police brutality, educational inequality, and economic exploitation. They evoked the Movimiento Chicano in all its rich complexities
and contradictions, a movement both nationalist *and* internationalist,
class conscious *and* culturalist, reformist *and* revolutionary. The posters
provided a rich repository of the iconography, idealism, and imagination
that propelled the movement to significant victories in the past and that
help account for its enduring presence in the hearts and minds of many
people to this day.[1]

The images in the exhibition were not just pictures, they were
posters: multiples designed for quick, inexpensive production and mass
distribution.[2] They were created for everyday use in homes and offices,
on bulletin boards and lamp posts, in schools and community centers.
Posters advertised art exhibitions, concerts, and theatrical productions
aimed at Chicano audiences. They alerted community residents about

forthcoming protest demonstrations and mass meetings. They nurtured and sustained collective memory by commemorating important moments of struggle in Mexican and Mexican American history. They proclaimed solidarity with other aggrieved communities of color in the United States and with nationalist struggles against colonial domination all around the world. The dazzling designs and accessible images that permeated these posters reflected the imagination and artistry of their creators to be sure, but they also owed much to the practical imperatives of the poster form: to attract attention, communicate clearly, and encapsulate a complex message in a compressed form.

Unlike art created primarily for the approval of critics or for display in galleries and museums, posters functioned as crucial components of a Chicano public sphere created by community-based artists and activists at the grass roots. No one invited the creators of these posters to become artists; they invited themselves. They acted in one of the few arenas open to them with the tools they had at hand. René Yañez explains the establishment of the Galeria de la Raza in San Francisco's Mission District as a matter of necessity. "Museums were not exhibiting Chicanos, galleries were not exhibiting Chicanos," Yañez recalls, "so we felt we had to take destiny into our own hands."[3] At a time when their enemies controlled almost all the major mechanisms of the public sphere—radio and television stations, newspapers, advertising agencies, schools, museums, conservatories, and art galleries—Chicano activist artists created forms of agitation and education through creative use of silkscreen and photo-offset images.

The art on display in the Santa Barbara exhibition was not just a secondary reflection of a social movement so powerful that it generated its own artistic images; rather, posters functioned as part of the movement itself, as vital mechanisms that performed important tasks in the struggle for social change. Today, they provide us with a "materials memory" as artifacts that helped call a movement into being through artistic expression. In addition to publicizing particular events and educating the community about individual issues, posters also played crucial roles as emblems of organic solidarity and as instruments of collective ideology.

Oppositional movements have to nurture and sustain an insurgent consciousness. They need to inventory the shared experiences and common conditions that make collective action necessary. They must create individuals capable of locating themselves inside the shared history of their social group, and they need to encourage people to take risks to bring about systemic change. Oppositional movements must talk back to power, they must oppose, invert, subvert, and ironicize ideas and images that support the status quo. They need to lead people toward affiliations and alliances that can sustain them in the present and lead to transfers of resources in the future. Movements have to create spaces for social change—figuratively by using memory and imagination to expand the realities and possibilities of the present, but also literally by creating physical places, institutions, and events where the hoped-for future makes itself felt in the present. Movement spaces are important as sites for direct oppositional activity, but they are also essential as crucibles for the creation of new kinds of people—activists, artists, and community leaders—individuals speaking clearly and acting confidently, people emboldened by the energy and the imagination of the moment. Within the Chicano movement, poster production emerged as one of the important sites where insurgent consciousness could be created, nurtured, and sustained.[4]

The posters presented an extensive array of images, icons, signs, and symbols evoking the shared social history and the common collective memory of people of Mexican origin in the United States. Victor Ochoa's *Border Bingo/Lotería Fronteriza* follows the format of a lottery card in presenting the perils that confront immigrants at the U.S.-Mexico border. Herbert Siguenza also uses a *lotería* motif in *Drug Abuse and AIDS: Don't Play Lottery with Your Life*. A zoot-suited *pachuco* stands in the spotlight in José Montoya's *Recuerdos del Paloma*. José Cervantes superimposes an Aztec/UFW eagle over a dove in *Que Viva La Paz*, while *La Virgen de Guadelupe* disguised in the form of Los Angeles's best-known civic building provides the central image in Alfredo De Batuc's *Seven Views of City Hall*. Ester Hernandez depicts *La Virgen* as a karate fighter in *La Virgen de Guadalupe Defendiendo los Derechos de los Xicanos* and as a tattooed image on a woman's back in *La Ofrenda*, a work that also testifies to the power and beauty of desire between women.[5] Cholos in baggy pants sporting headbands appear in Juan Fuentes's *Cholo Live*, while John Valadez features the Pendleton shirt in his humorous tribute to barrio style, *Cholo*.

Louie "The Foot" González and Ricardo Favela make a jalapeño pepper the central icon in their satirical *Royal Order of the Jalapeño*. This poster purports to be a certificate awarded to Chicanas and Chicanos who continue to display bicultural *locura* despite years in assimilationist institutions of higher education. The same artists mine collective memory and "insider" knowledge via an interlingual pun in their poster *Cortés Nos Chingó in a Big Way, the Hüey*.[6] A stunning display of graffiti calligraphy provides the focus for Chaz Bojórquez's *New World Order*, while home altars and photo displays inform the imagery of René Yañez's *Historical Photo Silk Screen Movie*, John Valadez's *Day of the Dead*, and Richard Duardo's *Zero, Zero*.

Connections between the historical struggles of the past and the political imperatives of the present permeate Chicano posters. Images from Mexican history punctuate Leonard Castellanos's *RIFA*, Ralph Maradiaga's *First Annual Arte de Los Barrios*, Manuel Cruz's *Viva Villa*, Victor Ochoa's *Border Mezz-teez-o*, and Rodolfo "Rudy" Cuellar's poster for Fiestas Patrias—*Celebración de Independencia de 1810*. Xavier Viramontes places Aztec imagery at the service of the United Farm Workers in his *Boycott Grapes: Support the United Farmworkers Union*. The memory of Los Angeles journalist Ruben Salazar is honored in Rupert Garcia's haunting 1970 silkscreen advertising the *Ruben Salazar Memorial Group Show* as well as in Leo Limón's poster announcing the 1979 opening of Teatro Urbano's play *Silver Dollar* about Salazar's murder during the 1970 Chicano Moratorium demonstration in Los Angeles.[7]

In addition to their inventory of images and their evocations of important moments in Mexican and Chicano history, these posters also make direct appeals for action. In their posters titled *Yes on 14*, Louie "The Foot" González and Max Garcia try to mobilize voters on behalf of a ballot initiative backed by the United Farm Workers. Similarly,

Andrew Zermeño's *Huelga!* and Ricardo Favela's *Huelga! Strike! Support the U.F.W.A.* employ art in the service of that union's picket lines and organizing drives. Works by as yet unidentified artists publicize boycotts against Gallo Wines and Coors Beer. Franco Mendoza's *Peligro! Deportación* invites people to a demonstration against proposed changes in immigration law.

Oppositional movements ask people to take risks, to imperil their security in the present in hopes of building a better future. Often it is not sufficient to stress shared cultural signs and symbols, the legacy of past struggles, or the urgency of impending actions. Building insurgent consciousness entails speaking back to power, subverting its authority, and inverting its icons as a means of authorizing oppositional thinking and behavior. Yolanda López accomplishes this by subverting and inverting a cluster of nationalist and nativist American icons in her compelling *Who's the Illegal Alien, Pilgrim?*

Through a poster designed to defend undocumented immigrants from the dehumanizing phrase "illegal aliens," López presents an indigenous Mexican warrior facing forward and pointing at the viewer in a manner reminiscent of the "Uncle Sam Wants You" recruiting posters that decorated public spaces in the United States throughout the twentieth century. The caption plays with a phrase made famous by John Wayne in the film *The Man Who Shot Liberty Valance* in which he referred repeatedly to the character played by Jimmy Stewart—a newcomer to the West—as "pilgrim." López's poster asks *Who's the Illegal Alien, Pilgrim?* Her question inverts the moral hierarchy of the discourse about "illegal aliens" by connecting the conquest of lands previously owned by Mexico to the actions of nineteenth-century Anglo "illegal aliens" who crossed the border to take Mexican land illegally. The intertextuality of López's poster makes a joke out of the icons of the dominant culture and uses laughter and ridicule to "uncrown power" and build insurgent consciousness. It turns "illegal aliens" into the aggrieved original residents of the region, and appropriates the ideological legitimacy and discursive authority of Uncle Sam and John Wayne for oppositional ends.

López's appropriation and inversion of icons from advertising and

Yolanda M. Lopez, "Who's the Illegal Alien, Pilgrim?" offset lithograph, Special Collections, University of California, Santa Barbara. In an attempt to question the meaning of "illegal alien," the most widely used anti-immigrant slur, Lopez's poster reveals that Anglos are the original border-crossers. Her imagery borrows from the "Uncle Sam Wants You" army recruiting posters traditionally displayed in U.S. government buildings, and the title borrows from a catchphrase made famous by John Wayne in the film *The Man Who Shot Liberty Valance*. Reproduced by permission of the artist.

entertainment evidences a strategy that emerges often in Chicano poster art. Ester Hernandez's 1982 *Sun Mad* illustrates the dangers posed to farm workers and consumers by indiscriminate use of pesticides on crops through a devastatingly effective parody of the Sun Maid raisin brand label. Hernandez echoes the design, lettering, and colors of the Sun Maid raisin box, but substitutes a skeleton for the usual image of an attractive young woman holding a basket of grapes. Lalo Alcaraz mocks advertising and politicians who foment fear of immigrants in *Fraid*, a poster that depicts a politician holding a can designed like the Raid brand insect repellent and boasting that "anti-immigrant spray" lasts for up to two elections![8]

Alcaraz's 1992 *White Men Can't (Run the System)* ridicules the responses by then Los Angeles Police Chief Darryl Gates and then President George Bush to the riots of that year. The poster parodies advertisements for the motion picture *White Men Can't Jump* by depicting Gates and Bush in the poses and costumes associated with Woody Harrelson and Wesley Snipes in the film. Similarly, Ricardo Duffy's *The New Order* appropriates imagery from Marlboro Cigarette billboards to portray George Washington against a border backdrop where the INS hunts down immigrants with the help of the barriers created by the passage of Proposition 187. Malaquias Montoya's moving *The Immigrant's Dream: The American Response* offers yet another inversion of dominant icons, depicting an immigrant firmly bound up inside an American flag in front of a barbed-wire fence. Alcaraz's 1997 *Che* contrasts the revolutionary aspirations of the past with the neoliberal realities of the present through a silkscreen depicting the Argentinian-born hero of the Cuban Revolution with a Nike "swoosh" on the front of his familiar black beret.

Poster images reinforced organic solidarity within the Chicano movement, but they also helped create connecting ideologies to link *chicanismo* with anticolonial nationalist struggles around the world. Informed by images of international solidarity prominent in Cuban poster art during the 1960s, infuriated by the massacre of protesting students in Mexico City shortly before the 1968 Olympics, and inspired by the affinities between antiracist campaigns in the United States and anticolonial movements overseas, Chicano artists gave broad exposure to international issues in their posters. Rupert Garcia's 1970 *Fuera de Indochina!* offers a graphic protest against the war in Vietnam, while Malaquias Montoya's *Chicano/Vietnam/Aztlan* emphasizes affinities between Chicanos and the Vietnamese people.[9] Linda Lucero pays tribute to the Puerto Rican struggle for independence in her 1978 *Lolita Lebrón*, a poster honoring the revolutionary nationalist who stormed onto the floor of the U.S. House of Representatives in 1954, fired shots at the ceiling, unfurled a Puerto Rican flag, and shouted "Free Puerto Rico now."[10] Hemispheric solidarity against totalitarianism takes center stage in Malaquias Montoya's silkscreen announcing a 1977 demonstration commemorating the first year of military dictatorship in Argentina and his 1979 serigraph protesting against loans made by Wells Fargo Bank to bolster the Pinochet dictatorship in Chile. In the wake of escalating U.S. military counterinsurgency in support of the right-wing government of El Salvador in the early 1980s, Herbert Sigüenza produced *It's Simple Steve...*, a parody of Roy Lichtenstein's 1960s parodies of popular comic strips. In Sigüenza's poster a dark-haired woman explains to a blonde Anglo male, "It's simple Steve. Why don't you and your boys just get the f—— out of El Salvador!" At about the same time, Louie "The Foot" González created a vivid poster for the Salvadorean People's Support Committee. Five years later Yreina Cervántes celebrated Chicano–Central American interactions with her poster *El Pueblo Chicano Con El Pueblo CentroAmericano.* Mark Vallen's *Sandinista* and an unidentified artist's *Poetry for the Nicaraguan Resistance* express solidarity with forces in Nicaragua under attack by the covert and overt support given to the "contras" by the U.S. government. These posters demonstrate the simultaneous nationalism and internationalism of the Movimiento Chicano. Although the movement has often been caricatured (in retrospect) as a product of "identity" politics, these posters show it to have entailed an intensely ideological effort to give an expressly political character to the term "Chicano." The internationalism, class consciousness, and solidarity with struggles for social justice among other aggrieved groups manifest in these posters reveals that the movement was an effort to convince people to draw their identity from their politics rather than drawing their politics from their identity.

Alliances with and affinities for struggles for social justice by other aggrieved groups in the United States also serve a central role for Chicano poster artists. Rolo Castillo's 1993 poster featuring two U.S. flags on fire and upside down announces a benefit concert for Leonard Peltier, a Native American activist wrongly convicted of murder in the aftermath of the American Indian Movement's 1973 direct action protest in South Dakota. One of the musical groups performing at the concert was Rage Against the Machine, a band fronted by Zach de la Rocha, son of Chicano artist Beto de la Rocha. In posters that did not appear in the Santa Barbara exhibition but are housed in the Special Collections at the University of California–Santa Barbara library, the San Francisco Poster Brigade publicized the international boycott of Nestle's because of that company's efforts to market infant formula to nursing mothers in Africa, supported efforts by elderly Filipinos to avoid eviction from San Francisco's International Hotel, and promoted solidarity efforts on behalf of striking coal miners in Stearns, Kentucky. Ricardo Favela announced a fundraiser for an African American politician in his 1972 *Announcement Poster for Willie Brown*, and José Montoya made an announcement poster in 1985 for the first annual American Indian–Chicano unity day. Montoya created a 1970 poster mobilizing public opinion against a pending piece of legislation in the California State Assembly, and Louie "The Foot" González did a poster for *International Women's Year* in 1975.[11]

Chicano posters signal the emergence of new spaces for oppositional activity. They create networks of people with the same images in their homes, in their neighborhoods, and at their places of work. Leonard Castellanos argued in 1975 that mural artists had turned the street into "the alternate educational system," into a place where "the *muralista* is rewarded with an audience reaction."[12] Just as gigantic murals turn empty walls at busy intersections into affirmations of community pride and expressions of collective history, posters call attention to the interiors of the places where Chicanos live and work. In dialogue with the art displayed on calendars circulated to Chicano families by bakeries and other small businesses in many barrios, poster artists turn to the calendar as a key form for inserting their visions into the home. Carlos Almaraz's *Corazon del Pueblo* uses black UFW/Aztec eagles to accentuate the orange and yellow colors of a calendar for February 1976. Gilbert "Magu" Luján's *April Calendar* for 1977 makes a dramatic plea for an end to gang warfare, while Manuel Cruz uses each bullet in Pancho Villa's ammunition belt to signify a different day in July 1977. Many posters draw on forms of representation controlled by Chicanas in working-class homes—especially religious and family altars, home decorations, healing kits, and personal fashions and styles.[13] The images of *La Virgen de Gaudalupe* by Ester Hernandez and Alfredo De Batuc, the Day of the Dead imagery of Willie Herrón, John Valadez, and Eduardo Oropeza, and the toys featured in Ralph Maradiaga's *Lost Childhood* all evoke the art of interior spaces in Chicano homes.

While refiguring domestic space for political purposes, Chicano poster art also calls attention to new kinds of public spaces and new roles for people to play within them. Juan Cervantes's 1975 silkscreen publicizes a Symposium for Third World Writers and Thinkers. Linda Lucero's *Expression Chicana* promotes an art show in the Mills College Dining Room in Oakland. Esteban Villa's *Cinco de Mayo Con El RCAF* advertises a southern California show by the Royal Chicano Air Force (Rebel Chicano Art Front) from Sacramento, a *centro* committed to inserting art into activist struggles. Yreina Cervántes's 1979 poster announces an exhibit of Raza Women in the Arts, but it also invites viewers to participate in "breaking the silence" about artistic production by Chicanas. Her extraordinary 1983 *Danza Ocelotl* calls attention to activities at the Self-Help Graphics centro in Los Angeles, an *atelier* established with the express purpose of encouraging Chicanos to purchase and display art prints in their homes. Artist Willie Herron used the small studio space upstairs at Self-Help Graphics in Los Angeles as a rehearsal room for his punk rock music aggregation, *Los Illegals*. With the help of Self-Help's director, Sister Karen Boccalero from the Order of Sisters of St. Francis, Herron founded and operated a nightclub at the site to encourage outsiders to come to the barrio to hear Chicano punk and to develop the skills and reputations of *punkeros* so they would have opportunities to play in venues in other parts of the city.[14]

Artistic and intellectual spaces are important to social movements because they create places where people can try out new ideas and new identities. They bring together artists and activists. They create a common fund of knowledge about tactics, techniques, and traditions of struggle. They function as "movement halfway houses"—eccentric places that are neither completely absorbed into the dominant power structure nor directly involved in activism for social change. Consequently, they appeal to community members, but are less vulnerable to the forms of repression that oppositional political organizations frequently face.[15]

Social movements also open up artistic production to people previously excluded from access to arts education and resources. Silkscreen serigraph poster production is often an entry-level art form, a method that inexperienced artists explore before moving on to oil painting, assemblage, and mixed-media productions. Part of the appeal of the silkscreen for activist artists stems from its economy and efficiency; it requires no printing press, enables large runs without deterioration of the matrix (the screen), and can be produced completely by hand. Many of the artists in the Santa Barbara exhibition made their first publicly exhibited art in the form of posters, and later took up careers as artists as a result. Louie "The Foot" González took his nickname because he was employed as a postal carrier when he started making posters. Ester Hernandez drew inspiration for her classic *Sun Mad* poster from political critiques of pesticide use advanced by the United Farm Workers union, but also from her own personal experiences as a farm worker who had suffered from exposure to pesticides in the fields.[16] Patssi Valdez participated in ASCO's famous "Instant Mural" and "Walking Mural" and in 1987 made the silkscreen *Scattered* that appeared in the Santa Barbara exhibition. Yet without the movement, she might never have become an artist. Valdez remembers her high school home economics teacher telling the "little Mexicans" in the class to pay special attention to the course because "most of you are going to be cooking and cleaning for other people."[17] Chicano artist Harry Gamboa Jr. remembers learning similar lessons at school and in the streets when he was growing up in Los Angeles in the 1950s. "We were taught that American society was a melting pot," he recalls, "but on closer inspection many of us were scalded and permanently scarred."[18]

The partisan, perspectival, and practical imperatives that permeate Chicano posters lead some critics and art historians to relegate poster production to the marginal status of "community-based art making." The "amateur" status of poster artists and art collectives and the historical, political, and social specificity of their images devalue posters as art in the eyes of many critics. Traditionalists tend to view posters as too commercial and contemporary to qualify as "folk art," while modernists tend to consider them insufficiently complex, novel, or difficult to be "modern art." As Néstor García Canclini observes, both traditionalists and modernizers seek "pure" objects—either works of folk art that express an "authentic" national culture uncontaminated by outsiders or modernist works that invoke art for art's sake through "autonomous experimentation and innovation."[19] Although the posters in the Santa Barbara exhibition reveal that their creators know a great deal about both modern and traditional art, for the most part, the posters do not have purity as their project. They aim instead at an art that builds audience investment and engagement by mixing modern and folk forms into a new synthesis. They combine the accessibility of commercial culture with "insider" signs and symbols based on common folk forms. They mix references to modern art with advertising logos and social movement slogans. They explore crossroads, connections, borders, and boundaries.

Standards of artistic evaluation that separate art from politics do a disservice to both. C. L. R. James reminds us that the classic dramatists of Greek antiquity—Aeschylus, Sophocles, Euripedes, Aristophanes—achieved greatness because they worked in popular forms to address the core crises and contradictions of their society. They wrote for the masses about the things that mattered in their lives.[20] Canons of criticism that validate art objects because they can be seen expressing a "pure" folk imagination or a "pure" modernist sensibility ultimately trivialize rather than elevate art. Fantasies that folk art emerges free from the constraints of commerce and history may make folk art objects valuable commodities in metropolitan centers, but they do so only by obscuring the actual social relations that shape artistic production and consumption. The dream of an art capable of reconciling individuals from antagonistic social positions into an appreciation of their common "humanity" depends upon treating one historically specific set of social experiences as if it were universal and human while discounting and devaluing experiences outside that realm as always inferior. An art safely insulated from social causes and consequences can be little more than embellishment or ornamentation. As García Canclini concludes, these ideologies about aesthetics leave little of importance to art except the task of representing disturbances and transgressions in such a way as to guarantee that "they do not disturb the general order of society."[21]

Rather than thinking about Chicano poster art as "community-based art making," I think it is more productive to view it as a form of art-based community making. This is not to claim, of course, that no Chicano community existed before the posters appeared. It is to say, however, that the emergence of the term "Chicano" (and the political and cultural activities that accompanied it) expressed a collective project of self-definition that helped give people of Mexican origin in the United States a radical and political definition of themselves that amounted to much more than a shared ancestry and country of origin. As David Gutiérrez demonstrates in his important book *Walls and Mirrors*, the rise of the Chicano movement provided a radical alternative to the assimilationist paradigm embodied in the term "Mexican-American." Over the years the hyphen in the word "Mexican-American" came to be seen as an arrow implying a desired and necessary movement from being "Mexican" to becoming "American." The term "Chicano" and the movement that emerged around it provided a way of rejecting the deracination and self-hatred embedded in the assimilation model, a way of forging alliances with other aggrieved communities of color, a way of ending antagonisms between new and old immigrant cohorts by describing Chicanos as a people united across borders, and a way of giving a working-class egalitarian accent to collective community politics.[22] Ruben Salazar encapsulated these complex processes in a crisp formulation in 1970: "A Chicano is a Mexican American who does not have an Anglo image of himself."[23]

Chicano poster art played an important role in articulating, illustrating, shaping, and refining the identity it expressed. As Laura Mulvey argues, moving from oppression and its mythologies to a stance of self-definition is a difficult process and requires people with social grievances to construct a long chain of countermyths and symbols.[24] For a people ridiculed, marginalized, and discounted by cultural signs they do not control, insurgent cultural production can be a great equalizer.[25] These posters are powerful because they speak to urgent needs and desires. It is an art that people create in order to stay alive, to view themselves as human, to speak back to power, and to envision a fulfilled future as a way of rendering the painful parts of the present as merely provisional, relative, contingent, and temporary.

Just as Chicano poster art is better art *because of* rather than *in spite of* its political dimensions, the politics of Chicano poster production are effective as politics in part because they rely so strongly on culture as a key category in people's lives. In recent years, Richard Rorty, Todd Gitlin, Martha Nussbaum, and others have attributed the weaknesses of contemporary movements for social justice to their inordinate preoccupation with culture. Rorty charges that "an activist" and political opposition has been replaced by a passive and "spectatorial, cultural" opposition.[26] Yet these posters show how cultural contestation and campaigns for social justice are mutually constitutive. People cannot enact new social relations unless they can envision them. But they cannot envision new social relations credibly unless they are enacted in embryonic form in their own lives. Often cultural creation bridges these needs.

Innovative forms of artistic expression often appear precisely because of social upheaval, ferment, and revolution. Chicano poster art fuses culture and politics in an art form that emerged because of the new possibilities produced by a social struggle that was itself augmented by a long history of cultural creativity and contestation.

In 1976, Louie "The Foot" González created the work of art that provided the University Art Museum in Santa Barbara with the title for their exhibition, "This Is Just Another Poster." González's title encapsulates the playful insouciance of an art that is modest, unassuming, and sometimes self-deprecating but at the same time provocative, powerful, and profound. The presentation of posters in an exhibition is a tribute to the artists who produced them, to be sure, but also to the social movement from which they emerged. The Chicano movement expressed the hopes and aspirations of people with unique perspectives on contemporary society. These posters bear witness to the things Chicano artists and audiences see with their own eyes: rural workers poisoned by pesticides in the fields and urban laborers undermined by union busting campaigns, low wages, and unsafe working conditions; school children taught to despise their language, history, and culture in overcrowded and underfunded schools; immigrants incarcerated, exploited, and brutalized by a society that wants their labor but refuses to recognize their humanity.

These harsh realities present a challenge to the honesty and integrity of everyone, but to artists most of all. As Harry Gamboa Jr. observes,

> The Chicano artist who chooses to make statements on the neocolonial quality of barrio life, who decides to express concerns over contemporary racist public/private policies, who comments on the unequal sharing of America's souring pie, is most certainly going to find it difficult to achieve the rewards which are available to less socially and politically threatening artists.[27]

Yet the movement and the conditions that made it necessary are not over. The circumstances Chicanos and all aggrieved social groups face are not the same as the ones that produced the Movimiento Chicano in the 1960s. The signs and symbols, the terms and tactics of struggle today cannot be encompassed entirely by the images in the Santa Barbara exhibition. But the struggle goes on. Social movements from the recent past—even those that fail—often play a crucial role in creating successful strategies, tactics, and ways of working in the present. As issues of identity and culture increasingly shape struggles for social justice, Chicano poster art and the movement from which it emerged become even more important models for transformative cultural and political work. They keep alive in the present the enduring example of a social movement that deftly combined cultural concerns and political projects, that attended to the economy and to the imagination, that incorporated nationalism and internationalism, and that inaugurated alternative academies where people without credentials from established institutions could develop their skills as artists and activists. For all of its shortcomings, omissions, exclusions, and tactical miscalculations, the Movimiento Chicano is not just another social movement from the past, but rather one of the most generative sources for social and cultural change available to us today.

CHAPTER 8

As Unmarked as Their Place in History

Genre Anxiety and Race in Seventies Cinema

> Genres hold the world in place, establishing and enforcing a
> sense of propriety, of proper boundaries which demarcate
> appropriate thought, feeling, and behavior and which provide
> frames, codes, and signs for constructing a shared social reality.
>
> —Michael Ryan and Douglas Kellner, *Camera Politica*

> Genres are at once fluid and static. Their boundaries continu-
> ally shift and adapt, but once they announce themselves, genres
> depend on distinct icons and codes. In addition, because
> generic icons encode ideology, a genre's form and content
> express ideological traces (what Fredric Jameson
> has called "sedimented ideologemes") through structure,
> plot, and characterization.
>
> —Paula Rabinowitz, *Labor and Desire*

Generic pleasures are familiar pleasures. Genre conventions encourage
the repetition, reconfiguration, and renewal of familiar forms in order
to cultivate audience investment and engagement. Created mostly for
the convenience of marketers anxious to predict exact sales figures by
selling familiar products to clearly identifiable audiences, genres also
have ideological effects. Their conventions contribute to an ahistorical
view of the world as always the same. The pleasures of predictability
encourage an investment in the status quo. Yet genres can also have
affinities with certain social positions. The serio-comic novel speaks to
aggrieved groups because it reverberates with a carnival-like laughter
that uncrowns power according to Mikhail Bakhtin. The romance novel,

in Janice Radway's analysis, appeals to women because it airs the injustices of domestic life and acknowledges the misrecognitions women encounter in relationships.

Sometimes, small changes in generic forms serve as a register of broader alterations in society at large. In moments of crisis, old stories may seem inadequate or at least incomplete. Pressing problems of the present may intrude into seemingly fixed genres. Even in less hectic times, the marketing imperatives of mass culture that generate genres in the first place can also encourage change because the need for novel ways to attract new audiences works against the promise of predictable pleasure implicit in any generic form.

Because genres involve classification and categorization, they have important ideological effects. Jacques Derrida connects generic thinking to the kinds of binary oppositions that divide people by gender, race, and class. "As soon as genre announces itself," he argues, "one must respect a norm, one must not cross a line of demarcation, one must not risk impurity, anomaly, or monstrosity."[1] Generic codes often connect activity to identity, reserving clearly defined roles for distinctly gendered, classed, and raced characters. Their conventions often encode social hierarchies as necessary and inevitable. In the United States, they emerge within what Nick Browne calls "a gender-racial-economic system built as much on what it prohibits as on what it permits."[2]

Race plays a crucial role in generic representations. Hollywood westerns, war movies, detective stories, melodramas, and action/adventure films often rely on racial imagery, underscoring the heroism of white males by depicting them as defenders of women and children against predatory Indians, Asians, blacks, and Mexicans. They use racial differences to signal zones of danger and refuge; they move toward narrative and ideological closure by restoring the white hero to his "rightful" place in the cinematic system. As Browne contends, race is the political unconscious of American cinema, and it is important to see that in any given time period consistent changes in cultural texts are not purely aesthetic gestures, but also reflections of broader structural and social changes. Browne points out, for example, how increased representations of Asians and Asian Americans in Hollywood films after World War II emerged in tandem with U.S. economic and political interests in Asia.

The racial crises of the 1960s in the United States gave rise to "genre anxiety," to changes in generic forms created by adding unconventional racial elements to conventional genre films.[3] The emergence of those films, their subsequent eclipse later in the 1970s by changes in Hollywood's marketing and production strategies, and their subsequent return in many films about "minority" issues during the 1980s and 1990s can best be understood not in aesthetic terms alone, but also as a sensitive register of dynamic changes in social relations.

Filmmakers from aggrieved racial communities have particularly complicated relationships with genres. To attract audience investment and engagement, they need to cater to the conventions of genre expectations. Often they find it necessary to displace the conservative effects of previous representations, not just by adding on new racial characters or settings, but by using race as a way of disrupting and restructuring genre conventions themselves.

Sidney Poitier's 1971 revisionist "western" movie *Buck and the Preacher* provides an emblematic example of genre anxiety in a moment of social crisis. It begins with a printed paragraph that scrolls down the screen, introducing the film as a story about one of the groups of freed slaves who fled to the West to build a home for themselves and their families during the 1860s and 1870s to escape the white supremacist terror in the postwar South. The scroll presents the film as a tribute to people resting "in graves as unmarked as their place in history."

By calling attention to the erasure of black migration to the West from history books, *Buck and the Preacher* announces its intention to make visible what has previously been invisible. But it is not only the black "exodusters" who went west after the Civil War who become visible because of this film. The departures in *Buck and the Preacher* from the norms established by previous western films and historical narratives make viewers self-conscious about the previous Hollywood films we have seen and the previous historical accounts we have read. After viewing Poitier's film, the western movie and the history of the West no longer seem invisible, but instead they become conspicuous as fabrications that direct our attention away from some stories in order to focus on others. After viewing this film, Hollywood films and historical accounts lose their innocence and their invisibility, but they become more visible as technologies of racialization.

The opening credits of *Buck and the Preacher* announce its revisionist intentions. Even before a single image appears on the screen, the film presents us with a musical pun. The sounds of harmonica, slide guitar, and jaw harp played by Sonny Terry and Brownie McGhee in traditional folk style sound ambiguously like the contemporary synthesizer and electric guitar scores of other 1970s films about African Americans like *Shaft* and *Superfly*. The music situates us in both the past and the present at the same time. The first visual images we see are sepia-tone "still" photos of nineteenth-century western buildings and landscapes with the names of the film's stars superimposed over them. Then photos of black settlers in wagon trains heading west follow underneath the remaining credits.

The invocation of hard times, physical repression, and the disillusioned aftermath of a period of turmoil announces a revisionist approach to the 1870s, but the musical sounds and social themes presented speak to the realities of the 1970s as well. The film's combination of story, music, and images thus announces an intention to do more than honor bodies marked in unmarked graves. The parallels between the 1970s and the 1870s—between the betrayal of the freedom won during the Civil War and the unfolding betrayal of the civil rights movement in the 1970s—make *Buck and the Preacher* a film that speaks to the present while purporting to depict the past. The interruptions that it attempts to enact on the nation's history take tangible and visceral form through its interruptions of the generic conventions of the Hollywood western movie. As the technologies of historical narratives become visible, as the lives of people lying in unmarked graves come into view, the politics of the present also appears before us in indirect and coded, but nonetheless unmistakably clear representations.

As the film's action begins, the stills turn to moving pictures. Poitier (as the character Buck) rides toward the camera, and the sepia turns to full color. Stillness turns to action, monochrome images give way to a broader palette of colors. Both of these visual and technical changes prefigure what will happen in the story; previously passive people take action and people of "color" (African Americans) oppressed by whites find that they must examine their relationships with other people of color—in this case, Native Americans—in order to win their battle.

A social crisis in society at large during the 1970s shaped the changes in the generic representations on the screen in *Buck and the Preacher*. Poitier's film contained many traditional icons of the western film—a wagon train of settlers heading west, Indians on the warpath, and a troop of armed men wearing blue coats and hats with crossed cavalry swords on them. In a generic western, the settlers would turn to the blue-coated riders to protect them from the Indians. But in *Buck and the Preacher*, the wagon train is made up of blacks running away from the post–Civil War South. The Indians on the warpath do not threaten the wagon train, indeed at a crucial moment in the film they ride to its rescue. The men in blue coats and cavalry hats are white racist thugs, "labor recruiters" from Louisiana, seeking to intimidate the settlers and make them return to work as sharecroppers for their former slave masters. "There's a whole way of life back there [Louisiana] that's going down the drain," one of them vows, "we don't aim to see it frittered away."[4] With enemies like these, the settlers see the Indians as potential allies.

An element of overdetermination infuses the impact of *Buck and the Preacher*. Its images have meaning for us, in part, because we have seen them so many times before. Poitier, for instance, brings his entire reputation and previous screen personas to his performance in the starring role. Having reaped critical and commercial reward for the dignified parts he played throughout the 1960s, Poitier found himself under attack by many race-conscious blacks by the early 1970s for the monotony and political complicity they saw in these roles. Poitier's critics lambasted him as the black man whites most loved to see, as "St. Sidney," because his roles always had an antiseptic quality to them, confining him to soft-spoken, quiet, patient, asexual, and unthreatening parts. With *Buck and the Preacher*, Poitier (the director) not only attempted to transform the conventions of the western genre, but he also tried to transform the image of Poitier (the actor) by departing from audience expectations and giving himself a role that enabled him to display physical strength and courage, that presented him as a devoted, loving, and sexual partner with his black wife.

In its challenge to historical narratives and Hollywood norms, *Buck and the Preacher* could not simply reverse racial roles, making white men the villains and people of color the heroes. Blacks and Indians cannot so easily assume the heroic roles reserved for whites in western lore, largely because the virtues imputed to whites in these films depend upon the denigration or demonization of people of color. We learn how poorly the conventional western fares in representing these realities in a dramatic scene, when the wagon master (Sidney Poitier as Buck) speaks through an interpreter and asks for aid from the chief of an Indian tribe whose land the settlers must traverse in their flight to freedom. After paying a sum of money to guarantee safe passage and to compensate for the game they will kill on their journey, Buck tells the chief his group needs guns to win their freedom. But the Indian leader refuses. Buck attempts to assert a bond between blacks and Indians, pointing out that his fellow blacks cannot return to Louisiana and will have to fight their way to freedom. Buck claims that they have the same enemies, but the chief reminds him that black soldiers fought for the United States Army against his people. "Tell him I ain't in the army no more," Buck tells the translator, but she just turns away and says, "He knows, Buck."

The scene has few parallels within the western genre. It also makes an uncanny connection to events off-screen. In the midst of the Vietnam War, the film challenges black soldiers to question how their inclusion in the U.S. nation-state through participation in the military might make them complicit in a war for the very white supremacy that oppresses them at home. Although Buck eventually leads the wagon train to freedom, we know that neither the blacks nor the Indians are really safe, that the broken promises of the Reconstruction era that send the wagon train west in the film persist in the present through the broken promises of the civil rights era. By challenging the integrity of the frontier myth and showing the internal and external contradictions of nineteenth-century U.S. society, *Buck and the Preacher* destabilizes the western itself, undercutting its status as a foundational story about origins in order to expose the contradictions it has always served to conceal. There can be no uninterrogated heroism in *Buck and the Preacher* because the heroism of the frontier always depends upon genocide.

The tasks confronting an oppositional filmmaker like Poitier come into sharp relief when we consider the images and genre conventions they have to displace in order to tell their stories their way. John Avildsen provides a particularly vivid example of what they are up against, of the conservative consequences of generic traditions, in the opening credits of his 1989 film, *Lean on Me*. Through a series of vignettes depicting a world out of control, the director introduces viewers to life at Eastside High School in Paterson, New Jersey. With a heavy metal song by Guns N' Roses ("Welcome to the Jungle") playing in the background, titles announcing the names of the actors and production personnel appear superimposed over scenes of violence in the graffiti-covered hallways and classrooms of the high school. Black thugs surround a white male and rough him up. A well-dressed black teacher opens his executive briefcase and takes out drugs to sell to a student. A group of black girls humiliate a white classmate in the bathroom, ripping her blouse off her body. When she runs screaming into the crowded hallway, a black female teacher tries to cover and console her, fending off the advances of leering and grinning black males who surround the two women. A white teacher tries to break up a fight in the cafeteria, but winds up getting his head cracked open as one of the students brutally pounds it against the concrete floor. Finally, older black boys push a rotund black youth into a locker, close the door on him, and walk away. As he pounds on the door and yells "Somebody help, please, somebody help," a black janitor reading a newspaper aimlessly ambles down the empty hall, unconcerned about the student in the locker or his cries for assistance.

In this montage, Avildsen offers us images that prefigure his film as a story about pollution and violation. Litter and graffiti in the school building provide a background of dirtiness and decay for the violations of persons, property, and propriety that follow. The student's plea for help that closes the credits prepares us for a drama about a black educator purportedly bringing law and order to this inner-city high school. Although the story is a contemporary one, the images that activate it rely on genre conventions that reach back to the early days of film.[5]

The scenes behind the opening credits for *Lean on Me* portray black people as boisterous, brutal, licentious, and lazy. In order to underscore the danger and disorder in Eastside High School, Avildsen employs imagery originally used by D. W. Griffith in his 1915 film *The Birth of a Nation* as a means of discrediting Reconstruction-era reforms that allowed blacks to vote, serve on juries, and hold elective office in the postbellum South. Drawing on minstrel show stereotypes, Griffith showed black legislators devouring pieces of fried chicken, sneaking nips of alcohol from flasks, propping their bare feet on their desks, and casting lascivious glances at white women when discussing legislation allowing interracial marriage. Griffith even depicts freedmen whipping a black "faithful soul" for remaining loyal to his old master, so that he can introduce the Ku Klux Klan as an organization formed to restore respectability to the legislature and to save "good" blacks from the physical brutality of the "bad" ones.[6]

In *The Devil Finds Work*, James Baldwin argues that *The Birth of a Nation* "cannot be called dishonest; it has the Niagara force of an obsession."[7] The obsessive force of the film comes as a logical consequence of its function as motion picture legitimating the "common sense" of white supremacy.[8] It has to go to great extremes in storytelling, turning racist vigilantes into innocent victims, presenting slave owners and the Ku Klux Klan as the "protectors" of African Americans and saving them from the evils of Reconstruction. But it also articulates the common sense of patriarchal power pervasive throughout American life on- and off-screen. The solitary white male figure whose heroism maintains social order and social boundaries needs both adversaries and dependents of other races and genders to secure his own status.

As Michael Rogin explains, *The Birth of a Nation* not only mobilizes patriarchal heroism in defense of white supremacy, but also recruits the narrative of white supremacy on behalf of patriarchy, underscoring the threat to the family and the need for patriarchal authority by making the threat racial.[9] The conventions of Hollywood film function here as Browne describes them—as nodes in a network of a racial-gender-economic system built on what it prohibits as much as on what it permits.

Avildsen updates Griffith's imagery without really revising it. He attributes the demise of discipline in Eastside High School to the 1960s—in the form of the power over school policy won by black female parents and teachers as a result of the civil rights movement. He substitutes a black principal for the role played by the Klan. "This is known as progress," explains James Baldwin sarcastically in describing a similar switch in the racial economy of the 1967 film *In the Heat of the Night*.[10] Both *The Birth of a Nation* and *Lean on Me* summon up patriarchal power as the necessary cure for a wide range of black misbehavior—from lascivious attacks on white women to the laziness of public employees, from boisterous sounds, body movements, and speech to uncontrollable brutality against white authorities and "innocent" blacks in need of white protection. Avildsen's use of the song "Welcome to the Jungle" as his theme invokes white racist associations between black people and "uncivilized" jungle life, although the song itself is actually a white heavy metal band's protest against exploitative and shallow commercial popular culture products like Avildsen's film.[11]

Like most Hollywood productions, *Lean on Me* borrows its conventions from more than one place. Elements of melodrama, comedy, and action-adventure characterize its key dramatic moments; story and spectacle combine to provide the pleasures of fused forms and genres. The plot and characters display clear debts to the "high school disruption" film genre including *The Blackboard Jungle* (1955), *High School Confidential!* (1958), *To Sir with Love* (1967), *Rock 'n' Roll High School* (1979), and *Fast Times at Ridgemont High* (1982), among others. Yet unlike most of the high school disruption films, *Lean on Me* has no sympathy for the subjectivity or subcultures of students, and offers no critique of the broader social conditions that create school disorder.

Instead, *Lean on Me* concerns itself solely with burdens that beset patriarchy, with the need to use physical force and intimidation to make teachers, parents, and students knuckle under to law and order as defined by Joe Clark. Although the film mixes elements of several genres, its role in the gender-racial-economic system is to insist on patriarchal power as the only answer to the disorder emblematized by the rampant subjectivity of black women and black teenagers.

The continuities that unite *The Birth of a Nation* and *Lean on Me* demonstrate the enduring power of genre conventions. Culture is cumulative; it builds like a barrier reef. Nothing from the past ever disappears completely; new stories often depend upon our knowledge of old ones. Moreover, the pull of the past is powerful. Representations from the present often appear credible in proportion to their resemblance to those from the past. Just as John Ford's western films struck many viewers as the "real West" because he derived his images from western paintings, lithographs, and Wild West shows, Avildsen's depictions of race attain credibility by redeploying images about race from the minstrel show and from previous films including *Gone with the Wind* and *The Birth of a Nation*.[12]

The rigidity of genre conventions in *Lean on Me* perfectly complements its ideological conservatism. The film purports to tell the "true" story of an actual high school principal, Joe Clark. Yet, it displays more allegiance to genre conventions than to historical accuracy. Clark rose to prominence in the 1980s as part of a coordinated campaign by neoconservatives to hide the consequences of cuts in government spending on education encouraged by the Reagan administration. Hailed as a national hero by Reagan's Secretary of Education, William Bennett, Clark blamed liberals and the civil rights movement for the sorry state of inner-city schools and offered his own record as an administrator who ruled with an iron hand as a way of improving the schools without spending any more money on education.

As principal at Eastside High School, Clark illegally expelled large numbers of "troublemakers," fomented factional fights among teachers, and roamed the halls carrying a baseball bat as a way of threatening students who misbehaved. Although all of these actions won praise from much of the press and from neoconservative pundits, Clark secured no increase in achievement on any level in his school. The costs exacted on students and teachers by Clark's incessant efforts at self-promotion became clear when he hired a stripper to perform at a school assembly and, even worse, was out of town on a speaking tour the day of the performance. Clark then took a leave of absence from his educational post to pursue more lucrative employment as a full-time speaker before neoconservative audiences.

The choice of Clark as the "hero" of Avildsen's film helped determine its ideological and narrative trajectory. Unlike Jaime Escalante, (the Los Angeles teacher celebrated in Ramon Menendez's 1987 *Stand and Deliver*), whose faith in his Chicano students actually produced improvement in their knowledge of math and led to subsequent educational achievement, Clark's record consisted purely of punishing black students in a manner more appropriate to a prison situation than a high school. Avildsen portrayed Clark as a hero by evading his real record at Eastside High School, by transforming the principal into a generic countersubversive patriarch saving white people from their own "fear of a Black planet." By placing blame in the film for the crisis in inner-city education on the mostly black and mostly female parents and teachers at Eastside, Avildsen absolves his viewers of any responsibility for the consequences of deindustrialization and neoconservative economics on inner-city youth. Instead he demonizes these young people and their parents, imagining that they would welcome a figure like Clark, a man who makes them cower by threatening them with a baseball bat and who forces them to learn to sing the school song on his command. In this respect, *Lean on Me* grafts parts of *Dirty Harry* and *An Officer and a Gentleman* onto *The Birth of a Nation*, providing an ideologically conservative message within an aesthetically conservative use of dramatic genre conventions.

The iconography shared by *Lean on Me* and *The Birth of a Nation* demonstrates the durability of socially charged stereotypes and the clear connection between the ways in which we have learned to tell stories and their ideological content. Many films since the 1970s have embraced generic forms and displayed the blend of generic and ideological conservatism at the center of *Lean on Me*. This aesthetic and political conservatism owes a great deal to the "blockbuster" films of the 1970s. Aimed at audiences in newly developed suburban multiscreen theaters and tailored for crossmarketing to upscale consumers in a variety of venues, the blockbuster films drew upon generic conventions to affirm continuity in an era of rupture and change.

For example, *Star Wars* (1977) affirmed patriarchal power through a recombinant mixture of generic icons from science fiction and western films, while the popularity of *The Godfather* (1972) and *Godfather II* (1974), *The Deer Hunter* (1978), *Close Encounters of the Third Kind* (1977), *Grease* (1978), *Jaws* (1975) and *Jaws II* (1978), and *The Exorcist* (1973) and *The Exorcist II* (1978) signaled similar resurgences in gangster and war films, musicals, action-adventure, and horror stories displaying the same tight fit between political ideology and fidelity to generic norms.

This emergence of blockbuster films firmly rooted in genre conventions during the 1970s and 1980s seems particularly surprising in retrospect, because they followed a period of filmmaking in the late 1960s and early 1970s characterized by the creative genre anxiety emblematized in *Buck and the Preacher*—by the intrusion of social tremors into cinematic representations in such a way as to render traditional genre icons unsatisfying and incomplete.

Anxiety here emerges as an epistemological principle, as a way of knowing. Like fear, anxiety recognizes that something is wrong even if we cannot fully formulate a description of the problem or of its solutions. Rather than presuming that culture simply reveals, conceals, reflects, or shapes social relations, anxiety as a focal point for analysis enables us to see how cultural creations indirectly engage social conditions by registering them in unexpected ways. The ambiguities illuminated by anxiety and the inability of anxious representations to suppress them may allow us important new insights into the utility of film as indirect evidence about social history.

Consider, for example, the contrast between *Lean on Me* and the 1972 American International Pictures release *Blacula* by director William Crain and the new spin that it puts on an old story. Like many other horror films, this one begins with an image of Count Dracula's castle in Transylvania (in 1780) on a stormy night. But on this particular evening the count's guests are a handsome black man and a beautiful black woman. "I've never before had the opportunity of entertaining guests ... from the darker continent," the count tells the couple. Dracula's statement locates the film within the history of previous Count Dracula movies, while simultaneously announcing its point of departure from them. Racial difference adds a new dimension to the Count Dracula story by bringing to the surface and to the present the legend's hidden metaphors about social relations. Vampires are, after all, aristocrats who terrorize and exploit ordinary people because they need to feed off of their blood. The history of racism in the United States adds an additional resonance to issues of "blood" and "blood sucking" in this film.[13]

The black couple has journeyed to Transylvania as representatives of their African nation, hoping to persuade the count to sign a petition calling for an end to the slave trade. The dignity and intelligence of the Africans (played by Shakespearean actor William Marshall and television favorite Denise Nicholas) contrast sharply with the boorish behavior of their host. When the black prince speaks about the "barbarity" of slavery, the count responds by enumerating its benefits and pleasures for slave owners—adding that he would not mind acquiring a possession like the African's wife.

Offended by Dracula's insult, the couple attempt to leave, but the count's henchmen subdue the prince and hold him down while Dracula sucks his blood. The count "curses" the prince, condemning him to replicate Dracula's own suffering—to hunger for blood without satisfaction. He then condemns the princess to an eternity of hearing her husband's anguished cries. To crown his victory, the count takes away the prince's African name and gives him a European one very much like his own, transforming Prince Mamuwalde into "Blacula."

As in its less-accomplished sequel *Scream, Blacula Scream!!* (1973), the racial specificity in *Blacula* transforms the horror film's generic conventions. Vampire films generally combine horror and sympathy; we fear the vampire even as we understand the sadness of his insatiable desires.

But connecting the count's power to white supremacist beliefs makes the victimization of the prince and princess all the more terrifying, while at the same time winning our sympathy for *their* hunger, which after all is only something imposed upon them by the white man. Accustomed to thinking of Dracula as European, this film makes us think of him as white. By addressing the context of inner-city life in the 1970s, *Blacula* also gestured to an even greater horror off-screen, to deindustrialization, disinvestment, capital flight, police repression—to the white racism of the 1970s that impacted black communities with "the Niagara force of an obsession," even if the film addressed it only indirectly through generic expressions of horror and comedy.

A low-budget "blaxploitation" film designed for inner-city theaters and the suburban drive-in circuit, *Blacula* presents a playful mix of the familiar and the unfamiliar; it attempts to create engagement and invest-ment among audiences by inserting contemporary social concerns into a familiar genre. Although some exceptionally attentive or imaginative viewers might have been able to develop more fully the film's intriguing premises about white responsibility for black criminality, Crain's film does not do so. Instead, it slips back into an uneasy amalgam of standard horror film conventions and 1970s urban black life. *Blacula* is not so much a fully realized social problem film as it is a spasm of genre anxi-ety—an uneasy hybrid created by the conflict between the conservative continuity reinforced by the persistence of generic forms and the cease-less pattern of social change that makes almost all generic representa-tions seem inadequate and obsolete.

The attempt in *Blacula* to inculcate new elements within an old genre raises important questions about the relationship between seem-ingly static generic conventions and the dynamic vicissitudes of social life. Of course, all genres change. Generic conventions offer basic guide-posts for character zones and narrative resolutions; changes in genre form offer opportunities for product differentiation and for fusing new audiences together through recombinant forms that blend the western with science fiction, the musical with the social problem film, action-adventure with comedy. Creative artists always cultivate audience interest through small changes in generic expectations, even in times of social stability. But more dramatic ruptures in genre form often appear in moments of great historical change.

In a sensitive study of 1940s film noir, Frank Krutnick argues that minor changes in the genre revealed significant stress in society at large over changing standards of masculine identity and behavior.[14] Similarly, Will Wright shows how tensions between individualism and community in western films between the 1930s and 1950s followed the contours of changes in corporate capitalism. Jonathan Munby's research reveals how Oedipal anxiety replaces ethnic anger as the motivating force in gangster films made between 1930 and 1949, while studies by Diane Waldman and Andrea Walsh demonstrate that Gothic romances tended to arbitrate tensions between female aspirations and male expectations during and after the Second World War with its dramatic changes in gender roles.[15]

These scholars provide examples of changes in single genres as clues about broader transformations and conflicts in society at large— about changes in gender roles brought on by wartime mobilization and postwar reconversion, or about changes in individual and group identity engendered by alterations in corporate capitalism and family form. All acknowledge the tendency for film genres to register and discursively transcode social tensions through slight variations in genre conventions.

But what happens when different genres show signs of the same anxiety? In the early 1970s, *Blacula* was not the only genre film displaying racial concerns. A number of westerns, comedies, and action-adventure dramas took unprecedented shapes by combining racial issues with generic conventions. Unlike self-consciously avant-garde and anti-racist films like *Sweet Sweetback's Baadasssss Song* (1971) and *The Spook Who Sat by the Door* (1973) these films added black characters and situations to traditional genres, and then traced the attendant consequences. By moving black characters out of their generic homes in comedies, social problem films, and action-adventure stories, they registered crises about racial relations in unexpected, yet powerful ways. In many cases, foregrounding race did more than desegregate previously all-white genres. In some cases, the prominence of race called the generic form itself into question, leaving filmmakers and audiences with no consistent guide to resolving familiar dilemmas.

Because the history of our own time has been so poorly told, the early 1970s may not seem like a particularly important period for examining the relationship between generic form and social change. But for black communities in the United States especially, the early 1970s presented a crisis of catastrophic dimensions. The Nixon administration's cessation of the War on Poverty, its abandonment of public housing, and its retreat from efforts to desegregate education, housing, and employment exacted terrible costs on communities of color. The Federal Bureau of Investigation's COINTELPRO program, coupled with repression by local police departments all across the country, destroyed the infrastructure and leadership of self-help and activist organizations from coast to coast. The cumulative consequences of wasteful spending on the Vietnam War, capital flight overseas, and the "planned shrinkage" and austerity imposed on municipal governments by finance capital in the 1970s combined to create a severe crisis for the entire country, but one that had particularly harsh consequences in inner-city communities.

The defeat of black power activism and the sudden devastation of the ghetto as a result of corporate disinvestment and government counterinsurgency rarely appeared directly in 1970s cinema, but one indirect reference to it in Berry Gordy's 1975 *Mahogany* enacted a crucial disturbance in a conventional generic romance. In the film, Diana Ross plays a fashion model courted by a community activist played by Billy Dee Williams. Ross's character has a chance to enter the world of high fashion which would enable her to leave the ghetto behind. Trying to explain his own desire to stay in the community—and hoping to entice Ross to stay as well, Williams takes her for a walk past a desolate row of empty lots and boarded-up buildings. He explains that this street used to be full of life, that only a few years ago things were getting better for black people—and for all people—but now things have changed. Williams's character contends he has to stay in the community to find out what happened, but the poverty and decay she sees only augments the model's desire to get out. *Mahogany* treads familiar ground when it presents a love affair imperiled by a conflict between community and career, but it adds enormously to its characters' dilemmas by placing them in the social world that the audience will go back to once the film ends.

The African American settings and characters that subverted genre conventions during that era in *Buck and the Preacher* and *Blacula* also manifested themselves in detective films (*Cotton Comes to Harlem*, 1970, and *Coffy*, 1973) in action-adventure movies (*Gordon's War*, 1973, and *Black Caesar*, 1973) and in comedy as well (*Uptown Saturday Night*, 1973, *Let's Do It Again*, 1975, *A Piece of the Action*, 1977) and most notably in Michael Schultz's 1975 Universal Pictures release *Car Wash*.

Slipping back and forth between a television-style ensemble comedy and self-contained short vaudeville performances by Richard Pryor, George Carlin, and Professor Irwin Corey, *Car Wash's* unstable form mirrors the precarious social realities faced by its black working-class characters.[16] A terrific rhythm and blues sound track helps move the action from one scene to another, but the film remains a series of vignettes rather than a coherent linear narrative. Like Robert Altman's *Nashville* (1975), the film's episodes simultaneously underscore the poignancy of individual stories while demonstrating the seeming impossibility of pulling them together into a coherent social vision. But as in *Blacula* and *Buck and the Preacher*, making race a central element changes the contours of the genre. Hollywood has long built comedies around groups struggling for success—most immigrant ethnic comedy involves dramatic representations of self-making and upward mobility. But while dominant film genres have not always shown these efforts to be successful, they have only rarely offered the level of fatalism and pessimism presented in *Car Wash*.

Like *Blacula* and *Buck and the Preacher*, *Car Wash* starts from the premise of promises unfulfilled—in this case expectations for upward economic mobility sparked during the prosperity of the 1960s and stoked by the utopian goals of the civil rights movement and the War on Poverty. Stifled by the tedium, monotony, and low pay they receive for their work, and divided from one another by jealousy, resentment, and petty rivalries, the characters in *Car Wash* plot an array of individual escapes. One assumes an Islamic name and presents himself as a black militant; another imagines himself as a comic-book superhero. The white boss's son quotes Chairman Mao and convinces his dad to let him work with the men, but they scorn his pathetic efforts to address them as fellow "revolutionaries." The script (by European American screenwriter Joel Schumacher) mocks all their efforts as foolish and self-deluding. Instead, it privileges the perspective of one character, a "family man" who pitches constructive ideas to the boss.[17] Denied the tragedy of *Blacula* or the heroism of *Buck and the Preacher*, the characters in *Car Wash* learn to accept their fate. Renouncing both individual and collective rebellion, the film implies that only obedience and resignation constitute appropriate responses to the social crisis that it addresses.

If the generic disruptions achieved in *Blacula* and *Buck and the Preacher* signal how racial identities can interrupt generic closure, *Car Wash* starts a new trend whereby the defeats suffered by aggrieved racial groups have instructive power for the rest of society. Although the film's conclusions clearly seem headed in a conservative direction, *Car Wash's* nonlinear uncentered story leads it to avoid the kind of narrative and ideological closure generally required of ensemble comedy films. Secure only in its cynicism, it ridicules the rebels and dreamers whose flamboyant actions engage our attentions most fully. Like the song by The Who responding to the 1960s with a vow not to be fooled again, the conclusions of *Car Wash* seem motivated less by conservatism than by the protective cynicism of disillusioned idealists facing defeat. By 1975, the fiscal crisis of the state, deindustrialization, and economic restructuring had already started to reverse the modest gains made by blacks and by all poor people before 1973. Factory shutdowns, cuts in social services, and a sharp decline in real wages undercut the infrastructure that sustained the civil rights movement, and increases in crime, delinquency, and drug addiction further fragmented the political and social fabric of Black America. In its recognition of that reality, and its resort to bemused detachment as a strategy for coping with—rather than conquering—community problems, *Car Wash* (in both its content and form) reflected the increasingly fragmented world inhabited by much of its audience.

Genre anxiety during the 1970s reveals a racial crisis so pervasive that it permeated films in genres usually isolated from political and social controversies. *Blacula, Buck and the Preacher,* and *Car Wash* challenged the conventions of horror, western, and comedy genres mostly because of the ways in which racial issues in the 1970s affected black people. But another set of films strengthened and reinforced genre conventions as a consequence of the racial crisis as seen by many whites in the early 1970s. In the wake of Richard Nixon's "southern strategy," which created an electoral majority by mobilizing white opposition to school busing, affirmative action, and other attempts at desegregation, urban crime films particularly took on a new tone and character.

Equally rooted in authoritarian and anti-authoritarian traditions, the urban crime drama has often been a contested zone of representation. It has been the domain of lone-wolf private detectives as well as large efficient crime-fighting bureaucracies, a forum for physical combat as well as for individual intelligence. Crime films of the early 1970s, including Don Siegel's 1971 *Dirty Harry* reflected "white anxiety" about the black self-activity and subjectivity of the 1960s, as well as about economic stagnation by reconfiguring the genre to present authoritarian white male heroes as the only remedy for a disintegrating society.[18] Although the urban crime drama has a long history of both celebrating and implicating the rogue cop, in *Dirty Harry* the specter of social disorder inscribes within the text a celebration of the hero's sadism as a preferred alternative to the specter of social disorder. Ambiguity disappears and sharp simple binary oppositions distinguish the good guys from the bad guys. Crime comes from bad people, coddled by insufficiently authoritarian rules and regulations, while extralegal displays of force and violence by authority figures bring order and presumably justice. Gender serves as a major organizing principle in *Dirty Harry* as criminals and civil libertarians alike of both genders are coded as "female" forces undermining patriarchal power and its ability to protect the populace from harm.

With a voyeurism bordering on envy, *Dirty Harry* details the brutality and sadism of criminals in order to sanction violent revenge by the hero. But the scenario has racial implications as well. At a crucial moment in the film, Harry Callahan foils a bank robbery by a black gang. Firing his enormous .44 magnum he disables the getaway car and wounds several of the robbers. Walking over to one lying on the pavement outside the bank, he stands over him as they both spot a gun lying near the robber's hand. The camera gives us Callahan's view of the black criminal cowering on the ground, looking up at the detective. A quick cut reverses the view and lets us look over the criminal's shoulder into the barrel of the officer's gun. Coolly taunting the robber, Harry softly raises the question whether he has expended all six bullets in his gun or whether he has one left. Confessing that he can't remember himself, Callahan reminds his victim that he is carrying the most powerful handgun in the world and encourages the thief to make a move for the gun on the ground, but first to ask himself, "Do I feel lucky?" Smiling, Harry asks softly, "Well, do you, punk?" When the criminal relents and lets Harry get to the gun, he tells the officer in exaggerated black dialect, "I gots to know." Harry raises his gun and points it at the wounded man on the ground. We see the criminal's mouth open wide and his eyes pop in terror as Callahan pulls the trigger, but there are no bullets left. Harry smiles triumphantly and walks away. We see the black man mutter, "Son of a bitch," and then the camera directs our gaze back to Callahan. Just in case we've missed the phallic power of this scene, Harry carries the two long guns by his sides, while a fire hydrant smashed by the foiled getaway car spews bursts of water up into the air.[19]

To offset the racist pleasures provided by this scene, Siegel switches immediately to a hospital ward where a black doctor tends to Harry's wounds. We find that they are friends who grew up together, "absolving" Harry of any racist intentions in the previous scene. But Siegel takes an additional step. When Harry starts to tell the physician about how to treat his wound, the doctor asks affectionately, "Do I come down to the station and tell you how to beat a confession out of a prisoner?" We see that "good" blacks not only don't mind Callahan's actions, they approve of them!

The depiction of a black criminal cowering before white male authority in *Dirty Harry* brings to the screen an image prefigured by thousands of law and order speeches by politicians, but it also relies on our absolute faith in the rigidity of genre boundaries. Harry's ruthlessness and contempt for the law mirror that of the criminals; they are so evil, he must become just like them. Harry Callahan is a hero only because the strict binary oppositions of the urban crime drama establish him as one. But in order to win us to this position, Siegel cannot isolate the genre from events off-screen. He has to summon up the specter of social disintegration in order to have Harry protect us from it. At the conclusion of *Dirty Harry*, Callahan reenacts the "feel lucky, punk?" scene with an effeminate longhaired serial killer. This time, the criminal resists and Harry kills him. But if our society needs Harry Callahan, it has already failed. *Dirty Harry*, *Blacula*, and *Car Wash* cannot present us with credible happy endings on-screen precisely because they have directed our attentions so effectively toward the seemingly irresolvable problems we face off-screen.

Callahan needs the threat of social disintegration to justify his assertion of white male power. But more than race is at work here. The irreversible entry of women into the paid labor force, the reach and scope of popular culture, declining real wages that threaten intergenerational transfers of wealth, and the emergence of a therapeutic/administrative bureaucracy of educators, psychologists, and social workers have all undermined the power of patriarchy in the United States since World War II. If the imagery summoned up by *Dirty Harry* evokes *The Birth of a Nation* in ways that are similar to *Lean on Me* it is not because patriarchy is triumphant and unquestioned, but rather that it must be affirmed all that much more emphatically in culture as it gradually loses its power in actual social life. Genre anxiety grows from social anxiety, but simply being aired to a wide audience does not automatically soothe anxieties.

The directors of these 1970s films had different agendas, ideologies, and interests. None of them intended either a purely ideological statement or a self-conscious innovation in genre form. Each wanted to attract audiences, and they allowed social problems to seep into their cinematic representations because they thought that would help them do so. Whether acknowledged overtly or covertly, the social crises of the early 1970s suffused these films with an instability that posed serious challenges to traditional genre conventions.

By comparison, contemporary Hollywood offerings seem exceptionally conservative in both ideological content and aesthetic aspiration. But it would be a mistake to connect genre forms with social relations without examining how the commercial matrix in which Hollywood films are made helps determine their ideological and aesthetic dimensions. In his indispensable research on the motion picture industry, Thomas Schatz reveals that between 1969 and 1973, film studio profits fell drastically.[20] In addition, until 1974, Hollywood depended largely on receipts from ten thousand theaters in older downtown districts. Under those circumstances, experimental and innovative films might be worth backing, and motion pictures with appeal to blacks in inner-city locations could play a significant role in studio earnings.

Key changes in the film industry after 1975, however, worked against the production of films like *Blacula, Buck and the Preacher,* and *Car Wash*. Changes in tax laws in the mid-1970s discouraged investors from risking money on smaller films, driving them instead to seek secure returns from high budget "calculated blockbusters" featuring well-known stars and displaying potential for crossmarketing opportunities as video games, toys, amusement park rides, and school lunch boxes. Justin Wyatt identifies another important development at this time, the rise of the "high concept" film starting in the mid-1970s, by which he means films carefully crafted around style in production and designed to integrate the film with its marketing—what Wyatt calls "the look, the hook, and the book."[21] In addition, the construction of more than twelve thousand new theaters between 1975 and 1990, most of them in shopping malls located in white suburban neighborhoods, undercut the economic importance of black consumers to the industry.[22] The growing gap between income and wealth acquired by whites as opposed to nonwhites after 1973 disenfranchised large sections of the population as consumers while giving special market power to others.

Many of the hits that emerged as blockbusters or high-concept successes in the 1970s and 1980s stuck closely to genre conventions, in part to facilitate the strategy of marketing films to children as something new, but selling those same films to parents as "nostalgia." *The Godfather, Jaws, The Exorcist, Grease, Saturday Night Fever, Star Wars*, and *Superman* suited the emerging financial structure of Hollywood better than small films with uncertain genre affiliations. As revenues from tape rentals have emerged as an increasingly important source of profits, producers have attempted to tailor their films to that market as well. Just as the content of D. W. Griffith's *Broken Blossoms* (1919) responded to the director's desire to market films to an elite audience, today's films follow the forms that filmmakers believe will win favor among young white suburban viewers.[23] Richard Shickel complains that the need for blockbuster star vehicles with sideline product potential has led to a merger of genres so that all Hollywood makes these days are comedies and action-adventure films.[24] If true, this would certainly prevent films displaying genre anxiety like those of the early 1970s from ever being made again.

Yet it is clear that the new economic realities of filmmaking have not permanently stifled genre anxiety. Schatz notes that the emphasis on producing a few blockbusters reduces the supply and increases the demand for new films. Low-budget mainstream and independent filmmakers have taken advantage of that opportunity to produce films that challenge absolute generic boundaries. Independent filmmaking especially has opened up new vistas for directors and writers from aggrieved racial groups, and these artists often deploy recombinant and genre-bending forms. Social power relations bleed into their films in intentional and unintentional ways, evoking resemblances to the genre anxiety films of the early 1970s.

Hollywood's gender-racial-economic system has always been more than a matter of black and white; representations of Native Americans, Asian Americans, and Latinos have also been staples of generic oppositions. When filmmakers from those communities starting trying to tell their own stories in the 1970s and 1980s, they often engaged generic forms and characters as stereotypes that needed to be displaced in order to allow for the emergence of new images and identities on- and off-screen. For example, Wayne Wang's low budget 1982 film *Chan Is*

Missing appears to be a mystery, but instead uses the conventions of the mystery genre to explore issues about identity among Chinese Americans in San Francisco. "I'm no Charley Chan," the narrator admits at one point, making reference to the screen detective that defined so many stereotypes of Asian Americans for film audiences. Throughout Wang's film, he highlights the disparity between Hollywood images of Chinese Americans and their lived experiences. In searching for the disappeared Mr. Chan, the heroes make their way through a Chinatown that resists easy characterization. The Chinese Americans in this film are divided by politics, age, gender, consumer tastes, and values. Mr. Chan is missing, but so is Charlie Chan. Instead, the community is made up of complex and complicated characters—a Chinese man who dances to mariachi music at a Filipino senior citizens center, a cook who drinks milk and wears a "Samurai Night Fever" T-shirt, a taxi driver who imitates Richard Pryor and Chicano gang members. The community is so composite that no picture can capture it accurately, certainly not the picture established in Hollywood's generic conventions. "I have Chan's picture," the narrator tells us at the film's conclusion, "but I still don't know what he looks like."

Similarly, Cheech Marin's 1987 *Born in East L.A.* engages with genre conventions only to call them into question. The film appears to be a comedy built around yet another version of the dope-smoking Chicano hustler that Marin has played throughout his comedy career. Yet in this film, the comedy takes a back seat to an inquiry into the meaning of the border for Mexicans and Chicanos, into Anglo insistence on seeing Chicanos as foreign, and on the plight of undocumented workers trying to enter the United States. Like Wang, Marin makes an affectionate film about his own ethnic group without essentializing them. The lead character speaks German better than Spanish, doesn't know why his community celebrates Cinco de Mayo, and only grudgingly acknowledges his ties to people from Mexico. Yet in the course of the film's action, he forges a profound solidarity with the immigrant border crossers that he sneered at when the film began.

Marin also depicts genre conventions in order to subvert them. He presents stereotypical representations of Chicano identity that originated in many films about gangs and barrio life, but parodies them at the same time. As Rosa Linda Fregoso notes, he draws upon "insider" knowledge of the parodic tradition of Mexican comedians Tin Tan and Cantinflas to insert a sense of shared history and social criticism into what might otherwise seem a simple stereotype.[25] At the same time, his film's title (and title song) parodies Bruce Springsteen's "Born in the USA," taking a comic approach to national identity on both sides of the border. Through a scene where Marin's character, Rudy, teaches a group of Asian immigrants how to pass as Chicanos, he reveals the constructed nature of Chicano stereotypes.

Jonathan Wacks's 1989 *Powwow Highway* combines the western, the social problem film, and the caper comedy into a new hybrid that also reveals ethnic identity to be unstable, constructed, contested, and composite. Although not made by Native Americans, its images and icons evoke the history of Hollywood's Indians only to demonstrate their inadequacy. Instead, we find that Native Americans are both united by a common history and divided by their responses to it, that social change requires diverse visions that address the entire community, and that just as some Native Americans can be villains, some Anglos can be allies to the Indian cause.

During the 1970s, films displaying genre anxiety gestured occasionally toward the growing perception that race in America did not just entail a binary opposition between black and white. Michael Schultz's *Which Way Is Up?* (1977), for example, depicted Richard Pryor as a black farmworker in the midst of militant Chicanos. In the 1980s and 1990s, filmmakers from aggrieved racial groups including Wang, Marin, and Spike Lee have emphasized the importance of intercultural communication and conflict, of recognizing the polylateral dimensions of racism and antiracism.

There can be no direct correspondence between political activity in any given era and aesthetic representations, no artistic form can remedy social problems all by itself, just as no movement for social change can guarantee a concomitant change in artistic representation. Challenges to generic conventions often serve emancipatory ends; renewals of generic conventions often signal social conservatism. But genre anxiety is more of a symptom than a critique; it can be a stimulus to social activism but not a substitute for it. Similarly, renewals of genre conventions signal a search for order in an unstable world. They may lead to reactionary politics, but at the same time they also display the anguish that people feel as they try to live what Robert Warshow described as "the life which happens to be possible to them."[26] The genre anxiety films of the 1970s reflected the demands of marketers and the needs of investors, but also the uncertainty and self-doubt of a society unable to face the political and social inequalities generated by the new economic realities of deindustrialization and economic restructuring.

Struggles over resources and power are always implicated in cultural stories. Instabilities in social life can never be divorced completely from aesthetic choices. Anxieties and tremors in generic forms do not necessarily signal social transformation, but they may provide the preconditions for it. Just as durable as the generic forms they challenge, efforts to alter genre conventions will continue as long as ordinary people discern the disparity between their aspirations for meaningful connection to other people and the poisonous legacies of hierarchy and exploitation that pervade our shared social lives.

PART III
FACING UP TO WHAT'S KILLING YOU

The three themes that have come together in cultural studies are: first, the central importance of gender studies and all kinds of "non-Eurocentric" studies to the study of historical social systems; second, the importance of local, very situated historical analysis, associated by many with a new "hermeneutic turn"; third, the assessment of the values involved in technological achievements in relation to other values.

—Immanuel Wallerstein et al., *Open the Social Sciences: Report of the Gulbenkian Commission on the Restructuring of the Social Sciences*

CHAPTER 9

"Facing Up to What's Killing You"

Urban Art and the New Social Movements

It is axiomatic that no social movement is as incoherent
as it appears from within, nor as coherent as it appears
from without.

—Troy Duster, in *Beyond a Dream Deferred*

In Toni Cade Bambara's story "The Organizer's Wife," members of a
radical commune compress their beliefs into a simple slogan emblazoned
across the front of a mural —"Face Up to What's Killing You."[1] The
indecent social order of our own day renders the urgent anxiety encapsulated in that slogan relevant to grassroots cultural creation all across
the globe. Performance artists and poets, graffiti writers and rappers,
photographers and filmmakers, car customizers and computer artists
create sights and sounds, poetry, prose, and performance art that turns
talking back into an art form and enables their audiences to confront the
new conditions that are killing them.

Since the start of the industrial era, the "old social movements"
(exemplified by trade unions, urban-reform coalitions, ethnic radicalism,
and socialist political movements) have based their strategies for social
change on struggles over space, on efforts to control the neighborhood
or the nation by trapping capital in one place in order to force those with
power to make concessions to them. But the present-day mobility of capital has rendered those strategies ineffective. Today, municipalities, trade
unions, and even nation-states compete to offer ever increasing subsidies
to capital in the false hope that benefits will trickle down to the majority
of the population. These arrangements inevitably fail, producing only

a downward spiral of lower wages, wretched working conditions, and unmet social needs.

"New social movements"—community-based coalitions that emphasize democratic participation and address issues of culture, identity, and the environment—have great potential for linking local concerns with global realities, but while they have emerged everywhere in the world over the past two decades, they remain embryonic in form and largely untested in their capacity to meaningfully interrupt, much less reverse the unprecedented power of transnational corporations and their agents like the International Monetary Fund (IMF) and the World Bank.[2]

The new social movements often address common cultural concerns and frequently make sophisticated strategic interventions on the terrain of culture, appropriating contemporary media technologies, forms of address, and channels of discourse for their own purposes. Yet, the new social movements are also a product of cultural change. The reach and scope of mass media and their role in producing the prestige hierarchies of consumer culture has undermined the authority of cultural arbiters connected to traditional institutions—universities, conservatories, art museums, and publishing houses. At the same time, global marketing, grassroots cultural creation, and mass migration have produced new axes of affinity and identification that undermine old social movements and the social world that gave them determinate shape. As Robert Dunn argues in work that makes productive use of the insights of Anthony Giddens and Zygmunt Bauman, contemporary cultural expressions emerge out of profound dislocations in social relationships, out of a perception of the compression of time and space, out of the ways in which abstract meaning systems augment social relations and push them beyond local experiences, and out of the ways in which new social relations make it quite difficult for most people to see the structures that shape their lives or to comprehend how they belong to something called "society" in any meaningful way.[3]

New social movements shape and are shaped by culture in particularly profound ways. Transformations in our understandings of space have particularly important implications for the creation, consumption, and circulation of culture in our postindustrial age. During the industrial era in the 1930s, blues singer Peetie Wheatstraw sang his music to black workers in taverns along Biddle Street in St. Louis. Industrial production created the precondition for Wheatstraw's career. Factory jobs lured rural blacks to the cities. Workmen's wages sustained the taverns and nightclubs where he played. His lyrics enabled Wheatstraw to identify himself as someone very much like his listeners. He sang to them about the factories where they worked and the streets on which they walked. Most of all, he reflected back to them their own toughness, determination, and courage. Wheatstraw billed himself as the "High Sheriff from Hell" and the "Devil's son-in-law" invoking images from African American folklore to stake his claim as someone who recognized what his audiences were up against and what kinds of postures and attitudes they had to adopt in order to survive the racism, poverty, and police repression that shrouded their lives.

In our postindustrial era, Michael Jackson makes music and images that entertain people on every continent. He has been a celebrity for as long as most of his fans can remember, but Jackson has assumed many different identities along the way. Starting out as a child star who sang like an adult, he has had different voices, different dance moves, and different clothes during his different periods of stardom. Peetie Wheatstraw labored to present his audiences with one clear and recognizable persona, to convince his listeners he was just like them. Michael Jackson's efforts, on the other hand, have proceeded in an opposite direction, to assume so many different identities that his fans could not possibly believe that he is like them. Jackson's hometown of Gary, Indiana, has much in common with Wheatstraw's depression-era St. Louis, but Jackson's no longer shows any connection to Gary or to Detroit where he had his first successes as an artist. He lives in California on a ranch named Neverland, which as Rita Gonzalez points out, bears some connection to those other American atopias—Disneyland and Graceland.

Postindustrial society has created a global market in need of commodities that can transcend the limits of immediate experiences and local conditions. Michael Jackson's skills as a singer and dancer, his superb sense of style and fashion, and his fascination with other celebrities plays to the needs and preoccupations of mass media in the postindustrial era. He is at the center of his family's success, but he is better known to the public as Diana Ross's friend and Lisa Marie Presley's ex-husband. Peetie Wheatstraw may have been the "High Sheriff from Hell" and the "Devil's son-in-law," but Michael Jackson has been the "King of pop" and Elvis's son-in-law!

More than matters of biography and personal idiosyncrasy divide Peetie Wheatstraw and Michael Jackson. Their different trajectories represent different systems of cultural production. The industrial communities, nation-states, social movements, and civic institutions that supported and subsidized cultural production in the industrial era have lost power and influence in the postindustrial age, while transnational corporate marketers and "philanthropic" foundations increasingly determine the nature, reach, and scope of the most available forms of art, music, drama, poetry, and prose.[4]

For new social movements, this means that traditions of cultural contestation based upon the creation of free spaces or liberated zones independent of commercial culture—for example, efforts to preserve preindustrial folklore and folkways, to fashion "oppositional" cultures out of common experiences of race, ethnicity, and gender, or to invent an avant-garde art capable of contesting the categories of commercial culture—now all seem decidedly obsolete. Artists from even the most aggrieved communities seem inescapably drawn to the networks, circuits, and sites of cultural production generated by the new transnational economy.[5]

Contemporary Los Angeles conceptual, performance, and spoken word artists Harry Gamboa Jr., Luis Alfaro, and Marisela Norte demonstrate the complexities and contradictions of cultural production in the postindustrial global city. Firmly grounded in the history, politics, and aesthetics of Chicano life in Los Angeles, their art engages with commodities and commercialized leisure, with the instabilities of identities, and with the ways in which new communication technologies and social relations erase old affiliations while generating new ones. They create an art that moves, that rides the circuits of commodity circulation but at the same time creates a new public sphere, a discursive space that has no fixed home.

As one of the "world" cities created by deindustrialization, economic restructuring, and globalization, Los Angeles has felt the full impact of urban austerity. By the early 1990s, some 40,000 young people (nearly 20 percent of the city's sixteen- to nineteen-year-olds) had no jobs and were not in school.[6] In poverty-stricken areas of the city, twenty-two out of every one thousand babies died in infancy, a figure far worse than that of many impoverished "Third World" countries.[7] Close to five hundred thousand full-time workers in the city earned less than ten thousand dollars per year, and one out of every four Los Angeles city residents had no health insurance of any kind.[8] The State of California tripled its prison population between 1980 and 1990. The state now spends more on corrections than on the state college system. Los Angeles police officers arrested more than fifty thousand young people during their well-publicized Operation Hammer, designed to identify and harass suspected gang members, although nearly every reliable study shows nowhere near that many gang members in the city. The ultimate effect of this action was not to reduce gang activity, but to tag as many inner-city youths as possible with "criminal" records to be used against them in the future, to disqualify them from employment opportunities, and to disenfranchise them politically.[9]

Home of the global film, music, and television industries, Los Angeles is also the home of innovative artists whose creations stem directly from the contradictions between local conditions and global realities. By facing up to the things that are killing them—and their communities—they have a great deal to teach us about the world that is emerging all around us.

Harry Gamboa Jr. grew up in a monolingual Spanish-speaking family living in East Los Angeles in the 1950s and 1960s. During his first day at school, the teacher ordered him to use scissors, construction paper, and glue to make a "dunce" cap for himself. Instead of writing the word "dunce," Gamboa was instructed to write "Spanish" on the cap and forced to wear it in front of the entire class until he learned to speak English. Looking back on the incident years later, he muses that ever since that day, he has been engaged in a crusade to undermine the English language.[10] Toward that end, his art features puns, double entendres, and ironic pronouncements that undermine the stability and reliability of terms we take for granted. An accomplished painter, filmmaker, and performance artist, Gamboa inserts his work into existing circuits and networks of public relations and mass media, slipping stories into community newspapers, creating spectacles that make the evening news reports. His art introduces contingency and chance into what otherwise might seem like reliable, authoritative, and objective narratives about civic life.

For one project, Gamboa shot photographs of strangers, gave them invented names, and wrote fictional stories about them that he then sent to local newspapers in the form of press releases announcing

Los Angeles street scene. Los Angeles is now the second-largest Mexican, Salvadoran, and Guatemalan city, the third-largest Canadian city, and home to some of the largest concentrations in the world of Koreans outside of Korea, Vietnamese outside of Vietnam, and Iranians outside of Iran. Photograph by George Lipsitz.

that so-and-so had received an award from the King of Sweden, retired from a distinguished career in the military, or planned a forthcoming speech before a service club. Community newspapers often published these stories in unedited form as if they were news because of the perpetual need for "local" copy by papers dependent on the advertising revenue they generate from local sources. Another project entailed making videos of real and staged street scenes, and then sending copies to the first twenty people in the telephone directory listed under the name Rodriguez. Some years ago, Gamboa pioneered the concept of "No Movies," staging scenes to make city streets look like sites of gang shootings or suicides in hopes of enticing local television news crews into covering events that had not happened. This tactic also enabled Gamboa to "make movies" at a time when he could not afford to buy cameras or film. On occasion, these staged events appeared on the evening news as purported "gang" shootings. By placing his "art" in community newspapers, home television screens, and on broadcast news, Gamboa feels that he is intervening in the circuits of communication that shape meaning for most people. If they discover his fabrications, he is delighted, assuming that he has succeeded in making them question their standard sources of information. Even when his artistry and authorship remain completely undetected, Gamboa feels that he is carrying out a guerrilla mission—injecting art into institutional spaces created solely for the convenience of commerce.

Gamboa tries to make his art as mobile and as ephemeral as the everyday life experiences of the postindustrial city. He now tries to carry a video camera at all times, so that he can record the random moments of danger, anger, and fear that occur on any given day. When family members or friends start arguing, he intervenes by asking them to extend those emotions by improvising for him about scenarios that he presents to them. These scenes often involve people negotiating the most desperate precincts of the inner city, attempting to fend off disaster in their personal lives as their support structures crumble around them.[11]

Why would a recognized artist whose works have been exhibited in museums and lauded by distinguished critics choose to work covertly and anonymously in sites that no one associates with art? Part of Gamboa's motivation stems from his resentment of the pervasive power of publicity and public relations, at the ways in which corporate communications media are used to obscure rather than illuminate the lives that people actually lead. "Horrible tragedies don't seem to be tragedies" once the media has processed them, he asserts. At the same time, the things that are held up to be desirable "are either things you would never want to do, or things that are completely unattainable anyway."[12] By luring newspapers and television stations into lies of his own making, Gamboa attempts to insulate himself and his audience from the lying that goes on every day under the guise of news, information, and entertainment. By creating sporadic but independent channels of production and reception, he hopes to dramatize how dependent people have become on sources, circuits, and sites controlled by others.[13]

Gamboa's art engages directly with the logic of time and space in the postindustrial city. He prefers photography, print, performance, and video art to painting, plays, and film because the former entail very short "turnaround" times: they emerge as finished products almost immediately. He chooses to emphasize transitory moments rather than monumental concerns because he senses that he lives in a world where the present obliterates much of the past and future. "Everyone feels they're in the line of fire," he explains. "There is no such thing as a long view, everything is a short take." Driving constantly on Los Angeles's freeways, Gamboa wonders how his auto trips can bring him in close proximity to millions of other residents of the city, but rarely lead him to any individual that he recognizes. "I've lived here since I was born in 1951, but sometimes I feel that maybe everyone I know is gone," he opines.[14] Gamboa's art emphasizes the immediacy of the moment rather than any sustained sense of project, reflecting the sense of dizzying and debilitating change engendered by fast capital.

At one time, Gamboa seemed to be an artist firmly connected to a place and to a community. He grew up in East Los Angeles, in a Mexican American community with distinct artistic practices displayed everywhere—in calendars distributed by local businesses, in graffiti and on murals, in the designs of low-rider cars, and in the colors and images used to decorate homes and advertise businesses. He participated in the Chicano movement as a student activist as well as an editor and contributor to the community journal *Regeneración*. Today, the neighborhood centers and youth clubs that taught him about art are closed due to the fiscal crisis imposed on the state by thirty years of neoconservative policies cutting taxes and social services. Compared to the 1970s, transportation to museums is more expensive, travel through inner-city neighborhoods more dangerous, and the museums themselves more costly to enter.

Migrants from Central America have changed what it means to be Chicano in Los Angeles. The Latino population has spread far beyond East Los Angeles, to what is known as South Central, as well as to industrial suburbs in the Southeast corridor where "Latinos" experience new kinds of coalition and conflict with African Americans, Asian Americans, Pacific Islanders, and Anglos. Rather than retreating back into the physical space of East Los Angeles and the art that it spawned thirty years ago, Gamboa carries East Los Angeles inside his art, fashioning a fugitive oeuvre that is at home everywhere precisely because it has no home, because it deals directly with displacement, circulation, and speed.

Gamboa draws artistic inspiration from changes that have come too quickly. In contrast, Luis Alfaro devises performance pieces that point to the changes that have not come quickly enough—the happiness that has never happened despite all the promises made in popular culture productions and in pronouncements by political leaders.[15] Alfaro's stories proceed from personal memories—of his aunt dying from cancer, of traveling to Delano as a child to march with Cesar Chavez and the United Farm Workers, of decorative objects in his childhood home, of the Los Angeles rebellion of 1992. He contrasts and correlates sentimental songs, popular television shows, and advertising slogans with the material and political deprivations of aggrieved communities. Alfaro puts on performances that address other performances—the popular culture stories that have been "performed" for us in romance novels, on television, and in the movies as well as the multiple social "roles" that we "perform" every day.

From his perspective as a gay Chicano, Alfaro explores the intersections of nationality, sexuality, and class in the postindustrial city. As David Roman demonstrates in his brilliant analysis and critique of Alfaro's work, the artist's stage persona explores the complications of intersectionality.[16] Alfaro's ethnicity inflects his sexuality; he approaches gay and lesbian issues from a Chicano/a perspective. At the same time, his sexuality shapes his relationship to race: he encounters *Chicanismo* through a "queer" critique. Sexual and racial identities intersect in his art, not so much as twin oppressions but rather as complicated sources of empathy and agony, insight and oppression Alfaro shows how diverse social forces shape sexual and racial identities, moving deftly through a broad range of institutions including the Catholic Church, commercial television, consumer culture, and social movements.

One of Alfaro's most popular and moving pieces concerns "The Huggy Boy Show," a televised rock 'n' roll dance party hosted by popular Los Angeles disc jockey, Dick Hugg. As a pioneer of rock 'n' roll radio in Los Angeles during the 1950s and the host for live shows in El Monte, Pomona, and other cities with large Chicano populations, to this day Huggy Boy holds special significance for Mexican Americans throughout southern California. Alfaro turns Hugg's stage name into a pun by recalling a teenage crush Alfaro developed on one of the males who appeared regularly on "The Huggy Boy Show." By wanting to "hug a boy" from "The Huggy Boy Show," Alfaro brings a Chicano accent to an articulation of gay desire, while revealing the sexual heterogeneity of the racially homogeneous Chicano audiences for many of Dick Hugg's shows.

Alfaro conflates popular culture, Chicano identity, and gay experience in a performance piece based on memories of watching televised roller derby matches as a child. Alfaro roller skates onstage (and often through the crowd) during this performance, while wearing a dress and talking about his memories of watching Ralph Valladares, a macho roller derby star of the 1950s and 1960s. In one of his most poignant pieces,

Alfaro dons a dress and speaks in thickly accented English to present himself as Lupe, a woman out for a good time on a Saturday night, a person whose self-affirmation and sense of style mask a desperate desire to block out the day-to-day realities of her life as a woman, as an ethnic "minority," and as a low-wage worker. Alfaro shows how dressing up, dancing, and looking for love on the dance floor help women like Lupe stay alive, to feel human, to endure the indignities of daily life, and to keep alive hopes for a better day tomorrow.

By working his way back through his memories of roller derby, "The Huggy Boy Show," and women claiming space for themselves on the dance floor in a neighborhood club, Alfaro situates himself as someone whose important artistic and public spaces have come from his diverse identities as a popular culture consumer, a part of an ethnic community, and a member of a sexual minority with a long and particular history of performance and spectatorship in dance and athletics. His recollections are not nostalgic hymns of praise to a lost community, but rather a conjuring up of lost possibilities, a reworking of spaces that were never comfortable to inhabit in the first place into scenes that can be used to call into being alternative spaces and social practices in the present and the future.

By demonstrating the conjunctural, composite, and intersectional nature of identities in his own life, Alfaro offers a constructive and instructive example of how to deal with the way the present era seems to produce plural subjectivities inside ourselves. He offers a model for making creative use of our contradictions and conflicts to augment rather than diminish our capacity to connect to a wider world. Yet Alfaro's performances offer no simple celebration of difference; on the contrary, they bring to the surface some of the "differences that make a difference," such as homophobia, racism, and class oppression. His performances expose the heterogeneity of all the groups that might claim his allegiance. They reveal that gays, Chicanos, workers, and popular culture consumers are not monolithic or homogenous groups, but rather coalitions of heterogeneous elements. His performances demonstrate the hybridity of his culture through memories that display equal attachments to commercial television programs and to the United Farm Workers union's Teatro Campesino, to gay "camp" and civil rights activism. Most of all, Alfaro's art displays the multiplicity of roles open to any one individual. He builds audience investment and engagement in his performances by showing how all the different identities that define us coexist uneasily with one another.

Like Alfaro and Gamboa, spoken-word artist Marisela Norte draws both the form and content of her work from the conflicts and communities she finds in the postindustrial city. In a city designed for automobile transportation, Norte has no driver's license. She writes her poems while riding the bus to work downtown every day from her East Los Angeles home. For many years, she let the length of her trip on the bus determine the length of her poems: when she reached her stop, the poem ended. This is not as hard as it sounds, however, since Los Angeles's public transportation system is generally so unpredictable that every form of poetry from the haiku to the epic would be possible. By making a moving bus her preferred site for artistic practice, Norte incorporates movement and circulation into the process of her poetry as well as into the final product.[17]

Norte populates her poems with the people she meets on the bus and those she watches through its windows. She blends their experiences together with images from popular songs ("Ninety-six Tears"), imaginary headlines from tabloid newspapers ("Bored Housewife Falls in Love with Jesus"), and advertising slogans ("976-LOCA, *Llamame*, I Speak Spanish"). In one of the world's greatest fashion centers and retail shopping cities, Norte goes to secondhand discount stores to document *las vidas de ellas*, the lives of the women of Los Angeles, especially the Latinas who compensate for the low-wage labor and sexual harassment in their lives by constructing "looks" for themselves with the makeup, attitude, and clothes that they purchase at discount stores.[18] She describes the clothes that her characters wear as items that have the label cut out, referring to the practice by discount stores of removing labels so they can sell brand-name items for less than the suggested retail price. But she makes a pun on that practice in describing her own aversion to being "labeled" simply as a woman, or as a Chicana, or as a worker, explaining "I'm the one that cut the label out."[19]

In spoken-word performances replete with Spanish, English, and interlingual puns, Norte details the dangers that await women in the city. Inadequate public transportation and street harassment make getting to work unpleasant, and render going out for pleasure practically impossible. Patriarchal attitudes in the Chicano community provoke her protests. "My father put bars on my bedroom before I was born" she asserts in one poem, referring to the "burglar bars" that people in poor neighborhoods use to protect their homes from criminals, but also to the psychic and emotional barriers to sexual pleasure that women like Norte experience within their own culture. In one poem, suppression of information about family planning and birth control lead to an unwanted pregnancy and an anguished abortion, the effects of which Norte's narrator describes eloquently in an interlingual rhyme "Estoy destroyed." ("I am destroyed.")

Norte learned English from the mass media, comic books, and public school classes because her Spanish-speaking father banned the use of English in their home. Her reminiscences about conversations with her Mexican cousins emphasize her discomfort with both Mexico and the United States, and they express her wonder at the misconceptions and mistranslations that binational identity engenders. Norte makes especially effective use of her off-centered reception of some English phrases as in a poem where the narrator talks about a frosty dinner with hostile prospective in-laws who serve her "punch" and "cold ... cuts."[20]

Although she has participated in Chicano art groups in East Los Angeles for nearly thirty years, Norte's art has been almost completely neglected by the cultural brokers of her city. She has never received support from Los Angeles's main artistic and cultural institutions, although appropriately enough she recently received a small grant for collaborating with a visual artist to make pieces for display on buses by the local Rapid Transit District.[21] She has never had her work published in a poetry journal or anthology, and has secured no visiting appointments as artist-in-residence at local colleges or universities. She does, however, have a devoted, indeed, a fanatical, following among young women who purchase compact discs and cassettes of her spoken word art at underground raves and at Norte's performances and readings. Her art reaches its listeners through conduits every bit as circuitous as the Los Angeles city bus routes that inspired it in the first place. Norte's devoted female fans, who see much of their own story registered for the first time in her spoken word art, regularly secure invitations for her to read her work before community and school groups, and her work is assigned often in college classrooms. But the poet who produces this work makes her living as an underpaid white-collar worker for precisely the kind of cultural institution that ignores artists like her.

Norte fills her work with references to popular culture, especially to Mexican and U.S. motion pictures, television programs, and popular music. She uses the unstable dialogue between cultures and countries as well as the peculiar preoccupations of people on each side of the border to bring to the surface all the inequalities, injustices, and private anxieties glossed over by both transnational and national cultures.

Gamboa, Alfaro, and Norte address issues of identity and culture of tremendous importance to the contemporary urban environment of Los Angeles. They proudly proclaim their Chicano identities, but refuse to be reduced to them, staking out roles for themselves as citizens, gendered subjects, and sexual beings as well as members of one ethnic group. They demonstrate knowledge about the past and display respect for it, but their art emerges out of present concerns and conditions. None of them work within mainstream commercial culture or within the avantgarde artforms favored by cultural institutions, but they repeatedly engage popular culture products and canonized artworks in the decisions they make about their art. They use the city itself as a space for art and as a source of inspiration, but they do so less to celebrate one urban area than to ask key questions about what kinds of communities do we have and what kinds of communities do we want?

Thirty years ago, artists with the commitments and interests of Gamboa, Alfaro, or Norte might well have thought of themselves as representatives of a discrete, homogenous, identifiable Chicano community.

But two decades of plant closings, economic restructuring, migration from Central America and Asia, declines in real wages, and defunding of community institutions have changed what it means to be Chicano. At the same time, the rise of feminism, gay and lesbian organizations, environmental coalitions, and interracial youth subcultures organized around punk rock and hip-hop have created new axes of identification and affiliation. Gamboa, Alfaro, and Norte work within widely recognized traditions of Chicano art, but their creations are also acclaimed and claimed by people who are not Chicanos, by cultural workers and intellectuals from many different social groups.

Gamboa describes Los Angeles as a place that is both real and unreal, a place where everyday life "surreality begins to resemble the movies, except that the extras are bleeding on the sidewalk."[22] In a city where low-wage labor, mass migration, racism, sexism, and homophobia compound the alienations and indignities of everyday life for millions of people, Gamboa, Alvaro, and Norte face up to the things that are killing them and their communities. They are not alone in their endeavors. The work they do is shared, not just by artists with access to the powerful publicity outlets surrounding commercial culture, but by visual and conceptual artists in other communities as well.

San Diego artists David Avalos, Louis Hock, and Deb Small produced a particularly creative and provocative means of using art to expose the hidden realities behind the emerging transnational economy in their "Art Rebate." Avalos, Hock, and Small secured federal funding for a project that enabled them to draw designs on dollar bills and hand them out to undocumented Mexican immigrant workers in San Diego. They used the normal processes of commercial circulation to spread their art around, as the migrants spent money, the artists' creation passed into new hands. The project was designed to reach "respectable citizens" and teach them that part of their incomes came from the exploitation of the low-wage immigrant laborers whom they frequently despise.

When neoconservatives in government attacked the federal arts agency that supported "Art Rebate," Avalos, Hock, and Small used local media coverage as an opportunity to include hostile reaction from parts of the public into the piece itself. Since their goal all along had been to challenge the invisibility of undocumented workers and California's reliance on them, even negative responses contributed to the success of their project.

In a previous collaboration, Avalos and Hock worked with Elizabeth Sisco to produce posters displayed on the back of city buses in San Diego. They created a parody of the city slogan most favored by San Diego boosters: "America's Finest City." Avalos, Hock, and Sisco displayed the words "Welcome to America's Finest Tourist Plantation" superimposed over a series of photographs of "brown working hands" in a variety of settings. One had the hands pointing to a sign that reads "Maid Service Please." Another had them scraping food off a plate. Yet another showed those working hands being placed in handcuffs by an officer from the Border Patrol. Asserting that no real public space existed in San Diego, the artists aimed to create "a public forum within conceptual space" using the circuits of advertising to attack other kinds of advertising and public relations. Securing their space on the buses at a time when San Diego hosted the Super Bowl, the bus poster project provoked extensive media coverage—most of it hostile, but the artists then worked that coverage into the art by making a video, a book, and a traveling exhibit incorporating attacks on their posters into the art project itself.[23]

As the nature of cultural production and consumption changes, as global austerity, deindustrialization, and economic restructuring continue to foment changes in grassroots community-based art making and art-based community making, scholars will need to develop new and better methods of cultural criticism. Artists are not just saying new things with their art; rather, they are calling into question the nature of art itself. Because validation in the university flows from within, scholars tend to be conservative, to repeat what has been done before, and to seek validation from the people who did it. But the dire emergency facing people around the world no longer allows us the luxury of this traditionalism, of scholarship that (to paraphrase Ulf Hannerz) is like Scandinavian cooking—something "passed down from generation to generation for no apparent reason."[24]

Those of us who work, teach, and study as "traditional intellectuals" in institutions of higher learning have an important role to play in analyzing and interpreting the changes that are taking place around us. We need to develop forms of academic criticism capable of comprehending the theorizing being done at the grassroots level by artists and their audiences, of building bridges between different kinds of theory. This kind of work is already in existence, even if in embryonic form.

An exemplary body of scholarship on culture by sociologists, for example, has illuminated complex connections linking cultural expressions to their social causes and consequences. Research on sexual racism by Roderick Ferguson, on memory, literature, and history by Avery Gordon, on nationalism and sexuality by Jacqui Alexander, on the politics of identity by Robert Dunn, on the American Dream and the popular novels by Elizabeth Long, on the evolution of romantic love by Steven Seidman, and on the emergence of new gendered identities during the 1950s by Wini Breines, all show how culture functions as a social force as well as the ways in which transformations in social relations call forth new forms of culture. Line Grenier's analyses of how the structure of the music industry in Quebec encouraged the emergence of the *chanson* as the emblematic icon of Quebecois nationalism and Herman Gray's splendid discussions about how the music recorded by small record companies stems as much from the industrial and commercial imperatives of their niche in the market as from aesthetic choices all serve to render relations between cultural structures and social structures in all of their proper complexity.[25]

Sophisticated work by these sociologists complements nicely the new interest in social structure among humanities scholars of culture. Feminist musicology shows how aesthetic choices often are actually social choices in disguise because musical compositions build affect, engagement, and investment among audiences through complex codes and metaphors that connote social roles including gendered identities, individualism, heroism, and danger.[26] Cinema studies scholars have developed stunningly successful schematizations of the race-gender hierarchies in romantic relations in Hollywood films of the 1950s by demonstrating the connections between the emergence of the United States as a global military and economic power after World War II and representations of Asians in such films as *Sayonara*.[27] Within Asian American studies, exemplary efforts include Jack Tchen's important study of D. W. Griffith attributing the difference between the filmmaker's overt antiblack racism in *The Birth of a Nation* and his condescending paternalism toward Chinese people in *Broken Blossoms* to the very different market niches Griffith hoped the two films would occupy.[28]

Social scientists and humanists have made important strides in theorizing the relations between cultural production and social life in recent years, but our work still speaks more to paradigms established during the industrial era than to the emerging realities and changing nature of the relations among culture, politics, and place in the postindustrial world. In this respect, we have much to learn from artists who are facing up to the things that are killing them and their communities. Cultural creators are also creating new kinds of social theory. Engaged in the hard work of fashioning cultural and political coalitions based on shared suffering, they have been forced to think clearly about cultural production in contemporary society. For example, Australian *yolngu* tribal musician, school principal, and internationally popular recording artist Mandawuy Yunupingu argues that some of his community's oldest traditions prepare them to face up to the peril and promise of postindustrial society. When devising a yolngu curriculum for the Yirrkala Community School, an elder in his tribe advised Yunupingu to think about the process of *ngathu*—the gathering of nuts to make bread. The nuts that grow in the rugged landscape of Arnhem Land contain a kind of cyanide, but by collecting, sorting, and cleaning them in the right way, the yolngu people wash away the poison and make bread that can feed many people. Yunupingu asserts that the ngathu process can serve as a model for disputes about school curricula or relations between social groups. "Remembering the preparation of *ngathu* reminds us that there are right and wrong ways," Yunupingu claims. "Hurry, and the poison will remain in the bread," but "there are ways of proceeding that, structurally, ensure that the interests of all are recognized and respected."[29]

Yunupingu's musical group named itself Yothu Yindi, a name that connotes the harmony and balance that indigenous Australians work to create. Their leader explains that the yolngu concept of *ganma* also offers a model for social relations. Ganma describes the brackish places where fresh water and salt water mix together. According to Yunupingu, non-aboriginal people "wrinkle up their noses" at this water because they find it distasteful, but "for us, the sight and smell of brackish water expresses a profound foundation of useful knowledge-balance."[30] Yolngu people know that brackish water contains a complex and dynamic balance that can serve as a way of thinking about relations between black and white Australians, and about other kinds of balance that need to be achieved in the world. "*Ganma* is a metaphor," Yunupingu explains. "We are talking about natural processes but meaning at another level. *Ganma* is social theory. It is our traditional, profound, and detailed model of how and what Europeans call 'society' works."[31]

According to Yunupingu, ganma allows us "to see European-type knowledge as just one sort of knowledge among many," to theorize the synthesis of seemingly incompatible cultures and forces, and to see that the knowledge needed to comprehend the world that is emerging is already here if we know how to find it. The cultural work that his theory has generated has been singularly effective in that regard: Yothu Yindi's song "Treaty" gained national and international attention, securing a power in the market that helped spark a successful struggle to force the Australian government to negotiate a new treaty between that continent's original inhabitants and the descendants of European settlers. On world tours, members of Yothu Yindi have met with Native Americans in Los Angeles and hip-hop activists in Marcus Garvey Park in Harlem to discuss "common" concerns among these disparate communities of color.[32] Artistic production plays a central role in Yunupingu's vision. "When you talk about the revolutionary things that have happened in the world," he argues, "it's always been connected with art and I think the Aboriginal people are in that process now. Our art is a mechanism for change."[33]

Yunupingu is not alone in theorizing about transnational culture from the grass roots, in facing up to the things that are killing him and his community. Singer and composer Jocelyne Beroad of the West Indian zouk band Kassav offers metaphors parallel to Yunupingu's in her story about how her group chose its name. Before the emergence of the band Kassav, musicians from Guadeloupe and Martinique rarely played music from their own communities, seeking commercial success with formulas that had been devised elsewhere. The success of Kassav in local and world markets with zouk music generated enormous local pride and helped build greater unity between the two islands. Kassav is the name of a cake made from cassava, also known as manioc, an edible root. But unlike African cassava, the kind that grows in Martinique and Guadeloupe cannot be eaten directly because it has a poison in it. As Beroad explains, "You've got to know how to extract this poison before you can eat it. It's a traditional family thing. So because they had to extract what was poisoning Martinquian and Guadeloupian music, they called it Kassav."[34] Beroad and her group knew about the presence of poison and the possibility of succumbing to it. But they used local knowledge and grassroots theorizing to "take the poison out" and play an unexpected role in transnational culture and economics.

All around the world, new social movements are forging unexpected and improbable coalitions. During the latter half of the 1990s, trade unionists organizing mostly Latino workers at the New Otani Hotel in Los Angeles confronted an employer (Japan's Kajima Corporation) advantaged by its global reach and scope. Yet the very power of their adversary enabled the New Otani workers to make unexpected affiliations—to ally with Korean nationals and Korean American groups who also had grievances against Kajima dating back to the company's use of Korean laborers during World War II. At the same time, Asian Immigrant Women Advocates waged a successful boycott against Jessica McClintock dresses by building a cross-class interracial coalition among women of color. The Haiti National Network connected U.S. human rights advocates with Haitian exiles to provide material aid and political support for social activists working on agrarian reform issues in that Caribbean country. In each of these endeavors, campaigns against injustice drew strength from the power of cultural expressions and ideas to forge alliances among people with distinctly different social roles and status.

Intellectuals have played an important role in each of these coalitions, in part because they have skills as attorneys, researchers, and writers that social movements need, but also because the writing and teaching of traditional intellectuals functions as a node in a network of oppositional discourse along with the cultural expressions and practices of organic intellectuals and community groups.

New cultural practices require scholars to develop new ways of studying and analyzing culture. As Néstor García Canclini argues in *Hybrid Cultures* we are ill-served in the present by categories that relegate the "traditional" and the "modern" to totally separate realms of experience. He asks us to move beyond paradigms that present "the cultured, the popular, and the mass-based" forms of culture as atomized and mutually exclusive endeavors. Canclini advises that "we need nomad social sciences, capable of circulating through the staircases that connect those floors—or better yet, social sciences that redesign the floor plans and horizontally connect the levels."[35]

The global disaster created by structural adjustment policies and transnational capital and culture may well be irreversible. But if change were to come, it would most likely emanate from people whose political and cultural practices flow from exploiting the contradictions in the new world order, whose theories about culture mix old and new insights for the purposes of popular democracy, and who look at the world without succumbing to either cynicism or sentiment: in short, from people who face up to the things that are killing them, and us.

CHAPTER 10

In the Sweet Buy and Buy

Consumer Culture and American Studies

> One of the illusions created by modern social science is that the
> commodity relations which exist among us today constitute the normal,
> natural, primordial, way in which society was always organized.
>
> —Walter Rodney, *One Hundred Years of Dependency in Africa*

During the fall semester of the 2000–2001 academic year, Native American students at San Diego State University mobilized against their school's use of the nickname Aztecs for university athletic teams and against the symbolism encoded in the school mascot—Monty Montezuma, a half-naked warrior in battle regalia. The protestors argued that marketing the school through this kind of imagery demeaned the actual Aztec people, reinforced negative stereotypes about Indians, and insulted the Native Americans in the SDSU student population by putting one of their cultures in a place that other schools usually reserved for animals.

One protestor found a particularly effective way of dramatizing the stakes of the debate. He wore a T-shirt emblazoned with a slogan that parodied the title of a country-and-western song popularized by Willie Nelson in 1980, from the sound track of the film *The Electric Horseman*, "My Heroes Have Always Been Cowboys."[1] In its original version, the song expresses a nostalgic reverence for the Old West and for the freedom it connotes. The message on the student's shirt changed just one word in the song's title, but to devastating effect. It read "My Heroes Have Always *Killed* Cowboys."

The shirt provoked a ferocious reaction from those opposed to changing the school's mascot. They charged that it promoted violence

235

and antiwhite racism. Yet heroic cowboys in fiction and film almost *always* kill Indians; indeed, their heroism usually rests precisely on their ability to do so. The western lands that cowboys love to roam fell into their hands through violent and bloody means—through war, conquest, forced removal, and relocation of native peoples. The "picturesque" qualities that make a native culture seem like an appropriate mascot to contemporary sports fans have little or nothing to do with that culture itself and everything to do with the relentless stereotyping of Native Americans over the years in songs, stories, film, photography, folklore, and spectacles like the Wild West Show.

The Native American activist at San Diego State wearing the "My Heroes Have Always *Killed* Cowboys" T-shirt used his antagonists' familiarity with popular culture and their devotion to it in order to make a political point. His provocative gesture disproved one of the arguments of his opponents who previously claimed that symbols do not matter very much, and their response underscored the fact that cultural images have an important impact on our understanding of ourselves, that attractive cultural icons and narratives can be used to occlude the ugliness of the unresolved hurts of history.

Yet the centrality of consumer items to the debate over Monty Montezuma at SDSU also revealed some sobering realities about contemporary consciousness and social membership. The university and many neighboring businesses opposed any change in the mascot only because the term "Aztecs" played a large role in their marketing activities. Neighborhood small businesses and the university alike had unused inventory of items that used the name Aztecs or the picture of Monty Montezuma. Their previous marketing campaigns gave the school's nickname and mascot a kind of "brand equity" that would be devalued if changes were made. Defenders of the name and the mascot cited their satisfaction as consumers and the value they derived from "tradition" as reasons to preserve the status quo, thereby relegating questions about human dignity and history that the Native American students presented to a status subordinate to consumer satisfactions and pleasures. Lectures about historical conquest, subordination, and attempted extermination drew little attention during the debate, but a T-shirt satirizing the title of a popular song became the vehicle through which a majority of people on both sides of the conflict began to understand the struggle.

This connection linking entertainment, commodities, and politics seems on the ascendancy in our society. The most prominent campaigner against the regulation and registration of firearms in the United States today is actor Charlton Heston, whose description of his progun politics as a "holy war" suggests that he failed to grasp the meaning of at least one of the commandments that he brought down from the mountaintop while portraying Moses in the 1956 film *The Ten Commandments*. Heston's most visible opponent on the gun control side of the debate is actress and television talk-show hostess Rosie O'Donnell. The most recognizable foe of the death penalty in the United States today is actress Susan Sarandon. The 2000 Republican National Convention punctuated the party's traditional commitment to family values by featuring an appeal for young people to register to vote from "The Rock," a celebrity from that notoriously pro-family institution, televised professional wrestling.

When anti-Castro Cubans in Miami discovered to their shock that a majority of the U.S. population opposed their campaign to keep six-year-old Elian Gonzalez in the United States and living with distant cousins in Miami rather than return to his biological father and step-mother and brother in Cuba, they called on actor Andy Garcia and singer Gloria Estefan to make their arguments for them in a press conference. During the several months that the case remained unresolved, at least six punk rock bands renamed themselves "The Miami Relatives," not because they sympathized with one side or the other in the Elian Gonzalez case, but rather because the media frenzy around the case made the term "Miami Relatives" a symbol of the power of the media to focus all attention on one story and to deflect attention away from others. Like the saturation reporting and melodramatic embellishments of the O. J. Simpson murder case, the killing of JonBenet Ramsey, and the affair between Monica Lewinsky and Bill Clinton, reporting on the Elian Gonzalez case blurred the lines dividing politics, entertainment, and commerce.

An emblematic incident may help us sketch out the full contours of the enormous reach and scope of commercial culture in our lives. During the 1980s, a Los Angeles disc jockey encouraged his listeners to tune in to the annual New Year's Day Tournament of Roses parade from Pasadena, but to turn down the sound on their televisons and listen instead to the counternarrative he provided on the radio. Instead of hearing game-show hosts and former beauty-pageant winners express child-like wonder and awe at parade floats featuring Disney characters made from daffodils or Budweiser bottles made from bachelor's buttons, the radio listeners were treated to a commentary that contrasted radically with the wholesome images on the television screen.

The disc jockey's narration would describe the Montebello High School Marching Band shown on-screen as the "Montebello Marching Sex Change Survivors," putatively a band composed entirely of musicians who had undergone sex-change operations. Baton twirlers on television might be described on the radio as the "Central Intelligence Agency's Martial Arts Marching Team" equipped with deadly batons to be thrown at terrorists at even the slightest provocation to keep the nation safe. Speaking in the same earnest, semiwhispered, tones of significant revelation that characterize parade narration on television, the disc jockey would transform the most spiffy drum and bugle corps into the "Mr. T Marching Band from I Pity the Fool Junior College."

Yet more than maliciousness and reverse snobbery lay behind the disc jockey's humor. The pleasures provoked by his commentary come from a cynical resignation about the inevitable reduction of all social activities to entertainment, coupled with the titillating transgression of imagining separate market segments layered on top of one another. The disc jockey's descriptions enabled marching bands and baton twirlers to become tabloid and talk-show oddities or secret agents out of action-adventure films. There was no point to his parody except to mock the pretense of a thoroughly layered commercial event presenting itself as a voluntary grassroots effort.

At least four layers of commercial transactions permeated the parade. Television executives interested in selling audiences to advertisers broadcast a parade that was initially created to advertise a football game that was originally designed as an advertising gimmick to promote winter tourism to California. The joke about the Mr. T Marching Band references this hypercommercialism by imagining the intrusion of still more commercial activities into the parade. The humor in this case depends on a multilayered and overdetermined relationship to commercial culture. The radio audience recognized the name of the actor Mr. T because he had become famous for his role on the television program *The A Team*. But Mr. T got that particular role because of the impression he made portraying boxer Clubber Lang in *Rocky III* (1982). The role in *Rocky III* came his way because of his real-life experiences as a sparring partner for Muhammad Ali, an Olympic hero and professional boxing champion whose appearances in motion pictures and sporadic efforts at becoming a recording artist only begin to explain his status as one of the most popular (and bankable) celebrities of all time. From *Rocky III* to *The A Team*, Mr. T maintained a distinct image through a recognizable style (Mohawk haircut, open vests, and lots of gaudy gold jewelry) and a recurrent catch phrase, "I pity the fool," as in "I pity the fool who thinks he can beat me in the ring." The phrase however, did not originate with Mr. T. "I Pity the Fool" served as the title of one of the biggest hit records by rhythm and blues singer Bobby "Blue" Bland in 1961.

Thus the maximally competent receiver of the joke about the Mr. T Marching Band would have to be someone well versed in the details of commercial culture. Such a person needs to know a lot to catch the full ramifications of a comment about a television and film actor who had been an athlete (Mr. T) and his use of the title of a blues song during a radio announcer's commentary about a television program created to broadcast a parade that was designed to call attention to a football game that originated in efforts to promote tourism! This is, I think, what we call postmodernism.

How did the purchase of commodities and the consumption of entertainment come to play such a central role in contemporary consciousness? What makes commercial culture so central to our understanding of the social? Apologists for the entertainment industry assert that commercial culture only gives people access to what they already desire. Free-market fundamentalists attribute the love of gain and the love of goods to human nature, and they depict commercial culture as a series of freely agreed upon transactions between buyers and sellers. But the ever increasing importance of commodity culture in U.S. society since World War II has largely been the product of state action, not private initiative. Government funds and government policies orchestrated the development of new technologies including radio, television, the Internet, and containerization in shipping along the lines most favorable to business and most amenable to commodification.

Corporate power has been the main source of government subsidies for consumption. Right-wing social movement organization during the Age of Balanced Budget Conservatism poured new money into politics and secured an even stronger base for probusiness policies like the telecommunications "reforms" of the mid-1990s. Corporate money not only enables business to secure favorable policies in the short run, but the profits from those endeavors fund future contributions to politicians that raise the costs of entry into the political sphere so high that social groups with interests directly opposite of corporate America are excluded from the process. Business desires have encouraged massive expenditures on "defense" that provide a steady flow of capital into the coffers of large corporations, but they have also created a plethora of "corporate welfare" subsidies for a variety of commercial endeavors. Business interests have shaped changes in the tax code to make investment income more valuable than wage income, that encourage investment in automation to cut labor costs and give management more control over production. Direct government subsidies and tax breaks channel capital to private firms for corporate acquisitions and real estate, while discouraging investment in enterprises likely to produce large numbers of high-paying jobs.

Government research and development spending has played an especially important role in creating the new economy of the twenty-first century. The Department of the Navy drew up the first plans for containerization in shipping, a technology that made it feasible to export heavy industrial production to low-wage countries. The government's National Labor Relations Board also took aggressive action against the rank-and-file longshore workers who protested against containerization, denying them any voice in determining whose interests the new technologies would serve. The Department of Defense drew up the first plans for computer communication networks like the Internet and supervised their development and implementation. Research and development efforts by the military transferred the economic risks of developing new technologies to the government while preserving the eventual profits that stemmed from that research for private interests. They also directed the technologies themselves along lines conducive to business needs.

The seeming contemporary eclipse of the state by the power of private capital and transnational corporations hides the crucial role of the state in promoting, protecting, and preserving the technologies, social relations, and economic interests of corporate capital and finance. As Dan Schiller demonstrates in his extremely important *Digital Capitalism: Networking the Global Market System*, building a "free market" for business requires enormous amounts of state intervention and invention.[2] This system also makes sure that the benefits and rewards of the new economy will flow to some social groups, but not to others. Free-enterprise fundamentalists always claim that profits for the wealthy eventually trickle down to the rest of society, but the ever increasing inequality and maldistribution of wealth in the United States and around the world in an era of enormous economic growth and record corporate profits indicates otherwise. This is no accident or anomaly, no temporary cost to be paid for future stability, but rather it is the intended consequence of deliberate policies enacted by the state in the interests of investors and owners.

Since concerted and consistent action by the state has been responsible for such serious declines in resources, life chances, and quality of life for most people, one might expect oppositional social movements to arise. Popular pressure could still coerce the state into fiscal policies that subsidize economic infrastructure rather than capital flight, which equalize rather than stratify economic opportunity, which enforce minimum-wage requirements and limits on the hours of work as a means of raising rather than lowering global working conditions. The state is still quite capable of setting up institutions aimed at equalizing power relations between capital and labor or between capital and consumers.[3] Why have social movements fighting for these changes been so slow to emerge?

Again, state policies hold some of the answers. The neoconservative politicians and ideologues who have worked assiduously to diminish the capacity of the state to serve as a source of social justice, have devoted enormous energies toward strengthening the state as an instrument of repression and incarceration to protect the interests of capital. At the same time, neoconservative political mobilizations have succeeded in enabling capital to evade responsibility for the policies that it has profited from, by blaming the ensuing social crises they cause on the allegedly deficient character and family structures of the new economy's worst victims. Ever since the Nixon presidency, neoconservative politics have relied on "moral panics" about crime, welfare, and "drugs, sex, and rock 'n' roll" to blame the social disintegration and economic decline caused by their own policies on its primary victims—working women, low-wage laborers, racialized minorities, the unemployed, and the homeless.

Yet as important as it has been for neoconservatives to mobilize state resources and to demonize the primary victims of their policies, they have also benefited from the success of previous state policies—including those of the New Deal and the New Frontier—promoting the primacy of consumer spending as the center of the social world. Their expressly political activities have succeeded in hiding and obscuring the workings of politics, making grievances that are actually collective and social appear individual and personal. We see evidence of this history all around us, even if we are unaware of its origins. In advanced capitalist countries at the start of the twenty-first century, activities associated with consumer spending occupy the center of the social world. Government fiscal policies privilege the confidence of consumers and the avarice of investors over the interests of ordinary citizens and workers. Developers destroy viable neighborhoods and demolish ecologically sustainable areas in order to secure maximal profits from luxury commercial and residential projects. Television programming divides families into market segments, colonizes intimate moments and personal spaces for advertising purposes, and promotes infantile narcissism and grandiose desires. Political campaigns revolve around manipulative media messages that project entertaining identities while demonizing opponents.

The "information superhighway" thus looks more like a shopping mall than a public thoroughfare. Educators and artists find themselves forced to deliver immediate gratifications and evoke familiar pleasures to sustain the attention of audiences in search of little more than amusement. Most important, the love of gain that lies at the center of contemporary culture and politics elevates the desire for individual advantage over the collective civic responsibility necessary for solving serious social problems.

The origins of today's problems lie in yesterday's solutions, especially the response by U.S. business and government to the mass mobilizations and egalitarian movements of the 1930s. The exercise of state power since then has favored a vision of consumption practices aimed at eliminating the sites and social relations most conducive to the emergence of oppositional social movements.

The Great Depression harmed the political reputation of capitalism and enabled the Left to position itself as a credible force for improving the material conditions of ordinary people. As the cult of the common person replaced the heroic rugged individual of the 1920s, general strikes, trade-union organizing, and populist politicians like Huey Long demanded action from the state to address the era's economic and social crises. Under the leadership of Franklin Delano Roosevelt, representatives of government, business, and labor created institutions of countervailing power like the National Labor Relations Board, the Works Progress Administration, and rural cooperatives. The New Deal also used government expenditures to stimulate consumption and promote asset accumulation. The National Housing Act of 1934 created the Federal Housing Administration and put the credit of the federal government behind home lending in order to encourage construction and real estate development. Provisions of FHA home-lending policies allowing lower down payments and self-amortizing loans were aimed at limiting excessive savings and encouraging immediate spending. The Social Security Act of 1935 addressed parallel issues: by assuring workers that they would have money available in their old age, social security made it possible for them to engage in less saving and more spending in the present. Many of the expenditures for public works during the New Deal created reservoirs, telephone and electric power lines, and paved roads aimed at stimulating suburban growth.[4]

Low wages and high unemployment during the 1930s undercut these measures, but when defense spending for World War II brought full employment and full production, and when postwar mobilization by workers won significant wage increases, a consumption-based policy of economic growth became possible.[5] At the end of World War II, workers sought to reap the rewards of the prosperity that their labor had helped to create. They waged the largest strike wave in American history between 1944 and 1949. In the summer of 1945, United Auto Workers local union representatives called for conversion of defense plants into government-run factories geared toward meeting consumer needs for housing and transportation. During the 1945–1946 General Motors strike, one popular demand from the rank and file was to make the company pay wage increases out of profits intended for stockholders rather than from price increases that would be paid by workers and consumers. Business and government officials worked hard to contain working-class demands for a role in shaping decisions about the postwar economy and for a greater share of the national wealth. They made concessions, but only in ways that guaranteed expanded opportunities for private profit—highway construction rather than rapid transit, loans for single family detached suburban houses rather than federally funded public housing or loans for renovating existing units, private pension plans and government loans for veterans rather than universal plans securing housing, medical care, pensions, and education like those adopted in other industrialized countries. Most important, they tried to divide unionized

workers from the unorganized, to encourage workers to think of themselves as atomized consumers rather than part of a collective body of
workers or citizens.[6]

Some economic theorists had identified underconsumption as
a serious problem for the U.S. economy as early as the 1880s, and sophisticated corporate liberals devised diverse schemes based on welfare
capitalism throughout the twentieth century. But only the confluence of
successful social movements in the 1930s and 1940s with the crisis of
capitalism during depression and war, coupled with elite concerns about

Sumner High School majorettes with Gemini spacecraft. The consumer society of the
Fordist 1950s was fueled by cold war "defense" spending aimed at broadening the
market for U.S. goods and subsidizing a high-wage/high-employment economy. The
consumer society of flexible accumulation at the turn of the twenty-first century will be
fueled by state-organized and subsidized "digital capitalism" designed to "deepen" the
market by connecting consumers to high-capacity computer/television hookups and
relegating the majority of the population to low wages, few benefits, and little job
security. Photograph by Lester Link, courtesy of Missouri Historical Society, St. Louis;
reprinted by permission.

reverting back into depression after the war generated the levels of government spending, the increased wages, and the business-government-labor agreements required for implementation of those earlier visions. Government spending during World War II doubled the size of the economy and brought especially impressive gains to big business. As they looked to government for direct defense spending as well as help in securing raw materials and markets overseas after the war, big business leaders accepted labor-management agreements and government programs aimed at stimulating consumption as necessary legitimation for the capital accumulation they secured from the state.

Between 1947 and 1953, federal spending on highways, home loans, and infrastructure enabled nine million people to move to suburbs, a 43 percent growth that expanded the suburban population to nearly thirty million people. Three quarters of suburban units were owner occupied, and advertisers noted with relish the higher spending patterns among young families in the newer suburbs.[7] Federal home-loan policies that restricted down payments to 5 percent or 10 percent and the home-owners mortgage tax deduction gave these families increased disposable income, while easy credit and installment buying made a wide range of commodities more affordable. Builders created thirty million new housing units in the two decades following World War II. Federal subsidies helped increase the percentage of home owners in the population from below 40 percent in 1940 to more than 60 percent in 1960. Spending on automobiles averaged $7.5 billion per year in the 1930s and 1940s, but approached $30 billion by 1955.[8] Residential mortgage debt accounted for less than 20 percent of disposable income in 1946, but climbed to 55 percent by 1965.[9]

As Vice President Nixon's "kitchen debates" with Soviet Premier Khrushchev demonstrated, the cold war also shaped the strategy of mass consumption. During World War II, government officials and private advertisements had emphasized postwar prosperity as a crucial aim of the war, presenting images of full refrigerators, powerful automobiles, and new homes more often than appeals based on the ostensible aims of the war—victory over fascism and the triumph of the Four Freedoms.[10] In the postwar period, material abundance in the United States presented an alternative to communism, democratic access to consumer goods implied a broader democracy of life chances. Increased consumption served as a barrier against radicalism at home, but also as an image that might keep other nations out of the Soviet orbit. State department policy makers urged European allies to adopt policies of mass consumption and mass production as an alternative to the kinds of authoritarian rule that raised memories of prewar fascism, but also as a convenient way of preparing European markets for the goods that U.S. corporations wished to sell to them.[11]

During the 1950s real wages increased by 20 percent, and by 1966 half of all workers and three-fourths of those under the age of forty had moved to suburban areas.[12] Workers secured regular vacations with pay, pensions that freed up more money for current spending, and expectations of intergenerational upward mobility. But these state-subsidized improvements in material wealth also helped reconstruct the political and social world of the worker. Government-financed urban renewal destroyed urban ethnic neighborhoods that had been sources of support and solidarity for striking workers during the 1930s and 1940s. Strict promanagement provisions in union contracts and the Taft-Hartley law transformed trade unions into disciplinary agents guaranteeing shop-floor peace to management in return for higher wages. These measures deployed the power of the state to eclipse the trade union or the ethnic inner-city neighborhood. They offered participation in a commodity-driven way of life as reparations, seeking to create a world in which people's identities as consumers would become more important than competing identities as workers, citizens, or ethnic subjects. While relying on the power of the state, they also hid the state, privileging private acts of consumption over collective behavior, and presenting the carefully constructed world of commodity relations as if it were the product of democratic choices.

Urban renewal and suburban growth played particularly important roles in transforming identities in the postwar era by creating new spatial relations among communities and families that encouraged the internalization of consumer desires. Similar to the processes in Germany described by Michael Wildt, new configurations of public and private space in the United States emerged as part of a project that created new patterns and expectations within consumer practices.[13] Nowhere was this new configuration of domestic and public space more evident than in the combination of commercial network television and Disneyland, two seemingly private enterprises that benefited from enormous subsidies from the state.

Throughout its history, commercial television has offered relentless and unremitting messages elevating the purchase of consumer goods in the private sphere over nearly every other human endeavor, yet television too was made possible only through action by the state. State expenditures on research and development during World War II helped perfect the technology of home television, while federal tax policies allowing corporations to deduct the costs of advertising from their incomes solidified the medium's economic base. Government antitrust action against Hollywood studios broke up monopoly in the motion picture industry at the same time that Federal Communications Commission rulings sanctioned the network system for television. Government action restricted stations to the narrow VHF band, granted networks ownership and operating rights to key franchises in major cities, and insulated early broadcasters against competition by putting a freeze on the development of new stations between 1948 and 1952. The private investors who secured enormous profits from television and the media managers who exerted enormous influence on the country because of it owed their wealth, influence, and power to a state that they then sought to undermine at every turn.[14]

In her exemplary scholarship on consumer society and the introduction of commercial network television to U.S. homes, Lynn Spigel details an extraordinary movement of cultural performances from city streets into suburban living rooms. Attendance at motion pictures, sporting events, concerts, and other public performances plummeted between 1947 and 1955. Despite an unprecedented rise in disposable income for middle-class families, total recreational spending suffered a 2 percent decline during those years. Migration to the suburbs pulled customers away from traditional sites of public entertainment and encouraged the growth of home-based entertainments including television viewing and listening to high-fidelity phonographs. Department stores in suburban malls lured customers away from crowded downtown shopping by offering free parking, while suburbanization undermined mass transit, exacerbated traffic jams, and contributed to an increase in commuters and a corresponding shortage of parking spaces in the inner city.[15]

Spigel identifies "a profound preoccupation with space" as an important characteristic of the postwar period. Realtors and home builders proclaimed the advantages of detached single-family homes with spacious backyards over the bungalows, duplexes, and apartments of central cities, while urban renewal, highway construction, and FHA home-loan policies all contributed to impose drastic penalties for living in the city and lavish subsidies for suburban dwelling. The modernist goal of "merging spaces" found powerful expression in suburban homes, argues Spigel, in picture windows, glass walls, landscape paintings, scenic wallpaper, and continuous dining-living areas. Television became an important part of the new suburban space. Manufacturers marketed television sets as a form of "going places," as a way of maintaining connections with a wider world while inhabiting the secure spaces of suburbia. Interior settings used in early television programs emphasized depictions of outside spaces as they might appear through windows, displaying city skylines or suburban hillsides. Popular authors echoed advertising rhetoric when they saluted the new medium for "bringing the world to people's doorsteps."[16]

Television advertisers boasted that their medium offered "not just a view, but a perfect view." Unlike the cinema or other spectator amusements that entailed the risk of bad seats or unruly neighbors, television claimed to place the spectator at the scene of the action with a perfect view and freedom from outside distractions. In that way, television echoed the appeal of suburbia itself, just as it echoed the spatial logic of a place that soon came to stand as the symbolic center of the new social world—Disneyland.

In 1952 Walt Disney purchased land for his theme park for $4,500 per acre, but due to his own enterprise and to the appreciation of land values in California it was worth $80,000 per acre by 1965.[17] Located at the confluence of major freeways in a suburban area certain to grow because of FHA home-loan policies and federal government defense spending, Disneyland guaranteed satisfaction through predictably perfect views and regimented experiences, just like both television and suburbia. If television was an indoor medium aspiring to the complexity of the world outside, Disneyland emerged as an outdoor place emulating the predictably and security of the safe suburban home and the scripted commercial television program.

Walt Disney raised the capital for Disneyland by selling a Sunday night series to the American Broadcasting Company, but television provided him with the amusement park's guiding aesthetic as well as its start-up capital. Nearly every decision about Disneyland grew from a concern about vision. Disney engineers regraded the terrain so that visitors would not see the outside world once inside the park, and they made sure that each "theme" land would be self-contained and not visible from the others. Disney insisted on one central entrance to the park because he believed that people would become "disoriented" if they entered by different gates. He wanted the spectacle of Sleeping Beauty's Castle to pull visitors down through the Main Street shops into the rest of the park. Underground tunnels hid power lines from view and enabled costumed "characters" from each theme land to travel to their destinations without being seen in "inappropriate" locations.[18]

Biographer Bob Thomas underscores the desire to control vision as the dominant aesthetic behind Disney's amusement park. "He wanted everyone to be channeled in the same way, to have their visit to Disneyland structured as part of a total experience," and "he saw the need for Disneyland to flow, as did a movie, from scene to scene." To secure that controlled flow, Disney decided upon mechanical animals rather than real ones for the jungle boat ride, "so that every boatload of people will see the same thing."[19] In this case, and many others, the copy could be better than the original. For the Main Street section of the park, he ordered buildings scaled full-sized on the ground floor, but reduced to five-eighths scale on the second story to make them seem larger and deeper, "to give an illusion of intimacy and an aura of play."[20] Five-eighths scale for the second stories of buildings also gave adults a view that resembled what a child would see.

The managed gaze of the Disneyland experience had commercial as well as aesthetic purposes. As visitors entered the park, they passed through Main Street on their way to Sleeping Beauty's Castle. This corridor led them (visually and physically) into the inviting shops along the street. The turn-of-the-century decor and charming scale of the buildings disguised their commercial purpose with a veneer of wholesome fantasy. Indoor passages made it easier to move from shop to shop than to travel back out to the street, inscribing shopping as the recommended first activity of a day at Disneyland. Purchases of Disney artifacts further advertised the films, comic books, and television projects of the host corporation, while food and drink purchases directly and indirectly enriched concessionaires who paid Disney large sums to give their products monopoly status on Main Street, not only securing a captive clientele, but also advertising their importance by associating their brand names with the "family fun" for sale at the park.

Retailers everywhere copied Disney's success. One developer and department store magnate concluded, "Main Street's purpose (in Disneyland) is exactly the same as Korvette's [department store] in the Bronx, but it manages to make shopping wonderful and pleasant at the same time. I'm sure people buy more when they're happy."[21] Promotional literature for Disney tried to distance itself from television viewing but appeal to its aesthetic contours at the same time, claiming, "Up until now, audience participation in entertainment was almost non-existent. In live theater, motion pictures and television, the audience is always separate and apart from the actual show environment.... Walt Disney took the audience out of their seats and placed them right in the middle of the action, for a total, themed, controlled experience."[22]

The "total, themed, controlled" experiences of Disneyland and of television fit perfectly with the spatial relations of the suburban communities, which they both reflected and shaped. Suburbs also offered "a perfect view" for a price—an exclusive lawn and backyard for each household. Backers of Disneyland, television, and the suburbs all stressed their benefits to the "family," but all three entities helped bring into being a new kind of family unit. Children needed their parents' money to gain access to the wonders of Disneyland, television, or suburbia. Disneyland and television hailed young viewers as consumers, presenting them with advertising messages disguised as play. Suburban communities characterized by sprawling distances and private residential spaces left little room for children to design or appropriate play sites of their own. The formally organized recreational center replaced the spontaneity of the street, just as the station wagon came into use as an antidote to suburban distances and the dearth of public transportation.

The preoccupation with controlling social and physical spaces at Disneyland corresponded to the aura of exclusivity sought in the suburbs. Local zoning and deed restrictions guaranteed suburban homeowners control over space, and not so coincidentally over the racial and class composition of their neighborhoods. Homogeneous visual stimuli underscored this homogeneity of race and class, as suburban landscapes sought to control the contradictions displayed freely in urban areas. Designer John Hench explained Disneyland's "language of vision" in much the same way. "Most urban environments are basically chaotic places," Hench complained, "as architectural and graphic information screams at the citizen for attention. This competition results in disharmonies and contradictions that serve to cancel each other. A journey down almost any urban street will quickly place the visitor into visual overload of ali the competing messages into a kind of information gridlock." By contrast, Hench described Disneyland as a locus of harmony, as a site that aspired to linear precision. He boasted of the park's "orderly progression," which he described as "similar to scenes in a motion picture."[23]

The motion picture analogy is not quite right, however. Disney-land's four- and five-minute rides interspersed among innumerable concession stands bear less resemblance to the closed and complete narratives of film than they do to the spasms of storytelling that serve to capture television audiences for commercial advertising. Just as television programs serve to naturalize the world of consumer goods by turning even domestic dramas into de facto fashion shows and shopping catalogues, the entertainment at Disneyland is itself a commercial, a simulation of stories sold by Disney in other media.[24]

The Disney organization creates narratives that place shopping at the center of human activity. For example, Disney World's publicist Charles Ridgway describes that park's Cinderella Castle by asking readers to "imagine a full-size fairy-tale castle rivaling Europe's finest and all the dream castles of literary history in space-age America. A castle without age-crusted floors and drafty hallways—a palace with air-conditioning, automatic elevators, and electric kitchens. A royal home grander than anything Cinderella could have imagined."[25] From this perspective, the story of Cinderella is no longer about class barriers, sibling rivalry, Oedipal conflicts, or even romance. The "dream castles of literary history" lose their connection to political history, but instead, fairy tales and literary history function as deficient precursors of the present. This vision connects the past with dirt and bodily discomfort, celebrating the present most of all for its air-conditioning and electric kitchens.

Disneyland quickly established itself as an extraordinarily successful commercial space. Three years after the park's opening, Disneyland attracted more visitors every year than the Grand Canyon, Yosemite, and Yellowstone National Parks combined. In its first decade of operation, an estimated 25 percent of the U.S. population had visited the park. Disneyland helped restructure citizenship as well as spectatorship. It provided narratives about the American past carefully designed to erase politics, depicting a turn-of-the-century town with no workers and no immigrants; Abraham Lincoln but no slavery; Aunt Jemima but no Nat Turner. More important, architects and urban planners turned to

Disneyland and Disney World as models for turning ceremonial public space and historic buildings into themed and controlled shopping malls as anchors for urban redevelopment.

The design aesthetic pioneered at Disneyland thrives in the shopping malls developed by James W. Rouse and his imitators, first in the suburbs, but now in the center of many of the nation's largest cities. Like Disneyland and Disney World, Rouse shopping centers display a modernist faith in besting nature via artificial landscapes and climate control. They reframe public space as shopping space, and they pursue exclusivity and segregation through active security patrols and through their preference for high-priced specialty shops maximizing sales per square foot over merchandisers selling staples. They build upon the managed gaze developed in Disneyland, on television, and in suburbs by presenting "perfect" views of local landmarks like the harbors in Boston, Philadelphia, New York, and Baltimore as stimuli for shoppers.

Publicity by the Rouse Corporation and its admirers in magazines including *Fortune* and *Business Week* frequently touted Rouse's success as proof of the superior abilities of the private sector in solving social problems. In actuality, Rouse relied on extensive state subsidies for his projects. Urban Development Action Grants provided Rouse with more than $110 million in federal aid during the 1980s, and records of the Department of Housing and Urban Development show another $168 million in public money funneled into twelve of Rouse's projects. In Toledo, local investors and city officials provided Rouse $13 million for improvements, dedicated payback receipts from a $10 million federal grant, and secured a $9.5 million loan from a local bank for Rouse's Portside project. But when half of the tenants left the development in two years and the project failed, Rouse walked away unaffected, having invested none of his own money.[26]

A profile in *People* in 1981 presented Rouse as a businessman capable of "saving cities" by building low-cost housing for minorities, quoting his prediction that "by the end of the '80s a black family will be able to live comfortably wherever it wants in almost every American city."[27] But the foundation that Rouse created and expected to provide

$10 million a year for low-cost housing by 1990 (and eventually $20 million per year) *lost* more than $1.5 million in 1985, nearly $2.6 million in 1986, and more than $5 million in 1987.[28] By the end of the decade, black families had worse access to decent housing opportunities than ever before.

In New York's South Street Seaport, the Rouse Corporation angered local residents and community groups by leaving the public only a six-foot-wide walkway along the harbor, reserving the rest for private businesses. Architecture critic Craig Whitaker notes that the imperatives behind this usurpation of public resources come from the demands of commerce, explaining, "In order to create a market, the developer often needed to control (architecturally and financially) some of the public domain, and in order to keep the developer interested, the politician needed to give up some of that same domain."[29] Consequently, a development celebrated for bringing citizens back to the harbor actually restricted their access to it. In this kind of situation, the harbor becomes a marketing lure, and the shopping mall near it offers privileged views of public resources only to those with the money to pay for condominiums and meals at fancy restaurants.

These festival malls present what J. B. Jackson terms "other-directed architecture"—self-conscious spaces directed toward tourists. They turn everyone into a spectator and offer sociability only under terms conducive to maximizing profits. They presume permanent divisions among places for work, residence, and shopping. They demand huge subsidies from taxpayers in the form of land clearance, tax abatement, and tourist promotion, but undercut the local merchants with the closest ties to the broader community. They divert public monies for police, fire protection, and basic services to commercial districts and away from residential zones. They refashion local history and community memory into novelty shopping opportunities under climate-controlled conditions, much like television and Disneyland do. They sell back to people (in diluted form) an image of the social life that they helped destroy in the first place. They turn urban sites into urban sights, and encourage a public life based on private insulation from fearful contradictions.

Not every Rouse mall is the same. The company's projects in Boston and Baltimore have been economically viable and much-used facilities. Yet the failure of many of Rouse's festival malls, the enormous subsidies they receive from the state, their negative effects on neighborhood businesses and local tax burdens, and their inability to generate any funds to deal with urban problems has not led to any serious rethinking of the relationship between consumer spending and the public interest. When Community Employment Training Act projects lose money or fail to produce jobs, they appear again and again in public discourse as "proof" of the failure of the state to solve social problems. But when massive subsidies to private developers and individuals produce real debacles, the reputation of the private sector remains untarnished. In part, this disparity exists because contributors to political campaigns and media conglomerates benefit personally even from failed projects using public money, but also because welfare capitalism during the postwar period and the reorganization of social space in the suburbs ever since have established consumer desire as the central unifying narrative of our nation, a narrative tapped most fully by Ronald Reagan in his years as president.

As cohost of the televised opening ceremonies at Disneyland, as a performer in commercials for General Electric, and as President of the United States, Reagan sacralized consumer desire with extraordinary skill. At the 1988 Republican National Convention he read a letter from a small boy who announced that he loved America because it had just about every flavor of ice cream you could want. As president, Reagan offered more for less, enacting tax cuts but promising no decline in government revenues, increasing defense spending but declaring no need for deficit spending, and ending regulation of the savings and loan industry by promising that market-based love of gain could solve the nation's problems more successfully than government regulation. When this hubris enabled the government to accumulate a larger national debt during Reagan's terms in office than it had accumulated in the entire previous history of the nation, when it produced massive unemployment, homelessness, unchecked health hazards, and substantial sums wasted on bailing out the speculators in the savings and loan industry, Reagan concluded that his policies were working just as he had intended.

Ronald Reagan's performance in what he called "the role of a lifetime" depended upon the strength of the neoconservative political mobilizations that brought him to power. For almost fifty years, memories of the Great Depression and conservative complicity with fascism hindered the Right in the United States. The fiscal crisis of the state in the 1970s, however, and the emergence of globalized capitalism enabled Balanced Budget Conservatives to successfully portray private capital as the engine of economic growth, while dismissing social welfare spending as a drain on productive resources. The failure of conservative economics to deliver the prosperity it promised to most Americans or to confront the consequences of the economic inequality it exacerbated leaves individuals with few options other than consuming commodities as distraction from serious structural problems and as reparations for the national failure to resolve them. In this context, the extent to which commercial popular culture places consuming commodities at the center of the social world has enormous import for whether oppositional social movements are possible. If commercial culture makes us think that politics are impossible, that state support of capital is productive but social welfare spending is wasteful, then we may well have become the people that those interested in unlimited freedom for capital want us to be. On the other hand, if commercial culture contains contradictions that may yet connect us to a broader social world, then consumer culture is only one of many terrains where political struggle may yet take place.

Commercial popular culture affects the forms of cultural expression that we see as well as the terms by which they come to us. It is not just that every piece of entertainment comes accompanied by advertising messages or must win the approval of advertisers or investors in order to appear in the first place, but rather that the commercial and industrial matrices in which popular culture is located go a long way toward shaping the identity of its products. In consumer society, cultural expression emerges directly from the search for market segments, the psychology of market sites, the exigencies of market practices, and the experiences of market pleasures. To the extent that we accept the definition of ourselves encouraged by market segmentation, that we accept the social relations mandated by the sites of commercial reception and production, that we attune our intellects and moral standards to the dictates of market practices, that we succumb simply to market pleasures as the ultimate horizon of cultural and social experience, the chances for oppositional social movements will certainly be slim.

The search for market segments in consumer society gives rise to specific cultural creations that hail us as part of target populations desired by advertisers. For example, the television program *Sixty Minutes* came into being because of the Columbia Broadcasting System's desire to fuse their Sunday afternoon football-watching audience with their Sunday night viewers of mystery stories. They created a program that combined the confrontation (and sixty-minute time clock) of competitive sports like football with the processes of investigation, induction, and deduction common to murder mysteries and dramas. Previously programmers had viewed the late afternoon and early evening on Sundays as a kind of sacred family time, addressed through children's programming or "wholesome" family entertainment. But the search to fuse together distinct market segments led the network to create a new social group whose visible demographics made them more attractive to advertisers and more lucrative to the networks than a mere family audience could ever be.

Similarly, *Made for Television Movies* in the 1970s began to draw their determinate shape from similar demographic considerations. Because the American Broadcasting Company's *Monday Night Football* games attracted overwhelming numbers of male viewers, rival networks began counterprogramming movies with women's themes (and often protofeminist viewpoints) in order to effectively deliver to advertisers the potential market segment completely unaddressed by advertisers on *Monday Night Football*. In the 1980s, advertisers found a way to cater to two previously distinct demographic groups at once by programming shows that parents and children would both like, but for different reasons. *Family Ties* depicted an adult couple in the 1980s whose youthful experiences in the 1960s shaped their values. By contrast, their children, and especially their son reflected the "values" of the 1980s, in this case ardent conservatism and reverence for Ronald Reagan. In similar fashion, *The Wonder Years* centered on the experiences of a child, but positioned him in the present looking back at adolescence in the 1960s from the viewpoint of a 1980s adult. This kind of fused marketing appeared in motion pictures as well, in the 1987 film *Dirty Dancing*, set in the 1960s, and previously in *Grease* (1978), a musical evoking nostalgia for the 1950s but starring contemporary stars John Travolta and Olivia Newton-John singing pop songs destined for album sales and the pop charts in the present.

Market sites also help determine the forms that commercial culture takes. Janice Radway explains that romance novels appear in small paperback form because they can be held with one hand by mothers with young children or by busy housewives who might need one hand free to attend to household responsibilities while they read.[30] Tania Modleski's studies of televised daytime game shows reveal a similar connection between text and context. Familiar theme songs, loud bells and buzzers that signal correct and incorrect answers, and loud bursts of audience applause signal the fate of contestants to women whose work in the home draws them away from continuous visual contact with the screen.[31] Radway and Modleski focus on the physical sites of reception, but the social site that a cultural expression occupies can also shape its content. Horace Newcomb points out that the serial narrative form of television soap operas, nighttime dramas, and even situation comedies stems from commercial rather than aesthetic causes. Advertisers interested in associating their product with popular performers prefer serial narratives because they enable audiences to build consistent identification with stars and entail situations that make it easier to predict the number and nature of a program's viewers.[32]

Market practices also help determine the aesthetic content of commercial culture. In his innovative work on "hooks" in popular music, Gary Burns shows how producers try to make a strong impression at the beginning of a recording because they know that many radio programmers test hundreds of songs at a time and will continue listening only if something strikes them strongly at the start. The programmers claim that the same practice guides their listeners; if a song starts inconsequentially they fear it will lead listeners to switch to another station. As a result, devices like the electric sitar beginning on B. J. Thomas's "Hooked on a Feeling" or the "misleading" orchestral introductions to 1970s disco songs come from the market practice of the industry niche in which they are located rather than from the inspiration or intuition of composers.

In other cases, advertising messages become products themselves—sometimes intentionally as products plugging other products such as baseball cards or music videos, sometimes unintentionally as commercials whose production values make them desirable on their own, such as Irma Thomas's singing commercials for Gulf Coast Loan Corporation in New Orleans, or the White Port Lemon Juice commercial that became a rhythm and blues hit under the title "WPLJ." Sometimes, this occurs in completely calculated fashion, as in the case of the professional ice hockey team in Anaheim owned by the Disney Corporation and named after that firm's motion picture hit *The Mighty Ducks*. Other times, toys appear as investment opportunities, advertisements for motion pictures and books, and repositories of the specialized knowledge of a generational cohort as in the case of Pokemon cards.

Many of the policies promoting consumption by business and government in the post–World War II era aimed at overcoming the social warrant of the Great Depression, at making a life built around the accumulation of goods both feasible and ideologically legitimate. They had to overcome cultural resistance to buying on credit (because of the devastating effects of mortgage foreclosures and personal indebtedness during the 1930s) as well as political resistance to government policies designed to "prime the pump" of the economy by channeling capital to business and safeguard the predictability, stability, and security that investors desired but that could not be produced by market forces alone.[33] Their main task during this era was to *broaden* the market by encouraging residents of the United States to spend more and by opening up markets overseas to U.S. firms.

The imperatives of the postindustrial era and its practices of "flexible accumulation" compel government and business today to seek to *deepen* the market. The power of transnational capital and the end of the cold war has extended consumer marketing to every corner of the globe, and eliminated most of the systems of government and social movements that might offer alternatives to the pursuit of commodities as the center of the social world. The greatest profits no longer come from marketing the same item to more and more consumers, but rather from the creation of specialty markets that derive their profitability from differentiation. During the 1960s, artist Andy Warhol explained his silkscreen prints of hundreds of identical Coca-Cola bottles as a tribute to American democracy because the millionaire and the pauper drink the same beverage: no matter how rich you get you can't get a better Coke. Today, specialized production for luxury markets guarantees that people from different social strata consume different products. Those at the high end of the consumption scale enjoy the greatest differentiation.

During the 1950s, television producers and networks sought the largest aggregate audiences, the high ratings that appealed to advertisers. Starting in the 1960s they turned instead toward targeted marketing in order to reach the groups that spent the most, that had the demographic profiles most valued by advertisers. Thus the preferred form of television address, and by today all forms of market address, hailed upwardly mobile salaried suburban professionals and their families as the implied recipient of media messages directed toward the "mass" audience.

The *deepening* of the market entails very different practices from those followed when the goal was largely to *broaden* the market. Having already conquered what geographer Neil Smith calls "absolute" space, consumer marketing now looks to the expansion of "relative" space, largely by creating more opportunities for sales to the same audiences. Massive government subsidies and policy interventions have guided the development of standards for linking high-definition television receivers with home computers in order to guarantee a market focus for the new technologies. As the important research of Maribel Paredes demonstrates, international trade agreements negotiated by governments and investment strategies guided by the International Monetary Fund and the World Bank have seen to it that television receivers produced in low-wage countries like Mexico will supply affluent consumers in North America, Europe, and Asia with cheap access to a new kind of consumer experience.[34]

Unlike television advertising, which attempted to shape future buying patterns once the consumer left the home, digital television and radio will encourage purchases in the home at the moment when consumer desire has been aroused. Multiple channels will not be used to diversify programming or create access to more and different cultures, but rather to create layers of market opportunities through which the purchase of one product will lead to the purchase of others. This perpetually expanding space for shopping realizes in life the kind of exaggerated hypercommercialism that functioned as parody when invoked by the Los Angeles disc jockey in his comic simulcast descriptions of the Rose Bowl Parade in the 1980s.

With the advent of digital capitalism, it may seem like nothing else remains of culture, politics, or social life except for profit-based commercial transactions. Yet all social systems have their contradictions. The very same processes that undermine the effectiveness of political opposition in any one national setting make it necessary for aggrieved groups to establish cross-border and transnational networks and alliances. The very same technologies of flexible accumulation and on-time production that lessen the bargaining power of workers at the point of production make capital more vulnerable to resistance at the points of distribution and reception.

The Australian dock strike of 1988 provided a clear demonstration of the ways in which new forms of production and distribution can promote new forms of resistance. Flexible accumulation and on-time production tip the balance in favor of management at the point of production because low inventories, outsourcing, and computer-generated automation make it easy to close down a plant and shift production elsewhere if the workers strike in any one location. But the same system relies on rapid delivery of perishable items, component parts for the assembly of other products, and commodities with a large part of their value compressed into their "timeliness" such as this year's fashions, motion pictures, or popular music. During the Australian Dock Strike, workers in that nation and around the world started to see how workers in transport and other distribution jobs acquired more leverage under the new system rather than less.

Shortly after successful strikes by the International Brotherhood of Teamsters in North America and by the International Transport Workers Federation in France, corporate executives at the Patrick Stevedore Company in Australia attempted to crush the Maritime Union of Australia. The company shifted more than three hundred million dollars in assets to subsidiaries so that it could plead poverty if convicted of violating Australia's fair labor practice laws. A Hong Kong management firm supplied ten million dollars to train a mercenary force of commandos to take over the docks and operate the sophisticated cranes usually operated by the longshore workers. With the help of military veterans from the Australian armed forces (and very likely with covert help from the Australian government itself), the company sent recruits to the Persian Gulf ports of Rashid and Jebel Ali in Dubai for special training in supervising killer dogs, handling weapons, and operating automated longshore equipment. Executives from other corporations and businesses raised twenty million dollars for a secret "war chest" to help the Patrick Stevedore Company break the union and dismantle the working conditions and wages that workers had won through collective bargaining and on-the-job action over the years.

On April 7, company managers ordered a team of commandos to eject the firm's entire twenty-one hundred person workforce from the docks in Melbourne. Before retreating from their posts, however, the dock workers quickly "misplaced" some twelve thousand containers, almost all of which remained "lost" until the strike ended. When the company tried to deploy a force of seven hundred security personnel and police officers to take control of the docks in Freemantle, workers brought twenty-five hundred community residents to the waterfront in time to mount a successful blockade. Although the media and the business community supported the company, much of the public at large supported the strikers, including members of other unions, the cast of one of the most popular television soap operas in the country, and the national snooker champion.

Workers in ports large and small around the world demonstrated clear solidarity with the Australian "wharfies." In San Pedro, California, dock workers refused to unload the Columbus Canada because the ship carried beef and lamb loaded by strike breakers in Australia. The longshore workers in Papua, New Guinea, placed an indefinite hold on all goods handled by nonunion personnel in Australia and the Swedish dock workers soon followed suit, announcing a complete embargo on cargo from Australia. The Japanese waterfront unions proved particularly effective, voicing support for an all-port strike that threatened to leave large amounts of perishable fruits, vegetables, fish, and beef to sit and rot on the docks in both countries.

Despite the wealth and power of employers and intense ridicule and opposition from the media, the Australian dock workers turned back the company offensive and defeated the lockout. While it remains to be seen if the gains won during militant collective action can be secured by the processes of collective bargaining, the lessons learned by the strikers during this dispute have important implications for workers in other places.

Solidarity from workers around the world, support at the local level from labor and community groups, mastery over the complicated technical knowledge needed to operate automated equipment, and decades of small- and large-group discussions about the social effects of new technologies all enabled the Australian dock strikers to win their dispute. They discovered that containerization links together workers from all continents into an integrated system that gives them leverage at the point of distribution and that makes transnational networks and alliances possible, practical, and productive.

Just as globalization alters power relations at the point of distribution, it also alters the relationships at the point of consumption. The "value" of a line of clothing endorsed by television star Kathie Lee

Gifford lies less in the material or labor costs of each item than it does in the value of Gifford's image as a loving mother who cares about her children. Consequently, when activists called for a boycott when they discovered that the clothing marketed with Gifford's endorsement was made by child labor, they were able to materially affect the present and future value of the commodity on the market. Similarly, "anti-sweatshop" student activists all across the United States have been able to raise demands that their universities refrain from joint marketing of athletic wear and other souvenirs bearing the school logo unless the products are made for fair wages at decent and safe conditions. Community groups in many cities have started "clean clothes" campaigns by asking municipal governments to ban the local sale of clothing made under sweatshop conditions. Precisely because so much of the value of these items lies in their cultural image, campaigns to contextualize, challenge, and change that image can be very effective.

Even at the microlevel of reception, market pleasures can shape new kinds of cultural expressions. Hip-hop artists have been especially adept at turning consumers into producers, displaying their knowledge about songs from the past by redeploying them as samples for current musical productions. The Bomb Squad, which produced samples for Public Enemy, tried to "work in the red zone"—that is, to program samples that would break the speakers on which they were played. The Bomb Squad's Hank Shocklee preferred recorded samples over drum machines because the machines were too good, too wed to the beat and too clean in their sounds. Shocklee wanted to capture the way real drummers slide drumsticks along the skins, play slightly late, or make other mistakes that make music more interesting from his perspective. Shocklee even used the audio hiss that sampling puts underneath hip-hop music as another musical sound in the mix, because he thought "the hiss acts as glue and holds everything together." [35]

The search for market segments, the significance of market sites, the function of market practices, and the creative fusions made from market pleasures all encode commercial culture with the imperatives of commerce. They teach us to take pleasure in our own inscription as consumers. They naturalize materialism and artifice, and encourage us to aspire to the identities that fit the categories most convenient for marketers. Most important, they give us identities as consumers that cut us off from the responsibilities and opportunities of citizenship by dividing us into separate market segments, by elevating consumer time over historical time, and by colonizing our imaginations to make us more malleable as consumers.

Yet the very need for novelty and the global appetites of consumer culture also make other fused identities and practices possible. Especially in the post-Fordist era, capital creates contradictory identities, stoking consumer desire and grandiose hopes for autonomy, fulfillment, and pleasure while at the same time delivering austerity, social decay, and fragmentation. In the short run, even these frustrations can work to promote yet another round of consumer identities and choices, but in the long run, they may open up the very wounds that they claim to heal.[36] If the current moment in world history offers us precious few examples of what scholars call the "old social movements"—that is, movements with a common ideology, rooted in struggles over places like factories, cities, and states, and seeking political power for themselves, it nonetheless offers us ample opportunity to observe "new social movements" characterized by immediate interests, coalition politics, shared cultural concerns, and a perceived necessity to work through the contradictions of existing institutions rather than an effort to seize old ones or create new ones.

The Lavalas Movement in Haiti, for example, made use of popular music that combined traditional rara rhythms, vodou practices, and commercial recordings to bring people into the streets in support of agrarian reform and against the nation's military dictatorship and its complicity with transnational capital. On January 1, 1994, in Chiapas, Mexico, the Zapatista Liberation Front emerged out of ten years of liberation theology discussion groups into armed struggle, which they augmented with the use of the Internet, English-language graffiti in Los Angeles and Mexico City, and fax machines. U.S. rhythm and blues records broadcast on Radio Bantu by the South African government as a means of attracting listeners to racist government propaganda inadvertently helped make the English language the lingua franca capable of uniting tribal groups speaking different languages and providing the opportunity for expressly politicized readings of songs whose lyrics seemed to contain no overt political message.[37] The same shared expectations and market identities that make displaced Andean Indians in South American cities consumers of new cultural commodities like chicha music also have given rise to thousands of neighborhood associations and political campaigns to secure social services.

For all their reach and scope, market segments, market sites, market practices, and market pleasures do not yet determine our social being totally. Commercial culture provides an inescapable terrain for social connection and identity formation, but contradictions among members of the same market segment, the differential access to power revealed in the style and prestige hierarchies of the mass media, the creative subversion and inversion of market practices by consumers, and the utopian aspects embedded within market pleasures all provide potential sources of contradiction and conflict. The disintegration of the social fabric under neoconservatism and the increasingly apparent inability of market-oriented solutions to meet individual and collective needs increases conservatism's stake in cultural issues, mandating countersubversive witch hunts against the very popular music and films that a consumer-oriented economy relies on for its economic well-being, as well as hysterical and counterproductive crusades against imagined foreign enemies and demonized domestic villains.

For scholars in American studies, the reach and scope of commercial culture in contemporary society requires us to develop new and better theories about the relationships linking entertainment, consumption, and social identities. The globalization of entertainment markets compels us to study transnational circuits and networks of communication as integral parts of any one national culture. The proliferation of new market identities and desires challenges us to search for sources of unity in an economy and culture increasingly dependent on generating new forms of differentiation and division.

Scholarly work on consumer culture, globalization, and the emergence of new identities does not guarantee a critical stance toward those processes. Without clear connections to oppositional social movements, such scholarship might well succumb to the temptation to become a research and development arm of global capital. At the same time, oppositional movements need the knowledge, information, and analysis that scholars have if they are to succeed.

To be sure, any oppositional social movement in the future will have to move beyond the present hegemony of consumer identities. It will need to challenge the enduring significance of the state as an instrument of repression and capital accumulation, to identify the human and economic costs of the transnational economy, and to struggle for employment, education, health care, and political rights for the increasingly disenfranchised and disinherited population of the world. This will not be easy. A recent experience presented me with a vivid illustration of just how difficult it may be.

Shortly before the completion of this book, I delivered a lecture at a large midwestern state university on globalization, commodification, and inequality. As I spoke, one member of the audience frowned at me, shook his head in disagreement, and had his hand up signaling he wanted to challenge me even before I finished speaking. I fully expect disagreements when I present my views, and in fact I have learned a great deal over the years from those with whom I disagree, but this time would be different.

The man's name was Jim. He responded to my remarks by taking off his watch and holding it up for the audience to see. He explained that the global economy I critiqued had made it possible for him to own that expensive watch, and that made it all worth it. I suggested that he think about the real costs of his timepiece, not the price he paid in the store, but the price paid by those who mined the minerals that went into it, the price paid by those who assembled it, the price paid by those who went hungry or without medical care because the same system that brought him that watch denied them food and medicine.

Jim would have none of it. He thought that I was unfairly trying to make him feel guilty, that the global economy had given him something of value, and that I was trying to take it away. He related how some friends of his who had vacationed in Costa Rica had gotten robbed. If I wanted to do something about conditions in the rest of the world, he suggested, I should teach people in Costa Rica not to take money from American tourists. Other members of the audience tried to help me out. They suggested to Jim that his ownership of a watch could hardly compensate for living in a society that failed to educate its children adequately, that allowed corporations to destroy the natural environment, that left some people in all parts of the world with so little hope and so little self-respect that they lashed out at others in violent and destructive ways. Jim was unmoved. Holding his watch up high and displaying it to the rest of the room, he asked, "What about this?"

Perhaps Jim was just playing with us. Maybe he is a performance artist whose métier involves having fun with visiting lecturers. Perhaps my talk struck a nerve and made him feel defensive, and talking about his watch was the best way he could think of to defend himself. The funny thing is, I buy products, too. Everyone does. Many of them are enjoyable. But they are inadequate compensation for having to live in a society that values things more than it values people. I don't begrudge Jim his watch. But I do wish he had a better sense of what time it is.

CHAPTER 11

Taking Positions and the
War of Position

The Politics of Academia

Hegemonizing is hard work.

—Stuart Hall

It is perhaps a measure of the inescapable irony of our time that the ideas of Antonio Gramsci have gained popularity among scholars largely as a means of explaining the futility of efforts to change past and present capitalist societies. Above all else, Gramsci was a revolutionary strategist, an individual who instructed others to temper their "pessimism of the intellect" with an "optimism of the will." He knew about defeat and domination from personal experience and systematic study, yet Gramsci still championed a political and ideological struggle *for* hegemony. He described "a war of position," in which aggrieved populations seek to undermine the legitimacy of dominant ideology, rather than just a "war of maneuver" aimed at seizing state power. To counter the hegemony of ruling historical blocs, Gramsci sought to fashion oppositional coalitions capable of struggling for a world without exploitation and hierarchy. He described traditional intellectuals as "experts in legitimation," but called for the development of "organic intellectuals" able to give voice to the repressed needs and aspirations of oppressed groups.[1]

Yet the Gramsci who appears in much contemporary scholarship is less a strategist of social struggle than a coroner conducting an inquest into the blasted hopes of the past. John Patrick Diggins uses Gramsci's concept of hegemony to explain the seemingly unchallenged primacy of liberal individualism in American political culture, while T. J. Jackson

Lears cites Gramsci's work on "contradictory consciousness" as an explanation why American workers in the nineteenth century exercised a "half-conscious complicity in their own victimization." In their challenging and eloquent analyses, Diggins and Lears focus on the undeniable triumphs of liberal individualism and consumer capitalism over oppositional movements dedicated to equality, collectivity, and mutuality. But they present hegemony less as something to be struggled for than as something imposed on society from the top down. Most important, they present the failures of oppositional movements in the war of maneuver as if they were also failures in the ideological and political war of position.[2]

Of course, defeat does matter. Institutional economic and political power means a great deal; oppositional movements pay a terrible price for failure. But as Stuart Hall observes, "hegemonizing is hard work."[3] Dominant groups must not only win the war of maneuver by controlling resources and institutions, they must win the war of position as well. They must make their triumphs appear legitimate and necessary in the eyes of the vanquished. That legitimation is hard work. It requires concessions to aggrieved populations. It mandates the construction and maintenance of alliances among antagonistic groups. It always runs the risk of unraveling when lived experiences conflict with legitimizing ideologies. As Hall observes, it is almost as if ideological dogcatchers have to be sent out every morning to round up the strays, only to be confronted by a new group of loose mutts the next day. Under those conditions, dominant groups can ill afford to assume their own society is wholly pacified, although of course it is in their interest to have others think that all opposition has been successfully precluded or contained.

Leon Fink's analysis of the Knights of Labor offers a refreshing alternative to the institutionalized pessimism of Diggins and Lears. The concrete struggles for power waged by the Knights of Labor in the late nineteenth century displayed an opposition to liberal individualism much greater than Diggins believes was possible, and the self-activity of masses in motion during that era belies the "half-conscious complicity" in their own victimization that Lears alleges to have been characteristic of the American working class. If the power of dominant ideology forced the Knights into addressing demands for individual, private, and material advancement, nonetheless, the lingering legitimacy of republican ideology enabled them to pose credible and popular demands for collective, public, and moral gains. Dominant ideology imposed costly contradictions on their project, but political activism enabled the Knights to expose and to benefit from the contradictions within that dominant ideology as well.

Even defeat did not mean an end to struggle; the institutional failure of the Knights did not preclude subsequent labor militancy and radical politics. In fact, the lessons of struggle taught by the Knights created the social and individual preconditions for future political contestation by millions of Americans. Fink learns from the people he has chosen to study, and he finds important evidence underscoring the activist implications of Gramsci's writings about the instability of bourgeois hegemony, the struggle for legitimation essential to all oppositional movements, and the enduring culture of opposition in America that survives any individual episode of struggle.

In my view, however, Fink does not go far enough. He does not follow his argument to its logical conclusion. He presents a scenario about how the Knights might have emerged victorious in the nineteenth century, proving that they may have been closer to taking power than historians have recognized. It is proper and constructive to call attention to one of the many "roads not taken" from the past that continues to characterize possibilities for the present. But the scenario Fink spins undercuts his earlier insights about the war of position. It places too much reliance on the short-term institutional struggle for power and too little emphasis on the long-term ideological work of constructing counterhegemonic ideas and institutions. By defining victory in terms of specific concessions to be wrested from the ruling class, Fink relegates consciousness to a secondary role as either an obstacle to, or an instrument for, concrete social changes. Yet consciousness is also an end itself.

Long traditions of working-class self-activity have properly focused on concrete material gains, on desired forms of social organization. Yet we have learned from hard and bitter experience that even the seizure of state power by oppositional movements does not necessarily entail victory for aggrieved populations. No single material or structural improvement has meaning by itself; it depends on whether it advances a process of radical democracy that allows people to participate in making the important decisions that influence their lives. Constructing that world requires a political process through which people change themselves and others at the same time that they change the social distribution of wealth and power.

Some examples may make the point clearer. In the early stages of the civil rights movement, Malcolm X spoke disparagingly of a movement that encouraged black people to risk their lives for the "privilege" of drinking a cup of coffee at a lunch counter next to white people. He argued that such a struggle sought "equality" rather than "justice," pathetically replicating and reinforcing the values and hierarchies of the oppressor within the minds of the oppressed. Yet as the movement unfolded, he changed his mind. Malcolm X came to see that the process of self-activity intrinsic to social movement mobilization led individuals to take direct action against the conditions that oppressed them. In the process, it allowed them to live in the world as if they had a right to participate in shaping it. The goals of the movement might have been reformist and reflective of bourgeois hegemony, but the process of struggle itself involved a radical reconstruction of both individuals and society.

Similarly, in *The Civil War in France*, Karl Marx could write approvingly of the Paris Commune, even though its specific achievements were objectively reformist, entailing only an end to night work for bakers and setting up a structure for direct democracy rather than relying on elected representatives to make most decisions. Even though the commune provoked brutal and total repression by the state, Marx could endorse it, not because its policies transcended the norms of bourgeois ideology, but because they expressed the self-activity of ordinary citizens transforming themselves and others through mutuality and collective action. To dismiss either the civil rights movement or the Paris Commune as examples of the power of liberal individualism or the workings of contradictory consciousness is to miss their role in the war of position. They represent instances where human self-activity manifested and legitimated the most radical kinds of oppositional thought and action. One need not imagine how those two insurgencies might have succeeded in taking state power to understand how they helped shape a prefigurative counterhegemony with enduring historical and ideological import.[4]

As the examples of the American civil rights movement and the Paris Commune demonstrate, victory and defeat are not mutually exclusive categories. The civil rights activists who waged a reformist struggle for juridical equality also nurtured and sustained more radical possibilities in the processes of struggle. In terms of concrete concessions, they secured little more than the 1964 Civil Rights Act and the 1965 Voting Rights Act. The ideological and political forces set in motion by that movement, however, reverberated to every corner of the world in subsequent years, serving as an impetus for oppositional action on innumerable fronts. The Paris Commune failed miserably to achieve its own ends, but as an example of what workers could do and as a guide toward the kind of world people might yet one day build, it continued to "succeed" long after the communards themselves were dead.

Even failure has its uses; it brings to the surface necessary information about the shortcomings and contradictions of oppositional movements. Sara Evans shows how the male-dominated civil rights movement subverted its own ideals and interests by failing to understand and correct its own sexism. Yet that very failure convinced women that an autonomous struggle over gender issues had to be waged, and their self-activity led to profoundly radical challenges to existing ideology and power.[5] Similarly, Paul Buhle explores the ways in which radical political parties and oppositional movements have imperfectly understood organic ethnic and class angers, cultural radicalisms, and utopian aspirations in America.[6] To ask how these parties and movements might have attained power is less important than to ask what they might have done better to understand the grassroots interests and aspirations on which they relied.

It is also difficult to identify exactly when oppositional ideology and action fails or succeeds. In 1859 it might have seemed that Afro-American resistance to slavery had had little effect. By 1865, when nearly two hundred thousand black soldiers had joined the Union army, when slaves in the South had staged a general strike in the fields, the legacy of Afro-American resistance before the war took on new significance. The differences between 1859 and 1865 did not depend solely on the events of those six years. They stemmed as well from the hidden yet enduring consequences of resistance that had been going on for centuries. Likewise, in Jack Conroy's wonderful novel of the Age of the CIO, *The Disinherited*, the narrator remembers that his father's union lost every strike along the way, but that even as the workers lost, conditions somehow gradually got better for them because they had been willing to fight. Their job actions never seemed to bring any tangible victories in the short run, but they served as an enduring threat to management, as a warning that enmity might interrupt production at any time and consequently they functioned as an incentive for concessions that might preempt future strikes.

In this context, the memory of previous "failed" efforts at class struggle informs the self-definition and willingness to take risks that brings Conroy's hero into one of the most important mass mobilizations in history, the union organizing drives of the 1930s.[7] Even in failure, social contestation changes the material and ideological balance of power in society. Conversely, even when social contestation succeeds, it is only setting the stage for future changes.

The literary critic Mikhail Bakhtin tells us that there is no such thing as a pure monologue, that every utterance is part of a dialogue already in progress.[8] As much as anyone, historians know the wisdom of that formulation. We turn to the past to understand the hidden dimensions of current discussions; we enter into dialogue with other historians to build true and useful understandings of events and issues that escape us as individuals. Fink builds on the insights of Lears and Diggins in his understanding of the past, just as those two scholars build on Gramsci and others in their analyses. But the habit of dialogue is not the property of historians alone, or of traditional intellectuals who write books and articles; it is an essential way of understanding the world for all historical actors. The organic intellectuals engaged in past and present social contestation can never be static entities embodying a pure consciousness. Rather, they are participants in a dialogue, authors of an ongoing narrative whose final chapter is never written.

Yet waging the war of position is easier said than done. Intellectuals and artists today often live disconnected from active social movements in a way that would have been difficult to predict two decades ago. They work within hierarchical institutions and confront reward structures that privilege individual distinction over collective social change. The painful contradictions confronting socially conscious artists and intellectuals in our society are most often experienced individually, but they stem from the systematic and structural imperatives that give cultural workers contradictory social roles. By their very nature, creative and critical endeavors allow and encourage identification with others. Intellectuals often work in solitude, but rarely in isolation. Empathy emerges within artistic and intellectual work as a crucial way of knowing, as a tool for understanding things outside our own experience. In times of tumult and change, artists and intellectuals can often experience their connections to others as both an honor and a responsibility. On the other hand, the routine conditions of training, employment, and evaluation in jobs that rely on "mind work" encourage a competitive individualism rooted in the imperative to distinguish oneself from others and to surpass others in accomplishment and status. Artists and intellectuals who have never experienced directly the power of social movements in transforming social relations can easily become isolated in their own consciousness and activity, unable to distinguish between their own abstract desires for social change and actual social movements. Taking a position is not the same as waging a war of position. Changing your mind is not the same as changing society.

Artistic and intellectual work takes place today in a contradictory context, and it produces people with a contradictory consciousness. Many intellectual and cultural workers appear to have the privileges of professionals, receiving yearly salaries rather than hourly wages, and controlling many decisions about the nature, purpose, and pace of their jobs. Yet these workers lack the prerogatives of professionals in many ways; they do not control the supply of new labor, their reliance on institutions limits their mobility, and many of them are part of large units of employees whose compensation and working conditions are determined more by bureaucratic fiat than from any accessible political process. Intellectuals and artists are allowed, and even encouraged, to take positions in opposition to prevailing ideology and power, but they are also pressured to segregate themselves from aggrieved communities, and to work within the confines and ideological controls of institutions controlled by the wealthy and powerful.

Intellectuals and artists unable to analyze and act upon their own structural positions in society often seek surrogates for their own alienations in subaltern social groups whom they imbue with uncomplicated and heroic oppositional consciousness. The search for solutions outside one's own sphere is not inherently unhealthy. Indeed, the enduring utility of critical, contemplative, and creative work is its ability to augment our understanding of the world by transcending the limits of immediate personal experience. Yet people unable to understand or appreciate their own contradictions are unlikely to recognize contradictions in others. Political solidarity motivated mostly by a desire to escape the painful complications of one's own life forces the objects of that solidarity into an instrumental position not likely to serve their own historically specific needs and aspirations.

What passes for politics on college campuses can be especially frustrating and futile. Academics need to take the written and spoken word seriously as a basic condition of their labor. Yet excessive preoccupation with political expression and analysis, with finding the right word for the right situation, and discovering the correct context for one's own thought can lead academics away from the kinds of thinking and action needed for social change. On the other hand, in a desire to escape this contradiction, many swing to the other extreme, to a glib anti-intellectualism that privileges any action over critical thinking, that ignores the very important structural role that educators can play through teaching and writing by expressing, validating, disseminating, and legitimating oppositional ideas with direct relevance for counterhegemonic political action.

Proclamations and position papers can be found in abundant supply on campuses, but the actual practice of politics often remains limited to the written and spoken word, to the expression of opinions, ideas, and attitudes. Under these conditions, it is easy for moral posturing to take the place of social analysis, for conclusions to count because they conform to people's desired self-images of themselves as "radical" or "political" rather than because of their actual utility in bringing about transformative social change. Minor disagreements over tactics and strategy easily escalate into mutual recriminations and condemnations. Even when the content of academic discussions concerns life and death issues, their form still seems to flow from more prosaic considerations about who gets the last word and who gets to be the center of attention. Repeated failures and frustrations rarely lead to reassessments of the nature of academic politics, because each instance can be blamed on the moral or intellectual imperfections of individuals (preferably from the opposing camp) rather than on the structural context in which the actions of individuals occur. Moreover, people not participating in political struggles of their own become ill-attuned to the struggles of others, writing books and articles that concentrate on personal alienation as the most important problem for politics to solve instead of examining the prospects for collective and coordinated movements for change. A discourse of personal injury and alienation that could be the starting point for transformative collective action all too often becomes an end in itself in academic life.

Students involved in campus politics experience contradictions very much like those of the faculty, but in different forms. As community organizer Danny HoSang (of People United for a Better Oakland) points out, at the student level, "political" organizing often emphasizes (1) educational events that replicate many of the practices of the classroom, (2) confidence-building confessions and dialogues that replicate therapeutic practices, and (3) cultural events aimed at building unity and pride that replicate the practices of commercialized leisure.[9] Only rarely does student activism take the form of efforts to exercise collective control over institutions that affect student's lives or to connect students to aggrieved groups off-campus engaged in direct–action struggles. Student politics on campus entails endless preparation for struggles that never happen because they so rarely move from talk to action. Activist Sonia Pena (of Denver Action for a Better Community) reminds us, "The goal of direct action organizing is not only to teach people that something needs to be done, but to show them that something can be done and that they can do it."[10] Students sometimes seem to think that once they have changed *themselves* they have changed society; but for all the emphasis on leadership training and development on campus, it is hard to see exactly what these students will be able to lead if they have no practical experiences with collective strategic struggles for resources and power.

The contradictory consciousness that pervades the lives of academic intellectuals, artists, and cultural workers presents specific impediments to progressive politics. Efforts to be radical—in the sense of getting to the root of social problems by creating practices and institutions antithetical to them—often end up as merely extreme, as actions that replicate the very values and prestige hierarchies they aim to overturn. Oppositional intentions do not insulate one from desires for domination over others or from the egoistic individualism endemic to our society. All too often "progressive" political organizations become sites for enacting distinctly unprogressive attitudes and ambitions.

Within academic politics, the same destructive practices emerge again and again to thwart the democratic potential of oppositional movements. These practices carry on the work of dominant ideology under the disguise of oppositional activity. Identifying them, and changing them, should be a high priority for people interested in a more democratic future. Although each time they appear they may seem like evidence of individual shortcomings, as proof of someone's bad character or bad intentions, these practices actually emerge from systemic structural forces that reward self-interest and self-glorification, that limit the

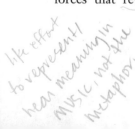

life effort
to represent/
hear meaning in
music, not the
metaphor.

consciousness of intellectuals and artists by preventing us from seeing the world through the many perspectives described by Toni Cade Bambara in her discussion of how to "tell the truth and not get trapped." [11]

The traps waiting within progressive political organizations are multiple and often take one or more of the following forms:

1. Waiting for the perfect bus.

It is often difficult for academics trained to think critically and argue energetically to find actual social movements that live up to their ideal standards. All political projects contain contradictions and pose possible

strike vote December 1, 1966

Strike Vote, University of California, Berkeley, December 1, 1966. Marshall Berman remembers the 1960s as a time that created new kinds of spaces. The intimacy among strangers that he recalls as central to the politics of that decade emerged from mass demonstrations like this one at the University of California, Berkeley. Photograph by Harawitz-Weir Photographers; reprinted by permission of Stan Weir.

risks. "Waiting for the perfect bus" describes an argumentative strategy that insists that all dangers be neutralized in advance *before* political action occurs, guaranteeing inactivity and effectively surrendering before the battle begins. While waiting for a bus, one can find fault with any vehicle that comes along—this one has worn tires, that one is not air-conditioned, this one has a driver we may not trust, and so on. But if we wait for a perfect bus to arrive, we will never get anywhere. Social movements do not start, survive, or succeed because they proceed from perfect knowledge of their own problems. Instead, social movements initiate a process identified by sociologist Michael Schwartz as "organizational learning"—a blend of action and analysis that emerges from within struggle as participants reshape their practical and theoretical ambitions and horizons.

2. Using a megaphone when you really need a hearing aid.

Because intellectual labor encourages the production of eloquent speech and elegant analysis, because the academic reward system evaluates individuals on the basis of their ability to draw attention to the discoveries they have made through research, academic activists often make a monologue out of what needs to be a dialogue. Reporting the results of research to aggrieved communities can provide them with crucial strategic insights and advantages, but *listening* is usually a more important organizing skill than speaking. People learn best what they see for themselves, but intellectuals and artists are sometimes so taken with their own conclusions that they do not work hard enough to provide institutional spaces and sites where other people can see for themselves. To borrow a phrase from Patrick Chamoiseux, they do provide illumination, but they do so like fireflies—with only enough light for themselves.

3. Elevating personal subjectivity over social analysis.

Artists and intellectuals who wait for the perfect bus or who use a megaphone when a hearing aid is required suffer from seeing things from too far away, from their distance from the communities they most wish to

ethnography insists upon listening

help. The opposite problem plagues those who elevate personal subjectivity over social analysis. Understandably wary of the procedures within intellectual life that construct artificial distances, they overcompensate by privileging first-person experience and expression over social analysis. It is not misguided for intellectuals and artists to employ empathy and emotion as ways knowing or as antidotes to their own alienation. It is not misguided to be sensitive to the suffering of others or to establish venues where people get the opportunity to express themselves. Yet cathartic expressions of personal feelings may leave oppressive social structures in place; in fact, they may even make them stronger by encouraging us to think about our anguish as personal rather than collective, as subjective rather than structural. The problems of distance are not solved by seeing things solely from close-up either. The problems of proximity are not solved by seeing things solely from far away. Social analysis and social activism both succeed best when contradictions remain alive, nettling, and generative, not when they are avoided or suppressed. Active scholars and scholar activists need to see things from close-up *and* far away.

4. Embracing terminal marginality.

(Radway)

People who have no direct experience with victorious social struggles can find it difficult to believe that fundamental changes are actually possible. Accustomed to marginality in existing institutions, they may become comfortable with it, and confuse embittered marginality with genuine opposition. Consequently they expect to lose, and sometimes even use their defeats as proof of their virtue, arguing that the only people who could succeed in a corrupt system are those who have internalized its broader corruption. While understandable, this stance becomes a self-fulfilling prophecy, depriving actual and potential allies of the organizational learning that comes in the process of struggle for transformative change, while limiting recruitment to oppositional positions by making them synonymous with powerlessness, defeat, and at best, martyrdom. It makes sense to be wary of the price one pays for succeeding in a corrupt system, but failure is hardly proof of virtue, and a strategy that allows for no ameliorative victories is unlikely to lead anywhere.

5. Acting like the last radical in town.

In times of repeated defeats for egalitarian social movements, previous eras of struggle can inhibit current action as much as they inspire it. Veterans of previous struggles can play a valuable role in sustaining social movements by passing along the lessons they have learned to new generations. On occasion, however, these veterans create memories of the past designed to dwarf the present, using their experience to judge the movements of the present as completely inadequate and inferior to those of the past. A kind of melancholy for past movements and a palpable bitterness about their eclipse often leads to a characterization of present movements as reformist and accommodationist in comparison with the purportedly revolutionary past.

While much can be learned by careful attention to the different possibilities available in different historical moments, and while perspective from the past always holds the potential to augment our understanding of the present, people acting like the last radical in town often embrace their alienation and isolation as a means of making themselves feel morally superior and as a means of making others feel morally inferior. Behavior like this caused one group of young people in Pennsylvania some years ago to form an organization dedicated to curtailing talk about the 1960s. They called their group, the National Association for the Advancement of Time.

6. Climbing like crabs in a barrel.

Hatred of oppression and recognition of one's own powerlessness can easily lead to self-hatred and self-destruction. The reality of repeated defeats, the recognition of what is at stake, and an inability to lash out at one's real enemies exacerbates factional disputes into moral crusades, turning minor disputes into loaded accusations of betrayal. At this stage, righteousness easily turns into self-righteousness, one's allies become surrogates for one's enemies, and instead of fighting oppression, aggrieved groups fight each other. Aggrieved groups often reserve their worst wrath for their own members; oppositional political groups frequently do more harm to their allies than to their enemies. On the individual level, this leads to personal attacks against anyone on one's own side who appears to be getting attention and recognition. Like crabs in a barrel, some activists attempt to climb up by pulling others down, not realizing that this ensures that everyone remains on the bottom. Activists who support other activists, push them forward, and help them do their work in the most effective ways and under the best possible conditions will have strong allies. Those who live in fear that someone else will get a little bit of recognition or reward can prevent this by making their allies weaker, but in the process they undercut themselves.

7. Poisoning the well you have to drink from.

During the worst stages of anticommunist Red-baiting in the United States during the early 1950s, some members of the Communist Party started to use party mechanisms to bring charges against one another, to hold inquisitions about party loyalty or character defects of members of their own group. Having been battered by outside enemies, they developed a desire to do the battering themselves, replicating even the form favored by their oppressors. Institutions and structures of struggle are precious resources for social movements; oppositional groups have to fight hard to build their own associations, organizations, networks, and journals. Yet these institutions are often imperiled and sometimes even destroyed when members of social movements conduct vendettas that impose on their allies the sanctions they would really like to impose on their enemies. Open criticism and debate is essential for the future of democratic organizations, but Manichean oppositions that turn non-antagonistic disagreements into winner-take-all battles imperil the very institutions needed for struggle, poisoning the well from which we all have to drink.

8. Drawing politics from identities instead of drawing identities from politics.

The emergence of the New Left during the 1960s and the survival of oppositional movements ever since has depended in no small measure on the recognition of race, gender, and sexual orientation as important axes of identity and as important arenas for oppositional politics. Significant in themselves as struggles for social justice, political mobilization by gays and lesbians, feminists, and communities of color have also led the way in showing other social movements the value of situated knowledge, the intersectional nature of identity, the forces that link microsocial experiences with macrosocial structures of power, and the need for social movements to enact what they envision—to be therapeutic as well as subversive.

In the contradictory context of academic politics, however, many of these strengths can become weaknesses. The same sense of a common identity that builds solidarity among women, gays and lesbians, or racialized "minorities" can also obscure the heterogeneity of all groups. There is no single way to be gay or lesbian, to be a woman, or to be a member of a racialized group. In addition, movements for social justice organized around the banners of women's liberation, gay liberation, or ethnic nationalism have always been forced to go beyond simple identity; indeed much of the project of these groups has been to battle within their identity category for a politicized definition of what it means to be gay or lesbian, to be a woman, to be a member of an aggrieved group. Efforts at self-naming such as claiming the terms "gay" or "queer," affirming an identity as Asian American, Chicano, or Black, or fighting against sexist language reveal the degree to which these movements have never presumed a unified politics stemming from a common identity, but rather have attempted to create identities based upon politics.

The practices of waiting for the perfect bus, using a megaphone instead of a hearing aid, elevating personal subjectivity over social analysis, embracing terminal marginality, acting like the last radical in town, climbing like crabs in a barrel, poisoning the well you have to drink from, and basing politics on identity rather than crafting identities based on politics stem less from the imperfections of individuals than from the contradictory condition and contradictory consciousness of middle-class academic life. The strengths and weaknesses of people in this position are closely related; like the pharmacon in the pharmacist's window (the snake coiled around a stick that symbolizes the healing effects of what might under other circumstances be considered poisonous), the disease and the cure can be very closely connected, sometimes even sharing the same identity. The things that can kill you can also cure you—if you know the right way to use them.

Living with these contradictions is not easy, and the temptations to seek more stable, secure, and "pure" positions are many. But it is precisely through dynamic negotiation of social contradictions that progressive political practice is most likely to emerge. Conversely, individuals who attempt to solve complex and contradictory problems by reciting rules and running for refuge within stable and pure positions are least likely to make contributions to progressive social change.

For all of its pitfalls, academic politics still matters. Professors and students, like all artists and intellectuals, can play crucial roles in collective social struggles. Schools are important social institutions; their policies and procedures help influence broader social debates about what is forbidden and what is permitted, who is included and who is excluded, who speaks and who is silenced. Scholarly analysis of social conditions and social movements helps frame the political context in which activists work. It communicates activist concerns to new audiences, and brings to social movements greatly needed evidence, analysis, and arguments. Academic work can be especially important when connected to activist struggles outside the academy because established educational and cultural institutions are not the only sites from which critical and creative thinking emerge; indeed, these institutions have been greatly enriched over the years by the innovative analyses and arguments about important issues that emanate from social movements themselves. Issues that can be avoided in the academy take center stage in collective action campaigns and mass mobilizations. Moreover, the ways in which social movements resolve their contradictions can offer important insights about the contradictions faced within academic politics.

Movements for social change often need to develop both organic solidarity within a core group and a connecting ideology to link its struggles with the aspirations and energies of potential allies. Creating organic solidarities and devising connecting ideologies require skills that intellectuals and artists often possess, but frequently ignore until they are pressed into service on behalf of a specific cause. Participation in actual organizing campaigns can produce more sophisticated thinking by artists and intellectuals, while at the same time opening up possible roles for them that are proscribed within the institutions in which they are usually employed. Social movements shake up social life by proposing redistribution of resources and opportunities and struggling for concrete goals, but they also produce a kind of organizational learning within movement activity that transforms people themselves, opening up new horizons for participants in the process of collective struggle. Organizational learning is a kind of intellectual work, a kind capable of connecting people employed as intellectuals to the creative and critical thinking done everywhere in society by people lacking the privileges accorded to traditional intellectuals.

Toni Cade Bambara's observation, that it is difficult to believe in social change if you have not actually seen social movements on your side seize power and redistribute resources, is particularly relevant at the present time.[12] For nearly three decades the decisive social movements in the United States have come from the right, from mobilizations organized, funded, and guided by the wealthiest and most powerful people in our society. A series of "think tanks" and corporate-front public relations operations masquerading as social movements have dramatically transformed the terms of political and cultural work in the United States, often by attacking and eclipsing the "expertise" previously vested in public educational and cultural institutions.[13]

The Right has been successful in building organizations and institutions that give full-time employment to intellectuals, allowing them to devote all of their time to serving as "experts in legitimation" for the wealthy corporations and individuals who pay their salaries.[14] The John M. Olin Foundation, Heritage Foundation, American Enterprise Institute, and the Scaife Foundation provide a form of corporate welfare for intellectuals willing to turn out arguments that conform to the Right's current political line. Charles Murray, Dinesh D'Souza, Abigail Thernstrom, and David Horowitz (among others) have secured lavish funding for producing "research" that would not pass the standards of scholarly peer review, but that successfully serves the interests of the "spin control" and public relations operations of their employers. There is of course a delicious irony in the spectacle of these defenders of the "free" market subsisting on handouts from wealthy patrons, in the production by staunch anticommunists of propagandistic pseudoscholarship worthy of the crudest fabrications of Stalinist Russia, and in attacks on "politically correct" doctrinaire college teachers coming from corporate *apparatchiks* afraid to submit their work to the processes of academic peer review, afraid to face actual students, and dependent for their livelihood on adjusting their thoughts to meet the political imperatives of the moment as determined by the think tanks that employ them. Yet while incapable of producing generative intellectual work, the right-wing mobilization of intellectuals has proven itself very successful at obscuring the kind of vision necessary for oppositional intellectual and cultural work—the ability described by Toni Cade Bambara as the ability "to see what the factory worker sees, what the prisoner sees, what the welfare children see, what the scholar sees ... what the ruling-class mythmakers see as well."[15]

Neoconservative intellectuals and other ruling-class mythmakers have disseminated ways of knowing that obscure "what the factory worker sees, what the prisoner sees, what the welfare children see, what the scholar sees" in order to encourage everyone to see as the ruling-class mythmakers want them to see. As Sidney Plotkin and William Scheuerman argue in their generative book *Private Interest, Public Spending: Balanced Budget Conservatism and the Fiscal Crisis*, a key goal of conservative political work over the past three decades has been to hide public concerns while foregrounding private interests—to encourage people to think of themselves as taxpayers and homeowners rather than as citizens and workers, to depict private property interests and the accumulated advantages accorded to white men as universal while condemning demands for redistributive justice by women, racial and sexual minorities, and by other aggrieved social groups as the "whining of special interests."[16]

In this context, scholarly analyses of how actual social movements work—why they win, how they lose, what legacies they leave—contain tremendous relevance for the politics of the present. Superb historical studies such as Robin D. G. Kelley's *Hammer and Hoe* and *Race Rebels*, Robert Fisher's *Let the People Decide*, David Gutiérrez's *Walls and Mirrors*, Charles Payne's *I've Got the Light of Freedom*, and Vicki Ruiz's *Cannery Women, Cannery Lives* offer indispensable evidence and argument about the nature of contesting for power under unequal conditions. Judith Halberstam's efforts to document and preserve the "queer" spaces and temporalities brought into being by drag kings and other subcultural dissenters from normative gender roles demonstrate clearly the utility of combining scholarly research and writing with the needs of cultural workers and activists from aggrieved communities.[17]

Our time does not lack for activists or activism. Three decades of neoconservative and neoliberal assaults on the victories of the egalitarian movements of the past ensure that the communities we come from and the institutions we inhabit will remain in crisis for the foreseeable future. Efforts to create new sources of private profit within the educational system through privatization, charter schools, vouchers, patent sharing, technology-based instruction, and schemes to turn universities into research and development arms of private corporations threaten the institutional future of education at all levels. It may be that rather than serving as crucibles for a more democratic future that educational institutions will be phased out as useless anachronisms in a society devoted to making maximum possible profits out of all social endeavors. Yet intellectual and artistic work will remain important even if they largely take place outside of schools, even if it is the work of social movements to re-create them in new sites.

Similarly, social movements will remain under assault in a society that allocates resources and opportunities along group lines yet insists on structuring legal, educational, and political debates along individualistic lines—as if sexism, racism, class subordination, and other collective axes of power suppress us individually rather than collectively. Yet social movements are proscribed in this culture precisely because they are so powerful, because we know more together than we know apart, because we are stronger collectively than we can ever hope to be as individuals. It is a burden—but also an honor and a responsibility to attach ourselves to social movements, to see what others see, to live out the dream of Toni Cade Bambara—"to tell the truth and not get trapped."

CHAPTER 12

Don't Cry for Me, Ike and Tina

American Studies at the Crossroads

If this is true, then everything we know is up for grabs, and
"what comes next" is anyone's guess.

—Kathryn Verdery, *What Was Socialism, and What Comes Next?*[1]

On a December night in 1992, I sat awake all night on board a jetliner
traveling to Frankfurt, Germany. The crew kept the cabin lights dim for
most of the flight. Nearly everyone else seemed to be sleeping, but I sat
up straight in my seat with my eyes wide open. Images, ideas, and arguments raced through my mind, making it impossible for me to sleep.

My trip to Germany came about in response to an invitation to
participate in an international conference on racist violence, assimilation,
and otherness. Three young editors from a German publishing house
organized the conference in conjunction with the German Society for
Christian-Jewish Cooperation as a way of focusing international attention on interethnic antagonisms in Germany and around the world. Earlier that year, teenagers and adults in the German Baltic port of Rostock
spent more than two days surrounding a hostel housing Vietnamese
immigrants. They threw rocks at the inhabitants and jeered them with
racist epithets. In November, two German youths in the town of Molln
threw firebombs into the home of a Turkish woman, igniting a fire that
killed her and her two granddaughters. Hate crimes against immigrants
and other "foreigners" of non-German ancestry killed at least sixteen
people in Germany in 1992, and authorities recorded at least eighteen
hundred other separate racial incidents.[1]

I knew next to nothing about the situation in Germany, but racial violence was very much on my mind. At the time I was living in Los Angeles, conducting research on race and urban space, on the ways in which social and spatial distance between races in U.S. cities comes to exert a determining influence on opportunities and life chances. At the end of April and the beginning of May in 1992, thousands of poor and working-class people living in the racially segregated inner-city neighborhoods of Los Angeles rose up in a violent rage. Provoked in part by the acquittal of four police officers charged with the brutal beating of an African American motorist, Rodney King, but generated as well by decades of declines in wages, employment opportunities, and social services, people threw rocks, set fires, smashed windows, ripped pipes and electric wires out of walls, and destroyed nearly eleven hundred buildings. Looters broke into some four thousand stores, walking away with necessities like bread, milk, cereal, baby diapers, and shoes. Businesses resented for their high prices and shabby goods suffered special devastation. The insurrection left sixty people dead and close to two thousand injured, while law enforcement authorities arrested and incarcerated more than ten thousand individuals.

My German hosts invited me to report on "the actual state and possible future of the U.S.-American multicultural experiment," especially in respect "to Los Angeles after the recent riots."[2] I accepted their offer promptly because I was eager to defend the intercultural and interracial qualities of life in Los Angeles as I had come to know and treasure them. Racists in Germany and all around the world pointed to the violence in Los Angeles in 1992 as an indictment of diversity. They pointed to the conflagration as justification for imposing cultural uniformity on diverse and heterogeneous populations, for denying asylum to refugees, and for depriving immigrants of legal and human rights. I knew they were wrong. Our problems in Los Angeles—and in the United States at large—did not stem from too much diversity, but rather from too much oppression, too much exploitation, and too much inequality. We suffered from too little justice, not from too much multiculturalism.

Yet while I was eager to speak out about racism and injustice, I was not eager to go to Germany. As someone raised in a Jewish American household in the years immediately following the Second World War, the specter of German racism held a special meaning for me. When I was growing up, Hitler's Germany was the negative example against which everything else could be judged. In my parents' home, it was important to remain Jewish because Hitler had tried to eliminate the Jews. It was important to be grateful that my grandparents found refuge in America, because if they had remained in Europe they would most likely have died in the Nazi concentration camps. It was important to speak out on controversial political issues, because "good Germans" had remained silent as Hitler rose to power.

Stories about anti-Nazi resistance instructed us about the importance of fighting back. My maternal grandfather often recounted a story that he received second- or third-hand about a man in his native village in Lithuania. Instead of going peacefully to the camps, this man choked a Nazi soldier to death with his bare hands before being killed himself. The grandfather who told me this story was a hardworking, quiet, and peaceful man, but he wanted his grandchildren to honor this act of violent resistance. The specter of Nazism remained at the forefront of his consciousness throughout his life. Decades after the end of World War II he remained astonished that anyone would purchase a Volkswagen automobile. If a symphony orchestra played a composition by Richard Wagner, my grandfather walked out of the concert hall because he knew that Nazi officers played Wagner's music in the concentration camps.

It was impossible for me *not* to think about the Nazi era as I traveled to Frankfurt. The demise of Communism in the East and the subsequent reunification of Germany seemed to inflame some long dormant aspects of German nationalism. Citizens of Germany seemed eager to welcome into their country ethnically German immigrants from former Communist states in Eastern Europe, but at the same time they seemed to be turning against forty years of postwar policies that extended asylum and residency to non-Germans from all parts of the world.

Racist violence in the form of firebombings, stonings, and even sexual assaults compounded the problems people of Vietnamese, Turkish, and Iranian origin faced in the newly reunified Germany. Young people born in Germany, some of them members of the third generation in their families to attend German schools, still found themselves considered foreigners. Women from immigrant and non-German ethnic families felt particularly excluded by the ascendancy of German nationalism; women's groups reported recurrent instances where these women felt silenced, isolated, and ill because of the new political and cultural climate in their adopted country. Many of them had surrendered traditional social roles in their home communities, but were still not accepted into the roles available to other German women. Entrepreneurs from immigrant and non-German ethnic backgrounds employed thousands of German workers in their businesses but still could play no role in shaping public policy. "Foreign" workers almost always performed the hardest jobs for the most meager remuneration.

The German view of citizenship—as a matter of race and culture rather than purely of politics—further complicated matters. Some four million immigrants lived in Germany in 1991, but less than 3 percent of the Spanish and Italian populations and less than 1 percent of the Turkish population had secured naturalized citizenship. In addition, the law governing naturalization was not immigration law, but "foreigner's law" dating back to the Nazi era, even though it had been modified slightly in the early 1990s.[3] Perhaps it was my grandfather's influence that made me laugh nervously at comedian Dennis Miller's analogy comparing German reunification to the possibility of the reunification of the comedy team of Dean Martin and Jerry Lewis. Speaking of both "acts"—Martin & Lewis and East & West Germany, Miller explained that since he had never been a fan of their previous work together, he found little joy in the prospect of their reunion.

I realized just how insecure I felt about traveling to Germany when I looked at the music tapes I had selected to listen to on my trip. I carried along cassettes by Ike and Tina Turner, Chuck Berry, Albert King, Billy Peek, and Fontella Bass—every one of them from St. Louis, the U.S. city where I have spent the most time and to which I feel most attached. This music conjures up an entire social world for me, and I feel "at home" when I listen to it, no matter where I am. I learned to love these musicians' music by listening to them play live in nightclubs on both sides of the Mississippi River, by listening to their songs on jukeboxes in neighborhood restaurants and taverns, by watching the ways in which their recorded and live performances made hardworking people forget their day jobs and dance the night away. The sound of Albert King's guitar on "I'll Play the Blues for You" evokes for me the smell of fish frying at North St. Louis church socials. When Fontella Bass sings "Rescue Me" I can taste a cold beer on a hot St. Louis night. Chuck Berry's flamboyance and self-assurance always remind me of the Ville neighborhood in which he was raised. Most of all, Ike and Tina Turner's

The Eads Bridge spanning the Mississippi River in St. Louis. According to Mark Twain, the Mississippi River at St. Louis was "too thick to drink, but too thin to plow." Rhythm and blues clubs on the Missouri side of the river used to close at 1:30 A.M. by law, but clubs in Illinois stayed open until five A.M. At these clubs Albert King, Chuck Berry, Little Milton, and Ike and Tina Turner played some of their best shows. Photograph by George Lipsitz.

rhythms bring back memories of their drummer "Stumpy" Washington and the way he could get people moving at the Riviera Lounge on Delmar Boulevard, at George Edick's Club Imperial on West Florissant Avenue, and in all those clubs on the east side of the river in Illinois.

We knew we lived in Ike and Tina Turner's town, in Miles Davis's town, in Josephine Baker's town. It never mattered to us what the rest of the world thought. We knew that we never saw our city on television programs or in the movies. We understood that hardly anybody anywhere else in the world knew much about us, or thought about vacationing where we lived, even though we were proud that we came from the city that housed the International Dog Museum, the Bowling Hall of Fame, and the Museum of Medical Quackery. We knew our city was old, that the smells from its factories made some people turn up their noses, and that Mark Twain once described our drinking water as "too thick to drink, but too thin to plow." We even knew that Ike and Tina had moved away to Los Angeles and no longer lived in St. Louis. Yet none of that mattered. We knew that we lived in Ike and Tina's town, and when we heard them play, we knew they were playing our music.

In an airplane high above the ocean on my way to Europe, I turned my walkman on loud and let Chuck Berry's "Livin' in the USA" blast in my ears. As always, his music made me smile, made me move to the beat even in an airplane seat, and his lyrics painted word pictures of the St. Louis that he and I both knew well—a city of corner cafés with names like "Mammer Jammer" and "Take It and Git," with signs in their windows like BRAINS, TWENTY-FIVE CENTS, which, we used to joke, told you what they had on the menu and how much it was worth to be smart in St. Louis.

This social world in St. Louis was also a political world for me. The CORE youth center at the corner of Spring and Cottage in a black neighborhood was where I first heard Little Milton Campbell singing the blues on the radio. It was also where I received my first sustained exposure to civil rights activism and organizing. The Melrose Tavern on McCausland Avenue in the Italian American "Hill" neighborhood gave me my first opportunity to hear local country-and-western singer

Barbara Fairchild's records on a jukebox, but was also the place where I learned about working-class interracial solidarity at meetings of RAFT, an oppositional rank-and-file caucus within Teamsters Local 688. To this day, I never hear B. B. King's playing or singing without thinking of the many nights I sat up talking with Ivory Perry, a grassroots activist from St. Louis who taught me so much about politics in long conversations that inevitably got around at some point to our mutual conviction that B. B. King's playing and singing topped everybody else's.

I know that these same songs have very different meanings for other people, but for me, listening to the music I listened to in St. Louis during those years always arms me with an energy and an optimism that I find in few other places. Not all of the organizing I participated in at that time succeeded; in fact, we lost many more battles than we won. But music has the power to cheat time by keeping alive past moments and meanings. And you never know when you might need them.

I thought I needed to take part of St. Louis with me when I went to Germany in 1992. I wanted to make sure I spoke from a standpoint grounded in the things that I had seen for myself in my life. The field hands and factory workers I observed in civil rights struggles in the 1960s, and in rank-and-file trade union insurgencies in the 1970s certainly taught me more about race and power than I ever learned in libraries or classrooms, much less from the systematic misrepresentations that permeate mass-mediated journalism, advertising, and entertainment.

Yet our strengths and weaknesses often come from the same sources. The same memories that can conjure up courage in a moment of danger can also create a kind of cowardice that keeps us confined to the limits of our own direct experiences and perceptions. Part of my anxiety about going to Germany came from my parochialism. How could lessons I learned in the United States be useful to people in countries with different histories, different population mixtures, and different understandings of race and ethnicity? What I could say about racist violence in the United States that could have any utility in explaining, interpreting, or curtailing attacks on Vietnamese, Turkish or Iranian people in Germany?

Even more troubling, what reason exists to trust that the things I learned in the 1960s and 1970s are still relevant even to the United States? The St. Louis that I lived in back then no longer exists. Capital flight, computer-generated automation, and economic restructuring have obliterated much of the city I knew. Between 1979 and 1982 alone, forty-four thousand manufacturing workers in St. Louis lost their jobs. The Pruitt-Igoe Housing project (where I did door-to-door voter registration canvassing in 1964) was so structurally flawed and so poorly maintained and had developed such a bad reputation, that the local housing authority blew it up with dynamite one day in 1973. The factories where I passed out leaflet after leaflet have all closed. The neighborhoods that housed a rich array of institutions and social networks now look abandoned and empty.[4]

In both St. Louis and Frankfurt, the globalization of economic production, distribution, and consumption, the emergence of new communications technologies, and the destruction and displacement of established social worlds mean that all of us are facing fundamentally new situations in respect to race. No matter how much North Americans or Germans are haunted by the hate, hurt, and fear of our respective pasts, we have no guarantee that the lessons of history will prepare us adequately for the future.

Right before the plane began its descent into Frankfurt, I had been listening to Chuck Berry's "Roll Over Beethoven," probably not the most respectful song to play to prepare for a visit to Germany. My hosts had arranged lodging for me at the Hotel Mozart. I wondered what kind of music they played there.

Almost as soon as the conference began, it became evident that many of the things that people around the world had discovered about race, racism, and the state during the industrial era did not apply to the new realities of a postindustrial world characterized by fluidity rather than fixity, by flexible accumulation rather than by Fordist production methods. Many of the presentations emphasized comparisons between different national conceptions of racialized citizenship. Others compared the treatment of specific minorities in different countries.

Rather than confronting one universal racism, we saw that we faced many racisms, each with their own complex combinations and permutations. We began to see that our different histories and different intellectual traditions made us view race and racism differently in each national context. None of us could claim that we came from countries that had the answer. Each of us came to Frankfurt burdened with sadness because of the antiforeign demagoguery and racial scapegoating we had been grappling with at home. I started to see that more than my own parochialism was at stake; *any* analysis of racism from a purely national perspective was too limited.

Most of us at the conference made some acknowledgment of the need to develop new and transnational ways of knowing. But the way we made our claims exposed our enduring ties to the places that had shaped our intellectual formations. The German speakers all presented elaborate theoretical models of racism, complete with diagrams, and urged us to make law-like generalizations. The French speakers offered precise definitions of words, making subtle distinctions among different kinds of racial enmity. They wanted us to develop a transnational typology of racism unified by a common terminology. The North Americans all presented narrative stories and illustrative anecdotes. We asked our colleagues to root their discussions in empathetic understanding of the experiences of others. Despite these clearly national differences, nearly all of us wound up doing the same thing—explaining how the racism in our nation differed from the racism faced by others in the room.

The attention paid to different models of citizenship in these talks led logically to a comparative consideration of *which* models of citizenship contributed most to racism. Yet that very discussion prevented us from inquiring about the ways in which citizenship *itself* always functions as a form of exclusion. Our discussions did not enable us to apprehend citizenship as a construct that shapes people as political subjects partly to hide their identities as economic subjects with antagonistic interests. Our discussions did not encourage us to consider how citizenship as a construct leaves the pursuit of justice solely to the state. Even at an international conference, we remained wedded to mostly national ways of knowing in a world that has become irreversibly transnational and international.

Purely national perspectives, while still indispensable, offer inadequate epistemologies for understanding the comparative and relational nature of racism in an age of transnational commerce and culture. Prohibitions against naturalized citizenship for non-Germans, for example, effectively racialize and marginalize Turkish, Iranian, and Vietnamese residents of Germany. Yet the abstract promises of universal inclusion offered by the United States—an approach that seems like the polar opposite of the German method—blends inclusionary promises with exclusionary practices in such a way as to racialize and marginalize immigrants as effectively as the German approach.

To my German hosts, it seemed evident that German nationalism rested on a common ethnic heritage and a common culture. But I noticed that some of the "Germans" had names that were clearly Italian, probably because their ancestors had migrated to Germany from the south. The German language spoken by people in Frankfurt sounded completely different to me than the German spoken by conference delegates from Saxony or Mecklenberg. When I asked people to identify for me something that represented the core culture of Germany, they often mentioned the music of Bach. But musically speaking, Bach's "German" compositions are replete with French and Italian forms, figures, and devices.

The more we talked at the conference, the more evident it became that racism in each of our countries did not exist in isolation. The Vietnamese families under siege in Rostock came to Germany in the first place because of the long-term consequences of the U.S. war in Vietnam. The victims of the recent racist attacks in Germany did not differ all that much from the five Cambodian and Vietnamese children murdered in a Stockton, California, playground in 1989 when a white male, Patrick Purdy, fired an AK-47 assault rifle into a crowded schoolyard.[5] The United States and Germany both produced individuals who hate people and attack them because they are from Southeast Asia.

The United States and Germany have also been partners in con-structing each other's national racism. Nineteenth-century white suprem-acists in the United States justified their presumed superiority over blacks, Native Americans, and Mexicans by imagining themselves as the heirs to traditions of intellectual and political life that they traced back to Germany. Some of Hitler's most devoted admirers lived in the United States and some of the most important investments in Nazi Germany were made by U.S. corporations pleased by the stability and profitability of Hitler's system. At the same time, eugenics "research" conducted in the United States claiming to prove the superiority of some races over others proved extremely popular in shaping German law and public pol-icy throughout the 1920s and 1930s.

The influence of U.S. attitudes and policies about "foreigners" in the 1920s on German policy in the 1930s offers a clear case in point. When my grandparents immigrated to the United States from Lithuania and Russia in the early years of this century, popular books like Madison Grant's 1916 *The Passing of the Great Race* celebrated the superiority of white people and evaluated "Nordic" whites as even more superior than "Alpine" or "Mediterranean whites." Industrialist Henry Ford waged a constant campaign against the "international Jew" in his *Dearborn Independent* magazine. Theodore Lathrop Stoddard's 1920 publica-tion, *The Rising Tide of Color against White World Supremacy* described immigration to the United States from Asia and from eastern and south-ern Europe as deadly threats to the country's future as a "white" nation.

Racist ideas quickly evolved into racist policies. Government measures supported popular racism in diverse ways, especially through increasingly restrictive and even exclusionary immigration laws in 1917, 1920, and 1921, as well as through massive deportations of alleged labor radicals in 1919 and continuing through the 1920s.[6] In testimony before a Congressional committee in 1924, eugenicist Harry Laughlin identified Jewish immigrants as a special threat to the United States. Asserting that intelligence tests revealed that 83 percent of Jews were feebleminded, Laughlin advocated an immigration policy that would prohibit the entry of nonwhites into the country and that would limit other groups to no more than 2 percent of their 1890 population. The National Origins Act of 1924 followed Laughlin's lead and enacted these standards into law. Laughlin went on to become the first president of the racist Pioneer Fund, a still-influential eugenics foundation. Some of his biggest admirers lived in Hitler's Germany. In 1936, the University of Heidelberg honored Laughlin for authoring an earlier U.S. law requiring forced sterilization of "incompetents," a piece of legislation that served as a model for subsequent Nazi sterilizations of more than two million people.[7]

During the 1930s, the "culture of unity" in the United States emerged out of interethnic alliances within trade unions to transform millions of European American immigrants and their children from unwanted aliens to redemptive insiders, from guests in someone else's home to architects of a new society. Through electoral coalitions, cultural expressions, and activist politics, the culture of unity enabled millions of people to challenge centuries of Anglo-conformity and claim the U.S. nation as their own. Emboldened by the ways in which the Great Depression discredited the moral authority of dominant groups' views of themselves as "one hundred percent Americans" whose lineage entitled them to primordial privileges—the 1930s culture of unity emphasized the longstanding currents in national culture that made the United States "a nation of nations," a place putatively destined for inclusion and egalitarianism. The social crisis engendered by the Great Depression played an important role in creating interethnic alliances in pursuit of social democratic reforms. At the same time, the rise of fascism in Europe badly undermined the legitimacy of racism and antisemitism in ways that had important repercussions for America's own highly racialized past and present.

The New Deal culture of unity and subsequent war against fascism enabled people like my grandparents and parents to feel fully "American" for the first time. Like other immigrants and their children, they found their own experiences and aspirations resonating in the inclusive "America" celebrated in magazines like Louis Adamic's *Common Ground*, in regionalist art, documentary photography, and musical compositions like Aaron Copland's "Appalachian Spring" and "Billy the Kid."[8] Nazism and its genocidal campaigns against the Jews cemented their identification with America. The United States became solidified as a site of refuge at a time when Europe resumed its role in their eyes as a place of persecution and pogroms.

The Popular Front nationalism of the New Deal culture of unity left many European Americans with a passionate enthusiasm for "America" and its culture. At its best, this nationalism produced a new respect for the grassroots creations of culture by white working-class communities as well as by aggrieved communities of color. The popular music made in St. Louis during the 1950s and 1960s that meant so much to my own intellectual and emotional formation found expression in mass-mediated commercial channels in part because of the ways in which the prior New Deal culture of unity celebrated American regional and folk forms.

Yet part of this zeal for things American came from a desperate effort to escape the humiliating stigma of feeling foreign. Assimilation was not merely a voluntary strategy among European American immigrants; to many it seemed a necessity. Howard Sachar notes that in the aftermath of World War II, Jews in the United States feared that anything that called attention to the distinctiveness of Jewish identity might reawaken antisemitism and "somehow lend credence to Hitler's racial theories."[9] In 1952 alone, some 160,000 Jewish Americans changed their names—shortening them, Anglicizing them, or replacing them entirely. Name changes were not new, but their volume doubled in the postwar period.[10]

My own lifelong immersion in U.S. popular music, film, and sports reflects genuine enthusiasm and approval, but I suspect it all stems in part from impulses communicated to me about the importance of becoming "American." The baseball cards I collected had meaning for me in part because they were like little passports into the national culture. They provided information about individual players and the history of baseball, but also a list of places where players were born that defined for me the picturesque diversity and plurality of the United States. I loved the names of these ballplayers' hometowns: Ed Bailey's Strawberry Plains, Tennessee; Earl Torgeson's Snohomish, Washington; Bill Voiselle's Ninety-Six, South Carolina; and Jim McAndrew's Lost Nation, Iowa. The physical places and cultural spaces for which I have such poignant nostalgia are mine by adoption, and the increasing pain of losing them that I feel has everything to do with the hopes of my family that embracing this nation-state and its culture would enable us to feel at home.

The role of the U.S. government in defeating world fascism while promoting the celebratory nationalism of the culture of unity obscured for many European Americans like the members of my family the degree to which the U.S. nation-state was still a racial state. Ethnic inclusion in the rewards and benefits of American society made possible by New Deal social welfare measures made it nearly impossible for them to recognize their simultaneous role as defenders of new forms of racial exclusion. The triumphant U.S. forces that liberated concentration camps were themselves racially segregated armies. The social democratic reforms won by the culture of unity owed their existence to militant actions by members of all aggrieved groups, but the fruits of victory went almost exclusively to the "white" members of that coalition. The celebratory nationalism of the culture of unity encouraged the national chauvinism and American Exceptionalism that fueled the cold war. At the same time it absolved the nation of its racialized past (and present) at the very moment when U.S. residents most needed to confront the central role of race in the life of the nation. The enormity of Nazi racism—and the good will accruing to the U.S. nation-state for fighting against it—made it difficult for many Americans to see the degree to which their own country remained a racial state. Because the United States clearly opposed Nazi aggression during World War II, the imperial dimensions of U.S. foreign policy in places like Vietnam became more difficult for many citizens to discern.

Today, Harry Laughlin's Pioneer Fund is alive and well in the United States, sponsoring racist research and exerting inordinate influence on public policies about immigration, welfare, and education.[11] The renewal of racism enacted by conservatives in the United States has served as a useful diversion in deflecting the public's attention away from the disastrous consequences of the ever increasing power of multinational corporations. Immigrants and refugees in Germany and other nations around the world pay a terrible price for a global economy that funnels 150 times as much income to the richest fifth of the world's population living in countries like Germany and the United States as it does to the poorest fifth who live primarily in Africa, Asia, and Latin America.[12] The United States and Germany have a mutually constitutive as well as contrasting relationship in respect to race. New epistemologies are needed to give full weight to distinctly national circumstances, but also to see beyond them. Struggles within distinct national contexts will remain vitally important for the foreseeable future, but it is equally important to now envision forms of identification and insurgency that display what Dipesh Chakrabarty calls "other narratives of self and community that do not look to the state/citizen as the ultimate construction of sociality."[13]

What Chakrabarty expresses so abstractly on the level of social theory made itself manifest concretely and directly in the everyday life of Frankfurt outside the 1992 conference. Every time we dined, shopped, or walked the streets, the complexity of our situation came into clearer relief. I was a foreigner in Frankfurt, but Frankfurt did not feel foreign to me. I recognized the downtown railroad station as the one Elvis Presley sang about in "G.I. Blues," a film loosely based on Presley's actual stint in the army at one of the many U.S. military bases near Frankfurt. One of those bases near my hotel, the Creighton Abrams Complex, was named in honor of one of the highest-ranking U.S. generals during the Vietnam War. What did the name Creighton Abrams mean to Vietnamese immigrants to Germany? The African American soldiers in camouflage uniforms that I saw outside the base reminded me of home. What memories did they evoke for the Vietnamese? The era of activism in St. Louis that I longed for nostalgically was for them the era when the U.S. military used napalm, fragmentation grenades, and saturation bombing to take the lives of more than two million people in Southeast

Asia. The same past united us all, but in different ways, with uneven and differentiated effects.

My nostalgia for St. Louis and the social warrant won there in the Age of the Civil Rights Movement has nurtured and sustained me for many years. Yet it also contains the seeds of dangerous omissions and occlusions. The culture and politics of St. Louis in the 1960s and 1970s that provide me with foundational truths were themselves ephemeral entities constructed in the midst of frantic and dynamic change. Ike Turner moved to St. Louis from Clarksdale, Mississippi. Tina Turner came from Nut Bush, Tennessee. To me, Lovejoy, Illinois, holds significance as the home of Albert King. But for King himself, Lovejoy was one stop on a long journey. Born in Indianola, Mississippi, he lived in Osceola, Arkansas, and Gary, Indiana, before he moved to Lovejoy. He did his most important recording in Memphis, and secured his first mainstream commercial success as a result of a performance at the Fillmore Auditorium in San Francisco. By the time he died in 1992, he had moved back to Memphis.

It would also be a mistake to underestimate the desperate conditions that gave birth to the music that provides me with so much delight. A bitter struggle lay beneath Albert King's rise to prominence as a musician. He was so poor as a child that owning a guitar was out of the question. He learned to play music by making his own instruments: a "Diddley Bow" (a broom wire nailed to the side of a building played with the neck of a glass bottle) and a wooden cigar box and twig "guitar" strung with six strands of identical wire. When he graduated to playing actual guitars he did not know that they made models for left-handers like himself, so he played his instrument upside down and backward his whole career. Uncomfortable using a finger pick, he used the meat of his thumb to pluck the hard metal strings.

King did not learn to read or write until late in life. He went to jail in the early 1950s for a highway accident that was not his fault, but because the crash resulted in the deaths of white passengers in another vehicle, the authorities thought they had to blame someone so they blamed him. King's life experiences sometimes made him a harsh employer. Musicians who played with him reported that sometimes he would correct their mistakes by slapping them in the face with one hand, and firing his pistol in the air at the same time with the other hand. Band members were often not quite sure if they had been slapped or if they had been shot. It was wonderful to be someone who could *hear* Albert King, but it was probably not always wonderful to be someone working for him. Most important, it could not have been easy to be Albert King, no matter how much joy he provided for members of the audience like me.

During the conference in Frankfurt, we knew that as a matter of geography we were in Germany. Yet many different national cultures shaped what we saw and heard in that country. In a restaurant operated by Italian immigrants around the corner from the conference, the jukebox featured Bob Marley and the Wailers from Jamaica. National Basketball Association games being played in the United States appeared on German television every night. I went looking for something distinctly German in the local music stores and came away with some examples of "Indoesiche Kapellen"—music played by Ambonese, Moluccan, and Indonesian immigrants to the Netherlands that was popular in Germany in the early 1960s. It was from these pieces of music that I received a glimpse of one possible source of a new epistemology for thinking about racism in the contemporary world.

The most important group of the Indoesiche Kapellen craze was the Tielman Brothers. The Tielman family left Indonesia in 1957 and moved to Breda in the Netherlands, the birth city of Elvis Presley's manager, Colonel Tom Parker. The battle between the Netherlands and its Asian colonial possession that later became Indonesia led to the migration of 12,500 Moluccans to the Netherlands in 1951, with more coming in later years as the conflict in Asia became increasingly violent.[14] Unlike Dutch youths whose musical training generally limited them to expertise on the accordion or piano, the Tielman Brothers and other Asians had extensive experience with Indonesian string instruments and electric guitars. When the guitar-based sounds of U.S. rock 'n' roll and rhythm and blues became popular in the Netherlands, Indonesian Eurasians and

Polynesian Moluccans were well positioned to become local interpreters of this imported music. The first Dutch teenage rock 'n' roll star, Lydia Tuinenburg, came from Indonesia, and the Indoesiche Kapellen enjoyed extraordinary popularity in Germany and the Netherlands between 1959 and 1964. Accustomed to hearing Indonesian folk music influenced by Portuguese fado and saudade music (as well as American popular music broadcast on armed forces radio stations from Australia and the Philippines), and lacking certification for many jobs outside of music, Ambonese and Eurasian musicians quickly became prominent interpreters of U.S. black music in Holland.[15]

The Tielman Brothers secured a spot at the 1958 Brussels World's Fair as a relief band in the Hawaiian Village section of the Dutch Pavilion. Originally scheduled only for fifteen-minute performances when the Hawaiian band took a break, the brothers stole the show with their wild rock 'n' roll songs and acrobatic antics. They tossed guitars to each other across the stage, played the guitar and electric bass with their teeth and their toes, and put their instruments behind their backs and played them flawlessly. Although popular everywhere in Europe, they developed a particularly strong following in Germany because the presence of U.S. military bases there created a constant demand for competent back-up bands for touring rock 'n' roll and rhythm and blues acts from "home." In Hamburg, they exerted a particularly strong influence on Tony Sheridan, an artist who played with the British musicians who eventually formed the Beatles. Indorock fans credit the Tielman Brothers with originating the "jumpy" bass style played by Paul McCartney on "I Saw Her Standing There" and characteristic of players who make the switch between lead guitar and electric bass.[16]

The Tielman Brothers originated in Indonesia, moved to the Netherlands, and gained their greatest success playing U.S. black music to white European audiences in Holland and Germany. The histories of Dutch and U.S. military combat in Asia and Europe shaped the musical worlds from which they emerged, as did the internal racialized histories of the United States, the Netherlands, and Germany. Often unwanted as workers, as citizens, or as neighbors, Indonesian and Eurasian Dutch youths found an opportunity to insert themselves into the national spot-light through commercial culture. Their prominence in popular music in turn, helped redefine the "nation" and its boundaries. Important within the national context of the Netherlands, their existence nonetheless can only be explained in transnational terms, by the ways in which their popularity transformed what it meant to be Asian in Europe largely because of the influence of Africa on music from North America.

The disruption between culture and place—and the transnational dimensions of national identity—exemplified by the Tielman Brothers reveals a pattern that is being repeated all around the world today. Contemporary bhangra music in Britain reveals parallel instances of the interconnections between national and transnational traditions. Bindu Sri performs in the United Kingdom, but she is an ethnic South Asian from East Africa. She fuses reggae music from Jamaica with bhangra music from the Indian subcontinent, embodying in her songs contrasts and comparisons between British colonialism in Kingston and Kashmir, in East Africa and the West Indies. Her music calls attention to the presence of Asian Indians in East Africa as well as the Caribbean, of "coolie" labor in Jamaica and Trinidad, of Asian Indian shopkeeping and low-wage labor in East Africa. Complex connections from the past remain an important part of her music in the present because, as a writer for the *Times* of London recently observed, "bhangra seems to cut across the tight racial divides of inner-city Britain."[17]

While conserving distinctly national song forms and sometimes even championing traditional social norms, bhangra in Britain is not a pure expression of British, Indian, or Punjabi national culture. Bhangra performers sing in English, Urdu, and Punjabi. The Safri Boys use samples and break beats from rap music behind their lyricism while the group Asia fuses bhangra with house music. XLNC blends Hindi folk melodies with hip-hop samples, while combining Middle Eastern ululation with African call and response. Traditional gender roles also come into question through bhangra, especially in the performances of female vocalists Asha Bhosie, Sasha Hindocha, and Bindu Sri.[19] The band Fun-Da-Mental, consisting of four youths born in Pakistan and India but raised in Northern British cities, became one of the first music groups of any kind to tour post-Apartheid South Africa. They titled their first album, *Seize the Time*, a slogan gleaned from their study of writings by U.S. Black Panther Bobby Seale, and they injected antiracist messages in their eminently danceable hit recordings.[19]

Today, the Tielman Brothers live in Australia. They moved back to the Pacific from Europe out of bitterness with the racism in the Netherlands that they believe deprived them of the credit and reward they deserved for their music. But a new generation of immigrants in the Netherlands now uses African American hip-hop to stake a claim for themselves and their culture in a way that echoes the trajectory of the Tielmans thirty years ago. Def Rhymes, an immigrant rapper from Surinam, delineates the experiences of the large part of the population of Surinam (almost 50 percent) that lives in Dutch cities by layering lyrics in English, Dutch, and Sranan (a creole language from Surinam) over Afro-Latin rhythms. Popular rapper El Jay brings together two colonized cultures from different parts of the world as the daughter of Moluccan and Surinam parents. She accentuates her identity in performance by donning a batik head shawl worn the "Asian" way. Another immigrant from Surinam, Patrick Tillion, offers an inventory of British and U.S. subcultural icons with his hip-hop stage name—Rude Boy Remington Colt .45. Turkish and Moroccan immigrant youths have also been active in Netherlands hip-hop.

These rap artists flaunt their identities as racialized outsiders from South America, North Africa, and the South Pacific as a peculiar way to assimilate into the mainstream of commercial culture in their country. Racialized immigrant hip-hop artists in the Netherlands announce themselves as the local residents most like the prestigious outsiders who perform African American culture. Although they have complicated histories that make them very different from African Americans, they also recognize and adopt for themselves African American strategies for crafting prestige from below within commercial culture. The culture of Surinam blacks and Asians colonized by the Dutch is not the same as the culture of inner-city African American youths, but it displays some distinct family resemblances.

Commercial culture products by contemporary immigrant rappers in the Netherlands, by bhangra artists in Britain like Bindu Sri, or by the Tielman Brothers in Belgium, Germany, and the Netherlands in the 1960s reveal lives and art that are determined by both national and transnational contexts. They provide us with the kinds of narratives Chakrabarty encourages us to seek, narratives that include but go beyond the national citizen-subject. Hip-hop, bhangra, and Indorock artists have emerged within historically specific national contexts, yet their art and audiences can never be bound within only one national context. Within their work, hidden histories come to the surface—histories of European imperialism and colonialism in Asia and Africa, of the role of imperialism in constituting the metropolis as well as the periphery, of the unexpected affinities among similarly racialized people in America, Asia, and Africa. Like the music from St. Louis that I treasure most, these forms of cultural expression emanate from social worlds and ultimately from political worlds. But they are not worlds that can be confined to one locality, one consciousness, or one epistemology. Some of them may exist nowhere else except within recorded music and the imagined affinities among people from very different places. Like the conference participants I met in Frankfurt, hip-hop, bhangra, and Indorock musicians have to master discrete national cultures in themselves as well as in comparison with one another. But they also need to acknowledge the mutually constitutive relations between nations, the flows of commerce, culture, and capital that make our experiences local *and* global simultaneously.

Approaches that imagine purely national or purely transnational solutions to problems of unequal power and unjust social relations are sure to fail in the present era, but approaches able to imagine other kinds of identities contain considerable promise. My experiences with racism in the United States turned out to be very different from those confronting my German or French colleagues at the 1992 Frankfurt conference, but our experiences contained many connections and similarities as well. The Vietnamese who left their homeland after the United States dropped more tons of explosives on it than had been used in the entire previous history of warfare, only to find themselves besieged by Germans throwing rocks at them in Rostock, knew some important things about both Germans *and* Americans that we might generally hide from ourselves and from each other. The music that made me feel at home by evoking cultural and social relations in a St. Louis that no longer existed might have been better understood by Ambonese/Dutch musicians in Germany than by me. The Germans my grandfather feared and hated derived part of their faith in eugenics from Harry Laughlin and the Pioneer Fund's other willing accomplices in the United States. It was impossible for me to feel any superiority over the Germans attacking Vietnamese immigrants in Germany when my path to the Frankfurt conference took me past the Creighton Abrams Complex every single day.

Shortly before the end of the conference I noticed a poster on a Frankfurt street advertising a forthcoming performance by James Brown. Like my tapes by Ike and Tina Turner or Chuck Berry, this reminder of African American culture felt like something that belonged to me personally. But then I realized that James Brown was no more "mine" than anyone else's, simply because we happened to be born in the same country. I remembered the part in Brown's autobiography where he reveals himself to be something more than "American," the part where he describes his family tree. "On my mother's side there is a strong Asian element," he wrote, "and some American Indian. My mother is Asian-Afro, but she's more Asian because her father, Mony Behlings, was highly Asian. I never thought that was possible until I visited Surinam right next to Guyana north of Brazil and I saw dark-skinned Asians there."[21] James Brown is most likely linked to Surinam in the way that Def Rhymes is linked to the United States, as a direct descendant and inheritor of the history of racialization, imperialism, and exploited labor, but also as a part of diasporic populations whose histories and futures cannot be contained within any one national narrative. In the U.S. national context, few people think of James Brown as "Asian," but his self-identification is logical and correct if one thinks outside a purely national frame and acknowledges the mobility of people as well as products in the modern capitalist economy. That this movement produces unexpected affiliations as well as irrepressible antagonisms is important to remember.

All political and cultural problems are now both local and global at the same time. The increasingly indecent order of globalization compels us to envision more than we can currently enact. We need to develop new ways of knowing as well as new ways of working together to generate a social warrant suited to the circumstances of the twenty-first century. Within national boundaries and across them, we now confront many dangerous crossroads—places of conflict and creativity where we, the people of the world, find ourselves paradoxically both closer together and farther apart than ever before. As national citizens and national subjects our perspectives may be too limited to imagine the kinds of unexpected alliances we will need in the years ahead. If we expect either a purely national or seamlessly international consciousness about racism and exploitation to emerge we will surely be disappointed. Contemporary capitalism creates ever new forms of differentiation and division rather than imposing a uniform oppression on a global working class.

Like contemporary national categories, contemporary knowledge paradigms separate our lives as political subjects from our experiences as embodied subjects and cordon off our existence as social subjects from our existence as epistemological subjects. Within the conduits of commercial culture and contemporary scholarship, however, we can find already-existing identities and identifications that are not bound by traditional definitions. Collisions occur at the crossroads. You can lose your way at the crossroads. The crossroads is a place of danger. But as Yoruba elders in West Africa have long advised their children, the trickster at the crossroads is always the master of possibility.

Notes

Introduction

1. See George Lipsitz, *Rainbow at Midnight: Labor and Culture in the 1940s* (Urbana and Chicago: University of Illinois Press, 1994).

2. Apologies to baseball player Graig Nettles who as far as I know invented this formulation with his famous quip, "At Yankee Stadium tradition was monuments to Babe Ruth, Lou Gehrig, and Joe DiMaggio. In San Diego, tradition is Nate Colbert trying to sell you a used car."

3. During my sojourn in the state, Rudy Perpich was governor and Rudy Boschwitz served as a senator. Of course, as I write this today, the governor of Minnesota is Jesse Ventura, a former professional wrestler. I think that wrestlers have as much right as anyone else to run for high public office, but it is disturbing to say the least to recognize that Ventura got elected governor without having to change the simplistic appeals or stylized cynicism that made him a successful entertainer in the wrestling industry.

4. Lizabeth Cohen, *Making a New Deal: Industrial Workers in Chicago* (Cambridge: Cambridge University Press, 1990).

5. William Pilcher identifies a new "social treaty" as one of the victories of the West Coast dock workers in the 1934 strikes. I think "social warrant" better describes the change in self-perception and social expectations that often results from social movement activism. See William Pilcher, *The Portland Longshoremen: A Dispersed Urban Community* (New York: Holt, Rinehart, and Winston, 1972). See also George Lipsitz, *A Life in the Struggle: Ivory Perry and the Culture of Opposition* (Philadelphia: Temple University Press, 1995).

6. Sidney E. Plotkin and William E. Scheuerman, *Private Interests, Public Spending: Balanced Budget Conservatism and the Fiscal Crisis* (Boston: South End Press, 1994), especially 67–96, 127–57.

1. In the Midnight Hour

1. Jenny Cathcart, "Our Culture," in *World Music: The Rough Guide,* ed. Simon Broughton, Mark Ellingham, David Muddyman, and Richard Trillo (London: Rough Guides, 1994), 271.

2. This is, of course, an old theme within American studies, but I owe my understanding of its importance to the original insights of David W. Noble.

3. For a discussion of the Pocahontas story and its relationship to subsequent stories of conquest in Asia, see Robert Lee, *Orientals: Asian Americans in Popular Culture* (Philadelphia: Temple University Press, 1999), 171–72, 179.

4. Joyce V. Millen and Timothy Holtz, "Dying for Growth, Part 1: Transnational Corporations and the Health of the Poor," in *Dying for Growth: Global Inequality and the Health of the Poor,* ed. Jim Yong Kim, Joyce V. Millen, Alec Irvin, and John Gershman (Monroe, ME: Common Courage Press, 2000), 185. On Pocahontas, see Rayna Green, "The Pocahontas Perplex," in *Unequal Sisters: A Multicultural Reader in U.S. Women's History,* ed. Ellen Du Bois and Vicky Ruiz (New York: Routledge, 1990).

5. Millen and Holtz, "Dying for Growth," 190.

6. Daniel Zoll, "Enemy of the State," *San Francisco Bay Guardian,* 2 August 2000, 27.

7. Philip Martin and Jonas Widgren, "International Migration: A Global Challenge," *Population Bulletin* 51:1 (1996): 2.

8. Joyce V. Millen, Alec Irwin, and Jim Yong Kim, "Introduction: What Is Growing? Who Is Dying?" in *Dying for Growth: Global Inequality and the Health of the Poor,* ed. Jim Yong Kim, Joyce V. Millen, Alec Irwin, and John Gershman (Monroe, ME: Common Courage Press, 2000), 5.

9. Jean-Bertrand Aristede, *Eyes of the Heart* (Monroe, ME: Common Courage Press, 2000), 5.

10. Carlos Fuentes, *A New Time for Mexico* (Berkeley: University of California Press, 1997), xiii.

11. George Lipsitz, *The Possessive Investment in Whiteness: How White People Profit from Identity Politics* (Philadelphia: Temple University Press, 1998); Ghassan Hage, *White Nation: Fantasies of White Supremacy in a Multicultural Society* (New York and London: Routledge, 2000).

12. Jorge del Pinal and Audrey Singer, "Generations of Diversity: Latinos in the United States," *Population Bulletin* 52:3 (1997): 15; Philip Martin and Elizabeth Midgley, "Immigration to the United States," *Population Bulletin* 54:2 (1999): 14.

13. Martin and Midgley, "Immigration to the United States," 25.

14. Kelvin M. Pollard and William P. O'Hare, "America's Racial and Ethnic Minorities," *Population Bulletin* 54:3 (1999): 13.

15. Pollard and O'Hare, "America's Racial and Ethnic Minorities," 3, 10.

16. John Beverly, *Against Literature* (Minneapolis: University of Minnesota Press, 1993).

17. Del Pinal and Singer, "Generations of Diversity," 2, 27.

18. Silvio Torres-Saillant and Ramona Hernandez, *The Dominican Republic* (Westport, CT: Greenwood Press, 1998), 61, 63; Patricia Pessar, *A Visa for a Dream: Dominicans in the United States* (Boston: Allyn and Bacon, 1995), 22; del Pinal and Singer, "Generations of Diversity," 24.

19. Peter Manuel, *Caribbean Currents: Caribbean Music from Rhumba to Reggae* (Philadelphia: Temple University Press, 1995), 51; del Pinal and Singer, "Generations of Diversity," 9, 15.

20. Linda Miller Matthei and David A. Smith, "Belizean 'Boyz in the 'Hood?' Garifuna Labour Migration and Transnational Identity," in *Transnationalism from Below*, ed. Michael Peter Smith and Luis Eduardo Guarnizo (New Brunswick and London: Transaction Publishers, 1998), 275.

21. Anthony P. Maingot, "Immigration from the Caribbean Basin," in *Miami Now! Immigration, Ethnicity, and Social Change*, ed. Guillermo J. Grenier and Alex Stepick III (Gainesville: University Press of Florida, 1992), 33.

22. David Nicholls, *From Dessalines to Duvalier: Race, Color, and Independence in Haiti* (New Brunswick, NJ: Rutgers University Press, 1996), xxii, xxiii, xxv.

23. Roger Waldinger and Mehdy Bozorgmehr, "The Making of a Multicultural Metropolis," in *Ethnic Los Angeles*, ed. Roger Waldinger and Mehdi Bozorgmehr (New York: Russell Sage Foundation, 1996), 14.

24. Max Castro, "The Politics of Language in Miami," in *Miami Now! Immigration, Ethnicity and Social Change*, ed. Guillermo J. Grenier and Alex Stepick III (Gainesville, FL: University of Florida Press, 1992), 109–32; del Pinal and Singer, "Generations of Diversity," 12.

25. Michel S. Laguerre, *Diasporic Citizenship: Haitian Americans in Transnational America* (New York: St. Martin's Press, 1998), 29.

26. David E. Lopez, "Language: Diversity and Assimilation," in *Ethnic Los*

Angeles, ed. Roger Waldinger and Mehdi Bozorgmehr (New York: Russell Sage Foundation, 1996), 142.

27. Robert Alvarez, "Mango Production and the U.S. Mexico Border" (oral presentation, San Diego, California, February 7, 2000). Author's notes.

28. Winston James, "Migration, Racism, and Identity: The Caribbean Experience in Britain," *New Left Review*, no. 193 (1992): 36–37; Jorge Duany, "Popular Music in Puerto Rico: Toward an Anthropology of Salsa," *Revista de Musica: Latino Americana* 5:2 (1985): 195.

29. Manuel, *Caribbean Currents*, 241.

30. Lucie Cheng and Philip Q. Yang, "Asians: The Model Minority Deconstructed," in *Ethnic Los Angeles*, ed. Roger Waldinger and Mehdi Bozorgmehr (New York: Russell Sage Foundation, 1996), 308; David E. Lopez, Eric Popkin, and Edward Telles, "Central Americans: At the Bottom Struggling to Get Ahead," in *Ethnic Los Angeles*, ed. Roger Waldinger and Mehdi Bozorgmehr (New York: Russell Sage Foundation, 1996), 281.

31. Hamid Naficy, *The Making of Exile Cultures: Iranian Television in Los Angeles* (Minneapolis: University of Minnesota Press, 1993), 5.

32. Mehdi Bozorgmehr, Claudia Der-Martirosian, and George Sabagh, "Middle Easterners: A New Kind of Immigrant," in *Ethnic Los Angeles*, ed. Roger Waldinger and Mehdi Bozorgmehr (New York: Russell Sage Foundation, 1996), 352.

33. Naficy, *The Making of Exile Cultures*, 5.

34. Pollard and O'Hare, "America's Racial and Ethnic Minorities," 11, 14.

35. Joane Nagel, *American Indian Ethnic Renewal: Red Power and the Resurgence of Identity and Culture* (New York: Oxford University Press, 1997), 89; Pollard and O'Hare, "America's Racial and Ethnic Minorities," 26.

36. Karen Brodkin, "Global Capitalism: What's Race Got to Do with It?" *American Ethnologist* 27:2 (May 2000): 237.

37. Robin Wright, "A Revolution at Work," *Los Angeles Times*, 7 March 1995, H1, FH4; H. Davidson Budhoo, "IMF/World Bank Wreak Havoc on the Third World," in *Fifty Years Is Enough: The Case Against the World Bank and the International Monetary Fund*, ed. Kevin Danaher (Boston: South End Press, 1994), 21–22; Walden Bello, "Global Economic Counterrevolution: How Northern Economic Warfare Devastates the South," in *Fifty Years Is Enough: The Case Against the World Bank and the International Monetary Fund*, ed. Kevin Danaher (Boston: South End Press, 1994), 19; Charles Kernaghen, "Sweatshop Blues: Companies Love Misery," *Dollars and Sense*, no. 222 (1999): 18.

38. Julie Sze, "Expanding Environmental Justice: Asian American Feminists' Contribution," in *Dragon Ladies: Asian American Feminists Breathe Fire*, ed. Sonia Shah (Boston: South End Press, 1997), 92.

39. Neferti Tadiar, "Domestic Bodies of the Philippines," *Sojourn* 12:2 (1997). See also Tadiar's "Manila's New Metropolitan Form," *differences* 5:3 (Fall 1993): 154; and her important forthcoming book based on her manuscript, "Fantasy-Production: Dynamics of National and Transnational Development."

40. Donald Lowe, *The Body in Late Capitalist USA* (Durham: Duke University Press, 1995), 28.

41. John Miller, "Economy Sets Records for Longevity and Inequality," *Dollars and Sense*, no. 229 (2000): 17, 18.

42. Sidney E. Plotkin and William E. Scheuerman, *Private Interests, Public Spending: Balanced Budget Conservatism and the Fiscal Crisis* (Boston: South End Press, 1994), 29.

43. Akhil Gupta and James Ferguson, "Beyond 'Culture': Space, Identity, and the Politics of Difference," *Cultural Anthropology* 7:1 (February 1992): 6–22.

44. Aristede, *Eyes of the Heart*, 22.

45. Etienne Balibar and Immanuel Wallerstein, *Race, Nation, Class: Ambiguous Identities* (London: Verso, 1991).

46. David W. Noble's critique of nationalism has been crucial to my thinking on this issue. See his forthcoming book, *Death of the National Landscape* (Minneapolis: University of Minnesota Press, 2002).

47. See David W. Noble, *The End of American History* (Minneapolis: University of Minnesota Press, 1985).

48. Katherine Verdery, *What Was Socialism and What Comes Next?* (Princeton: Princeton University Press, 1996), 37.

49. Ken Jowitt, *New World Order* (Berkeley: University of California Press, 1992); Verdery, *What Was Socialism*, 38.

50. Lipsitz, *Possessive Investment in Whiteness*, 24–46.

51. Arjun Appadurai, "Disjuncture and Difference in the Global Cultural Economy," *Public Culture* 2:2 (1990): 1–24.

52. C. L. R. James, *American Civilization* (New York and London: Blackwell 1994).

53. Americo Paredes, *With His Pistol in His Hand* (Austin: University of Texas Press, 1958).

54. Grace Lee Boggs, *Living for Change: An Autobiography* (Minneapolis: University of Minnesota Press, 1998), 255.

55. Noble, *The End of American History.*

56. Martin Luther King Jr., *Strength to Love* (Philadelphia: Fortress Press, 1981), 66.

2. Sent for You Yesterday, Here You Come Today

1. Charles Hamm, *Putting Popular Music in Its Place* (Cambridge: Cambridge University Press, 1995), 117.

2. The American Studies Association has become the academic home for scholars who find unique ways to interact with artists and audiences such as Michelle Habell-Pallan, Tricia Rose, Suzanne Smith, Brenda Dixon-Gottschild, and Nan Enstad. It has also served as an important locus for scholar-artists George Lewis, Roberta Hill, and Elizabeth Alexander. The preconvention collaboratives at the organization's annual meeting in Detroit in October 2000 explored the links between scholarship and historic preservation, ethnic alliances, art and citizenship, public history, performance, cultural history, popular journalism, the culture of activism, material culture, labor history, ethnic history, maritime communities, local and community history, religion, educational assessment, and student internships.

3. E. Durham, J. Rushing, and W. Basie, "Sent for You Yesterday," on *Count Basie: The Golden Years, Volume 4, 1944–1945,* Jazz Archives CD 158082.

4. Michael Denning, *The Cultural Front* (New York and London: Verso, 1996), 69–70.

5. Denning prefigured this argument more than a decade ago in "'The Special American Conditions': Marxism and American Studies," *American Quarterly* 38:3 (1986). Journalist Louis Adamic played a key role during the 1930s in mobilizing immigrants and their children to think of themselves as "redemptive outsiders" rather than as unwanted aliens, while the visual art of Thomas Hart Benton, the photographs of the Farm Security Association photographers, the musical compositions of Virgil Thompson and Aaron Copland, the folklore of B. A. Botkin, and the literary creations of Langston Hughes and John Dos Passos among others celebrated a new sense of national unity. David Peeler identifies the iconography of the "common man" as the common currency of New Deal culture, while Lizabeth Cohen emphasizes the importance of the "culture of unity" fashioned through the activist efforts of the CIO. Denning fuses these arguments together by delineating the ways in which what he calls the Age of the CIO forced a fundamental reformulation within U.S. culture and politics.

6. Denning, *The Cultural Front,* 237, 273, 281.

7. Ibid., 277, 208.

8. Among the best previously written accounts are Paula Rabinowitz, *Labor and Desire: Women's Revolutionary Fiction in Depression America* (Chapel Hill: University of North Carolina Press, 1991); Alan Wald, *Writing from the Left: New Essays on Radical Culture and Politics* (London: Verso, 1994); Douglas Wixson, *Worker-Writer in America: Jack Conroy and the Tradition of Midwestern Literary Radicalism, 1898–1990* (Urbana: University of Illinois Press, 1994); Robin D. G. Kelley, *Hammer and Hoe: Alabama Communists during the Great Depression* (Chapel Hill: University of North Carolina Press, 1990); and Paul Buhle, *Marxism in the United States: Remapping the History of the American Left* (London: Verso, 1991).

9. Antonio Gramsci, *Selections from Cultural Writings* (Cambridge, MA: Harvard University Press, 1985), 98, quoted in Denning, *The Cultural Front*, 135.

10. See Lizabeth Cohen, *Making a New Deal* (New York and Cambridge: Cambridge University Press, 1991); George Sanchez, *Becoming Mexican American* (New York: Oxford, 1991); April Schultz, *Ethnicity on Parade* (Amherst: University of Massachusetts Press, 1994); and John Higham, *Send These to Me* (Baltimore: Johns Hopkins University Press, 1984).

11. Denning, *The Cultural Front*, 65, 217, 222, 225, 235, 447.

12. Ibid., 239.

13. See Jill Quadagno, *The Color of Welfare* (New York: Oxford University Press, 1994) and my *The Possessive Investment in Whiteness: How White People Profit from Identity Politics* (Philadelphia: Temple University Press, 1998).

14. George Lipsitz, *A Rainbow at Midnight: Labor and Politics in the 1940s* (Chicago and Urbana: University of Illinois Press, 1994).

15. See Gary Gerstle, *Working Class Americanism: The Politics of Labor in a Textile City, 1941–1960* (Cambridge: Cambridge University Press, 1989) for one version of this story, but see also *Cultures of U.S. Imperialism*, eds. Amy Kaplan and Donald Pease (Durham: Duke University Press, 1991) and Jonathan Arac, *Critical Genealogies: Historical Situations for Postmodern Literary Studies* (New York: Columbia University Press, 1987).

16. Denning, *The Cultural Front*, 145, 217, 222, 396.

17. Ibid., 130.

18. Ibid., 450, 453, 131.

19. Kenneth Burke, *Permanence and Change: An Anatomy of Purpose* (New York: New Republic, 1935), 145–46; C. L. R. James, *American Civilization* (New York and London: Blackwell, 1994), 127, 148, 158; Denning, *The Cultural Front*, 122.

20. Denning, *The Cultural Front*, 231.

21. Ibid., 179, 180; John Dos Passos, "Whom Can We Appeal To? *New Masses* 6 (August 1930): 8.

22. Dennis R. Judd and Todd Swanstrom, *City Politics: Private Power and Public Policy* (New York: HarperCollins, 1994), 65.

23. Langston Hughes, *A New Song* (New York: International Workers Order, 1938).

24. Amy Kaplan, "Left Alone with America: The Absence of Empire in the Study of American Culture," in *Cultures of United States Imperialism*, ed. Amy Kaplan and Donald E. Pease (Durham and London: Duke University Press, 1993), 9.

25. Kaplan, "Left Alone with America," 15.

26. W. E. B. Du Bois, *Black Reconstruction in America* (New York: Simon and Schuster, 1992), 704, 706.

27. Du Bois, *Black Reconstruction in America*, 728.

28. David W. Noble, *The End of American History* (Minneapolis: University of Minnesota Press, 1985).

29. Eric Foner, *Free Soil, Free Labor* (New York: Oxford University Press, 1970); David Montgomery, *Beyond Equality: Radical Republicanism, 1862–1872* (New York: Knopf, 1967); Lawrence Goodwyn, *The Populist Moment: A Short History of the Agrarian Revolt in America* (New York: Oxford University Press, 1978).

3. Dancing in the Dark

1. Marshall Berman, "Eternal City," *Village Voice Literary Supplement*, 1 November 1989, 12.

2. Tom Daykin, "McConnell: Sloane Is Mired in the Past," *Lexington Herald-Leader*, 10 June 1990, B8.

3. The Montgomery Bus Boycott of 1955–1957 succeeded because of judicial intervention, not popular pressure. The 1964 Civil Rights Act and the 1965 Voting Rights Act implemented important institutional changes, but these watered-down legislative acts fall far short of the demands that Dr. King in particular and the civil rights movement in general advanced in the 1963 March on Washington or during the 1965 voter registration campaigns. The weaknesses written into the 1964 Civil Rights Act and the 1968 Fair Housing Act protected white privileges, while the 1965 Voting Rights Act did more to protect the Democratic Party in the South than to advance the actual interests of black voters and

communities. After 1964, public opinion polls consistently revealed that a majority of whites felt that the civil rights movement was asking for too much too fast. See George Lipsitz, *The Possessive Investment in Whiteness: How White People Profit from Identity Politics* (Philadelphia: Temple University Press, 1998).

4. Alice Echols, *Scars of Sweet Paradise: The Life and Times of Janis Joplin* (New York: Henry Holt, 2000).

5. Steve Chapple and Reebee Garofalo, *Rock 'n' Roll Is Here to Pay* (Chicago: Nelson Hall, 1977), 172.

6. Chapple and Garofalo, *Rock 'n' Roll Is Here to Pay*, 75.

7. Vincent Harding, "Responsibilities of the Black Scholar to the Community," in *The State of Afro-American History: Past, Present, and Future*, ed. Darlene Clark Hine (Baton Rouge: Louisiana State University Press, 1986), 281.

8. Kirkpatrick Sale, *SDS* (New York: Random House, 1973).

9. Robin D. G. Kelley, *Hammer and Hoe* (Chapel Hill: University of North Carolina Press, 1990).

10. Daniel Horowitz, *Betty Friedan and the Making of the Feminist Movement: The American Left, the Cold War, and Modern Feminism* (Amherst: University of Massachusetts Press, 1998).

11. Ernest Galarza, "The Mexican American: A National Concern: Program for Action," *Common Ground* 10:4 (1949): 27–38.

12. Stan Weir, *Singlejack Solidarity: Work, Culture, and Job Based Unionism* (Minneapolis: University of Minnesota Press, forthcoming, 2002).

13. Bruce Kuklick, "Myth and Symbol in American Studies," *American Quarterly* 24:1 (October 1972): 435–50.

14. Leo Marx, "Reflections on American Studies, Minnesota, and the 1950s," *American Studies* 40:2 (Summer 1999): 46. Marx uses this particular phrase to describe one of the core contributions made to American Studies by what Michael Denning calls the Cultural Front of the 1930s, but I think it also defines a clear point of overlap and agreement between the American Studies founders and their antagonists among the New Critics and Southern Agrarians.

15. Marx, "Reflections on American Studies, Minnesota, and the 1950s," 49.

16. Ibid., 44, 49, 50.

17. Ibid., 49.

18. I borrow the concept of "social warrant" from William Pilcher's account of the 1934 strikes in the West Coast longshore industry. He argues that

the strikes enabled workers to fashion a "social treaty" guaranteeing them rights and dignity in relation to management. Although never written down in any individual labor-management agreement, the "treaty" functioned in the minds of workers as a new set of social expectations and demands. See William Pilcher, *The Portland Longshoremen: A Dispersed Urban Community* (New York: Holt, Rinehart, and Winston, 1972).

19. Marx, "Reflections on American Studies, Minnesota, and the 1950s," 47.

20. George Mariscal, *Aztlan and Vietnam: Chicano and Chicana Experiences of the War* (Berkeley: University of California Press, 1999).

21. See Lipsitz, *The Possessive Investment in Whiteness.*

22. Stephen E. Ambrose, *Nixon*, vol. 3, *Ruin and Recovery, 1973–1990* (New York: Touchstone, 1991), 12.

23. Bruce Springsteen, "Dancing in the Dark" on *Born in the USA* (Columbia 38653).

4. Listening to Learn and Learning to Listen

1. Michel Crozier, Samuel P. Huntington, and Joji Watamiki, *The Crisis of Democracy: Report on the Governability of Democracies to the Trilateral Commission* (New York: New York University Press, 1975).

2. See George Lipsitz, *The Possessive Investment in Whiteness: How White People Profit from Identity Politics* (Philadelphia: Temple University Press, 1998).

3. See Thomas Sugrue's Bancroft Prize–winning book *The Origins of the Urban Crisis: Race and Inequality in Postwar Detroit* (Princeton: Princeton University Press, 1996).

4. Clarence Lo, *Small Property Versus Big Government: Social Origins of the Property Tax Revolt* (Berkeley: University of California Press, 1990), 57–60.

5. Sidney E. Plotkin and William E. Scheuerman, *Private Interests, Public Spending: Balanced Budget Conservatism and the Fiscal Crisis* (Boston: South End Press, 1994), 21, 75, 131.

6. Michael Rogin, "The President, the Cousin He Was Having an Affair with, the Cousin He Was Married to, and Her Girlfriend," *London Review of Books*, 21 September 1993, 9.

7. Michael Rogin, "Christian v. Cannibal," *London Review of Books* 1 April 1999, 18.

8. Michael Rogin, "How Dirty Harry Beat the Ringo Kid," *London Review of Books* 9 May 1996, 3.

9. Michael Rogin, "Ronbo," *London Review of Books* 13 October 1998, 7.

10. Harold Evans, *The American Century* (London: Cape), 1998; Rogin, "Christian v. Cannibal," 18.

11. If Clarence Thomas is to be believed (admittedly an unlikely possibility), as a college student he sympathized with the views of black militants in groups like the Black Panther Party. But believing Thomas means that we trust the testimony of a man who swore under oath during his confirmation hearings that he had no opinion on abortion and had never discussed it with anyone despite having belonged to a right-wing Christian fundamentalist church for ten years, having attended Sunday services regularly, and having been a prominent speaker on the conservative lecture circuit.

12. Thomas Ferguson, *The Golden Rule* (Chicago: University of Chicago Press, 1995), 293.

13. Thomas J. McCormick, *America's Half Century* (Baltimore: Johns Hopkins Universty Press, 1989).

14. Michael Holtzman, "The Ideological Origins of American Studies at Yale," *American Studies* 40:2 (Summer 1999): 71–99.

15. See Donald Pease's characteristically brilliant analysis in "Doing Justice to C. L. R. James's *Mariners, Renegades, and Castaways*," *Boundary 2* 27:2 (Summer 2000): esp. pp. 4, 7.

16. See especially the challenges raised within geography studies by Edward Soja in *Postmodern Geographies* (London: Verso, 1998); and in legal studies by Kimberle Crenshaw in "Race, Reform, and Retrenchment: Transformation and Legitimation in Antidiscrimination Law," *Harvard Law Review* 101 (May 1988): 1331–87, and Mari Matsuda in "Affirmative Action and Legal Knowledge: Planting Seeds in Plowed-Up Ground," *Harvard Women's Law Journal* 11 (Spring 1988): 1–17. George Marcus and Michael M. J. Fischer, *Anthropology as Cultural Critique: An Experimental Moment in the Human Sciences* (Chicago: University of Chicago Press, 1986); Michael Ryan, "The Politics of Film: Discourse, Psychoanalysis, Ideology," in *Marxism and the Interpretation of Culture*, ed. Lawrence Grossberg and Cary Nelson (Chicago and Urbana: University of Illinois Press, 1988), 478.

17. Toni Morrison, *Beloved* (New York: Knopf, 1987), 255.

18. Laura Mulvey, "Visual Pleasure and Narrative Cinema," *Screen* 16 (1975): 618; Stephen Heath, *Questions of Cinema* (London: Macmillan, 1981).

19. Stuart Hall, "The Toad in the Garden: Thatcherism among the Theorists," in *Marxism and the Interpretation of Culture*, ed. Lawrence Grossberg and

Cary Nelson (Chicago and Urbana: University of Illinois Press, 1988), 35–73; George Lipsitz, "The Struggle for Hegemony," *Journal of American History* 75 (June 1988): 146–50.

20. Jacques Derrida, *Of Grammatology* (Baltimore: Johns Hopkins University Press, 1976).

21. Michel Foucault, *The History of Sexuality* (New York: Pantheon, 1976) and *Language, Counter-memory, Practice* (Ithaca, NY; Cornell University Press, 1980). For an extraordinary application of Foucault's work to American culture, see Thomas L. Dumm, *Democracy and Punishment* (Madison: University of Wisconsin Press, 1987).

22. Jean-François Lyotard, *The Postmodern Condition* (Minneapolis: University of Minnesota Press, 1984).

23. Pierre Bourdieu, "The Aristocracy of Culture," *Media, Culture, and Society* 2 (1980): 225–54; Toril Moi, *Sexual/Textual Politics: Feminist Literary Theory* (London and New York: Metheun, 1985); Luce Irigaray, *This Sex Which Is Not One* (Ithaca: Cornell University Press, 1985); Jürgen Habermas, *Legitimation Crisis* (Boston: Beacon Press, 1975); Mikhail Bakhtin, *Rabelais and His World* (Bloomington: Indiana University Press, 1984). Bourdieu's great contributions have revolved around bringing a convincing sociological frame to aesthetic questions. Lawrence Levine's fine work in *Highbrow/Lowbrow* (Cambridge: Harvard University Press, 1989) on the changing status of diverse cultural objects reflects one manifestation of Bourdieu's influence. Irigaray and Hélène Cixous have raised vital questions about subjectivity and the body in feminist studies. Teresa de Lauretis in *Alice Doesn't: Feminism, Semiotics, Cinema* (Bloomington: Indiana University Press, 1984) and Tania Modleski in *The Women Who Knew Too Much* (New York: Metheun, 1988) demonstrate the importance of cultural theory within film studies. Habermas's *Legitimation Crisis* presents an important discussion of ideological legitimation and historical change. His work has influenced Fredric Jameson's extraordinary essay "Reification and Utopia in Mass Culture," *Social Text* 1:1 (1979): 130–48. Bakhtin is perhaps the most influential European theorist in American Studies. See Horace Newcomb's "Dialogic Aspects of Mass Communication," in *Critical Studies in Mass Communication* no. 1 (1984): 34–50 and Dana Polan's *Power and Paranoia* (New York: Columbia University Press, 1986).

24. Gayatri Chakravorty Spivak, "Can the Subaltern Speak?" in *Marxism and the Interpretation of Culture*, ed. Lawrence Grossberg and Cary Nelson (Chicago and Urbana: University of Illinois Press, 1988), 271–313. See also Spivak's *In Other Worlds: Essays in Cultural Politics* (New York: Metheun, 1987).

25. Michèle Lamont, "How to Become a Dominant French Philosopher: The Case of Jacques Derrida," *American Journal of Sociology* 93 (1987): 588–622.

26. Judith Lowder Newton, "History as Usual? Feminism and the 'New Historicism," in *The New Historicism*, ed. H. Aram Veeser (New York: Routledge 1989), 153–54.

27. See for example any of Lynne Cheney's uninformed and incoherent references to poststructuralism. One example is "Report to the President, the Congress, and the American People," *Chronicle of Higher Education* 35 (21 September 1988): 18–23, especially pages 18–19 where she is at her most antiintellectual. An example of reified theory comes in Sande Cohen, *Historical Culture* (Berkeley: University of California Press, 1986).

28. I thank Reda Bensmaia for this phrase although he should not be blamed for its deployment here.

29. Jon Wiener, "The De Man Affair," *The Nation* 246 (9 January 1988): 22.

30. Hall, "The Toad in the Garden," 69–70.

31. In British Cultural Studies, "articulation" has two meanings. One refers to speech acts of enunciation. The other refers to a state of connectedness or jointedness. Thus, ideology can be seen as a product of utterances, as well as a device for connecting individuals, groups, structures, and ideas.

32. David W. Noble, *The End of American History: Democracy, Capitalism, and the Metaphor of Two Worlds in Anglo-American Historical Writing, 1880–1980* (Minneapolis: University of Minnesota Press, 1985).

33. Giles Gunn, *The Culture of Criticism and the Criticism of Culture* (New York: Oxford University Press, 1987), 160–162.

34. Henry Nash Smith, *Virgin Land* (Cambridge: Harvard University Press, 1971), ix, 11.

35. Alan Trachtenberg, *Brooklyn Bridge* (New York: Oxford University Press, 1965), 117.

36. Bruce Kuklick, "Myth and Symbol in American Studies," *American Quarterly* 24 (October 1972): 435–50.

37. Gene Wise, "'Paradigm Dramas' in American Studies: A Cultural and Institutional History of the Movement," *American Quarterly* 31 (Bibliography Issue, 1979): 293–337.

38. Ralph Ellison, "Editorial Comment," *The Negro Quarterly* (Winter–Spring, 1943): 301.

39. Chester Himes, *If He Hollers Let Him Go* (New York: Doubleday, 1945).

40. Ben Sidran, *Black Talk* (New York: Da Capo Press, 1981), 18.

41. Albert Murray, *The Omni Americans* (New York: Vintage, 1983), 22.

42. Ralph Ellison, "Society, Morality, and the Novel," in *The Living Novel: A Symposium*, ed. Granville Hicks (New York: Macmillan, 1957), 66. I am indebted to John S. Wright for calling this quote to my attention.

43. David Riesman, "Listening to Popular Music," *American Quarterly* 2 (Winter 1950): 359–72; Russell Roth, "The Ragtime Revival: A Critique," *American Quarterly* 2 (Winter 1950): 329–39; Charles Seeger, "Music and Class Structure in the United States," *American Quarterly* 9 (Fall 1957): 281–94; Parker Tyler, "Hollywood as a Universal Church," *American Quarterly* 2 (Summer 1950): 165–76; Gene Balsley, "Hot Rod Culture," *American Quarterly* 2 (Winter 1950): 353–58.

44. Mark Schwed, "Don't Mind Murdoch," *Los Angeles Herald-Examiner*, 21 December 1988, A2.

45. Horace Newcomb, "Untold Stories," presentation at the University of Southern California, Los Angeles. November 20, 1989. Author's notes.

46. Morrison, *Beloved*.

47. Ian Angus and Sut Jhally, eds., *Cultural Politics in Contemporary America* (New York: Routledge, 1989); Paul Buhle, ed., *Popular Culture in America* (Minneapolis: University of Minnesota Press, 1987); Richard Butsch, ed., *For Fun and Profit* (Philadelphia: Temple University Press, 1990); Donald Lazare, ed., *American Media and Mass Culture* (Los Angeles: University of California Press, 1987); Lary May, ed., *Recasting Postwar America* (Chicago: University of Chicago Press, 1989); Tania Modleski, ed., *Studies in Entertainment* (Bloomington: Indiana University Press, 1987). See also Michael Denning, *Mechanic Accents* (London: Verso, 1988); Janice Radway, *Reading the Romance* (Chapel Hill: University of North Carolina Press, 1984); Elizabeth Long, *The American Dream and the Popular Novel* (London: Routledge, Kegan Paul, 1985); Lynn Spigel, "Television and the Home Theater," *Camera Obscura* 16 (1988): 11–46; John Fiske, *Television Culture* (London: Metheun, 1987); David Marc, *Comic Visions* (Boston: Beacon, 1989); Polan, *Power and Paranoia*; Michael Ryan and Douglas Kellner, *Camera Politica* (Bloomington: Indiana University Press, 1988); Rosa Linda Fregoso, "Born in East L.A. and the Politics of Representation," *Cultural Studies* 4 (October 1990); Lisa Lewis, "Form and Female Authorship in Music Videos," *Communication* 9 (1987): 355–77; Herman Gray, *Producing Jazz* (Philadelphia: Temple University Press, 1989); Jeff Sammons, *Outside the Ring* (Urbana: University of Illinois Press, 1987); Elliott Gorn, *The Manly Art: Bare Knuckle Price Fighting in America* (Ithaca:

Cornell University Press, 1986); Bright at Rice University, Shank at the University of Pennsylvania, Austin at the University of Minnesota, Rose at Brown University, and Jenkins at the University of Wisconsin.

48. Marcus and Fischer, *Anthropology as Cultural Critique*, 7.

49. Peter Steinfels, *The Neo-Conservatives: The Men Who Are Changing America's Politics* (New York: Simon and Schuster, 1979), 51.

50. Jodie T. Allen, "Moynihan Pushes Administration to 'Fess Up' to Social Security Tax Scam," *Washington Post*, 10 January 1990, B3.

51. The study by the American Council of Education revealed that the percentage of low-income black high-school graduates going to college fell from 40 percent to 30 percent and that the percentage of low-income Latinos fell from 50 percent to 35 percent. In addition, the study showed that even among middle-income blacks, the rate of college participation fell from 53 percent to 36 percent in 1988. For middle-income Latinos, the rate of college participation fell from 53 percent to 36 percent.

52. See Leonard Minsky and David F. Noble, "Corporate Takeover on Campus," *The Nation* 249 (30 October 1989): 494–96.

53. National Center for Education Statistics, *1988 Digest of Educational Statistics* (Washington, DC: Department of Education, 1988), 258; Chris Raymond, "Social Scientists Used to Drastic Reagan-Era Fund Cuts, Hoe Worst Is Over," *The Chronicle of Higher Education*, 17 May 1989, A20. I am grateful to Charles Betz for calling these statistics to my attention in his undergraduate honors thesis, "Reconstructing the Academy: The Political Economy of Higher Education," (University of Minnesota, 1989).

54. Not all of these individuals and groups had exactly the same agenda. But Bennett's attacks on student loans, Cheney's condemnations of critical theory, new curricula, and virtually any ideas not already congruent with her own, and Helms's demagoguery about the National Endowment for the Arts all aim at limiting access to public resources for people opposed to the corporate or conservative view of America. At the same time, tax-exempt neoconservative foundations have been important in funneling private funds (themselves tax-deductible donations) to ideologically compliant intellectuals. The John M. Olin Jr. Foundation channeled $3.6 million to Allan Bloom, $1.4 million to Samuel P. Huntington, $1 million to J. Clayburn LaForce and James Wilson, $376,000 to Irving Kirstol, $200,000 to Walter Williams, and $5.8 million to various law schools willing to establish programs in "Law and Economics" that apply "free market" principles to

legal studies. Jon Wiener, "Dollars for Neocon Scholars," *The Nation* 250 (1 January 1990): 12–13.

55. Michael Denning, "The Special American Conditions: Marxism and American Studies," *American Quarterly* 38 (Bibliography Issue, 1986): 356–80.

56. Barry Ulanov, *Duke Ellington* (New York: Harper, 1946), 276.

57. Poststructuralism might seem to ignore the nation as a unit of study because processes like the social construction of gendered subjects, the medicalization of sexuality, and the tyranny of univocal narratives all transcend national boundaries. Yet they are inflected differently in each national context. Postmodernism is a category most often associated with the United States by European theorists because of the ethnic diversity and social dynamism of U.S. society. Todd Gitlin quips, "Postmodernism is born in the USA because juxtaposition is one of the things we do best." Todd Gitlin, "Postmodernism and Politics," in *Cultural Politics*, ed. Ian Angus and Sut Jhally (New York: Routledge, 1989), 355.

5. Like Crabs in a Barrel

1. Yen Le Espiritu, *Asian American Women and Men* (Thousand Oaks, CA: Sage, 1997), 90.

2. Mitchell Landsberg, "Wide Ethnic Health Disparities Found in County," *Los Angeles Times*, 25 July 2000, B7.

3. Robert Bullard, ed., *Confronting Environmental Racism: Voices from the Grassroots* (Boston: South End Press, 1993). Laura Westra and Peter S. Wenz, *Faces of Environmental Racism: Confronting Issues of Global Justice* (Lanham, MD: Rowman and Littlefield, 1995); George Lipsitz, *The Possessive Investment in Whiteness: How White People Profit from Identity Politics* (Philadelphia: Temple University Press, 1998), 8–10.

4. Lisa Lowe, "The International within the National: American Studies and Asian American Critique," *Cultural Critique* 40 (Fall 1998): 30.

5. Yen Le Espiritu, "Colonial Oppression, Labour Importation, and Group Formation: Filipinos in the U.S.," *Ethnic and Racial Studies* 19:1 (January 1996): 29–45; William Wei, *The Asian American Movement* (Philadelphia: Temple University Press, 1993); Elaine Kim, *Asian American Literature: An Introduction to the Writings and Their Social Context* (Philadelphia: Temple University Press, 1982).

6. Gary Okihiro, *Margins and Mainstreams: Asians in American History and Culture* (Seattle: University of Washington Press, 1994).

7. Lisa Lowe, "Work, Immigration, Gender: New Subjects of Cultural Politics," in *The Politics of Culture in the Shadow of Capital*, ed. Lisa Lowe and David Lloyd (Durham: Duke University Press, 1997), 369.

8. Chester Himes, *If He Hollers Let Him Go* (New York: Thunder's Mouth Press, 1986).

9. Patrick Chamoiseau, *Texaco* (New York: Vintage International, 1998), 54.

10. Michel S. Laguerre, *Diasporic Citizenship: Haitian Americans in Transnational America* (New York: St. Martin's Press, 1998), 1–2, 64–70.

11. Laguerre, *Diasporic Citizenship*, 1, 67–68.

12. Ibid., 1–5, 31–70.

13. Winston James, *Holding Aloft the Banner of Ethiopia: Caribbean Radicalism in Early Twentieth Century America* (London and New York: Verso, 1998), 9–13, 40.

14. James T. Campbell, *Songs of Zion* (New York: Oxford University Press, 1995), 33.

15. Quintard Taylor, *In Search of the Racial Frontier: African Americans in the American West, 1528–1990* (New York: W. W. Norton and Company, 1998), 46, 49, 60.

16. Angela Davis, "Interview with Lisa Lowe: Reflections on Race, Class, and Gender in the USA," in *The Politics of Culture in the Shadow of Capital*, ed. Lisa Lowe and David Lloyd (Durham: Duke University Press, 1997), 303–23.

17. Lowe, "Work, Immigration, Gender," 362.

18. Randall Robinson, *The Debt: What America Owes to Blacks* (New York: Dutton/Plume, 2000).

19. James R. Barrett and David Roediger, "Inbetween Peoples: Race, Nationality, and the 'New Immigrant' Working Class," *Journal of American Ethnic History* 16:3 (Spring 1997): 3–44.

20. Glenn Omatsu, "The 'Four Prisons' and the Movements of Liberation: Asian American Activism from the 1960s to the 1990s," in *The State of Asian America: Activism and Resistance in the 1990s*, ed. Karin Aguilar-San Juan (Boston: South End Press, 1994), 19–69.

21. Laura Pulido, "Multiracial Organizing among Environmental Justice Activists in Los Angeles," in *Rethinking Los Angeles*, ed. Michael J. Dear, H. Eric Schockman, and Greg Hise (Thousand Oaks, CA: Sage, 1996), 171–89; Robert Bullard, "Decision Making" and Clarice E. Gaylord and Elizabeth Bell,

"Environmental Justice: A National Priority," in *Faces of Environmental Racism: Confronting Issues of Global Justice*, ed. Laura Westra and Peter S. Wenz (Lanham, MD: Rowman and Littlefield, 1995), 3–28, 29–39.

22. Manning Marable, *The Crisis of Color and Democracy: Essays on Race, Class, and Power* (Monroe, ME: Common Courage Press, 1992).

23. Frantz Fanon, *The Wretched of the Earth* (New York: Grove Press, 1968), 243.

24. Gerry Meraz, "Culture for the Cause," *Urb*, no. 42 (May 1995): 69.

25. C. Ondine Chavoya, "Collaborative Public Art and Multimedia Installation: David Avalos, Louis Hock, and Elizabeth Sisco's 'Welcome to America's Finest Tourist Plantation,'" in *The Ethnic Eye: Latino Media Arts*, ed. Chon Norriega and Ana M. Lopez (Minneapolis: University of Minnesota Press, 1996), 208–27; Michelle Habell-Pallan, "No Cultural Icon," manuscript, 1995; Tricia Rose, *Black Noise* (Hanover: Wesleyan/University Press of New England, 1994).

26. Josh Parr, "Young Laotian Women Build a Bridge in Richmond," *Shades of Power* 1:4 (1999): 7.

6. The Lion and the Spider

1. Consider the Thompson Twins: not twins, not named Thompson, and always made of more than two members.

2. Much discussion of popular music remains wedded to considerations of taste and evaluation, as if by talking about a particular kind of music, authors must be recommending its purchase. I want to emphasize here that I am reading popular music diagnostically, as a symptom of changed social relations, that it does not matter if I like or dislike any of the music I discuss. The question is what can we learn about social relations by taking musical expressions seriously.

3. Alex Stepick III and Guillermo Grenier, "Cubans in Miami," in *In the Barrios: Latinos and the Underclass Debate*, ed. Joan Moore and Raquel Pinderhughes (New York: Russell Sage Foundation, 1993), 81, 83.

4. Sheila L. Crouch, *Imagining Miami: Ethnic Politics in a Postmodern World* (Charlottesville: University Press of Virginia, 1997), 121, 144.

5. Marvin Dunn and Alex Stepick III, "Blacks in Miami," in *Miami Now! Immigration, Ethnicity, and Social Change*, ed. Guillermo Grenier and Alex Stepick III (Gainesville: University Press of Florida, 1992), 49; Alejandro Portes and Alex Stepick, *City on the Edge: The Transformation of Miami* (Berkeley: University of California Press, 1993), 176–202.

6. Diane Lindquist, "Moving In on Miami Trade," *San Diego Union Tribune*, 15 June 1998, A1, A14.

7. For more about Lisa M see the insightful discussions in Frances R. Aparicio, *Listening to Salsa: Gender, Latin Popular Music, and Puerto Rican Cultures* (Hanover: Wesleyan/University Press of New England, 1998), 150, 160, 168–69.

8. Lydia Martin, "New Crew Cut Angers Latin Women's Groups Who Call It Offensive," *Miami Herald*, 3 August 1990, 4B.

9. See Andrew Ross, *Real Love* (New York: New York University Press, 1998), 35–69.

10. Gustavo Perez Firmat, *Life on the Hyphen: The Cuban American Way* (Austin: University of Texas Press, 1994), 127.

11. Fernando Gonzalez, "A Half-Century of Hits from Father of Real Miami Sound," *Miami Herald*, 2 July 1995, ARTS section, 11; Joel Whitburn, *Joel Whitburn's Top R&B Singles, 1942–1988* (Menomonee Falls, WI: Record Research, 1988), 258–59.

12. Fred Bronson, *The Billboard Book of Number One Hits* (New York: Billboard, 1988), 414; Donald Clarke, *The Penguin Encyclopedia of Popular Music* (London: Penguin, 1989), 643.

13. After recording with the Delmiros on Dade Records in the early 1960s, Reid reached the charts with "Nobody But You Babe" and "I'm Gonna Tear You a New Heart" in 1969, "Good Old Days" in 1972, and "Funky Party" in 1974. Joel Whitburn, *Bubbling Under the Hot 100, 1959–1981* (Menomonee Falls, WI: Record Research, 1982), 137; Joel Whitburn, *Top R&B Singles, 1942–1988* (Menomonee Falls, WI: Record Research, 1988), 347.

14. Perez Firmat, *Life on the Hyphen*, 116.

15. D. Aileen Dodd, "Joseph Kolsky, 77, Pop Music Record Executive," *Miami Herald*, 12 May 1997, 4B.

16. Sharony Andrews, "'Uncensored Story' Nasty, But History Is Interesting," *Miami Herald*, 26 February 1992, 3E; John D. McKinnon, "2 Live Crew Verdict Comes as No Surprise," *Miami Herald*, 9 March 1994, 5B.

17. Chuck Phillips, "The 'Batman' Who Took On Rap," *Los Angeles Times*, 18 June 1990, F1.

18. Chuck Phillips, "The Anatomy of a Crusade," *Los Angeles Times*, 18 June 1990, F4.

19. Associated Press, "Rap Group Members Arrested Over 'Nasty' Lyrics," *St. Paul Pioneer Press*, 11 June 1990, 2.

20. Amy Binder, "Constructing Racial Rhetoric: Media Depictions of Harm in Heavy Metal and Rap Music," *American Sociological Review* 58 (December 1993): 753; Phillips, "The Anatomy of a Crusade," F4.

21. Chuck Phillips, "Boss Apparently Oks Crew's Use of 'U.S.A.'" *Los Angeles Times*, 26 June 1990, F10.

22. Jordan Levin, "Dancehall DJs in the House," in *Reggae, Rasta, Revolution: Jamaican Music from Ska to Dub*, ed. Chris Potash (New York: Schirmer Books, 1997), 230.

23. Levin, "Dancehall DJs in the House," 228–30.

24. John Leland, "When Rap Meets Reggae," in *Reggae, Rasta, Revolution: Jamaican Music from Ska to Dub*, ed. Chris Potash (New York: Schirmer Books, 1997), 187–88.

25. See George Lipsitz, "The Hip Hop Hearings," in *Generations of Youth*, ed. Joe Austin and Michael N. Willard (New York: New York University Press, 1998), 395–411.

26. Norman C. Stolzoff, *Wake the Town and Tell the People: Dancehall Culture in Jamaica* (Durham and London: Duke University Press, 2000), 6.

27. Stolzoff, *Wake the Town and Tell the People*, 232.

28. Robin D. G. Kelley, *Race Rebels* (New York: Free Press, 1994); Carolyn Cooper, *Noises in the Blood: Orality, Gender, and the "Vulgar" Body of Jamaican Popular Culture* (Durham: Duke University Press, 1995).

29. See Lisa Lowe and David Lloyd's introduction to *The Politics of Culture in the Shadow of Capital*, ed. Lisa Lowe and David Lloyd (Durham: Duke University Press, 1997), 1–32.

30. Louis Chude-Sokei, "Postnationalist Geographies: Rasta, Ragga, and Reinventing Africa," in *Reggae, Rasta, Revolution: Jamaican Music from Ska to Dub*, ed. Chris Potash (New York: Schirmer Books, 1997), 222.

31. Chude-Sokei, "Postnationalist Geographies," 222.

32. Ross, *Real Love*, 55.

33. Yen Le Espiritu, *Asian American Women and Men* (Thousand Oaks, CA: Sage, 1997), 8.

34. Pirrette Hondagneu-Sotelo, *Gendered Transition: Mexican Experiences in Immigration* (Berkeley: University of California Press, 1994).

35. Ross, *Real Love*, 63.

36. Lynn Bolles, "Kitchens Hit by Priorities: Employed Working Class Jamaican Women Confront the IMF," in *Women, Men, and the International Division of Labor*, ed. June Nash and Maria Patricia Fernandez-Kelly (Albany:

State University of New York Press, 1983), 138–60, quoted in Ross, *Real Love*, 220.

37. Steve Barrow and Peter Dalton, *Reggae: The Rough Guide* (London: Rough Guides, 1997), 306.

38. Jacqui Alexander, "Not Just (Any)body Can Be a Citizen: The Politics of Law, Sexuality, and Postcoloniality in Trinidad and Tobago and the Bahamas," *Feminist Review* 48 (Autumn 1994): 5–23; Jacqui Alexander, "Redrafting Morality: The Postcolonial State and the Sexual Offenses Bill of Trinidad and Tobago," in *Third World Women and the Politics of Feminism*, ed. Chandra Talpede Mohanty, Ann Russo, and Lourdes Torres (Bloomington: Indiana University Press, 1991), 173-96.

39. Ross, *Real Love*, 66–67.

40. Walter Rodney, *Walter Rodney Speaks* (Trenton, NJ: Africa World Press, 1990), 11.

41. Ross, *Real Love*, 69.

42. Chude-Sokei, "Postnationalist Geographies," 218.

43. For an excellent discussion of gender and sexuality in salsa music, see Aparicio, *Listening to Salsa*, 142–53.

44. Levin, "Dancehall DJs in the House," 230; Ross, *Real Love*, 49.

45. George Lipsitz, *Dangerous Crossroads* (New York and London: Verso, 1994), 39.

46. Colin Larkin, *The Guinness Who's Who of Rap, Dance, and Techno* (Middlesex, UK: Guinness Publishing, 1994), 162.

47. Andrews, "'Uncensored Story' Nasty," 3E.

48. Wendell Logan, "Conversation with Majorie Whylie," *The Black Perspective in Music* 10:1, 86, 92.

49. Timothy White, *Catch a Fire* (New York: Henry Holt, 1998), 418.

50. See Donald Clarke, ed., *The Penguin Encyclopedia of Popular Music*, 2d ed. (London: Penguin, 1998), 690; Rose Ryan, "Aboriginal Music," in *Our Place Our Music: Aboriginal Music*, ed. Marcus Breen (Canberra: Aboriginal Studies Press, 1989), 121; Bruce Weber, "Reggae Rhythms Speak To an Insular Tribe," *New York Times* 19 September 2000, 1.

51. Adrian Anthony McFarlane, "The Epistemological Significance of 'I-an-I' as a Response to Quashie and Anancyism in Jamaican Culture" in *Chanting Down Babylon*, ed. Nathaniel Samuel Murrell, William David Spencer, and Adrian Anthony McFarlane (Philadelphia: Temple University Press, 1998), 115–16.

52. Roger Steffens, "Bob Marley: Rasta Warrior," in *Chanting Down Babylon*, ed. Nathaniel Samuel Murrell, William David Spencer, and Adrian Anthony McFarlane (Philadelphia: Temple University Press, 1998), 256; Ennis B. Edmonds, "Dread 'I' In-a-Babylon: Ideological Resistance and Cultural Revitalization," in *Chanting Down Babylon*, ed. Nathaniel Samuel Murrell, William David Spencer, and Adrian Anthony McFarlane (Philadelphia: Temple University Press, 1998), 19, 24, 33; McFarlane, "The Epistemological Significance of 'I-an-I,' " 108; Walter Rodney, *The Groundings with My Brothers* (London: Bogle-L'Ouverture Publications, 1996), 66–67.

53. McFarlane, "The Epistemological Significance of 'I-an-I,'" 116.

54. Neil J. Savishinsky, "African Dimensions of the Jamaican Rastafarian Movement," in *Chanting Down Babylon*, ed. Nathaniel Samuel Murrell, William David Spencer, and Adrian Anthony McFarlane (Philadelphia: Temple University Press, 1998), 130.

55. Barry Chevannes, "The Origin of the Dreadlocks," in *Rastafari and Other African-Caribbean Worldviews*, ed. Barry Chevannes (New Brunswick, NJ: Rutgers University Press, 1998), 88, 92; Savishinsky, "African Dimensions of the Jamaican Rastafari Movement," 133.

56. Leonard Barrett, *The Rastafarians* (Boston: Beacon Press, 1977), 139.

57. Stolzoff, *Wake the Town and Tell the People*.

58. Roger Steffens, "Bob Marley: Rasta Warrior," 252, 254, 255, 262.

59. Soul Vibrations from Nicaragua; Alpha Blondy, Yasus Afari, and Majek Fashek in Africa; Yothu Yindi, No Fixed Address, and the Warumpi Band in Australia; and Herbs in Oceania provide examples of the global appeal of reggae.

60. Chude-Sokei, "Postnationalist Geographies," 218.

61. Peter Manuel, *Caribbean Currents: Caribbean Music from Rumba to Reggae* (Philadelphia: Temple University Press, 1998), 177.

62. Stolzoff, *Wake the Town and Tell the People*, 113; Trainer, "Buju Banton: Dancehall's Cultural Griot," in *Reggae, Rasta, Revolution: Jamaican Music from Ska to Dub*, ed. Chris Potash (New York: Schirmer Books, 1997), 212.

63. Barrow and Dalton, *Reggae*, 311.

64. Raquel Rivera, "Rapping Two Versions of the Same Requiem," in *Puerto Rican Jam: Essays on Culture and Politics*, ed. Frances Negron-Muntaner and Ramon Grosfoguel (Minneapolis: University of Minnesota Press, 1997), 253.

65. Manuel, *Caribbean Currents*, 92.

7. Not Just Another Social Movement

1. For the history of the Chicano movement see Rudolfo Acuna, *Occupied America: A History of Chicanos*, 2d ed. (New York: Harper and Row, 1981); David Gutierrez, *Walls and Mirrors: Mexican-Americans, Mexican Immigrants, and the Politics of Ethnicity in the Southwest, 1910–1986* (Berkeley: University of California Press, 1995); Carlos Muñoz, *Youth, Identity, and Power: The Chicano Movement* (New York: Verso), 1989; Vicki Ruiz, *From Out of the Shadows: Mexican Women in Twentieth Century America* (New York: Oxford University Press, 1998); Ramon Gutierrez, "Community, Patriarchy, and Individualism: The Politics of Chicano History and the Dream of Equality," *American Quarterly* 45 (March 1993): 44–72; Ernesto Chavez, "Creating *Aztlan*: The Chicano Student Movement in Los Angeles, 1966–1978" (Ph.D. dissertation, University of California, Los Angeles, 1994).

2. As a member of the curatorial team, my tendency was to refer to all the art in the exhibit as "prints" until the art historians in the group noted the inaccuracy of that term. Although all of the works in the exhibit were multiples, they were not all prints. Chon Norriega asked if it wouldn't solve the problem of terminology to refer to the exhibit as focused on "the art form formerly known as prints." To this day, I do not understand why his suggestion was not adopted.

3. Philip Brookman, "Looking for Alternatives: Notes on Chicano Art, 1960–1990," in *Chicano Art: Resistance and Affirmation, 1965–1985*, ed. Richard Griswold del Castillo, Teresa McKenna, Yvonne Yarbro-Bejarano (Los Angeles: Wight Art Gallery, UCLA, 1991), 185.

4. My arguments about social movements owe much to the important scholarship of Robert Fisher. See his "Grass-Roots Organizing Worldwide: Common Ground, Historical Roots, and the Tension between Democracy and the State," in *Mobilizing the Community: Local Politics in the Eras of the Global City*, ed. Robert Fisher and Joseph Kling (Newbury Park, London, and New Delhi: Sage, 1993), 6–17.

5. The tattoed woman is being offered a rose extended by a female hand.

6. The most polite translation I can give for a general audience is that it means Cortez messed us over in a big way, the dummy. See Shifra Goldman, *Dimensions of the Americas: Art and Social Change in Latin America and the United States* (Chicago and London: University of Chicago Press, 1994), 169.

7. See Edward Escobar, "The Dialectics of Repression: The Los Angeles Police Department and the Chicano Movement, 1968–1971," *Journal of American History* 79:4 (March 1993): 1483–1514.

8. The caption in the balloon in Alcaraz's poster has the politician using the phrase "S.O.S." which he explains means "Spray on Spicks." SOS was the acronym for "Save Our State," the organization formed to mobilize support for Proposition 187, a 1994 California ballot initiative designed to throw a half million children out of school, deny needed medical services to children of undocumented workers, and mandate teachers, nurses, and other professionals to become informants to the Immigration and Nationalization Service by "turning in" children and adults "suspected" of undocumented status. See Kitty Calavita, "The New Politics of Immigration: 'Balanced Budget Conservatism' and the Symbolism of Proposition 187," *Social Problems* 43:3 (August 1996): 284–306; George Lipsitz, *The Possessive Investment in Whiteness* (Philadelphia: Temple University Press, 1998), 47–54.

9. For discussions of the term *Aztlan*, see *Aztlan: Essays on the Chicano Homeland*, ed. Rudolfo A. Anaya and Francisco Lomeli (Albuquerque: University of New Mexico Press, 1991).

10. Ronald Fernandez, Serafín Mendez Mendez, and Gail Cueto, *Puerto Rico Past and Present: An Encyclopedia* (Westport, CT: Greenwood Press, 1998), 191–93; Ronald Fernandez, *Prisoners of Colonialism* (Monroe, ME: Common Courage Press, 1994).

11. Originals in the California Ethnic and Multicultural Archives Special Collections at Donald C. Davidson Library at the University of California, Santa Barbara.

12. Leonard Castellanos, "Chicano Centros, Murals, and Art," *Art and Society* 12:1 (1975): 40.

13. See Amalia Mesa-Bains, "El Mundo Femenino: Chicana Artists of the Movement — A Commentary on Development and Production," in *Chicano Art: Resistance and Affirmation, 1965–1985*, ed. Richard Griswold del Castillo, Teresa McKenna, Yvonne Yarbro-Bejarano (Los Angeles: Wight Art Gallery, UCLA, 1991), 132–40.

14. David Reyes and Tom Waldman, *Land of a Thousand Dances: Chicano Rock 'n' Roll from Southern California* (Albuquerque: University of New Mexico Press, 1998), 136.

15. See Aldon Morris's discussion of "movement halfway houses" in his book, *The Origins of the Civil Rights Movement: Black Communities Organizing for Change* (New York: Free Press, 1984), 139.

16. Amalia Mesa-Bains, "El Mundo Femenino," 136–37.

17. Ruiz, *From Out of the Shadows*, 103.

18. Harry Gamboa, Jr., *Urban Exile: Collected Writings of Harry Gamboa, Jr.*, ed. Chon Noriega (Minneapolis: University of Minnesota Press, 1998), 56.

19. Néstor García Canclini, *Hybrid Cultures: Strategies for Entering and Leaving Modernity*, trans. Christopher L. Chiappari and Silvia L. Lopez (Minneapolis: University of Minnesota Press, 1995), 4.

20. C. L. R. James, *American Civilization* (Cambridge, MA, and Oxford, UK: Blackwell, 1993), 149–58.

21. Canclini, *Hybrid Cultures*, 27.

22. David Gutierrez, *Walls and Mirrors*.

23. In his splendid chapter "Space, Power, and Youth Culture: Mexican American Graffiti and Chicano Murals in East Los Angeles, 1972–1978," Marcos Sanchez Tranquilino identifies the origins of this quote in Ruben Salazar, "Who Is a Chicano? And What Is It That Chicanos Want?" *Los Angeles Times* 1970, reprinted in Jacinto Quirarte, *Chicano Art History: A Book of Selected Readings* (San Antonio: Research Center for the Arts and Humanities, University of Texas, 1984), 5.

24. Laura Mulvey, "Myth, Narrative, and Historical Experience," *History Workshop* vol. 23 (Spring 1984): 3.

25. The definitive explanation of insurgent cultural creation is Americo Paredes, *With His Pistol in His Hand: A Border Ballad and Its Hero* (Austin: University of Texas Press, 1958).

26. Richard Rorty, *Achieving Our Country: Leftist Thought in Twentieth Century America* (Cambridge: Harvard University Press, 1998), 75–107; see also Martha Nussbaum's unprincipled and uncomprehending critique of Judith Butler, "The Professor of Parody," *The New Republic*, 22 February 1999, 37–45; Todd Gitlin, *The Twilight of Common Dreams* (New York: Metropolitan Books, 1995).

27. Gamboa, Jr., *Urban Exile*, 54.

8. As Unmarked as Their Place in History

1. Jacques Derrida, "The Law of Genre," *Glyph* 7 (1980): 202–3.

2. Nick Browne, "Race: The Political Unconscious in American Film," *East-West Film Journal* 6:1 (January 1992): 10.

3. See Browne's important argument about how heterosexual coupling between white men and "non-white" women form a semiotic subtext for this system in his "Race," 5–16.

4. *Buck and the Preacher*, dir. Sidney Poitier, 102 min., RCA/Columbia Pictures Home Video (60148), 1971.

5. *Lean on Me*, dir. John Avildsen, 109 min. [prod. comp.], 1988.

6. *The Birth of a Nation*, dir. D. W. Griffith, 159 min. [prod. comp.], 1915.

7. James Baldwin, *The Devil Finds Work* (New York: Dell, 1976, 1990), 53.

8. Herman Gray, "Jammin' on the One," presented at the Emerging Majority or Warring Minorities Conference, Santa Cruz, California. March 5, 1994.

9. Michael Rogin, *Ronald Reagan, the Movie: And Other Episodes in Political Demonology* (Berkeley: University of California Press, 1987).

10. Baldwin, *The Devil Finds Work*, 61.

11. Rob Walser, *Running with the Devil* (Hanover: Wesleyan/University Press of New England, 1993).

12. William Howze, "John Ford's Celluloid Canvas," *Southwest Media Review* no. 3 (1985).

13. *Blacula*, dir. William Crain, 92 mins., Canon Video (TVB3242), 1972.

14. Frank Krutnick, *In a Lonely Street* (London: Routledge, 1993), 88.

15. Will Wright, *Sixguns and Society* (Berkeley: University of California Press, 1976); Diane Waldman, "At Last I Can Tell It to Someone," *Cinema Studies* (1982); Andrea Walsh, *Women's Film and Female Experience* (New York: Praeger, 1984); Jonathan Munby, *Public Enemies, Public Heroes: Screening the Gangster from Little Caesar to Touch of Evil* (Chicago: University of Chicago Press, 1999).

16. Mark A. Reid, *Redefining Black Film* (Berkeley: University of California Press, 1993), 30, 31.

17. For conflicting interpretations of *Car Wash* see Michael Ryan and Douglas Kellner, *Camera Politica* (Bloomington: University of Indiana Press, 1988),124, and Reid, *Redefining Black Film*, 30–31.

18. I first encountered this thesis in Ryan and Kellner, *Camera Politica*, 46.

19. *Dirty Harry*, dir. Don Siegel, 102 min., Warner Home Video (1019), 1971.

20. Thomas Schatz, "The New Hollywood," in *Film Theory Goes to the Movies*, ed. Jim Collins, Hilary Radner, and Ava Preacher Collins (New York: Routledge, 1993), 16.

21. Justin Wyatt, *High Concept: Movies and Marketing in Hollywood* (Austin: University of Texas Press, 1994), 21.

22. Schatz, *"The New Hollywood,"* 20.

23. John Kuo Wei Tchen, "Modernizing White Patriarchy: Re-Viewing D. W. Griffith's Broken Blossoms," in *Moving the Image*, ed. Russell Leong (Los Angeles: University of California at Los Angeles Asian American Studies Center, 1991), 256.

24. Quoted in Schatz, *Hollywood Genres*, 33.

25. Rosa Linda Fregoso, "Born in East L.A. and the Politics of Representation," *Cultural Studies* 4:3 (1990).

26. Robert Warshow, *The Immediate Experience* (New York: Atheneum, 1971), 56.

9. "Facing Up to What's Killing You"

1. Toni Cade Bambara, *The Sea Birds Are Still Alive* (New York: Viking Books, 1982), 16.

2. Robert Fisher, "Grass Roots Organizing Worldwide: Common Ground, Historical Roots, and the Tension Between Democracy and the State," in *Mobilizing the Community: Local Politics in the Era of the Global City*, ed. Robert Fisher and Joseph Kling (Newbury Park: Sage, 1993), 5–7.

3. Robert Dunn, *Identity Crises* (Minneapolis: University of Minnesota Press, 1998).

4. Néstor García Canclini, "Cultural Reconversion," in *On Edge: The Crisis of Contemporary Latin American Culture*, ed. George Yudice, Jean Franco, and Juan Flores (Minneapolis: University of Minnesota Press, 1992), 33.

5. David Harvey, *The Condition of Postmodernity* (Cambridge: Basil Blackwell, 1989); Fredric Jameson, *Postmodernism, or the Cultural Logic of Late Capitalism* (Durham: Duke University Press, 1991); George Lipsitz, *Dangerous Crossroads: Popular Music, Postmodernism, and the Poetics of Place* (London: Verso, 1994).

6. Maxine Waters, "Testimony before the Senate Banking Committee," in *Inside the L.A. Riots*, ed. Don Hazen (New York: Institute for Alternative Journalism, 1992), 26–27.

7. Cynthia Hamilton, "The Making of an American Bantustan," in *Inside the L.A. Riots*, ed. Don Hazen (New York: Institute for Alternative Journalism, 1992), 20.

8. Eric Mann, *L.A.'s Lethal Air: New Strategies for Policy, Organizing, and Action* (Los Angeles: Labor/Community Strategy Center, 1991), 7.

9. Marc Cooper, "L.A.'s State of Siege," in *Inside the L.A. Riots*, ed. Don Hazen (New York: Institute for Alternative Journalism, 1992), 15.

10. Harry Gamboa Jr., interview by the author, Los Angeles, California, 12 August 1993.

11. Harry Gamboa Jr., *Urban Exile: Collected Writings of Harry Gamboa Jr.* (Minneapolis: University of Minnesota Press, 1998).

12. Gamboa Jr., interview by the author, Los Angeles, California, 12 August 1993.

13. See "Light at the End of Tunnel Vision," in Gamboa Jr., *Urban Exile*, 97–120.

14. Gamboa, interview by the author, Los Angeles, California, 12 August 1993.

15. Luis Alfaro, "*La Virgen*," "Huggy Boy," "Ralph Valladares," all performed August 8, 1994. Bonaventure Hotel, Los Angeles.

16. David Roman, *Acts of Intervention: Performance, Gay Culture, and AIDS* (Bloomington: Indiana University Press, 1998).

17. George Lipsitz, "Word Power," *Public Art Review* 9:1 (Fall–Winter 1997): 13–15.

18. Marisela Norte, *NORTE/word* (Los Angeles: New Alliance Records, 1991), audiocassette. See also Michelle Habell-Pallan, "No Cultural Icon," in *Women Transforming Politics*, ed. Kathy Jones, Cathy Cohen, and Joan Tronto (New York: New York University Press, 1997): 256–68.

19. Marisela Norte, "976 LOCA," on *NORTE/word* (Los Angeles: New Alliance Records 1991), audiocassette.

20. Michelle Habell-Pallan, "No Cultural Icon." Habell-Pallan introduced me to Norte's work (and to Norte) and I am deeply indebted to her for that great gift to my life.

21. Perhaps my great interest in someone known as the "Bus Poet" of L.A. stems from the frequent description of my own artistic efforts as "pedestrian."

22. Gamboa, *Urban Exile*, 106.

23. C. Ondine Chavoya, "Collaborative Public Art and Multimedia Installation: David Avalos, Louis Hock, and Elizabeth Sisco's *Welcome on America's Finest Tourist Plantation*" in *The Ethnic Eye: Latino Media Arts*, ed. Chon A. Norriega and Ana M. Lopez (Minneapolis: University of Minnesota Press, 1996), 208–27.

24. Ulf Hannerz, *Cultural Complexity: Studies in the Social Organization of Meaning* (New York: Columbia University Press, 1992), 42.

25. Roderick Ferguson, "The Nightmares of the Heteronormative," *Cultural Values* 4:4 (October 2000): 419–44; Avery Gordon, *Ghostly Matters* (Minneapolis: University of Minnesota Press, 1996); Jacqui Alexander, "Erotic Autonomy as a Politics of Decolonization: An Anatomy of Feminist and State Practice in the Bahamas Tourist Economy," in *Feminist Genealogies, Colonial Legacies, Democratic Futures*, ed. M. Jacqui Alexander and Chandra Talpede Mohanty

(New York and London: Routledge, 1997), 63–100; Dunn, *Identity Crises;* Elizabeth Long, *The American Dream and the Popular Novel* (Boston and London: Routledge, Kegan Paul, 1985); Herman Gray, *Producing Jazz* (Philadelphia: Temple University Press, 1988); Steve Seidman, *Romantic Longings* (New York: Routledge, 1991); Wini Breines, *Young, White, and Miserable* (Boston: Beacon Books, 1992); Line Grenier, "The Aftermath of a Crisis: Quebec Music Industries in the 1980s," *Popular Music* 12:3 (October 1993): 209–28.

26. Susan McClary, *Feminine Endings* (Minneapolis: University of Minnesota Press, 1991).

27. Nick Browne, "Race: The Political Unconscious of American Film," *East-West Journal* 6:1 (January 1992): 5–16.

28. John Kuo Wei Tchen, "Modernizing White Patriarchy: Reviewing D. W. Griffith's *Broken Blossoms*," in *Moving the Image*, ed. Russell Leong (Los Angeles: UCLA Asian American Studies Center, 1992), 133–43.

29. Mandawuy Yunupingu, "Yothu Yindi: Finding Balance," *Race and Class* 35 (4): 117–18.

30. Yunupingu, "Yothu Yindi," 118.

31. Yunupingu, "Yothu Yindi," 118.

32. John Castles, "Tjungaringanyi: Aboriginal Rock," in *From Pop to Punk to Postmodernism: Popular Music and Australian Culture from the 1960s to the 1990s*, ed. Philip Hayward (North Sydney, Australia: Allen & Unwin, 1992), 31; Marcus Breen, "Desert Dreams, Media, and Interventions in Reality: Australian Aboriginal Music," in *Rockin' the Boat*, ed. Reebee Garofalo (Boston: South End, 1992), 150; Karl W. M. Neueunfeldt, "Yothu Yindi and Ganma: The Cultural Transposition of Aboriginal Agenda through Metaphor and Music," *Journal of Australian Studies* no. 38 (September 1993): 1, 2, 4, 7, 11.

33. Mandawuy Yunupingu[e], "Yothu Yindi Band," in *Aboriginal Voices: Contemporary Aboriginal Artists, Writers, and Performers*, ed. Liz Thompson (New York: Simon and Schuster, 1990), 103.

34. Banning Eyre, "Kassav," *Rhythm Music Magazine* 3:3 (1994): 15.

35. Néstor García Canclini, *Hybrid Cultures: Strategies for Entering and Leaving Modernity* (Minneapolis: University of Minnesota Press, 1995), 2.

10. In the Sweet Buy and Buy

1. The film itself was clearly patterned after David Miller's 1962 motion picture *Lonely Are the Brave*, which features a brilliant script by Dalton Trumbo based on Edward Abbey's novel *Brave Cowboy*.

2. Dan Schiller, *Digital Capitalism: Networking the Global Market System* (Cambridge: MIT Press, 1999).

3. Simon Head, "The New, Ruthless Economy," *New York Review of Books* 43:4 (February 19, 1996): 51.

4. Kenneth Jackson, *Crabgrass Frontier: The Suburbanization of the United States* (New York: Oxford, 1985); Jill Quadagno, "Welfare Capitalism and the Social Security Act of 1935," *American Sociological Review* 49 (1984): 632–47; M. Patricia Fernandez-Kelly, "Migration, Race, and Ethnicity in the Design of the American City," in *Urban Revisions*, ed. Russell Ferguson (Los Angeles: Museum of Contemporary Art, 1994), 17.

5. George Lipsitz, *Rainbow at Midnight: Labor and Culture in the 1940s* (Urbana and Chicago: University of Illinois Press, 1994).

6. Lipsitz, *Rainbow at Midnight*, 253–57.

7. "The Lush New Suburban Market," *Fortune* (November 1953), 128.

8. Susan Hartmann, *The Home Front and Beyond* (Boston: Twayne, 1982), 165–68. John Mollenkopf, *The Contested City* (Princeton: Princeton University Press, 1983), 111.

9. Michael Stone, "Housing: The Economic Crisis," in *America's Housing Crisis: What Is to Be Done?* ed. Chester Hartman (London: Routledge and Kegan Paul, 1983), 122.

10. Robert Westbrook, "'I Want a Girl Just Like the Girl That Married Harry James': American Women and the Problem of Political Obligation in World War II," *American Quarterly* 42:4 (December 1990): 587–614.

11. D. W. Ellwood, "The Impact of the Marshall Plan on Italy; The Impact of Italy on the Marshall Plan," in *Cultural Transmissions and Receptions: American Mass Culture in Europe*, ed. Rob Kroes, R. W. Rydell, D. J. F. Bosscher (Amsterdam: VU University Press, 1993), 100–24.

12. David Brody, *Workers in Industrial America: Essays on the Twentieth-Century Struggle* (New York: Oxford University Press, 1980), 192.

13. Michael Wildt, "Changes in Consumption as Social Practice in West Germany during the Fifties," in *Getting and Spending: European and American Consumer Societies in the Twentieth Century*, ed. Susan Strasser, Charles McGovern, and Matthias Judt (New York: Cambridge University Press, 1998), 301–16.

14. George Lipsitz, *Time Passages: Collective Memory and American Popular Culture* (Minneapolis: University of Minnesota Press, 1990), 45.

15. Lynn Spigel, "Installing the Television Set: Popular Discourses on Television and Domestic Space, 1948–1955," *Camera Obscura* no. 16 (1988): 20.

16. Spigel, "Installing the Television Set," 14, 15, 17, 18.

17. Leo Litwak, "A Fantasy That Paid Off," *New York Times Magazine* 27 June 1965, p. 25

18. Paul Goldberger, "Mickey Mouse Teaches the Architects," *New York Times* 22 October 1972, pp. 40, 92; Margaret I. King, "Disneyland and Disney World: Traditional Values in Futurist Form," *Journal of Popular Culture* 15:1 (September 1981): 120.

19. Bob Thomas, *Walt Disney: An American Original* (New York: Simon and Schuster, 1976), 251, 252.

20. Sonja K. Forbes and Ann Gill, "Michel Foucault's Theory of Rhetoric as Epistemic," *Western Journal of Speech Communication* 51:4 (Fall 1987): 393.

21. Goldberger, "Mickey Mouse Teaches the Architects," 94.

22. Quoted in Mark Gottdiener, "Disneyland: A Utopian Urban Space," *Urban Life* 11:2 (July 1982): 161.

23. Quoted in Randy Bright, *Disneyland: The Inside Story* (New York: Harry N. Abrams, 1987), 48.

24. See Michael Sorkin, "See You in Disneyland," in *Variations on a Theme Park: The New American City and the End of Public Space*, ed. Michael Sorkin (New York: Noonday Press, 1992), 205–32.

25. Goldberger, "Mickey Mouse Teaches the Architects," 40.

26. Robert Guskind and Neal Pierce, "Faltering Festivals," *National Journal* 17 September 1988, 2310.

27. Andrea Pawlyna, "James Rouse, a Pioneer of the Suburban Shopping Center, Now Sets His Sights on Saving Cities," *People* 6 July 1981, 71.

28. Guskind and Pierce, "Faltering Festivals," 2309.

29. Craig Whitaker, "Rouse-ing Up the Waterfront," *Architectural Record* 174:4 (April 1986): 67.

30. Janice Radway, *Reading the Romance* (Chapel Hill: University of North Carolina Press, 1984).

31. Tania Modleski, "Rhythms of Reception," in *Regarding Television: Critical Approaches — An Anthology*, ed. E. Ann Kaplan (Los Angeles: American Film Institute, 1983), 67–76.

32. Horace Newcomb, "Television Form and Serial Narrative," oral presentation at a colloquium at the Annenberg School of Communication, University of Southern California, Los Angeles, December 1, 1989. Author's notes.

33. Lipsitz, *Rainbow at Midnight*.

34. Maribel Castaneda Paredes, "The Development of the US Advanced

Digital Television System, 1987–1997: The Property Creation of New Media" (Ph.D. dissertation, University of California, San Diego, 2000).

35. Tom Moon, "Public Enemy's Bomb Squad," *Musician* no. 156 (October 1991): 76.

36. Fredric Jameson, "Reification and Utopia in Mass Culture," *Social Text* 1:1 (1979): 130–48.

37. Charles Hamm, *Putting Popular Music in Its Place* (Cambridge and New York: Cambridge University Press, 1995), 210–48.

11. Taking Positons and the War of Position

1. Antonio Gramsci, *Selections from the Prison Notebooks*, ed. Quintin Hoare and Geoffrey Nowell Smith (New York: International Publishers, 1971), 9–10, 60–61, 173–75.

2. John Patrick Diggins, "Comrades and Citizens: New Mythologies in American Historiography," *American Historical Review* (June 1985): 624–38; T. J. Jackson Lears, "The Concept of Cultural Hegemony: Problems and Possibilities," *American Historical Review* (June 1985): 567–93.

3. Stuart Hall, oral presentation, University of Minnesota, Minneapolis, April 3, 1987. Author's notes.

4. See Harvard Sitkoff, *The Struggle for Black Equality, 1954–1980* (New York: Hill and Wang, 1981), 165, 186; George Breitman, ed., *Malcolm X Speaks* (New York: Pathfinder, 1985); Karl Marx, *The Civil War in France* (New York: International Publishers, 1940).

5. Sara Evans, *Personal Politics: The Roots of Women's Liberation in the Civil Rights Movement and the New Left* (New York: Vintage, 1979).

6. Paul Buhle, *Marxism in the United States: Remapping the History of the American Left* (London: Verso, 1987).

7. Jack Conroy, *The Disinherited* (Westport: Lawrence Hill, 1982).

8. Mikhail Bakhtin, *The Dialogic Imagination: Four Essays*, trans. Michael Holquist and Caryl Emerson, and ed. Michael Holquist (Austin: University of Texas Press, 1981), 410.

9. Danny HoSang, "Who's Got the Power? Does Anyone? Many Youth Organizations Try, But Few Succeed," *Third Force* 3:4 (September/October 1995): 19–23.

10. HoSang, "Who's Got the Power?" 22.

11. Bambara quoted in Alice A. Deck, "Toni Cade Bambara (1939–)," in

Black Women In America: An Historical Encyclopedia, ed. Darlene Clark Hine, Elsa Barkley Brown, and Rosalyn Terborg-Penn (Bloomington: Indiana University Press, 1993), 80.

12. Toni Cade Bambara, "What It Is I Think I'm Doing Anyhow," in *The Writer on Her Work,* ed. Janet Sternburg (New York: W. W. Norton, 1981), 160.

13. John Stauber and Sheldon Rampton, "The Public Relations Industry's Secret War on Activists," *Covert Action Quarterly* no. 55 (Winter 1995–96): 18–25, 57; Sidney Blumenthal, *The Rise of the Counter-Establishment: From Conservative Ideology to Political Power* (New York: Times Books, 1987); Jerome L. Himmelstein, *To the Right: The Transformation of American Conservatism* (Berkeley: University of California Press, 1990); Alan Crawford, *Thunder on the Right* (New York: Pantheon Books, 1980); Thomas Ferguson and Joel Rogers, *Right Turn: The Decline of the Democrats and the Future of American Politics* (New York: Hill and Wang, 1986); Russ Bellant, *The Coors Connection: How Coors Family Philanthropy Undermines Democratic Pluralism* (Boston: South End, 1991).

14. Jean Stefanic and Richard Delgado, *No Mercy: How Conservative Think Tanks and Foundations Changed America's Social Agenda* (Philadelphia: Temple University Press, 1996).

15. Bambara quoted in Alice A. Deck, "Toni Cade Bambara (1939–)," 80.

16. Sidney Plotkin and William E. Scheuerman, *Private Interest, Public Spending: Balanced Budget Conservatism and the Fiscal Crisis* (Boston: South End, 1994).

17. Robin D. G. Kelley, *Hammer and Hoe: Alabama Communists during the Great Depression* (Chapel Hill: University of North Carolina Press, 1990), and *Race Rebels: Culture, Politics, and the Black Working Class* (New York: Free Press, 1994); Robert Fisher, *Let the People Decide: Neighborhood Organizing in America* (Boston: Twayne, 1984); David Gutierrez, *Walls and Mirrors* (Berkeley: University of California Press, 1995); Charles M. Payne, *I've Got the Light of Freedom: The Organizing Tradition and the Mississippi Freedom Struggle* (Berkeley: University of California Press, 1995); Vicki Ruiz, *Cannery Women, Cannery Lives: Mexican Women, Unionization, and the California Food Processing Industry, 1930–1950* (Albuquerque: University of New Mexico Press, 1987); Judith Halberstam, *Female Masculinity* (Durham: Duke University Press, 1998).

12. Don't Cry for Me, Ike and Tina

1. Stephen Kinzer, "Vietnamese Easy Target, Fear Ouster by Germany," *New York Times* 6 December 1992, 1, 6; "Two Germans Admit Arson Attack That

Killed 3 Turkish Nationals," *New York Times* 2 December 1992, p. 6. See also Nora Rathzel, "Germany: One Race, One Nation?" *Race and Class* 32:3 (January–March 1991): 31–48.

2. Undated letter to George Lipsitz from Friedrich Balke, Rebekka Habermas, and Patrizia Nanz, September 1992, in author's possession. My remarks and all the presentations at the conference can be found in Friedrich Balke, Rebekka Habermas, Patrizia Nanz, and Peter Sillem, eds., *Schwierige Fremdheit: Uber Integration und Ausgrenzung in Einwanderungslandern* (Frankfurt: Geschichte Fischer, 1993).

3. Rathzel, "Germany," 32, 33.

4. George Lipsitz, *The Sidewalks of St. Louis: Places, People, and Politics in an American City* (Columbia and London: University of Missouri Press, 1991), 126–27.

5. Yen Le Espiritu, *Asian American Panethnicity: Building Institutions and Identities* (Philadelphia: Temple University Press, 1992), 155–56.

6. Jean Stefanic and Richard Delgado, *No Mercy: How Conservative Think Tanks and Foundations Changed America's Social Agenda* (Philadelphia: Temple University Press, 1996), 35; Thomas F. Gossett, *Race: The History of an Idea in America* (New York: Oxford University Press, 1997), 372.

7. Stefanic and Delgado, *No Mercy*, 35–36.

8. Lizabeth Cohen, *Making a New Deal: Industrial Workers in Chicago* (Cambridge: Cambridge University Press, 1990); Michael Denning, *The Cultural Front: The Laboring of American Culture in the Twentieth Century* (London and New York: Verso, 1996).

9. Howard Sachar, *A History of the Jews in America* (New York: Vintage, 1992), 553.

10. Alvin Kugelmass, "Name-Changing and What It Gets You: Twenty-Five Who Did It, *Commentary* 13 (August 1952); I thank Josh Kun for alerting me to this article and to Howard Sachar's book.

11. Steven J. Rosenthal, "The Pioneer Fund: Financier of Fascist Research," *American Behavioral Scientist* 39:1 (September/October 1995): 44–61.

12. Davison Budhoo, "IMF, World Bank Wreak Havoc on the Third World," in *Fifty Years Is Enough: The Case Against the World Bank and the International Monetary Fund*, ed. Kevin Danaher (Boston: South End Press, 1994), 20–23; Dan Gallin, "Inside the New World Order," *New Politics* (Summer 1994): 106–23; Robin Wright, "A Revolution at Work," *Los Angeles Times*, 7 March 1995, H1, H4.

13. Dipesh Chakrabarty, "Postcoloniality and the Artifice of History? Who Speaks for the 'Indian' Pasts?" *Representations* 37 (Winter 1992): 10. I thank Lisa Lowe for calling my attention to the significance of this formulation.

14. Dirk Jacobs, "Discourse, Politics, and Policy: The Dutch Parliamentary Debate about Voting Rights for Foreign Residents," *International Migration Review* 32:2 (Summer 1998): 364.

15. Mel van Elteren, *Imagining America: Dutch Youth and Its Sense of Place* (Tilburg: Tilburg University Press, 1994), 99–111.

16. Lutgard Masters, "Indorock: An Early Eurorock Style," *Popular Music* 9:3 (1990): 307–20.

17. Kevin J. Aylmer, "British Bhangra: The Sound of a New Community," *Rhythm Music Magazine* 4:2 (1995): 16.

18. Kim Burton and Sairah Awan, "Bhangra Bandwagon: Asian Music in Britain," in *World Music: The Rough Guide*, ed. Simon Broughton, Mark Ellingham, David Muddyman, and Richard Trillo (London: Rough Guide, 1994), 229–31; Aylmer, "British Bhangra," 15–16.

19. Colin Larkin, ed., *The Guinness Who's Who of Rap, Dance, and Techno* (Enfield, UK: Guinness Publishing Company, 1994), 230.

20. James Brown (with Bruce Tucker), *James Brown: The Godfather of Soul* (New York: Thunder's Mouth Press, 1997), 2.

Permissions

The University of Minnesota Press is grateful for permission to reprint the following previously published essays in this volume.

Part of the introduction appeared as "No Shining City on a Hill: American Studies and the Problem of Place," *American Studies* 40:2 (Summer 1999): 53–69.

Part of chapter 1 appeared as "America at the Crossroads: An Introduction," by George Lipsitz and Jonathan Munby, in *Cultural Values* 4:4 (October 2000): 383–88. Reprinted with permission from Blackwell Publishers.

An earlier version of chapter 2 appeared as "'Sent for You Yesterday, Here You Come Today': American Studies Scholarship and the New Social Movements," *Cultural Critique* 40 (Fall 1998): 203–25.

An earlier version of chapter 4 appeared as "Listening to Learn and Learning to Listen: Popular Culture, Cultural Theory, and American Studies," *American Quarterly* 42:4 (December 1990): 615–36. Reprinted with permission from The Johns Hopkins University Press.

Part of chapter 6 appeared as "World Cities and World Beat: Low Wage Labor and Transnational Culture," *Pacific Historical Review* 68:2 (May 1999): 213–31. Copyright 1999 by Pacific Coast Branch, American

Historical Association. Reprinted with permission from the University of California Press.

Chapter 7 originally appeared in the exhibition catalog *Just Another Poster? Chicano Graphic Arts in California*. The exhibit was organized by the University Art Museum in collaboration with the California Ethnic and Multicultural Archives, Department of Special Collections, Davidson Library, University of California, Santa Barbara, and the Center for the Study of Political Graphics. Reprinted courtesy of the University Art Museum, University of California, Santa Barbara.

An earlier version of chapter 8 appeared as "Genre Anxiety and Racial Representation in 1970s Cinema," in Nick Browne, ed., *Refiguring American Film Genres* (Berkeley: University of California Press, 1998), 208–32. Reprinted with permission from the University of California Press. Copyright 1998 The Regents of the University of California.

An earlier version of chapter 9 appeared as "Facing Up to What's Killing You: Artistic Practices and Grassroots Social Theory," in Elizabeth Long, ed., *From Sociology to Cultural Studies* (Malden, Mass.: Blackwell Publishers, 1997), 234–57. Reprinted with permission from Blackwell Publishers.

An earlier version of chapter 10 appeared as "Consumer Spending as State Project: Yesterday's Solutions and Today's Problems," in Susan Strasser, Charles McGovern, Matthias Judt, and Daniel S. Mattern, eds., *Getting and Spending: American and European Consumer Society in the Twentieth Century* (Cambridge: Cambridge University Press, 1998), 127–47. Reprinted with permission of Cambridge University Press.

Part of chapter 11 appeared as "Academic Politics and Social Change," in Jodi Dean, ed., *Cultural Studies and Political Theory* (Ithaca: Cornell University Press, 2000), 80–92. Reprinted with permission of Cornell University Press.

Index

George Lipsitz is professor of ethnic studies at the University of California, San Diego, where he serves as director of the Thurgood Marshall Institute. He is the author of *Time Passages* (Minnesota, 1990), *The Possessive Investment in Whiteness, Dangerous Crossroads, Rainbow at Midnight, The Sidewalks of St. Louis,* and *A Life in the Struggle.*